NEOCONSERVATISM

NEOCONSERVATISM

AN OBITUARY FOR AN IDEA

C. BRADLEY THOMPSON
WITH YARON BROOK

Paradigm Publishers
Boulder • London

Copyright © 2010 Paradigm Publishers

Published in the United States by Paradigm Publishers, 2845 Wilderness Place, Suite 200, Boulder, CO 80301 USA.

Paradigm Publishers is the trade name of Birkenkamp & Company, LLC, Dean Birkenkamp, President and Publisher.

Library of Congress Cataloging-in-Publication Data

Thompson, C. Bradley.
  Neoconservatism : an obituary for an idea / C. Bradley Thompson, with Yaron Brook.
      p. cm.
  Includes bibliographical references and index.
  ISBN 978-1-59451-831-7 (hardcover : alk. paper)
  1. Conservatism—United States. I. Brook, Yaron. II. Title.
  JC573.2.U6T46 2010
  320.520973—dc22

                                                                2010008512

Printed and bound in the United States of America on acid-free paper that meets the standards of the American National Standard for Permanence of Paper for Printed Library Materials.

Designed and Typeset by Straight Creek Bookmakers.

14 13 12 11 10   1 2 3 4 5

David Foster
Lest we forget:
"He who sins against a child sins against God."

—Victor Hugo, *The Man Who Laughs*

Contents

PREFACE

This book is the culmination of a long intellectual journey that started when I was an undergraduate in college and first introduced to the ideas of Leo Strauss and Irving Kristol. Over the course of the last thirty years, I have experienced firsthand many of the ideas, policies, and postures described in this book, and I know personally many of the people whose names appear on these pages. This book is therefore written from the perspective of someone who was once associated with the Straussian school of political philosophy and, by default, with the neoconservative intellectual movement. I have studied and worked with many former students of Leo Strauss throughout my university career. I still have many friends and acquaintances who are Straussians in good standing, and I have come to know many neoconservatives over the years. I have learned a great deal from some of them, value their friendship, and, in some cases, admire their scholarly integrity and nobility of character. Indeed, they are among some of the best men and women I have ever known. This book is therefore written from the perspective of an insider.

I have always respected the intellectual seriousness that the Straussians and neoconservatives bring to studying the Great Books, and I have always admired their ability to identify the deepest moral and political challenges that confront our society. However, I have also always known that we ultimately share different philosophic and political principles, so despite the intellectual debt that I owe to many Straussians and some neoconservatives, I was never quite one of them. In many ways, therefore, this was not an easy book to write, at least not initially. From the beginning, I knew it would disappoint and even anger some of my friends and former teachers. It was with some reluctance and trepidation, then, that I set out on a journey to the center of that unique and complex intellectual world, and what I found there at first surprised and then ultimately disappointed me. Once fully revealed and understood, it became clear to me that I could not sanction such ideas and practices. This book is therefore written as a critical engagement with the neoconservatives in what Norman Podhoretz might call the "breaking ranks" tradition. My friends among Strauss's followers who know that I have been working on this project know that I undertook this journey with honorable intentions. They also know that once set on the trail, I would not turn back.

Though the original motive for this book began as something of a personal mission to better understand the intellectual world in which I had been educated, it very quickly took on a much larger significance. In the years immediately after 2001, I also came to see a radical dichotomy between the neoconservatives' political rhetoric and the actual policies they pursued. This dichotomy really came into focus during the administration of George W. Bush, in both its domestic and foreign policies. Ultimately, this is a book about America and its future direction. It was written during a time when neoconservative ideas and policies were ascendant and having a direct impact on American policy at home and abroad. Given the important intellectual and political role they have played in modern American culture, we owe it to ourselves and to our progeny to reflect on what the neocons thought, said, and did—and what they might have planned for the future. I have concluded that neoconservative political thought is based on a comprehensive worldview that is, to paraphrase and flip an Irving Kristol expression, outside the "American grain." Yaron Brook and I have written this book to alert Americans—and especially those who value our nation's founding principles—to the threat posed to this country by neoconservatism.

* * *

This book probably would not have been written—or at least not as quickly as it was—without the inspiration and wise counsel of several friends and colleagues. And although I am tempted to blame all its errors on my friends who should have known better than to encourage me to write it, I am, alas, responsible for its content. Eric Daniels, Robert Mayhew, Craig Biddle, Onkar Ghate, Steven Grosby, Michael Zuckert, Alexander Duff, and Justin Lesniewski read various parts of the manuscript and provided helpful and sometimes very critical comments. My Clemson colleague, Jeff Love, read several chapters, bled red ink all over them, and then pushed and probed over many wonderful lunches together. Yet another Clemson colleague, Brandon Turner, read and critiqued the entire manuscript just days before it went to press and made it better with his wise comments. Donna Montrezza did an excellent job of copyediting the entire manuscript.

Yaron's chapter on neoconservative foreign policy benefited from the assistance of several people. Alex Epstein played a crucially important role in helping Yaron to develop the central arguments of the chapter, and Don Watkins provided valuable editing assistance. Yaron's assistant, Kara Devar, kept him on task and provided important logistical support for our meetings around the country. Revital Brook, Yaron's wife, must also be thanked for permitting Yaron to take all my "urgent" early-morning, late-night, and weekend phone calls.

I owe a very special thanks to my old friend Peter McNamara, who read an early version of the entire manuscript and who offered many helpful and sometimes stinging comments that challenged me to rethink many of my arguments and conclusions. Peter and I met on the first day of graduate school many years ago and have been good friends ever since, despite my having wandered off the reservation. Several other friends contributed to this book by indulging me in conversations and by asking tough and probing questions. Bradford P. Wilson and I have been discussing many of the ideas presented in this book on Friday evenings via e-mail (and a good claret) for over a decade. He surely will not agree with some of what is written here, but he certainly helped me to clarify and deepen my arguments. Vanni Lowdenslager has always asked tough and probing questions during my visits to her mountain home. I also profited from and enjoyed my conversations with Chris Tollefsen about the Straussian interpretation of Plato. Special thanks are due to the reviewers for Paradigm Publishers, including the distinguished political scientist A. James Reichley, who helped to improve the manuscript through their informed and probing questions. Lastly, I should like to thank my copilot on this project, Yaron Brook, who read the entire manuscript several times over, took countless early-morning and late-night phone calls, and took time out of his remarkably busy schedule to meet with me in different cities around the country to discuss our project. He also contributed a fabulous chapter to this book.

Over the years, I have also collected some personal debts that are directly or indirectly relevant to the writing and publication of this book. I am honor-bound to thank two former teachers and mentors for whom I have enormous respect: Harvey C. Mansfield and Ralph Lerner. In 1989, I had the great privilege of auditing a course they taught together at Harvard University on "Revolutionary Constitutionalism." Their model of scholarly integrity has been a great inspiration to me ever since, and should they ever ask why I have written this book, here is my answer: not that I loved Strauss less, but that I loved truth more.

A special word of thanks is owed to my friend and former colleague, John Lewis. During several difficult years that we spent together at Ashland University, John was a fountainhead of intellectual and moral integrity. I am also deeply indebted to John McCaskey, who spent a whole year helping me to escape Ashland, and even more so to John Allison who actually made it possible for me to land in a much better place. In turn, Bruce Yandle, Bob Tollison, and Bobby McCormick brought me to Clemson University, where I am now most happily ensconced. I also owe thanks to our editor at Paradigm, Jennifer Knerr, who saw the importance of this project without necessarily agreeing with its perspective.

Lastly, I must thank four very special people. My three children, Henry, Samuel, and Islay, inspire me every day to fight the good fight. Most importantly, it was my wife, Sidney, who taught me a valuable lesson by her virtuous example during the Ashland years: that wickedness is ultimately banal and impotent. And yes, it's true, my dear, "good things happen to good people."

INTRODUCTION
THE NEOCONSERVATIVE PERSUASION

An obituary—so soon! Surely the reports of neoconservatism's death are greatly exaggerated. The neoconservatives have, after all, been a leading intellectual force in American politics for at least thirty or forty years, and the recent takeover of Congress and the White House in the 2008 elections by liberal Democrats hardly represents the death knell of this formidable movement. One election cycle does not kill off an intellectual movement that is deeply embedded in America's major think tanks, philanthropic foundations, media outlets, and universities. Not even the recent death of Irving Kristol, the founding father of neoconservatism and *éminence grise* to many powerful people around the United States, can diminish or retard the growing influence of neoconservative ideas on American culture today.

The fact of the matter is that the neoconservatives are far from irrelevant or dead; indeed, they are very much alive. Their ideas may not hold sway over the Obama administration in the same way they influenced the administration of George W. Bush, but few people on the Left or Right are prepared yet to discount the power of their ideas or the reach of their intellectual and political influence. They still wield enormous influence over the conservative intellectual movement and the Republican Party, and they continue to influence public opinion through their highly visible positions in the print and electronic medias. So when the GOP returns to power, as it surely will one day, it will take the neocons or some of their ideas with them. For now, though, the neocons are sitting patiently on the sidelines waiting to be called back into the game. The time has not yet come when they can be studied as a historical curiosity. Is it not premature, then, to write their obituary?

Several layers of irony are embedded in the title of our book. First, it plays off the title of an essay—"Socialism: An Obituary for an Idea"—by the most famous and influential of all neoconservatives, Irving Kristol. On one level, we hope to do for neoconservatism (if prematurely) what Kristol did for socialism—and then some. Kristol's obituary for socialism is itself, however, deeply ironic given the essay's subtle attempt to resuscitate and defend the moral ideal associated with the utopian socialists. Second, an obituary for an intellectual movement still very much alive suggests that something else is at work here. If this book is an obituary, it is an obituary of a peculiar sort. We know that professional obituarists will often write the biographical parts of a death notice long before their subject has expired. And so it is with us. At the very least, we have painted an intellectual portrait of a political philosophy that will in all likelihood eventually come to an end. But this book is more. If it is not an obituary in the strict sense of the term, it may be read as a prolegomena to any future obituary, or it may serve the rather ironic task of inspiring the need for some future obituary. Better yet, readers may better understand our ultimate purpose by considering the following image: Think of Charlotte Corday writing Marat's obituary on her way to Paris.

* * *

Neoconservatism: An Obituary for an Idea is an inquiry into the ever-shifting labyrinths of the neoconservative mind. Its purpose is to identify and examine the core ideas and principles that make up the neoconservative persuasion. This book asks and answers the *what* question: It explains what the "neo" is, what the "conservatism" is, and what the "ism" is in neoconservatism. Defining neoconservatism or making sense of it is not, however, an easy task. Despite the many books and articles that have been published on neoconservatism in recent years, we still lack the most important thing: a genuine knowledge of what neoconservatism is. We still do not know to which class of intellectual and political phenomena it belongs. Moreover, we do not know if neoconservatism is a genuine political philosophy with identifiable principles, or if it is a complex *mode* of thinking without any fixed principles.

Here is the challenge. Some neoconservatives have denied that there is such a thing as neoconservatism.[1] Irving Kristol—the man who has done the most to explain what neoconservatism is to the general public—has said that it does not actually exist as a formal movement: "It holds no meetings, has no organizational form, [and] has no specific programmatic goals." In fact, according to Kristol, "when two neoconservatives meet they are more likely to argue with one another than to confer or conspire." Curiously, though, Kristol has seen fit to write two books, *Neoconservatism: The Autobiography of an Idea* and *Reflections of a Neoconservative,* about a movement that does not exist! While some neoconservatives reject the label (e.g., Daniel Bell), Irving Kristol has embraced it. At his tongue-in-cheek best, Kristol has suggested that he accepted the neoconservative designation simply because, "having been named Irving, I am relatively indifferent to baptismal caprice." In fact, continuing the joke, he claims that he may very well be "the only living and self-confessed neoconservative, at large or in captivity."[2]

Some neoconservatives have written that neoconservatism died in the 1990s, and others have stated that it was absorbed into the larger conservative movement.[3] The truth of the matter is almost certainly the reverse—that the larger conservative movement has been absorbed into the neoconservative movement. The fact is that neoconservatism today *is* conservatism. The neocons have captured the conservative intellectual movement such that *New York Times* columnist David Brooks could quip a few years ago: "We're all neoconservatives now."[4] This is of course the same David Brooks who could write that neoconservatism is a political mirage that does not actually exist![5]

Ironically, despite its very real influence in Washington, neoconservatism is not and will almost certainly never be a mass political movement; indeed, it has no real interest in being a popular movement *per se*. It has no meaningful political constituency. There is no neoconservative "Joe Six-Pack." If one were to drive through "red state" America, most ordinary Americans would never have heard of neoconservatism but for the fact that the neocons have received a good deal of media scrutiny since the invasion of Iraq. "John Q. Public" does not self-identify as a neoconservative in the same way that he might think of himself as a libertarian or as a religious conservative. There would never be a neoconservative third party. Neoconservatism is an intellectual movement that is of, by, and for the intellectual, cultural, and political elite—i.e., professors, opinion-makers, policy wonks, and politicians. The neoconservatives seek to guide America from the top down.

Still, we are left wondering exactly what this neoconservatism is, if anything. Our job is compounded by the fact that virtually all neoconservatives say that neoconservatism is *not* a systematic political philosophy, and it is doubly compounded by the fact that the neocons regularly disagree with each other on a variety of issues. The founding fathers of neoconservatism—e.g., Irving Kristol, Daniel Bell, Nathan Glazer, and Norman Podhoretz—have been "arguing the world" with one another for more than fifty years. There are also, to be sure, several competing strands in neoconservative theory and policy, particularly relative to foreign policy. Second- and third-generation neoconservatives are different in some ways from the founding generation. In fact, some of the first-generation "neocons" prefer to think of themselves as "paleoliberals" rather than as neoconservatives.[6] There is, therefore, some truth to the claim that neoconservatism is not a monolithic or a unitary political movement in the same way that

Marxism, with its various Kautskyist, Bernsteinite, Luxemburgian, Menshevik, Bolshevik, Leninist, Trotskyist, Stalinist, and Maoist factions, is not and never has been a homogenous movement. The fact that neoconservatism is not a strictly homogenous or unified political movement does not mean, however, that it is not shaped by certain core ideas and beliefs in the same way that various communist factions have been shaped by the overriding philosophy of Karl Marx.

What, then, are the defining characteristics of neoconservatism? Those who are willing to call themselves neoconservatives (and not all are) typically describe neoconservatism as an "impulse," an "orientation," a "tendency," a "sensibility," a "persuasion," a "temperament," a "style of thought," or a "mode of thinking." Its proponents have described neoconservatism as a way of seeing the world as a state of mind and not as a systematic political philosophy. The eminent neo-conservative political scientist, James Q. Wilson, has downplayed the idea that neoconservatism is any kind of organized movement, intellectual or otherwise: "There is no such thing as a neoconservative manifesto, credo, religion, flag, anthem, or secret handshake." Instead, he calls neoconservatism "a mood, not an ideology."[7]

But how exactly does one define a mood or a state of mind? How does one argue with or against a sensibility, a persuasion, or a temperament? The short answer is that one does not. But maybe that is the point. Maybe—just maybe—the neocons do not want neoconservatism defined or limited by the straightjacket of permanent first principles—or any fixed principles, for that matter. If that is so, then we must ask the obvious question: Why not?

As if to deepen our quandary, Irving Kristol has also described neoconserva-tism as a *syncretic* intellectual movement—i.e., a movement that is an unsteady and perhaps even a confused amalgam of different ideologies. The neocons typi-cally pick and choose their principles from a wide variety of intellectual, political, and religious traditions. What are we to make of an intellectual movement that has drawn inspiration at one time or another from thinkers as diverse as Plato, Aristotle, Locke, Adam Smith, Burke, Tocqueville, Trotsky, Herbert Croly, Reinhold Niehbur, Milton Friedman, and Friedrich von Hayek? What are we to make of an intellectual movement that has praised statesmen as diverse as Jeffer-son, Lincoln, Bismarck, Disraeli, Teddy Roosevelt, Franklin Delano Roosevelt, Harry Truman, Henry "Scoop" Jackson, Ronald Reagan, George W. Bush, and Barack Obama? What are we to think of an intellectual movement that consists politically of socialists, liberals, and conservatives? What are we to make of an intellectual movement that draws on Jewish, Catholic, and Protestant theology, but whose members are most often nonbelievers? What are we to make of an intellectual movement whose principal spokesmen seem to disagree with one another on virtually every issue? What holds them all together? The dilemna of neoconservatism is probably best summed up by Daniel Bell's description of himself as "a socialist in economics, a liberal in politics, and a conservative in culture."[8] Bell's self-definition is, as we shall see, illustrative of neoconservatism as an intellectual movement, but it is nonetheless perplexing.

How can neoconservatism be all this and more? To what does it all add up? On the surface, neoconservatism appears to be a paradoxical mass of contradictions with no unifying structure or purpose. The obvious temptation is to suggest that the neoconservatives are confused or that neoconservatism is just a patchwork hash of ideas and policies that has no essence or defining principle—but that would be wrong. Untangling and reconstructing what the most self-consciously "neoconservative" neocons mean by neoconservatism is the guiding purpose of this book.

Neoconservatism *is,* as we shall argue, a complex political philosophy that defies easy description. There is, however, an inner core to neoconservative thought. It is more than just a "mood," a "temperament," or a "state of mind," and it is more than just a series of political strategies and policy prescriptions. By way of analogy, neoconservatism might be compared to a Fabergé egg that contains multiple layers, some of which are intentionally hidden. Readers should know at the beginning of this book that penetrating to the inner core of neoconservative thought requires considerable digging and heavy lifting.

Purposes and Themes

Neoconservatism: An Obituary for an Idea is unique because it is the first and only book to present neoconservatism as a comprehensive and integrated political philosophy with its own system of metaphysics, epistemology, ethics, and politics. It tells the story of how and why a small group of neoconservative intellectuals and policy strategists came to define and dominate the intellectual horizon of the American political Right in the last half of the twentieth century. Specifically, *Neoconservatism* illuminates for the first time in print what the neocons call their "philosophy of governance" and what they mean when they advise Republicans to "think politically"; it explicates their theory of statesmanship; it examines their call for a "conservative welfare state"; it details why they give only two cheers for capitalism and not three; it traces neoconservatism's deepest philosophic sources; it demonstrates how and why the neocons trace the origins of nihilism to Enlightenment liberalism; it unpacks the meaning of their so-called "classical-realist synthesis" of Plato and Machiavelli; it shows how the neoconservative foreign policy of "benevolent hegemony" is actually a branch of its "national greatness" domestic policy; it takes up the neocons' claim that neoconservatism is the only brand of conservatism that is truly "*in* the American grain"; it contrasts neoconservatism with and against the principles and practices of the American Founders' vision of a free society; and it reveals the ominous parallels between neoconservatism and certain authoritarian political theories that became prominent in the 1920s and 1930s.

Readers of this book should know up front that this is not a systematic *A* to *Z* study of neoconservative ideas or policies. It does not examine neoconservatism historically or sociologically; it does not explain how neoconservatism may or may not have changed over time; nor does it elucidate or dissect the various wings, factions, and personalities of neoconservatism. Others have done these things already—and sometimes done them reasonably well. This book is about the philosophic *essence* of neoconservatism. It is, to use Irving Kristol's felicitous expression, about the "neoconservative persuasion."

Ultimately, our purpose is to open up and to reveal the inner workings of the neoconservative mind and to reconstruct the broad parameters of neoconservative political philosophy. This is no easy assignment given the fact that there is no "Neoconservative Manisfesto" or party platform to which all neocons have sworn allegiance and doubly so given the fact that the neocons disagree with each other as often as the brothers Hitchens. It is precisely the syncretic nature of neoconservatism that makes it so hard to understand and to present accurately, which is why the neocons have been so successful in deflecting criticism and in mocking their critics who never quite seem to get it right. A truly serious and decisive examination of neoconservatism must therefore begin by transcending the flawed accounts of neoconservatism, of which there have been too many in recent years.

Our method for discovering and excavating the hidden recesses and deepest philosophic principles of neoconservatism begins with the surface of neoconservative thought—i.e., with their most accessible public writings on contemporary politics and culture. We begin, in other words, with their self-presentation. In particular, we start in chapters 1 and 2 with their attempt to make over and take over the Republican Party and the conservative intellectual movement. We then drill down—layer by layer, chapter by chapter—to the hidden core of neoconservative political thought. To slightly change the metaphor, we engage in an exercise of intellectual spelunking. A primary task of this book has been to identify the neoconservatives' *method* of thinking, which will in turn help us to reveal and explicate the most important philosophic principles of neoconservatism in terms of *fundamentals*.

We also tackle and devote several chapters to a related question that has vexed many scholars: What is the deepest philosophic source of neoconservatism? Different neoconservatives will claim philosophic allegiance to different ideas or thinkers, but at the heart of the neoconservative persuasion stands one thinker above all others: Leo Strauss. A central goal of this book is to elucidate the intellectual relationship between Strauss and neoconservatism. More to the point, we examine the ways in which prominent neoconservatives have applied Strauss's philosophic ideas to American domestic and foreign policy.

A good deal—and certainly a good deal of nonsense—has been written on this subject in recent years, but we do not believe the relationship between Strauss and neoconservatism has been properly understood or explained. Indeed, much that has been written on Strauss by friends and foes alike has only muddied the public's knowledge of the connection between Strauss and neoconservatism. One major problem in examining the relationship between Strauss and the neocons is that Strauss rarely spoke publicly about his political views. He left his students and readers with very little in the way of public-policy prescriptions. For instance, Strauss wrote almost nothing about economic or foreign policy. Consequently, making sense of his philosophic principles and his rare statements on contemporary political issues and their connection to neoconservative ideas and policies is no easy assignment.

What is most needed today is a reexamination of Strauss's thought that avoids the salacious gossip, distorted caricatures, and strained rationalizations that have defined many recent works on Strauss and his students. We also need a better understanding of Strauss's relationship to the neocons. Most importantly, Strauss cannot be either refuted or defended if he has not been understood properly. Thus we have attempted to read Strauss with the kind of care that his work deserves, and we have also labored to understand and present his perspective on its own terms (i.e., as he understood it himself), eschewing the role of either fawning toady or foaming critic. We began our study of Strauss by neither taking him for granted, as do so many of his students, nor by rejecting his premises out of hand, as do so many of his detractors. Like the great political philosophers that he studied, Strauss deserves to be examined with seriousness and respect, and we have attempted to do just that.

After reviewing all the evidence, we have concluded that the relationship between Strauss's thought and that of the neoconservatives is real, meaningful, and fundamental, but its deeper contours and significance are still largely unknown.[9] We argue that Leo Strauss's view of the world and man's place in it has inspired and guided neoconservative thinking (via Irving Kristol) in the most essential ways. On this score, foremost among the unique and important contributions of this book to neoconservative scholarship is our discovery of a Rosetta Stone–like document that reveals not only a previously unknown philosophic connection between Irving Kristol and Leo Strauss, but also the deepest recesses of neoconservative thought. If we examine the rise of neoconservatism in terms of essentials, if we look for that one decisive moment that turned and shaped the neoconservative mind, it would have to be Irving Kristol's first intellectual encounter with Leo Strauss. That moment represents the intellectual birth of neoconservatism.

In light of our discovery, we shall explore Strauss's influence on several key elements of neoconservative thought. In particular, we will show how Strauss's philosophical method and ideas shaped the neocons' diagnosis of and prognosis for Western society, their condemnation of Enlightenment liberalism, their ironic defense of America and the principles of its revolutionary founding, their call for a new form of statesmanship grounded in Machiavellian prudence, their call for a new political morality that promotes self-sacrifice and service as the highest virtues, their insistence that Americans devote themselves to religion and nationalism, their demand that government regulate both man's material and spiritual needs, and, finally, their call for a reconsideration of, if not a return to, classical natural right and Platonic political philosophy. At the heart of our study of neoconservatism, then, is a new reading of Strauss that focuses on two principal themes in his thought: first, his critique of the classical-liberal tradition and, second, his unique and controversial interpretation of Plato—and, more particularly, his interpretation of Plato's doctrine of Ideas.

In the end, the theme that animates this book will shock and outrage some: Neoconservatism is, we shall argue, a unique species of anti-Americanism. At the deepest philosophical level, neoconservatism stands for the repeal of 1776. For the past five decades, the neocons have devoted their considerable philosophical and polemical talents to analyzing and critiquing the ideas and policies of the liberal-Left as being anti-American. This is one of the attributes for which they are best known. Furthermore, they have also done important and sometimes path-breaking work in resuscitating the study of the American Founding. What is less well known, however, is that the neocons have also devoted considerable time and energy undermining (in very subtle ways) the principles of a free society. This will of course come as a surprise to some, as the neocons have likewise invested a great deal of time and energy mining the American past in search of usable traditions that will cast an Americanized veil over their core principles.[10] They have worked very hard to convince the American people that there is something in the national character that is naturally inclined toward the neoconservative way of viewing the world. We think not.

Neoconservatism: An Obituary for an Idea seeks to recover a somewhat forgotten but venerable literary genre that combines philosophical analysis with political criticism. Ultimately, we have written this book to alert Americans to the threat posed by neoconservatism to the principles and institutions of a free society. We take neoconservatism seriously as an important and influential intellectual movement, and we have judged the neocons' political philosophy and policy prescriptions on the basis of the merits or demerits of their ideas and actions. Responsible American citizens owe it to themselves and to their posterity to become acquainted with the ideas and political ambitions of this enormously influential but dangerously misunderstood intellectual movement. In the end, not only do we reject the false promises of neoconservatism, we judge and condemn it as a political philosophy that is fundamentally at odds with the heart and soul of Americanism and the spirit of American liberty.

Focus and Scope

Let us return—again—to the problem of how to understand neoconservatism and put to rest what we know will be a common criticism coming from some neoconservative and Straussian quarters. Some of our neoconservative critics will say that the neoconservatism presented in this book is too unitary and homogenous—that it does not do justice to the likes of Daniel Bell, Nathan Glazer, Seymour Martin Lipset, Daniel Patrick Moynihan, Norman Podhoretz, James Q. Wilson, and others. It is certainly true to say that there are different strains in neoconservative thought, that neoconservatism may have evolved on some issues over time (e.g., foreign policy), and that not all neoconservatives will recognize themselves in the portrait drawn in this book. It is self-evidently true that not all neoconservatives follow the same path all the time, but it is equally true to say that neoconservatism does have core principles and a method and, moreover, that the logic of those principles and that method does in fact lead somewhere.

The nitpickers and naysayers will also argue that not all neoconservatives are Straussians and not all Straussians are neoconservatives. True enough: Many first-generation neocons were in fact not Straussians, and although not all Straussians are neocons, we think it is fair to say that many are. However, as Irving Kristol might have asked, so what? This kind of potential criticism begs this more fundamental question. Those neocons who have been most self-reflective about what neoconservatism is have been connected directly or indirectly with Strauss and his students. As we shall demonstrate conclusively in later chapters, the most important and influential neoconservative, Irving Kristol, was profoundly in-fluenced by Strauss and became his most influential popularizer. (Kristol's son, William, is now one of the leading lights in the neoconservative world, and he is an out-of-the-closet Straussian, as are several of the writers for his magazine, *The Weekly Standard*.) To be precise: This is a book about those neoconservatives who have been most influenced by Leo Strauss via Irving Kristol.

Thus, although *Neoconservatism: An Obituary for an Idea* is not an exhaus-tive treatment of neoconservative thought, we have attempted to present the neoconservatives' political philosophy in its most salient essentials. In order to bring some intellectual coherence to such a big and messy topic, we have nar-rowed our research primarily to a handful of neoconservative thinkers who we think best represent the core spirit of neonconservatism. The founder and voice of the neoconservative movement—the man who has provided its intellectual and political direction—is, unquestionably, Irving Kristol. His ideas dominate our study. Although many other neoconservative intellectuals have contributed in important ways to the neoconservative synthesis (e.g., Daniel Bell, Nathan Glazer, James Q. Wilson, and Norman Podhoretz, all of whom make cameo appearances in this book), Kristol's intellectual impact on the neoconservative movement has been without rival. He is the recognized voice of neoconservatism.[11] With the recent passing of Irving Kristol, the neoconservative intellectual baton has been unofficially passed to David Brooks, Peter Berkowitz, and Kristol's son, William. And of course, standing behind Irving Kristol, as we shall prove beyond all doubt, is Leo Strauss.

Let us be clear: We do not treat neoconservatism as a conspiracy or a cabal (readers of this book will find no flowcharts starting at some office at the University of Chicago, moving through apartments in New York City, and ending in some dark bunker office in the White House), but rather as an important intellectual and political movement that deserves to be taken seriously. Unlike their critics on the Left and the Right, we have not engaged in rumor-mongering or salacious gossip, we have not engaged in the politics of personal destruction, and we have rejected the all-too-common temptation to see neoconservative cabals secretly pulling the strings of America's government. Instead, we bring the same intellectual seriousness to neoconservatism as the neoconservatives have brought to bear on so many other intellectual and political movements. At the end of the day, no matter how critical we might be of the neocons and their influence on American intellectual and political life—and we shall be quite critical—we have worked very hard to be honest in our presentation of their ideas and fair in our final judgment of them.

PART I
THE END OF IDEOLOGY

CHAPTER I
THE PATH TO POWER

During the 1990s and certainly in the years immediately after September 11, 2001, a *spectre* (to paraphrase Karl Marx) seemed to haunt America's intellectual and political landscape—the spectre of neoconservatism. All the powers of America's intellectual establishment entered into an unholy alliance to expose and exorcise this ominous threat: the liberal *New York Times* and *The American Conservative* magazine, the New Left and the Old Right, and Sidney Blumenthal and Pat Buchanan all sounded the alarm. The Left characterized the neoconservatives as crusading moralists and neo-fascists, and the Right denounced them as moral nihilists and neo-Jacobins.[1] Wherein lies the truth?

Unfortunately, despite the many books and articles that have been published on the neocons in recent years, the deeper meaning of neoconservatism is still largely unknown. Much of the current popular literature on the neocons is unpersuasively hostile, overwrought, superficial, paranoid, and wrongheaded. The neocons have been treated by both their Left- and Right-wing enemies in the press as though they were some sort of malevolent, Oz-like force secretly controlling and pulling the strings during the eight years of the Bush administration. More invidiously, some of the neocons' most hostile critics have suggested that the "neo" in neocon stands simply for "Jewish defender of Israeli interests." During the lead up to and following the second Iraq war, the *New York Times* and the trendy establishment magazines and newspapers around the world ran articles on the neocon "cabal" (usually a code word for "Jewish") and its quest for world domination. The French weekly *Le Nouvel Observateur* ran a six-page spread (under the headline banner "After Iraq, the World") on "*les intellectuels néoconservateurs*" and their imperialistic designs for world domination. The

British, never to be outdone by the French, ran an hour-long special on their offical government television station that began with the ominous words: "This is a story about people who want the world run their way, the American way."[2] Some news outlets even ran articles—replete with flowcharts—connecting all the conspirators, including to whom they were married and where and with whom they went to college. In the end, such articles often said more about those who wrote them than about their subjects.

Conspiracy theories were rife during this period. It all sounded very sinister, and the neocons were made to appear as though they were America's modern political Hydra, becoming more powerful with each attempt to weaken them. Amusingly, it turns out that much of the paranoid misinformation about the neocons came from Lyndon LaRouche, that perennially self-parodying kook of American politics. Surprisingly (or not), the press took what LaRouche fed them hook, line, and sinker. How ironic that the *New York Times* and much of the elite media had become a mouthpiece for LaRouche's army.[3]

Just as there has been a great deal of mendacious rubbish published about the neoconservatives in recent years, so the neocons in turn have written a string of self-pitying and self-justifying essays in their own defense. If the neoconservatives are to be believed, virtually *none* of their critics have properly understood or explained what neoconservatism is all about. As the neoconservative *New York Times* columnist David Brooks put it: "If you ever read a sentence that starts with 'Neocons believe,' there is a 99.4 percent chance everything else in that sentence will be untrue."[4] In 2004, leading neoconservatives published a collection of twenty-four essays, the purpose of which was to defend the realm from the naysayers and nattering nabobs of the establishment media. They treated their critics rather dismissively as "full mooners" and crackpots. Worse yet, some neoconservatives, such as David Brooks and Joshua Muravchik, have simply evaded serious intellectual engagement with their critics by dismissing them as anti-Semitic.[5]

The whole debate over neoconservatism has become rather unseemly. It is tinged with bitter partisanship that can only foster a high degree of intellectual evasion and dishonesty. We now live in a very strange intellectual world, where neocon means Jewish and where a critic of neoconservatism means anti-Semite. The nasty critics and the fawning sycophants alike have, for very different reasons, dimmed the lights on neoconservatism and prevented the general public from seeing the deepest levels of neoconservative thought and practice. More to the point, virtually all of the polemical studies of neoconservatism, both for and against, are characterized by a high degree of superficiality.

The critics of the neocons, for instance, tend to focus on personalities, organizations, and dark conspiracies. They operate at a rather gossipy level by identifying who studied with whom, who married and sired whom, and how they are connected through a labyrinthine network of universities, think tanks, magazines, foundations, and midlevel offices at the Pentagon. Likewise, the neocons and their supporters have purposely promoted a superficial and distorted view of their own movement by advancing the perception that neoconservatism is so ideologically and politically diverse and that it has changed so much over time that there is actually "no 'there' there." They resist any attempt to label—i.e., to identify or define—their views. Writing in *Commentary,* one of the neocons' house organs, James Nuechterlein, has said that "Neoconservatism is a movement that, as far as most of its adherents are concerned, would rather not speak its name."[6] In fact, several high-profile "neocons" have even denied that they are neocons, or at minimum they reject the label. At the very least, the neocons want you, the public, to believe that neoconservatism is something of an ideological and political mirage. They often hide behind a stylistic veil of writing that emphasizes ambiguity, paradox, and irony. Their style of public communication often appears as a carefully calculated web of equivocations, hints, approximations, and generalties that lead the reader in a certain direction without ever quite establishing objectively defined principles. Thus the neocons are specialists in the art of plausible deniability, which leaves them with an automatic escape hatch that renders them immune to meaningful analysis and criticism. Simply put, it is impossible to criticize what one can never quite see or know.

Let us, then, begin anew. Of this much we can be certain: Modern America's intellectual and political skyline has been shaped rather profoundly by neoconservative thinkers. As Norman Podhoretz, a leading neoconservative patriarch, has written rather modestly, "Neoconservatism has had a trickle-down effect on the political culture, and its influence on both major parties is evident even today."[7] For better or worse, the world in which we live bears the imprint of neoconservative thinking. Thus it is critically important that we know exactly what they stand for and where they are heading. Only then, as Abraham Lincoln once said in a different context, can we "better judge *what* to do, and *how* to do it."[8] What is therefore most needed today is a fresh study of neoconservatism that is both intelligently critical and cautiously respectful.

A Very Brief History of Neoconservatism

Who exactly are the neoconservatives, where did they come from, and what do they stand for? The history of the neocons is well known and need not be repeated here at great length. Their story is told in the wonderfully entertaining PBS documentary *Arguing the World* (2001), and several monographs have recounted the origins and developments of neoconservatism.[9] Legend has it that neoconservatism was born at Brooklyn College during the late 1930s. The first meeting of the men who would eventually become the founders of the neoconservative movement—men such as Irving Kristol, Daniel Bell, Seymour Martin Lipset, and Nathan Glazer—took place at Alcove One in the college lunchroom, which was the home of the college Trotskyists, and was notably distinguished from Alcove Two, home of the college Stalinists. The young men who would one day become advisers to Democratic and Republican presidents alike cut their first ideological teeth on the heated sectarian debates that defined the American Marxist movement during the later years of the Great Depression.[10]

Thus, although Neoconservatism was born and nurtured on the radical Left, its history is of a slow rightward drift over the course of thirty or forty years. The men and women who would one day become neoconservatives broke ranks first with Marxian socialism in the 1940s and '50s because of its *totalitarianism,* with liberalism during the 1960s because of its *appeasement* of the Soviet Union, and finally with the New Left during the 1970s because of its imperialistic *nihilism.* Thus over the course of forty years, they evolved rather seamlessly from neo-Marxists to neoliberals to neoconservatives.

During most of the 1960s, these soon-to-be neocons saw themselves as unsentimental, pragmatic liberals—as New Deal–Fair Deal–New Frontier–Great Society democrats in the tradition of Franklin D. Roosevelt, Harry S. Truman, John F. Kennedy, Lyndon Johnson, and Hubert Humphrey. Nathan Glazer, one of the first-generation neocons and coeditor with Irving Kristol of their flagship journal, *The Public Interest,* has described the political inclinations of these proto-neocons in these terms:

> All of us had voted for Lyndon Johnson in 1964, for Hubert Humphrey in 1968, and I would hazard that most of the original stalwarts of *The Public Interest,* editors and regular contributors, continued to vote for Democratic presidential candidates all the way to the present. Recall that the original definition of the neoconservatives was that they fully embraced the reforms of the New Deal, and indeed the major programs of Johnson's Great Society.... Had we not defended the major social programs, from Social Security to Medicare, there would have been no need for the 'neo' before conservatism.

The catalyst that pushed them into the conservative movement was the moral, cultural, and political implosion of liberalism during the late 1960s. The neocons saw an America that was being destroyed politically by liberalism's failed social policies and culturally by the moral chaos created by the New Left. The soon-to-be neoconservatives were appalled by the inability of liberal intellectuals to see the obvious failures of their Great Society programs and by their appeasement of student radicals on America's besieged college campuses. Unable to defend itself from the onslaught of the counterculture and the New Left, liberalism was therefore also unable to defend America—indeed, civilization itself—from the new barbarism. And so these disaffected and skeptical liberals broke very openly and publicly with liberalism. By the late 1960s, Irving Kristol's transformation was complete:

> I no longer had to pretend to believe—what in my heart I could no longer believe—that liberals were wrong because they subscribe to this or that erroneous opinion on this or that topic. No—liberals were wrong, liberals are wrong, because they are liberals. What is wrong with liberalism is liberalism— a metaphysics and a mythology that is woefully blind to human and political reality.[11]

At the same time that neoconservatives announced their disaffection from post-1960s liberalism, they also began a steady migration into the conservative intellectual movement and the Republican Party. In 1971 the editors at the *National Review* invited the neocons to "C'mon In, the Water's Fine," and to join their mainstream conservative movement.[12] Throughout the 1970s and early 1980s, Kristol was followed into the Republican Party and into the conservative movement by many of his liberal friends and colleagues (although not all and not all at once). And in the near three decades since Ronald Reagan's first term in the White House, the neocons have systematically taken over the conservative intellectual movement with remarkable speed, their ideas have come to dominate the Republican Party, and their policies have influenced the administrations of Ronald Reagan, George H. W. Bush, and George W. Bush. Scores of neocons have held high-level positions in the Reagan and Bush administrations of both father and son. Richard Perle, for instance, a leading neoconservative foreign-policy expert, has stated approvingly that President George W. Bush, "on issue after issue, has reflected the thinking of neoconservatives." The *New York Review of Books* ran an article in 2003 during the pinnacle of neocon influence under the ominous title "The Neocons in Power." And during the 2004 Democratic presidential primary, Howard Dean charged that "President Bush has been captured by the neoconservatives around him."[13]

The neocons' political influence is largely a result of their impressive intellectual accomplishments. They are, without question, the most intellectually sophisticated and ambitious faction of the postwar intellectual Right. They were accepted into the conservative intellectual movement during the 1970s and '80s largely because they came with a high degree of intellectual caché. They had the right stuff: academic standing and connections with the elite liberal culture. The neocons brought to the Right a kind of intellectual savoir faire and political savvy that it had lacked for several generations.

The neoconservatives teach at the best universities, including Harvard, Yale, Cornell, Johns Hopkins, Berkeley, Stanford, and the University of Chicago. They control the wealthiest conservative philanthropic foundations, such as the John M. Olin (recently defunct) and Bradley foundations; they manage the leading conservative think tanks, such as the American Enterprise and Hudson institutes; they run the leading conservative journals and magazines, such as *Commentary, The Public Interest* (recently defunct), *National Interest, The Weekly Standard, City Journal, The New Criterion,* and *National Affairs;* they have a presence in the major media, including at least one columnist at the *New York Times* and a strong presence at Fox News.

The neocons are also remarkably prolific. Over the course of the last sixty years, they have written what probably amounts to hundreds of books and articles on a remarkably wide range of topics, such as communism, capitalism, democracy, student radicalism, poverty, affirmative action, Central America, dictatorship, deviance, religion, the U.N., feminism, abortion, homosexual marriage, progressive education, judicial activism, pornography, modern art, and other subjects too many to list. Their books sometimes even sit atop the bestseller lists. The neocons write with a philosophical dexterity, a moral seriousness, and a literary verve and clarity that is rare in the academy. Their prose style is almost always high-minded, elegant, probing, earnest, witty, commanding, ironic, and often combative. The substance and literary style of an Irving Kristol essay is, for instance, reminiscent of the writing produced by the great nineteenth-century *belles-lettres* essayists Matthew Arnold, Thomas Babington Macaulay, and John Stuart Mill. A neoconservative essay or book typically draws on a remarkably wide range of ideas taken from specialized studies in political science, psychology, economics, and sociology, wrapped in images and metaphors borrowed from history, philosophy, and literature. A typical neoconservative essay by Daniel Bell or a *New York Times* op-ed by David Brooks might quote, for instance, an economic report from the RAND Corporation in one paragraph and then explain its meaning in the next with references to Aristotle, Rousseau, or Nietzsche. They also have an amazing ability to mask their normative claims in the descriptive and predictive language of the social sciences, which is one reason why the neocons can sometimes seem so slippery and impervious to criticism.

When they are in attack mode against their political enemies (e.g., the New Left, liberal appeasers, paleoconservatives, or libertarians), their literary efforts can be brutally mocking and intellectually devastating. They typically portray their ideological and political adversaries as intellectual lightweights, buffoons, and wicked power-lusters. Applying the lessons learned during their days as young Trotskyists, the neocons follow a "take no prisoners" approach to ideological and political combat. Of a particular form of liberal hypocrisy, Irving Kristol once wrote mockingly: "In the United States today, the law insists that an eighteen-year-old girl has the right to public fornication in a pornographic movie—but only if she is paid the minimum wage."[14] Regardless of whether one agrees or disagrees with the neocons, they almost always impress readers with their formidable learning and the clarity of their prose, and they certainly challenge readers to think more deeply about the most pressing issues confronting American society. By earned right, they must be taken seriously.

Academically, the neocons might best be described as philosophical sociologists, or sociologists of values. They are at their best when examining the ideological causes and cultural consequences of various social "problems," such as poverty, racism, crime, pornography, or anti-Americanism. They have a wonderful ability to explain *why* things happen and what it all portends for the future. The neocons are also self-described skeptics: They do not trust the viability of untested ideas and theories applied to society wholesale. They believe that society is akin to a fragile "organism" that often reacts to the introduction of new ideas or policies in all kinds of negative ways unintended by social reformers. Social reality is complex, they say, and to change or reform society in a truly positive way is difficult. The so-called laws of economics and social science are, according to the neocons, ultimately grounded on the "hard realities of morality, family, culture, and religion—the 'habits of the mind' and 'habits of the heart,' as Tocqueville said."[15] Public policy must begin, they argue, with the people as they are and have been; it must take into account the inherited qualities and character of the people for whom the reform is intended, and it must proceed cautiously and gently.

Ultimately, what makes the neocons so interesting and unique is the seriousness with which they take ideas. They take seriously Richard Weaver's old adage that "ideas have consequences." Neoconservatism is not a political party as much as it is an intellectual movement that seeks to shape and guide politics through ideas. "What rules the world," according to Kristol, "is ideas."[16] Thus the neoconservatives look to ideas—to philosophy—as the ultimate cause of various social facts, and from there they trace how those ideas work or will probably work in practice. They believe that men and women are shaped and moved by values (values consciously chosen or unconsciously accepted), and they examine the intersection—if not the collision—between the common and traditional values of a particular society and the philosophical blueprints for radical social change promoted by the intelligentsia. In the words of Daniel Bell, it is "moral ideas" that shape history by inspiring "human aspirations."[17] The neoconservatives frequently write grand and sweeping essays and books demonstrating how the ideas of, say, Adam Smith or Martin Heidegger have shaped Western or American culture. They have demonstrated better than just about anyone else in contemporary intellectual life that evil ideas have evil consequences. Kristol puts it this way:

The modern world, and the crisis of modernity we are now experiencing, was created by ideas and by the passions which these ideas unleashed. To surmount this crisis, without destroying the modern world itself, will require new ideas—or new versions of old ideas—that will regulate these passions and bring them into a more fruitful and harmonious relation with reality.... For two centuries, the very important people who managed the affairs of this society could not believe in the importance of ideas—until one day they were shocked to discover that their children, having been captured and shaped by certain ideas, were either rebelling against their authority or seceding from their society. The truth is that ideas are *all* important.[18]

But to which ideas are the neocons beholden? What "new ideas" do they propose as the anodyne to the "crisis of modernity"? What is their political philosophy, and what is their plan for governing America? Unfortunately, there are no easy answers to these questions.

Unlike traditional conservatives, neoconservatives do advocate some kinds of "progressive" reform and change. In this, they are more liberal than conservative. Irving Kristol, doyen of the neoconservatives, has said of neoconservatism that it is distinct from traditional conservatism in that it is utterly free of nostalgia for the past. Whereas traditional conservatives often seem trapped in the past and wanting to preserve old manners and mores, the neocons are, by contrast, progressive and forward-looking. This much they seem to retain from their youthful days as Trotskyists: They seek slow transformation rather than preservation. The neocons have always had a much less jaundiced view of government and the role it should play in human affairs than traditional conservatives. In their view, government is, or certainly can be, a positive good.

Irving Kristol has described himself and his friends as "realistic meliorists," by which he means they support government programs for the relief of man's estate, but they also are skeptical of government programs that ignore human nature, history, and experience.[19] The neocons might be best described as cautious or pragmatic liberals in that they think that reform should be modest, slow, and experimental, and it should be devised in such a way that it relies more on traditional social values and "mediating social structures" than on bureaucratic authority and ideological dogmas imposed arbitrarily from the top down.[20] They are skeptics without being pessimists. The neocons are also thoughtful students of human nature; they are moral anthropologists, as well as historians and sociologists of cultural and moral values. They are excellent at demonstrating how certain social policies cut against the grain of human nature or traditional values and why they are doomed to failure. But the neocons also think that, if done properly, human nature and traditional values can be "incentivized" with the proper inducements and guidance, and that social reform therefore is possible. We might say that the neocons apply John Dewey's pragmatic method of analysis to the social problems created by Dewey's liberal followers. They are what might be called nervous or conservative Deweyites.

Politically, the neoconservatives were skeptical of large social engineering projects, particularly Lyndon Johnson's Great Society welfare programs, and they were even more so once it became clear that these programs were the cause of serious social pathologies.[21] Through flagship journals founded in the 1960s, such as *The Public Interest,* the neocons exposed and criticized the failures of the welfare state and the disastrous consequences that ensued. In contrast to many liberal intellectuals, the neocons do believe in the Law of Unintended Consequences, which says that things never quite turn out the way you hope they will. According to the neocons, it was the failure of Great Society liberals in the 1960s to understand this law, that led to the social upheaval that followed in its wake. The neocons were and are particularly good at demonstrating the perverse incentives and outcomes generated by government social programs. They did pioneering studies demonstrating, for instance, how welfare programs such as Aid to Families with Dependent Children (AFDC) created a culture of dependence and perpetual poverty. Their scholarship showed how AFDC fostered an explosion of out-of-wedlock births and several generations of single-parent homes, particularly in the black community. They traced the effects of these policies all the way down to the street level. Their studies showed the relationship between welfare policies and the creation of a generation of fatherless boys who subsequently turned to gangs, drugs, crime, violence, and other forms of deviant and socially destructive behavior.

Intellectually, it was the neoconservatives who largely stood alone in America's universities speaking out about the moral crisis of the West. It was the neocons who wrote some of the best and most profound critiques of philosophic nihilism and its cultural consequences for Western civilization. It was neoconservative academics such as Allan Bloom who, in *The Closing of the American Mind,* demonstrated the relationship between the philosophies of Nietzsche and Heidegger and the moral nihilism of the New Left. The neocons have waged a matchless intellectual war against the pieties of America's tenured radicals. They have been trenchant critics of the major ideas that have dominated America's universities since the 1960s, such as nihilism, relativism, historicism, and egalitarianism; they have been on the front lines of the culture war, opposing intellectual trends such as feminism, multiculturalism, environmentalism, postmodernism, deconstructionism, and political correctness; and they have challenged the intellectual integrity of politically correct academic programs such as women's, black, Latino, and queer studies as well as any other kind of ideologically motivated academic programs that now define the modern American university. The neocons have been particularly good at demonstrating how these ideas have percolated through American culture to affect deleteriously the manners and mores of ordinary Americans.

To sum up: Neoconservatism was born and grew up as an *oppositional* movement. The neocons have always articulated quite clearly what it is they don't
like about modern American society. Neoconservatism is probably best known
for its opposition to 1960s-style liberalism and the radicalism of the New Left.
The neocons' critique of the Left has often been withering and sometimes even
brutal. It is the neoconservatives who, more than any other group on the political Right, have taken the fight directly to the New Left.

We now have a sense of what the neocons are against, but what are they for?
The neocons never could have achieved their notable successes without having
presented a positive political philosophy? So what is it?

From the 1960s to the present, the neoconservatives have reintroduced into
American intellectual life and culture a moral discourse that includes ideas and
principles such as natural law, freedom, capitalism, constitutionalism, statesmanship, virtue, and meritocracy. Academically, they have defended liberal education,
high academic standards, the "Great Books" tradition, and good old-fashioned
political history. They have also stood on the front lines of the culture wars in
defense of Western civilization. In foreign policy, they have advocated a muscular
national defense and a principled and tough-minded defense of Israel.

Most significantly, the neoconservatives present themselves as great defenders
of American ideals and institutions—of Americanism. They are the most unabashedly pro-American academics in several generations, and they have sought
to capture the moral high ground in defining what it means to be an American
against the attacks of the New Left. In contrast to America's tenured radicals,
the neocons have, according to James Q. Wilson, "great sympathy for and often
take their cues from the general and settled convictions of the average American." Their thinking and rhetoric have also helped to restore a moral clarity to
American domestic and foreign policy that had been lacking since at least the
1960s. Their patriotism comes prepackaged in the language of the American
Founding Fathers and Abraham Lincoln. The neoconservatives almost single-
handedly recaptured and resurrected the study of the American founding from
the hands of debunking Marxist scholars. As Irving Kristol once put it rather
pungently: "It is the self-imposed assignment of neoconservatism to explain to
the American people why they are right, and to the intellectuals why they are
wrong."[22]

There is certainly much that is laudable in neoconservative thought and
practice, and there are some admirable neoconservatives. But, as we shall argue
throughout this book, all is not quite as it seems with the neoconservatives.
On the surface, they *seem* to take ideas seriously, they *seem* to be principled,
they *seem* to support the principles on which America was founded (e.g.,
individual rights, limited government, and constitutionalism), they *seem* to
support capitalism, and they *seem* to support a strong national defense. And,

on one level, on the *exoteric* or political level, they do support these principles and policies. On a deeper level, however, on what they might call the *esoteric* or philosophical level, they eschew such ideas and principles. Ironically, despite all their interest in philosophical ideas, despite all their attempts to examine the moral conditions of civil society, and despite their lip service to capitalism and the principles of the American founding, the neoconservatives scorn reason, principles, morality, and capitalism, and, ultimately, they scorn America. In other words, they talk like Abraham Lincoln but act like Stephen Douglas.

Reforming the "Stupid Party"

The inner core of neoconservative political thought is best accessed by examining its surface or that which comes to sight first. Examining what the "neo" is in neoconservatism—i.e., examining how the neocons position themselves relative to traditional American conservatives and to the Republican Party—provides the initial doorway into the neoconservative intellectual universe. The rest of this chapter and all of the next are devoted to presenting the outer layer of neoconservative political thought.

In a much-discussed essay on "The Neoconservative Persuasion" published in 2003, Irving Kristol summed up the neocon agenda this way: Their aim is and has been, he wrote, to "convert the Republican Party, and American conservatism in general, against their respective wills, into a new kind of conservative politics suitable to governing a modern democracy."[23] The implication, of course, is that the GOP and their conservative leaders are and have been ill equipped to govern modern America. Historically, neoconservatives have always had a rather distant and uneasy relationship with traditional conservatives and Republicans. The neocons have tended to support the view of John Stuart Mill when he characterized conservatives as the "stupid party." They now aim, with all of their intellectual sophistication and liberal "street cred," to change that, and, to a very large extent, they have.[24] Over the course of the last two generations, the neocons have played a key role in giving the Republican Party and the conservative intellectual movement a total makeover.

Kristol's first task in converting the conservative intellectual movement into a political movement capable of governing America was to redefine its guiding principles and its relationship to traditional American values. Neoconservatism, Kristol boasts, is the *first* variant of twentieth-century conservatism that is "*in* the 'American grain.'"[25] At first glance, this is an extraordinary claim! What could he possibly mean by it? The implication, of course, is that traditional conservatism (let's call it Goldwater conservatism)—with its proclaimed attachment to Jeffersonian principles of individual rights, limited government, and the free-enterprise system—is *outside* the American grain or even *un*-American.

Following in Kristol's footsteps, the neoconservative columnist at the *New York Times,* David Brooks, has systematically laid out in the pages of *The Weekly Standard,* the *Wall Street Journal,* and the *New York Times* what he calls a plan for "creative destruction," which is his blueprint for purging the GOP of its attachment to what he mockingly dubs the "Leave Us Alone" philosophy of small-government conservatives. "Wishing to be left alone is not a governing doctrine," Brooks has written with neoconservative coauthor William Kristol. Brooks has proudly announced in an article titled "The Era of Small Government Is Over" that "reducing the size of government cannot be the governing philosophy for the next generation of conservatives." For more than ten years, Brooks has been the leading neoconservative obituarist for the "death of small-government conservatism." He applauds the fact that conservatives and the Republican Party are "now significantly less anti-state and more pro-community than two years ago." Conservatives have "become re-reconciled," Brooks is pleased to report, "to the idea of some government action."[26]

The neoconservatives have openly and proudly launched what they call "Big-Government Conservatism."[27] To that end, they have conditioned conservatives and Republicans to believe that some version of the welfare state is necessary today in order to deal with the complexities of modern life. They urge the GOP to embrace the post–New Deal welfare state and to use the government to help organize and regulate the economy. First Irving Kristol in the 1970s and '80s, then David Brooks beginning in the 1990s, and more recently Peter Berkowitz (a Senior Fellow at the Hoover Institution) have all encouraged conservatives to make their peace with big government and direct it toward conservative ends, although it is not clear what conservative ends would be left to pursue after they followed the neocons and abandoned their limited-government principles. Remarkably, Peter Berkowitz has appealed to the conservative philosophy of Edmund Burke to argue against pursuing a policy of "reversing and ultimately eliminating the New Deal," which "would require the dismissal of society's accumulated experience, knowledge, and traditions over the course of 80 years." The welfare state is now "rooted," he argues, "in shared American values" and "woven into the fabric of American sensibility." To seek to reverse it, he claims, would be to engage in the kind of "radical" politics to which Burke objected.

From Berkowitz's pseudo-Burkean perspective, then, American history begins in 1932. "Like it or not," Berkowitz intones, "the New Deal is here to stay," and so conservatives should abandon their core principles and make their peace with it. He argues that to do otherwise, or rather to fixate on the "utopian dream of cutting government down to 18th-century size can only derail conservatism's core and continuing mission of slowing and containing government's growth, keeping it within reasonable boundaries, and where possible reducing its reach." Translation: As we go forward into the early twenty-first century, the true conservative position will seek to manage and contain the growth of the Obama administration's various recent attempts to nationalize America's banking, auto, and health care industries. Neoconservatism means the abandonment of traditional conservative principles (to the extent that conservatives actually ever supported and acted in such principles) in order to become a moderating force within the modern liberal universe. By this account, neoconservatism provides the means to service liberal ends.[28]

The neoconservative critique of the Republicans' traditionally pro-freedom, limited-government philosophy is, more importantly, a critique of principles as such. In the place of guiding principles, the neocons advise Republicans to substitute a method and a temperament for thinking about politics. The two buzzwords that one most often hears coming from today's neoconservatives are "moderation" and "prudence."[29] Neoconservative political philosopher Peter Berkowitz calls moderation "an essential political virtue and a quintessentially conservative virtue." It is a valuable psychological and moral disposition, he writes, "which involves controlling passion so that reason can give proper weight to competing partisan claims, most of which contain some element of truth and some element of falsehood." Moderation provides the indispensible attitude necessary for the creation of a new politics of compromise between Left and Right. In fact, Berkowitz denounces those defenders of limited-government principles as imprudent revolutionaries who "appeal to abstract notions of natural right to justify a radical reversal of today's commonly held convictions about the federal government's basic responsibilities."[30]

In denouncing such radicals, Berkowitz is also quite intentionally denouncing the principles of 1776, which is a curious position to take for someone who claims to be a conservative, even if just a *neo*conservative. Thus the American Revolution, because of its dedication to "abstract notions of liberty," must surely be seen as "imprudent" from the neoconservative perspective. To repeat: The neocons do not want traditional conservatives thinking and acting on the basis of principles. Instead, they have replaced principles for a disposition or an attitude, and they preach moderation as a virtue so that ordinary Americans will accept compromise as inevitable and necessary. They want the American people to be moderate, which means open and pliable to compromise and change. Neoconservative moderation and prudence mean a defense of the status quo, which means a defense of our post–New Deal world.

Neoconservatism thus understands itself as a "third way" between the stale categories of Left and Right. It is all about "stealing ideas from both the left and right," as David Brooks has advised Republicans. In real political terms, that's what neoconservative "moderation" actually means. Put differently, the "art of government," writes Irving Kristol, is to translate the "liberal or radical impulse into enduring institutions," which means that liberal ends will be achieved with conservative means.[31] In other words, socialism-cum-liberalism is the motor, and conservatism the brake. In this tug of war between neoconservatives and liberals, it is only the speed or the degree of political change that is affected, not the direction. The neocons' advice to the Republican Party is to compromise and accept the moral ends of liberal-socialism, but with the caveat that conservatives can do a better job of doling out the goods and services. This, then, is the clue to the real meaning of the neocons' advice to the Republican Party: The principled approach to politics shall be abandoned for the art of compromise, which will be cloaked in the semiphilosophical language of moderation and prudence.

If the Jeffersonian-Goldwater tradition—i.e., if a dedication to a limited-government philosophy—is supposedly outside the "American grain" and imprudent, what conservative ideas are *in* the American grain? To whom do the neoconservatives turn for guidance and inspiration?

Kristol, Brooks, and several other neoconservatives have reinvented a usable past for conservatives that gives pride of place to big-government activism. Remarkably, at the top of the neocons' pantheon of American heroes are three individuals who did as much to destroy America's individual-rights republic as any three figures in American history: Herbert Croly, Theodore Roosevelt, and Franklin Delano Roosevelt.[32] This is the same Herbert Croly who bragged that his political philosophy was "flagrantly socialistic both in its methods and its objects," the same TR who once said that "every man holds his property subject to the general right of the community to regulate its use to whatever degree the public welfare may require it," and the same FDR who once said that all Americans must act "as a trained and loyal army willing to sacrifice for the good of the common discipline."[33] What unites Croly and the Roosevelt cousins is their support for the idea that the individual should be subordinated to a collectivistic, paternalistic, corporate State. That the neocons would turn to such a statist triumvirate for historical inspiration and guidance reveals much about their plan to "reform" the Republican Party.

The neocons are, relative to the "American grain" tradition associated with the limited-government philosophy of Thomas Jefferson, unabashed statists. They support, in the words of Ben Wattenberg, a "muscular role for the state," one that taxes, regulates, controls, orders, and redistributes—and, as we shall see, one that fights. In his *Weekly Standard* manifesto on the neoconservative persuasion, Kristol further indicates how he and his friends understand the role of the State in American public life:

> Neocons do not like the concentration of services in the welfare state and are
> happy to study alternative ways of delivering services. But they are impatient

with the Hayekian notion that we are on "the road to serfdom." *Neocons do not feel that kind of alarm or anxiety about the growth of the state in the past century, seeing it as natural, indeed inevitable.* Because they tend to be more interested in history than economics or sociology, they know that the 19th-century idea, so neatly propounded by Herbert Spencer in his "The Man Versus the State," was a historical eccentricity.[34]

Not only is Kristol indifferent to the growth of the State, he does not believe, as did virtually every thinker on the Right in the early post–World War II period, that the continuing growth of the State leads to serfdom. Certainly Hayek's and Spencer's defense of freedom was fatally flawed in many important respects, but surely they are preferable to Herbert Croly or Franklin Delano Roosevelt! Not so for the neocons. They much prefer the big governmentalism of Herbert Croly to the small governmentalism of Herbert Spencer.

Former Trotskyists in the 1930s and '40s and then liberals in the '50s and '60s, the neocons have never abandoned their deepest moral and political commitments (as we shall see below), and their cavalier acceptance of and support for the growth of the State remains unabated. This is precisely why the neocons' war against the "New Class"—that coalition of journalists, academics, and bureaucrats associated with the New Left—has never been a war against New Deal liberalism. By denouncing the cultural Left that grew out of the 1960s, the Kristolians hoped to preserve the principles and institutions of the New Deal Old Left. They reject the principles and policies of Tom Hayden, Jerry Ruben, and Huey Newton, but they support those of Rex Tugwell, Stuart Chase, and Franklin Delano Roosevelt.

The real problem with traditional conservatives and Republicans, according to the neoconservatives, is that they are too beholden to that old-fashioned Jeffersonian idea that the government that rules best, rules least. Irving Kristol and David Brooks believe that nineteenth-century ideas such as natural rights, individualism, limited government, and laissez-faire capitalism were historical "eccentricities"—myths better forgotten than defended. They criticize the GOP for being "overreliant on anti-statist rhetoric." The neocons therefore follow their hero Herbert Croly's admonition to his fellow Progressive socialists that "Reform is both meaningless and powerless unless the Jeffersonian principle of non-interference is abandoned."[35] David Brooks or Peter Berkowitz could have just as easily uttered such sentiments.

Not surprisingly, then, the Old Right's opposition to the New Deal appalls the neoconservatives. They reserve special scorn for those conservatives and libertarians who oppose the "positive" liberty principles of compulsory social insurance, increased taxes, economic and moral regulation, and other exercises of coercion by the State. David Brooks has advocated the transformation of the

Republican Party from one that celebrates "freedom and capitalism" and the "heroic individualist" to one that views America as a big family defined by its nurturing virtues and "its ability to rebuild families and communities." The neoconservatives' new Republican Party will not "fight for freedom," he opines, but it will fight for "compassion."[36] Irving Kristol has likewise described the traditional conservatives' desire of "returning to a 'free enterprise' system in which government will play the modest role it used to" as representing a dangerously utopian "counter-reformation." (Ironically, as Kristol denounces any attempt to return to the classical liberalism of the nineteenth century as dangerously utopian, he simultaneously calls on Americans to begin the "long trek" back to the classical political philosophy of Plato!) The very idea of a return to the laissez-faire philosophy of the previous century draws Kristol's scorn:

> There is no more chance today of returning to a society of "free enterprise" and enfeebled government than there was, in the 16th century, of returning to a Rome-centered Christendom.... One may regret this fact; nostalgia is always permissible. But the politics of nostalgia is always self-destructive.

Ironically, what really bothers the neocons about small-government Republicans is that they are too principled, too ideological, too beholden to an outdated Jeffersonian conception of government. The neocons regard such ideological nostalgia as fatally "doctrinaire" and as fostering "moral self-righteousness," which they see as the only thing worse than nihilism.[37] Ultimately, the neocons view any return to a pre–New Deal world as not only impractical and fanciful but, more importantly, immoral.

At a deeper level, Kristol and Brooks actually reject the fundamental principles of a free and liberal society. According to Kristol, principles such as individual rights, limited government, and economic freedom are neither morally edifying nor practically sustainable. "A society founded solely on 'individual rights' was," he wrote, "a society that ultimately deprived men of those virtues which could only exist in a *political community* which is something other than a 'society.'" Such virtues include

> a sense of distributive justice, a fund of shared moral values, and a common vision of the good life sufficiently attractive and powerful to transcend the knowledge that each individual's life ends only in death. Capitalist society itself—as projected, say, in the writings on John Locke and Adam Smith—was negligent of such virtues.[38]

On a deeper level, the problem with the Founders' liberalism, according to Kristol, is that it begins with the individual, and a philosophy that begins with the "self" must necessarily promote selfishness, choice, and the pursuit of personal happiness. A secular capitalist society—a society that enables its citizens to pursue their self-interest—inevitably degenerates, he argues, into a culture of isolated individuals driven solely by the joyless quest for creature comforts. A free society grounded on the protection of individual rights leads inexorably to an amiable philistinism, an easygoing nihilism, and, ultimately, to "infinite emptiness."[39] The bourgeois virtues associated with Adam Smith's "nation of shopkeepers" would lead eventually, according to Kristol, to a nation of shopkeepers selling girly magazines. In other words, according to Kristol and friends, the principles espoused by John Adams, Thomas Jefferson, and James Madison point toward the Marquis de Sade, Nietzsche, and Abbie Hoffman.

If the growth of the State represents the road to serfdom for Hayek, the demystification of the State represents the road to nihilism for the neocons. During the 2008 financial crisis that rocked the American economy, David Brooks described the actions of those Republican members of Congress who voted against a $700 billion bailout and the nationalization of the banking system as a "revolt of the nihilists," and he praised instead Henry Paulson's plan for transferring "nearly unlimited authority to a small coterie of policy makers" in order to control and regulate the banking system. "What we need in this situation," he opined, "is authority." He praised Paulson's plan precisely because it circumvented "any system of checks and balances" and relied instead on "the wisdom and public spiritedness of those in charge." Brooks's deepest hope is that some powerful and charismatic leader or some small band of properly educated statesmen will rise up, "amid all the turmoil," and "occupy the commanding heights" of political rule and governance.[40]

Thus the great political lesson that the neocons have successfully taught other conservatives and their Republican students over the course of the last thirty years is to stop worrying and to love the State. In the words of David Brooks, we have—with his blessing—entered a "political age built around authority rather than freedom." Our greatest challenge is, he writes, to "restore legitimate centers of authority." By this he means the assumption of power by the federal government in order to assume the task of shaping the moral and political culture of the nation. Brooks calls this new system of government "Progressive Corporatism."[41]

In what may be Irving Kristol's most shocking statement in defense of collectivist redistribution and statism, he has suggested that the "idea of a welfare state is in itself perfectly consistent with a conservative political philosophy—as Bismarck knew, a hundred years ago."[42] Incredibly, in addition to Theodore Roosevelt and Franklin D. Roosevelt, the neocons have proudly added Otto von Bismarck—the German chancellor who invented the welfare state and who laid the groundwork for the collectivist-authoritarian politics of the twentieth century—to their list of statesmanlike heroes![43] The neocons' new Republican

Party will, once firmly entrenched in power, seek to restore not a Jeffersonian model of government, but rather the policies of an Americanized form of Prussian welfare statism.

This, apparently, is what it means to be "in the 'American grain.'"

CHAPTER 2
A NEW GOVERNING PHILOSOPHY

In chapter 1 we scratched the surface of neoconservative thought and practice. In this chapter we dig down to the next layer to examine more closely how the neocons situate themselves relative to other conservatives and Republicans. Neoconservatism's leading rhetoricians, first Irving Kristol in the 1970s and 1980s and now more recently David Brooks, have long urged the Republican Party to reinvent itself by developing a new "governing philosophy."[1] Decoding what the neocons mean by this notion of a "governing philosophy" (a phrase frequently repeated in their writings but rarely discussed and never defined) is an important key to unlocking the deeper meaning of their long-term intellectual and political project. Surprisingly, no previous study of neoconservatism has seen or understood the critical importance that the neocons place on this seemingly innocuous political concept.

The great problem with the Grand Old Party, according to David Brooks, is that it has always lacked "a governing *philosophy,* a set of ideas to help Republican officials organize their thinking while they serve in government and use the power of government to conservative ends." Brooks's diagnosis of the GOP is, at face value, absurd. Conservatives and the Grand Old Party have long had a governing philosophy associated, at the very least, with the political platforms of Barry Goldwater and Ronald Reagan. So what Brooks really means to say is that he does not like the traditional Republican philosophy of governance. He clearly thinks that conservatives and Republicans have pursued and been guided by the wrong "governing philosophy." In Brooks's view, a proper "philosophy of governance" would connect "citizens to higher national aims" and organize "American behavior around the world."[2] A proper "philosophy of governance" would take a more active role in controlling what people think and the way they behave. Paradoxically, though, a "governing philosophy" for the neocons is not a set of fixed principles. Rather, it is a mode of thinking for restoring the Republican Party to political power.

Ironically, the neocons do not have—indeed, they are opposed to—a defined program of principles or policies. Instead, their notion of a "governing philosophy" is guided by concepts such as the "common good" or the "public interest," abstractions that are free-floating, open-ended, and ultimately indefinable. Let us be clear: The neoconservatives are not advising Republicans to develop a political philosophy grounded in absolute and certain moral principles. In fact, the truth is just the opposite. In their view that would be much too "doctrinaire" and much too limiting. Neocons do not like ideological straightjackets that limit their ability to act for the "national interest" in prudent, statesmanlike ways. For them, principles just get in the way. In fact, the neocons urge conservatives to stop thinking in principles. David Brooks has urged Republicans to "be policy-centric, not philosophy-centric."[3] The neoconservatives have, ironically enough, a distaste for arguments grounded in moral first principles, particularly arguments either *for* capitalism or *against* the welfare state. They openly scorn the necessity for moral and political consistency. For the neocons, the idea of first principles, moral absolutes, and principled consistency represents a kind of naïve foolishness. They cynically declare that the "age of ideology" is over, by which they mean that the self-righteous moralism of the Old Right and the New Left must be abandoned so that they, the neocons, can get on with the business of managing more efficiently the practical and inevitable realities of the modern welfare state.

A Philosophy of Governance

If the neoconservatives' "governing philosophy" is not about philosophic principles, then what exactly is it? A "philosophy of governance" is a philosophy for *how* to rule or govern. The problem with the Republican Party hitherto, according to Irving Kristol, is that it has no vision for how America ought to be governed. For too long, the GOP was guided by what he mockingly calls a "businessman's mentality," by which he means that for too long Republicans have been concerned with such mundane tasks as balancing the budget, lowering taxes, and cutting government spending. According to Kristol, focusing on such pedestrian issues with the eye of an accountant is not how one gets elected, nor is it how one builds a governing majority. Instead, he urges conservatives and Republicans to act less like political "accountants" and more like political "entrepreneurs."[4] Kristol maintains that the art of politics is learning how to acquire power creatively in the same way that the business entrepreneur acts creatively to acquire profits.

A governing philosophy is ultimately about developing strategies for getting, keeping, and using power in certain ways, which means that it is about developing a political rhetoric that will arouse the passions and loyalties of the voting masses. Thus the neocons are less interested in the particular content or the truth of an idea than they are in its political utility. They view ideas as weapons, as a means to a political end. The ultimate utility of an idea is whether it helps one to acquire power. What GOP strategists need most, according to Kristol, is a strong "dose of *Machiavellian shrewdness*," the characteristics of which are "quick-wittedness, articulateness, a clear sense of one's ideological agenda and the *devious routes* necessary for its enactment."[5] If compassionate conservatism injected Christian love into the hardened arteries of Republican politics, then neoconservatism infused blood-thinning cynicism into the Republican bloodstream.[6]

The neoconservative message to traditional conservatives and Republicans is, in effect: "Grow up! Get over your juvenile ideological hang-ups. Be clever. Improvise, modify, and adapt your principles to changing circumstances. Develop an ideological agenda that will get you elected and keep you in power." This mode of reasoning explains how and why neoconservatism seems to have no philosophical identity and why the neocons can appear to be all things to all people all at once. Once in power, says Kristol, the GOP must learn how to "shape" rather than balance or cut the budget. This means essentially that the Republicans should heed Machiavelli's advice and shape the budget in politically advantageous ways (i.e., in ways that buy votes and in ways that have a strong emotional appeal for the people).

For all of their supposed concern for ideas and philosophy, there is something profoundly antiphilosophical about the neoconservatives. They eschew moral first principles in favor of a technique or a mode of thinking, and they scorn absolute, certain moral principles for what "works." This means that for more than forty years they have fought an ideological war against ideology. Most importantly, the neocons do not want the GOP or the American people to take their own principles too seriously; the neocons do not want them to be principled defenders of a coherent, systematic philosophy, such as the individual-rights, limited-government philosophy associated with the classical-liberal tradition and the American founding. Ultimately, despite some of their rhetoric to the contrary, neocons do not want the American people to be fully self-owning, self-governing, or self-reliant. That would make ordinary Americans too ideologically rigid, independent, and resistant to the siren call of the "public interest." The neocons want a passive populace who is willing to follow the moral and political guidance of a specially trained corps of wise and benevolent "statesmen." As will be shown in chapter 7, however, the neocons do have a coherent, systematic philosophy beneath their surface pragmatism, but it is a philosophy that provides guidance for rulers only and not one that should be followed by the general public.

The neocons' pragmatic political strategy works something like this: They urge Republicans to drop their limited-government principles and to consider only the immediate problems of the present—one at a time, unconnected to all other problems, and without reference to objectively demonstrable and certain moral principles. Instead, the neocons advocate taking each and every extant political issue and treating it as though it were a separate and discrete phenomenon unconnected to larger principles. This is how they carve out political space for acts of high-minded, statesmanlike action. Shockingly, Irving Kristol has written that "there are moments when it is *wrong* to do the *right* thing." Consider Kristol's "First Law" of politics:

> There are occasions where circumstances trump principles. Statesmanship consists not in being loyal to one's avowed principles (that's easy), but in recognizing the occasions when one's principles are being trumped by circumstances.... The ... *creative statesman*, one who possesses some political imagination, will see such occasions as possible opportunities for *renewed political self-definition.*[7]

Consider what Kristol is saying here. He is telling Republicans to stop taking their principles so seriously. He is telling them that a consistent adherence to one's principles is "easy," a claim that most Americans, regardless of their political ideology, would surely find bizarre. He is telling them that politics trumps principles, and that the successful statesman is chameleonlike in his ability to redefine his principles in the light of changing circumstances. At any given moment and in any given situation, the neocons can pull out of their back pocket a playbook of ideas, policies, and political rhetoric that are appropriate to the situation, to the here and now. This is how and why they can draw on so many different and sometimes contradictory philosophic traditions; this is how and why they can call on the ideas of Bismarck one day for solutions to contemporary problems and then the rhetoric of Jefferson the next so as to address a new set of problems.

This view of an ever-changing political reality is the source for the neocons' firmly held position that it is wrong for political parties (and particularly for Republicans) to be guided by unbending philosophical principles. Instead, Republicans should identify and make their policies conform to the great streams of public opinion. In a revealing *Wall Street Journal* op-ed, Kristol expressed how the neoconservatives understand the nature of political reality and how political actors should respond to it:

> *Self-definition* is a permanent problem for political parties in a modern democracy. The advent of new generations, together with technological and social

change, challenge traditional principles. The initial, instinctive response of all parties is to change the people so as to match the party's principles. But changing people is hard, and is usually beyond the power of politics. Religion can sometimes manage it; politics, almost never. The decline of political parties is associated with a reluctance to match principles to people, lest the parties be vulnerable to an accusation of "pragmatism." But it is precisely this reluctance that makes for a "pragmatic"—i.e., grudging, defeatist—response rather than a bold, creative one.[8]

Notice once again Kristol's emphasis on the need for politicians to define and redefine their principles based on the changing tides of public opinion. Statesmen should not expect (or want) consistency in politics. Principles, which for Kristol are synonymous with mere opinions, do and must change with the times. It is in this context, then, that we can understand why the neocons advise Republicans to abandon fixed principles as a guide to action. The neocons think it impolitic and foolish for Republicans to begin their thinking about public policy hampered by the ideological straightjacket of moral first principles or principles that are out of date. (Of course, they do advocate old-fashioned principles when such principles suit their contemporary political needs.) The neocons view the kinds of principles associated, for instance, with Jeffersonian conservatives, the Old Right, and Goldwater Republicans as at best irrelevant and sometimes as dangerously utopian because they almost always conflict with the realities of political life. In the revealingly honest words of Michael Ledeen: "Most of the conventional wisdom about leadership is dangerously wrong, because it suggests that there is a set of unchanging principles which, if applied diligently, always give the best chance of success." Machiavelli, the neocons' guiding light on questions of political prudence, "rejects this," Ledeen approvingly tells us, and the neocons clearly also reject the idea that politicians should act on the basis of permanent principles.[9] Dedication to principles too often gets in the way of high-minded statesmanship.

The most remarkable aspect of the neocons' notion of a "governing philosophy" is that it is a strategy for governing without philosophy. They claim to be nonideological and free from dogma. The neocons tell Republicans that firm principles are unnecessary (indeed, they are usually a hindrance to gaining power), that prudence must always trump principle, and that *expediency* is the best guide to action. In fact, one might say that for the neocons, pragmatism (disguised as prudence) is a substitute for moral principles. Ultimately, the neocons' goal is to disarm the GOP of its adherence to the fixed philosophic principles associated with the classical-liberal tradition and the American founding.

The neocons describe themselves unabashedly as *pragmatists*. The philosophy of pragmatism—that uniquely American philosophy associated with Charles S. Pierce (1839–1914), William James (1842–1910), and, most importantly, John

Dewey (1859–1952)—rejects the idea that there is an objective reality, that there are fixed laws of logic, permanent truths, or absolute principles of morality and politics. The pragmatist, according to William James, "turns away … from fixed principles, closed systems, and pretended absolutes and origins"; he is opposed to "the pretense of finality in truth." Pragmatists and neoconservatives both claim that reality is fluid and indeterminate, that the truth of an idea is determined not by its connection to reality but by its "practical cash value," that what is true today may not be true tomorrow, that ideas are "instruments," and that philosophy must be practical, results-oriented, and meliorative. The neoconservatives' intellectual method is thus virtually identical to the pragmatic method (see the two block quotations above from Irving Kristol), which was summed up by James: It is the "attitude of looking away from first things, principles, 'categories,' supposed necessities; and of looking towards last things, fruits, consequences, facts."[10]

The neoconservatives' support for and understanding of pragmatism is seen clearly in Peter Berkowitz's 2009 essay "Pragmatism Obama Style" that appeared in *The Weekly Standard*. His tone in this essay clearly suggests that he approves of President Barack Obama presenting himself and acting "as a postpartisan pragmatist," but he chastises the president for being "anything but postpartisan." The problem with Obama, from Berkowitz's perspective, is that he is not a proper or a true pragmatist. Proper pragmatism, Berkowitz writes, "stands for flexibility in solving problems as opposed to insistence on solutions that conform to religious or metaphysical dogma or rigid moral and political agendas." Better yet, pure pragmatism "denies the very existence of objective truth, arguing that opinions we declare true are merely those that have proved useful to one interest or another," which is precisely the lesson that the neocons have been trying to teach the Republicans for the last two generations. Worse yet, President Obama has, according to Berkowitz, cloaked himself in a "deceptive form of pragmatism, where pretending to be nonpartisan is a pragmatic strategy for imposing far-reaching progressive policies on an unwary public." Obama's pragmatism is "unpragmatic because … it obscures its governing principles and ultimate intentions."[11] In other words, what Berkowitz does not like about the president's pragmatism is that Obama has taken a page directly out of the neocon playbook and out-neoconned the neocons by pretending to be nonpartisan in order to obscure his true governing philosophy.

Neoconservatism, like pragmatism, does not publicly advocate a set of doctrines or principles (except when it does for rhetorical purposes), but instead claims to be only a method or a way of thinking. In ethics and politics, for instance, pragmatism rejects the principles of the Declaration of Independence because of its "dogmatic" truth claims (e.g., "We hold these *truths* to be self-evident"), as do the neocons, despite their occasional rhetorical use of the Declaration's principles. (They do, however, support the idea that ordinary people should have something to believe in as a part of their civic religion.) In other words, it is pragmatically practical to espouse and use principles in the appropriate context, but contexts are always changing and thus so should the ideas used by neoconservative statesmen. It is one thing to use principles rhetorically for one's political advantage (e.g., during an election season), but it is an altogether different thing to actually act on those principles as if they were "true." To do so would, for the neocons, be prima facie evidence of one's ideological fanaticism and "extremism." The pragmatist and neoconservative therefore "turns," in the words of James, "towards action and towards power." The pragmatic neocon covets power—or rather the power to acquire power. That is what counts.[12]

As pragmatists, the neocons begin with the expediencies of the moment and with what works. They view political reality as in a state of constant flux and change, which means that political policies should not be framed in black and white. They advocate policies that relieve social pressures, anxieties, and tensions. They advise Republicans (and sometimes Democrats) to be moderate, to be flexible, to be adaptable, and, most importantly, to be *prudent.* The neoconservatives are certain—absolutely certain—that moderation and prudence are the *only* way to deal with reality. They occasionally characterize their intellectual and political method as "pragmatic," but they much prefer, as Kristol has written, to use the term "prudential" to describe their approach to politics.[13] In other words, they like to cloak their pragmatism behind the respectable veil of this important classical virtue. Prudence—i.e., the classical virtue of practical judgment and wisdom—is not only the queen of the virtues for the neocons, it is virtually synonymous with their philosophy of governance. Those neocons influenced by the political philosopher Leo Strauss very much like to talk about prudence as though they were talking about classical or Aristotelian prudence (see chapter 6).

Irving Kristol has described their method this way:

> The neoconservative approach has been called pragmatic. But I don't like the word. It implies a lack of values. The term I prefer is "prudential," which comes from Aristotle. Prudence is a virtue, a way of looking at the world and taking your principles from the world as it is. Not determining your principles first, then trying to shape the world to fit them.... When you apply the prudential view to politics, you see that the job of government is not to shape society according to some design of perfection but to cope. The business of government is *coping.*[14]

Notice what Kristol is doing here. The term *prudence,* unlike the term *pragmatism,* implies "values," but Kristol's definition of prudence as "coping" is value-free. In other words, Kristol has highjacked a value-laden concept such as prudence in order to disguise his pragmatism. Kristol's "prudential" view of politics is all about learning how to *cope* with an indeterminate, necessitous, ever-changing world. Coping means adaptation, compromise, and using different principles and policies as the need arises. As the Straussian neoconservative Carnes Lord has written, "statecraft is an art of *coping* with an adversarial environment in which actions generate reactions in unpredictable ways and chance and uncertainty rule."[15]

David Brooks has, likewise, grounded his philosophy of governance on a pragmatic understanding of prudence utterly disconnected from first principles. Prudence, he writes,

> is the ability to grasp the unique pattern of a specific situation. It is the ability to absorb the vast flow of information and still discern the essential current of events—the things that go together and the things that will never go together. It is the ability to engage in complex deliberations and feel which arguments have the most weight.[16]

The neocons like to present their "prudential" pragmatism as though it were a form of common sense grounded in practical "realism." But surely this is a corruption of the Aristotelian definition of prudence. Aristotelian prudence, properly understood, and certainly the prudence understood by Washington, Adams, Jefferson, and Madison, always acts in the service of some fundamental principle, but the neocons have abandoned fixed and morally certain principles for a technique or way of thinking and acting. Pragmatic compromise disguised as Aristotelian prudence is a way of life for the neocons.

Prudence for the neocons is clearly *not* the application of rational moral principles to a variety of particular circumstances as it was for, say, Aristotle or Washington, and it is more than just the art of coping. Prudence is, they argue, the virtue that balances, steadies, and elevates competing interests and arguments. The neocons' pragmatic method of statesmanship is grounded in two basic assumptions: first, the identification of the "public interest" with some kind of golden mean and, second, the conceit that they—and they only—have the necessary practical wisdom by which to know or determine the golden mean. Notice that Brooks's understanding of prudence is defined in such a way that it is the preserve of a very small group of high-minded statesmen. Ordinary people live by principles; neoconservative statesmen govern by prudence.

Armed with this method of political wisdom, the neocons believe it to be both necessary and possible to find the golden mean, to "strike a balance" between altruism and self-interest, duties and rights, "public goods" and "private goods," nationalism and individualism, regulation and competition, religion and science.[17] They "pride themselves" as being "non-dogmatic and willing to compromise," Ben Wattenberg has written, "choosing one from column A and one from column B as on a Chinese menu."[18] How does such a view cash out politically? Inevitably, Irving Kristol thinks it is both desirable and possible to figure out a workable "amalgam of the prevailing 'Left' and 'Right' viewpoints,"[19] which means searching for the golden mean and "striking a balance" between capitalism and socialism—an ever-shifting balance that will always favor socialism.

Politics, or what the neocons sometimes call the "art of politics"—or, better, the "art of statecraft"—is the art of balancing or compromising conflicting social claims.[20] The fundamental reality of politics, according to the neocons, is the fact that at any given moment in time there will always be competing ideological, political, religious, and economic factions within the polity or the regime. Although the factions that are dominant today may not be dominant tomorrow, competing visions of the good life will always animate politics. That is the basic reality of politics with which the neoconservative statesmen must deal.[21] What this means in practice is that the primary responsibility of the neoconservative statesmen is to balance, moderate, uplift, and ultimately ennoble these competing ideas, interests, and factions. Straussianized neocons regard ideological and political compromise not as a deadly sin, but as a special art.

The neoconservatives' so-called prudential method claims that properly trained public officials have the wisdom necessary to channel human action in certain socially desired directions by tinkering with and restructuring the incentive mechanisms of America's political, economic, and social institutions. David Brooks, for instance, has praised President Obama for his attempt to build a "new leadership class" that aims "to restructure incentives in order to channel the animal drives of the marketplace in responsible directions." Brooks sums up very nicely the standard neoconservative trope that the "market needs adult supervision—a leadership class made up of people who appreciate the market but who also have committed themselves to public service, and who therefore take the long view and are more conscious of the public good." Or consider the claim of Norman Podhoretz in defending the idea of a neoconservative welfare state. According to him, wise and prudent neoconservative statesmen should be able to figure out "the *precise point* at which the incentive to work" would be "undermined by the availability of welfare benefits, or the point at which the redistribution of income" would begin "to erode economic growth, or the point at which egalitarianism" would come "into serious conflict with liberty."[22] Identifying what Podhoretz calls the "precise point" between competing social claims is the essence of how the neocons would establish the public interest as a golden mean.

Not only do the neoconservatives believe that it is possible for this "new leadership class" to draw a line between the "public" and the "private," they also believe that properly educated neoconservative statesmen will have the necessary wisdom to know *where* and *how* to draw the line between personal freedom and public regulation, between egalitarianism and liberty, between wealth and poverty. The method by which one identifies the "precise point," or the point of balance, comes in the form of a cost-benefit calculation, which the neocons apply to all social programs. Writing in the neocon house organ, *The Weekly Standard*, Paul Mirengoff has warned conservatives that it would be "anti-pragmatic" to allow "ideology" to "replace or trump" what he calls the "calculation."

The classic example of how the neocons would use this method of governance is "supply-side" economics. This doctrine says that if you lower the marginal tax rate to a particular point, people will work more and thus create more wealth, which in turn will expand tax returns, thereby giving the government the revenue to sponsor its various social programs. In other words, supply-side tax cuts are a means to manipulate and control human behavior so as to help perpetuate the welfare state. The key here, of course, is that the neocons believe that they can identify that precise point at which lower tax rates will actually lead to an increase in government revenue. The neoconservative economist Irwin Stelzer has likewise chastised free-market conservatives for their opposition to antitrust laws and called for something that he calls "efficient regulation," which is the golden mean between the nationalization of industry and free enterprise.[23] According to Carnes Lord, "the management of prosperity is an inescapable imperative of contemporary statecraft."[24] In other words, prosperity can and should be planned and directed by the efficient regulation of the State and by sufficiently well-educated statesmen.

During periods of political normalcy, the principal job of neoconservative statesmen is, in the words of Carnes Lord, to practice "the art of regime management"—i.e., to manage and "fine-tune" public policy.[25] The neocons are willing, according to Irving Kristol, to "interfere with the market for overriding social purposes," but they much prefer "to do so by '*rigging*' the market, or even creating new markets, rather than by direct bureaucratic controls."[26] They believe that it is both possible and desirable to use government power to manipulate, incentivize, or nudge people to make socially beneficial decisions. At the exoteric political level, *this* is what the neoconservatives mean when they advise Republicans to adopt a governing philosophy. *This* is what they mean by "Machiavellian shrewdness." This is what it means to be "*in* the 'American grain.'"

"Thinking Politically"

A key component of the neocons' "governing philosophy" is their pragmatic intellectual method for gaining and keeping power. To use the neocons' terminology, they urge Republicans to "*think politically*," which means to assess and "confront the reality" of their immediate political situation and to "adapt" to changing political realities "in a self-preserving way."[27] By adaptation, the neocons are referring to the process of adjusting to the principles and policies of those who currently hold power, who threaten one's power or who can help one to gain power. The neoconservatives are ideological peddlers who have an uncanny ability to adapt, triangulate, mix, and adopt different political ideas for different audiences.

Let's examine what it really means to "think politically" in practice. Consider, for instance, the neoconservatives' public support of religion and, in particular, their alliance with the religious Right. Over the course of the last twenty-five years or so, they have been cynically defending religion as a show of their political solidarity with evangelical Christians. The neocons understand and accept the fact that most Americans are religious, and they also know that they need religious conservatives in their camp if they are ever to form a long-term governing majority, which is, of course, their ultimate political ambition. Irving Kristol stated the neoconservative position most clearly and succinctly when he said, "if the Republican party is to survive, it must work at accomodating these people."[28] By allying themselves with and speaking publicly for the politically dispossessed people of faith, the neocons saw a way to expand their political base. From the early 1980s, Kristol and others saw that the most important long-term social trend in American politics was the rise of the religious Right and the likelihood of a religious reawakening in America. The neocons reacted to this development by allying themselves with the religious Right in order to build a new Republican majority that they would control ideologically. The relationship was strictly one of political convenience. This kind of strategic thinking is precisely what Kristol means when he advises Republicans to "think politically," that is, "to "confront" and "adapt" to new political circumstances "in a self-preserving way."[29]

The neocons cynically support religion when they think that they can control and moderate the opinions and actions of religiously pious people, but they shudder in horror when religious people get too uppity politically or when they take their religion too seriously. Consider, for instance, the relations between the neocons and the religionists during the 1990s. It was at this time that the neocons attempted to forge a political alliance with the Moral Majority and conservative Catholics. The alliance ended (temporarily), however, when the neocons lost control of the alliance. In 1996, for instance, the neoconservative-influenced Catholic journal *First Things* published a series of articles bemoaning the corrupt state of American culture and denouncing the American regime as morally and politically illegitimate. This was too much for the neocons, who resigned *en masse* from the *First Things* editorial board.[30] The neocons seek to manage and moderate the apocalyptic extremism of religious folks, but they don't like it when such people take their religion too seriously and then act on it. That would be to turn religion into an ideology. The neocons make it very clear: "We're in charge of the ideas; you're in charge of voting."

"Thinking politically" is thus a synonym for compromise and developing strategies for gaining power: It means compromising with the secular Left when necessary (particularly when liberals claim the moral high ground on issues that concern the alleged "needs" of the people, such as health care), and it also means compromising with the religious Right when necessary (particularly when the religious conservatives can be rallied to challenge the cultural hegemony of the nihilistic Left). As a political strategy, it means that Republicans should co-opt the liberal message in order to expand their political base and to form a permanent ruling majority. As William Kristol has written: "A minority party becomes a majority party by absorbing elements of the other party."[31] In other words, the neoconservative method for defeating liberalism is to become a liberal.

The neocons' pragmatic rationale for this wholesale moral and political ca-pitulation is that, "If it's going to happen, why not take the credit?" That's what it means to "think politically." This is particularly true with regard to government spending. The problem with Republicans, according to Irving Kristol, is that the "merits of pre-emptive spending seem destined to remain forever incomprehen-sible to the conservative cast of mind."[32] Kristol and the neocons have therefore advised Republicans to adopt the following kinds of tactics so that Republicans might absorb elements of the Democratic Party in order to become the majority party. For example, if liberals launch a national campaign for socialized medicine, Republicans should steal the issue from the Democrats and advocate a system of universal health care but one that allows people to choose their own doctor or HMO. If liberals commence a public campaign against the profits of "big business" or the salaries of their executives, Republicans should neutralize liberal pretensions by encouraging "greedy" and "profiteering" corporate executives to voluntarily "donate" their profits to left-wing charities. If radical environmentalists launch a public relations campaign against global warming, Republicans should encourage American companies to hire environmentalists as advisors. If feminists propose to nationalize preschool child care, Republicans should go along but insist that par-ents be given vouchers to send their children to the day care facility of their choice.

The real meaning and trajectory of the neocons' philosophy of governance was on full display recently in a 2007 *New York Times* op-ed by David Brooks, whose column was written as a "how-to manual" for Republicans. His goal was to provide Republicans with pragmatic advice on how to regain political power. The first item of business, according to Brooks, is for the GOP to abandon the now passé "truths" and basic principles of the "Goldwater-Reagan glory days." They must reject their public image as the "minimal-government party, the maximal-freedom party, the party of rugged individualism and states' rights." This therefore means they must abandon their traditional principles, except of course when those principles are useful politically. In other words, the Republi-cans must abandon *their* philosophy of governance (i.e., their adherence to certain principles) and adopt the neocons' philosophy of governance (i.e., an adherence to Machiavellian prudence). Restoring Goldwater conservatism is, in Brooks's view, a nonstarter: It is the "wrong diagnosis of current realities and so the wrong prescription for the future." What the GOP needed in 2008 and beyond, according to Brooks, was an up-to-date public philosophy that deals with "current realities" and the politics of power.[33] Once again, neoconservative thinking is all about changing one's principles so as to acquire and keep power.

According to Brooks, there was a time (as there might be again in the future) when, under the appropriate circumstances, the principles of limited government made sense and were the avenue to political power:

> Back in the 1970s, when Reaganism became popular, top tax rates were in the 70s, growth was stagnant and inflation was high. Federal regulation stifled competition. Government welfare policies enabled a culture of dependency. Socialism was still a coherent creed, and many believed the capitalist world was headed toward a Swedish welfare model. In short, in the 1970s, *normal, nonideological* people were right to think that their future prospects might be dimmed by a stultifying state. People were right to believe that government was undermining personal responsibility. People were right to have what Tyler Cowen, in a brilliant essay in *Cato Unbound,* calls the "liberty vs. power" paradigm burned into their minds—the idea that big government means less personal liberty.[34]

In David Brooks's world, then, the small-government individualism of Barry Goldwater is no longer relevant in the twenty-first century because high taxes and oppressive regulations are apparently no longer a problem for most Americans. Many of the "old problems" that led to the election of Ronald Reagan have receded or been addressed. The deeper problem is that, as Brooks sees it, conservative intellectuals and Republican politicians have been too beholden to their old and outdated principles and have been too slow in recognizing "the change in their historical circumstances." Instead, *"normal, nonideological"* people in the twenty-first century must adjust themselves to *their* historical circumstances and address new problems in new ways. (Readers will notice that Brooks twice equates the "normal" with the "nonideological," which is to say to be without principles. Or, put the other way around, he equates the ideological with the abnormal.)

What Brooks and Irving Kristol fear most is a politics of principle, particularly political principles that support individualism, limited government, and laissez-faire capitalism. (We shall explain why in the chapters that follow.) They do not want the American people to think in "abstract principles," particularly those associated with the classical-liberal tradition. Instead, they want them to think pragmatically or, better yet, not at all. In the neoconservative world, to be morally principled is to be unbalanced psychologically.

What new realities, problems, and "big threats" does Brooks identify as requiring new modes and orders? The great challenges facing twenty-first-century Americans "come from complex, decentralized phenomena: Islamic extremism, failed states, global competition, global warming, nuclear proliferation, a skills-based economy, economic and social segmentation." In other words, many of the problems now afflicting twenty-first-century Americans were actually caused, according to Brooks, by the limited-government philosophy (e.g., its supposed inability to properly deal with Islamic extremism) and capitalism (e.g., its supposed role in promoting global competition, global warming, a skills-based economy, and economic and social segmentation).

The good news for Brooks is that the American people have, well ahead of conservative intellectuals and the GOP, groped their way toward a "new mental framework." They have abandoned the "'liberty vs. power' paradigm" and replaced it with an FDR-like "'security leads to freedom' paradigm.'" Brooks's curious reasoning in support of this claim goes something like this: If all Americans are guaranteed the basic necessities of life—e.g., food, clothing, shelter, education, and health care—they will have more freedom to pursue "a wider range of opportunities" in their day-to-day lives. Tellingly—indeed, in a shocking admission—Brooks reveals that the "'security leads to freedom' paradigm is a fundamental principle of child psychology." In other words, the American people are to be treated by their government as though they are helpless children in need of a government-as-nanny. Brooks's "new paradigm" for the Republican Party is therefore "oriented less toward negative liberty (How can I get the government off my back?) and more toward positive liberty (Can I choose how to lead my life?)."[35] Put more honestly, his solution to the problems of modern America is more redistribution and centralized-government control that is cloaked in the rhetoric of freedom and the soothing tones of child psychology.

A Neoconservative Welfare State

Lest we think that Irving Kristol and David Brooks are little more than conservative versions of John Dewey or that neoconservatism is just a technique, we must consider the very real possibility that the neocons actually do advocate some moral principles and a particular vision of the good society. Take, for instance, their advocacy of what Kristol calls a "conservative welfare state," which may very well be the neoconservatives' signature policy on domestic affairs. As Norman Podhoretz once put it, neoconservatives, "unlike the older schools of American conservatism," are "not for abolishing the welfare state but only for setting certain limits to it."[36] It is rare for the neocons to openly support a particular policy as though it were a nonnegotiable imperative, but this is precisely what the welfare state is for the neoconservatives. Ironically, their support for the welfare state seems almost dogmatic and ideological.

How do the neocons defend their welfare state? Do they support it simply on pragmatic grounds, or do they defend it morally?

On the surface, Kristol and the neoconservatives seem to support the idea of a welfare state begrudgingly, as an unfortunate reality of contemporary American politics that conservatives must learn to accept and use in order to remain politically relevant. "I shall, to begin with," Kristol notes, "assume that the welfare state is with us, for better or worse, and that conservatives should try to make it better rather than worse." In other words, why fight the tide of history when you can help guide it? In the view of Nathan Glazer, a neoconservative sociologist at Harvard, "There is no escape in a modern developed nation from the major social programs that were developed under Franklin D. Roosevelt and expanded in the years since." Or, as neoconsevative Ben Wattenberg has written, "I personally think the welfarists have probably gone too far and I am prepared to examine case by case, *pragmatically*, as Neo-Conservatives are supposed to do, what went wrong and how we ought to rectify it." At first blush, the neocons seem only to accept the necessity of the welfare state as an unfortunate reality of modern democracy, but one they think ought to be reformed piecemeal. They favor, in Wattenberg's words, "moderately high big-government spending provided the programs can be shown to work and can be changed if they don't."[37] The socially destructive unintended consequences associated with the welfare state can and must be ameliorated, but abolishing the system altogether as is advocated by some conservatives and most libertarians is a nonstarter for the neocons.

The neoconservatives' tentative support for the welfare state is also pragmatically political. Contrast, for instance, Kristol's critique of welfare programs such as Aid to Families with Dependent Children with his support for expanding many New Deal and Great Society entitlement programs, such as Social Security and Medicare. He supports reforming AFDC because it created a culture of dependence and perpetual poverty, which in turn led to increased crime, drug use, and gang activity. But Kristol actually favors expanding Social Security and Medicare on the expedient grounds that senior citizens are a powerful voting bloc and because they are socially "unproblematic," by which he means that welfare for seniors does not lead to the same kind of social pathologies (e.g., teenage pregnancy and crime) that it does for other groups.[38]

Kristol's seemingly reluctant acceptance of the welfare state as historically inevitable and politically necessary masks, however, what he really thinks, which is that the welfare state is a *moral* good. Kristol and virtually all of the other neoconservatives are deeply committed to the moral ends of the welfare state. The normative basis for Kristol's support of a "social insurance" welfare state stems, fundamentally, from the moral principle of *altruism* (the ethic that says that individuals have a moral duty to sacrifice their interests to the needs of others and for the greater good). He believes in this ethic, and he certainly has no scruples in demanding that such duties be enforced by the State. This is why he not only supports saving and perpetuating most New Deal welfare programs, but would also expand them to include new programs, such as universal medical and child care and increases in Social Security. In the 1960s, Kristol and his friends embraced the "desired aims" of Lyndon Johnson's Great Society programs (and presumably they still do), but he broke with liberals only over how to satisfy the people's needs and deliver their right to a welfare check. "What is needed," according to Kristol, is not to eliminate or even reduce welfare, but to create "better social programs."[39] The neocons have faith that properly trained social planners can figure out how to make various social welfare programs work without causing negative externalities and moral hazards, such as the breakdown of the family, teen pregnancy, the creation of a permanent underclass, rising crime rates, and various other social pathologies.

Before we go any further, though, we must put the neoconservatives' welfare state in some sort of broader historical perspective. Throughout American history, there have been two principal means by which to deal with poverty and misfortune: private charity and government welfare. The first system was dominant in the United States from the time of the founding up to the twentieth century, while the second was established principally with the New Deal in the 1930s. What distinguishes these two methods of poor relief? The system of private philanthropy was voluntary. It was inspired by personal benevolence and given as a gift, and it operated through a network of private institutions (e.g., families, churches, private charities, fraternal lodges, mutual-aid societies, etc.). The government welfare system is, by contrast, based on coercion and forced redistribution. It upholds "needs" as "rights" to which one is entitled, and it is funded through coercive taxation and operated through government agencies.

If forced to choose between these two systems of poverty relief, Irving Kristol and the neoconservatives reject the system of private philanthropy and advocate the government welfare system. On this point, Kristol has been nothing but clear and adamant. In spite of their frequent, rehearsed, and patriotic appeals to America's founding principles, we can be certain of one thing: The neocons' support of the welfare state cannot be defended or justified by an appeal to the principles of liberty and justice that are associated with the American Founding. The difference between the neoconservatives' "conservative welfare state" and the modern liberal welfare state is one of *degree* only, while the difference between the neocons' views on poverty relief and those of the Founders' is one of *kind*. Washington, Adams, and Jefferson would have considered it inconceivable to think that the "needs" of the poor would be the basis of State-mandated rights. They simply could not have imagined a government dedicated to feeding, clothing, housing, nursing, busing, or babysitting the "needy." They certainly would have viewed Kristol's moral principles as unjust and his political principles as much worse than those of George III.

Kristol and company support unequivocally the change in philosophical outlook and moral valuation brought about during the Progressive Era and institutionalized during the New Deal. This new philosophy embraced altruism as its moral ideal, it accepted a collectivist view of society, and it adopted a statist view of politics. Not surprisingly, it turns out that Kristol regards the "socialist ideal" not only as "admirable," but also as a "*necessary* ideal, offering elements that were wanting in capitalist society—elements indispensable for the preservation, not to say perfection, of our humanity."[40] Kristol has praised utopian socialism because it is "community-oriented" rather than "individual-oriented." He admires the socialist vision of an ideal citizen who transcends the "vulgar, materialistic, and divisive acquisitiveness that characterized the capitalist type of individual." The moral world created by Enlightenment individualism and laissez-faire capitalism is morally tainted from Kristol's point of view. Kristol knows very well that the moral system inherent in the welfare state is the morality of altruism. He also knows that the welfare state—including *his* conservative welfare state—is a form of involuntary servitude.[41] This from the author of *Two Cheers for Capitalism*, regarded by some as one of the most important moral defenses of capitalism written in the twentieth century.[42] Apparently Kristol saved his third cheer for the moral ideal associated with his first great philosophic inspiration, Leon Trotsky.

Likewise, Kristol's friend and colleague Nathan Glazer has stated publicly that the differences between socialists and neoconservatives are exaggerated. In fact, he says, they "agree on more and more":

> It is very hard for us to define what it is that divides us, in any centrally principled way. We might, depending on which socialists, and which neoconservatives are arguing, disagree about the details or the scope of health insurance plans; or about the level of taxation that should be imposed upon corporations; or how much should be going into social security.... But where are the principles that separate us?[43]

Where, indeed! Neoconservatives agree with the underlying moral principles of the socialists; they disagree merely over the best means to achieve their shared ends. Kristol and company share much more in common morally with the new liberalism of Franklin D. Roosevelt than they do with the old liberalism of Calvin Coolidge.

The neoconservatives, from Irving Kristol to David Brooks, accept the basic idea launched by New Deal liberals that those in need have a legitimate moral claim on their fellow citizens—a right, an entitlement that must be honored and enforced by the government. They believe that people have *rights* to the "pub-lic" provision of certain private goods and services—i.e., food, shelter, medical care, pensions, and similar such goods. The neocons insist that the welfare state can and should be demanded as a right because it is grounded in the people's "needs"—and, as Kristol explains, "needs" for the neocons are synonymous with rights. Adapting the Marxian principle—"From each according to his ability, to each according to his needs"—to the realities of modern American society, Kristol writes:

> In our urbanized, industrialized, highly mobile society, people *need* govern-mental action of some kind if they are to *cope* with many of their problems: old age, illness, unemployment, etc. They *need* such assistance; they demand it; they will get it. The only interesting political question is: *How* will they get it?[44]

The neocons camouflage their fundamental moral commitments—e.g., to satisfy people's "needs"—in the guise of pragmatism by insisting that the only meaningful question to ask is: "How"? We know, however, that Kristol sup-ports the welfare state for more than just pragmatic reasons. His not-so-veiled operating assumption is that "needs" trump rights—e.g., the rights to liberty and property. Simply put, he believes that one person's "need" provides a moral claim on the liberty and property of another. In his view, the fulfillment of a "need" is something to which one is morally entitled, which in turn makes it a "right." Further, this is a "right" that can and should be "demanded" without apology, responsibility, or gratitude, and that can be satisfied only through the redistributive and coercive power of the State. But having equated *rights* with *needs*, it is not clear how Kristol could resist the call to equate needs with *wants*. Though he would never publicly admit to this, his position, in effect, amounts to the following: Welfare recipients have a legitimate moral claim—an enforceable *ownership* claim—to their entitlement, which is to say, to the time, labor, and resources of those who subsidize their entitlement. More recently, Peter Berkowitz has defended the New Deal welfare state on, of all things, Burkean grounds. Ac-cording to Berkowitz, needs-as-claims-as-rights that have been recognized and enforced by the government for eighty years, regardless of their moral status, have the status and authority of prescriptive use and legitimacy.[45]

In a *Wall Street Journal* essay published several years ago, Irving Kristol joined many liberals and socialists in characterizing Bill Clinton's "two years and out" welfare proposal for able-bodied welfare recipients as a "cruel," "unfair," and "ruthless" policy. Such an emotionally and rhetorically unbuttoned response to Clinton's welfare reform reveals a much deeper moral commitment to altruism and to welfarist redistribution than the author of *Two Cheers for Capitalism* is typically wont to reveal. Throughout his career, Kristol supported unequivocally the moral spirit of entitlement created by the New Deal and the Great Society programs. And to the question of whether we have a right to be taken care of by others, Kristol answers unequivocally in the affirmative. He also knows that the entitlement regime he supports empowers the State by breeding dependence on it. Apparently he thinks that those denied a welfare check after two years on the dole have been denied their needs-as-rights and have therefore been abused by their government.

On the practical level, Kristol described the likelihood that the then-proposed Personal Responsibility and Work Opportunity Act would actually pass in Congress and then work in practice as a "fantasy."[46] Well, the fantasy became reality, but subsequent history has proved that Kristol's suggestion that the welfare reform law of 1996 would produce legions of starving mothers and children was foolishly wrongheaded. The fact of the matter is that Clinton's welfare reform legislation has been recognized by liberals and conservatives alike to be a moderate success story. Tens of thousands of Americans successfully transitioned from welfare dependency to self-reliance and work. More fundamentally, it turns out that a welfare check is *not* the "need"-cum-right for most people that Kristol thought it was.

Kristol's call for universal *economic security* as a right not only abrogates the laws of reality (such a thing is literally impossible), but it represents a denial of any philosophically legitimate concept of rights. Our Revolutionary Founding Fathers believed that individuals have a right to freedom of action—the right to be free from interference by others. Kristol and company, on the other hand, believe that rights are rights to *things*—rights that require the sacrifice of some in order to satisfy the needs of others. Ultimately, his position amounts to this: Some people have a "right" to the rights of others, which means that some people are the means to the ends of others. Let us be absolutely clear in identifying the precise moral meaning of the neoconservative position on welfare. No matter what rhetorical strategies neocons such as Kristol and Berkowitz use to defend the welfare state, their position—both morally and politically—can be reduced to one principle: They support the use of force to redistribute the wealth of *disarmed* citizens.

One wonders what kind of philosophical argument the neocons might provide to support their claim that the State has a right to force some to work involuntarily for the sake of others. Unfortunately, they have not left us with any such defense other than emotional assertions. They do not tell us how or why individuals have a fundamental human right, a moral and legal claim, to the wealth, ambition, ability, and values of others. One suspects, at least in part, that Kristol, Glazer, Bell, Brooks, and others ultimately appeal to their readers' feelings about what is right. David Brooks has even gone so far as to suggest that American judges should base their decisions on the basis of empathy rather than reason. "People without social emotions like empathy are not," he writes with stunning obscurantism, "objective decision-makers." Instead, those who rely on their reason to make important moral decisions rather than their emotions are likely to be, in Brooks's view, "sociopaths who sometimes end up on death row."[47] The neocons should not be permitted, however, to escape the moral meaning of their position. It is imperative that such philosophical jabberwocky be exposed and discussed publicly as a moral rather than a public-policy issue.

How, according to the neocons, would a conservative welfare state actually work in practice? Indeed, what makes it a *conservative,* as opposed to a liberal or a socialist, welfare state? How do they sell their welfare program to traditional conservatives? The neocons advocate a strong central government that provides welfare services to all people who need them while at the same time giving people a *choice* about how they want those services delivered. That is what makes it "conservative" in principle and practice, they argue. That's how they reconcile Hayek and Trotsky, Friedman and FDR.

In practice, this means that the neocons would use the coercive force of the State to redistribute wealth and to provide for all of the people's needs—from universal Social Security to health and child care to education. However, they would do it by maintaining the façade of a market economy: They would let the people choose their own "private" Social Security accounts; they would let them choose their own "private" health and child-care providers; and they would give parents vouchers to let them choose which schools their children will attend. But, of course, the choices given to the people would not be the unlimited, wide-open choices of a free market. Rather, the people are permitted to choose from among a handful of preauthorized providers. The neocons call this tinkering scheme a "free-market reform" of the welfare state.

The range of so-called choices associated with the neoconservatives' "free-market" reform of the welfare state is, however, a charade. To define "choice" as the freedom and the right of individuals to choose between a few government-approved programs is fundamentally dishonest and it destroys the concepts of "choice," "freedom," and "rights." Under such a corrupt definition of "choice," the only people truly free to choose are the government bureaucrats who decide which programs are government approved and which are not. By contrast, Kristol denies the right of individuals to make the ultimate choice: the choice to opt out of all schemes of welfare redistribution and to choose for themselves how they want to use the product of their own mental and physical effort. Morally, we should never forget that Kristol and the neoconservatives believe that some individuals should be forced to work to satisfy the needs-cum-rights of others, and that they deny the right of productive individuals to keep the fruits of their labor. Capitalism for the neocons does not mean an inalienable right to property or a policy of economic laissez-faire. Instead, it means a system in which property is held by permission, and choices within the economy are regulated by the government.

As economic "supply-siders," the neocons occasionally support tax cuts—but not because they want to return to taxpayers money that is rightfully theirs. Instead, they cleverly advocate lowering the marginal tax rate because it will provide an incentive for people to work harder, earn more money, and spur economic growth. It will thus generate more tax revenue that will then be used to fund their conservative welfare state. In other words, reduced tax rates translate into an expanded welfare state. Kristol sums up the neoconservative position this way:

> The basic principle behind a conservative welfare state ought to be a simple one: *wherever possible,* people should be *allowed* to keep their own money—rather than having it transferred (via taxes) to the state—*on condition that they put it to certain defined uses.* ... Policies such as these have the obvious advantage of *reconciling the purposes of the welfare state with the maximum degree of individual independence* and the least bureaucratic coercion. They would also have the advantage of being quite popular.[48]

Consider what Kristol is really saying here. First, in a neoconservative welfare state there is no such thing as an *inalienable* right to property: The people are allowed to keep and spend their property only by permission of the State, which is also to say that there is no principled recognition of property rights. The neocons are happy enough to retain some of the forms and formalities of private property, but they do think that the government should have some control—even ultimate control—over its use and disposal. Kristol and the neocons reject government ownership of the means of production, but they do support the idea of government *control* of the means of production. Second, notice the similarity here between Kristol's neoconservative view of government and the modern neoliberal view of government. In language remarkably similar to the views of liberal theorist Cass Sunstein, Kristol believes that the government should define for ordinary people the uses to which they will spend their money. In other words, the government should "nudge" the behavior and actions of people in certain predefined directions.[49] The only meaningful difference between Sunstein and Kristol is that they would use the coercive power of government to nudge the American people in slightly different directions and for slightly different reasons. In a neoconservative State, wise statesmen can somehow reconcile rights and duties, individualism and collectivism, freedom and socialism.

And what will happen to those people who do not spend their money according to properly "defined uses"? Kristol has left us with one chilling example of what he means: He favors an inheritance tax law that would prohibit any one individual from inheriting more than one million dollars and that would impose a 100 percent inheritance tax on the "undistributed portion" of a man's estate after his death. In other words, if a man with a wife and two children dies holding a $10 million estate, the State permits him to leave to his wife and children one million dollars each, but he must give away the rest to friends or to charity or else it will all be taken forcibly by the State.[50] This kind of policy is the inevitable result of elevating "needs" over rights.

In the end, the neocons' strategy and philosophy of governance—their public advice to the Republican Party—is to compromise and accept the moral ends of liberal-socialism, but with the caveat that they can do a better job of delivering liberal "social services" or that they can direct those services toward "conservative" social ends. For Kristol and the neocons, the moral ideal of capitalism is immoral, but its means and results are good, while the moral ideal of socialism is good, but its means and results are suboptimal. In other words, they seek a compromise between capitalism (the means) and socialism (the end). But observe *who* is being asked to compromise here. It is only the defenders of individual rights and capitalism who are being asked to compromise their ends or principles. Liberals, by contrast, are being asked to compromise only on the means—on the size of the welfare check and the manner in which it is delivered. Moral appeasement of this sort only serves to embolden the Left, a lesson that conservatives seem constitutionally unable to learn. They fail to grasp that compromising one principle inevitably leads to hundreds of little compromises in practice. In any such relationship, liberalism will always have the upper hand and it will always dictate the future. And so it has. Such has been the nature of American politics for the last seventy-five years.

This is precisely why the neoconservative position can offer no principled opposition to the creation of *new* welfare programs in the future. Without a moral argument against the regulatory-welfare state, the neocons have no principled grounds on which to oppose the creation of new social programs until they have actually been put into practice, at which point they typically argue that it would be imprudent to abolish programs that the people want, programs that have institutionalized bureaucracies and ready-made interest groups prepared to defend them. Having made this kind of concession, the neocons have sacrificed the right of self-ownership to the idea of "needs-as-rights." And what this means, of course, is that they have no moral grounds on which to object to the next depredation. They can offer no *moral* argument against liberal plans to socialize medicine and day care precisely because they accept the moral claims of liberalism.

Part II
The Crisis of Modernity

CHAPTER 3
THE STRAUSSIAN MOMENT

Leo Strauss (1899–1973) has emerged in recent years as the reputed philosophic mastermind of the neoconservative movement. The claim, however, is contested. It has raised the hackles of some and caused others to come unbuttoned in the search for nefarious conspiracies. Either way, both Strauss's defenders and his critics have given new meaning to Richard Hofstadter's claim that American politics is uniquely characterized by a certain "paranoid style."[1] No one can deny with a straight face that there is not some kind of intellectual connection between the neoconservatives and Leo Strauss, but the much more interesting and important issue is to define the nature and meaning of that relationship. With this in mind, over the course of this chapter and the next three, we shall drill down to the philosophic heart and soul of the neoconservative persuasion.

Let us begin with what is known: First, the relationship between Strauss and the neocons is complicated and its meaning is not immediately self-evident and, second, some sense and a good deal of nonsense have been written about Strauss's alleged connection to the neoconservatives.[2] The most obvious challenge in establishing the Strauss-neocon connection is that Strauss's philosophical and political views, like those of the neoconservatives, are difficult to pin down. An aura of mystery surrounds his political philosophy, which seems to have been cultivated not least of all by his own students, who have divided into self-designated "East Coast," "West Coast," and "Midwestern" factions according to how they interpret Strauss's philosophic project.[3] Commentators have characterized Strauss as everything from a moral absolutist to a Nietzschean nihilist, from a Jewish religious thinker to a philosophic atheist, from a conservative partisan to a liberal skeptic. More recently, he has been portrayed as the evil genius behind the Bush administration's foreign policy curtain—a dead man pulling the strings of his warmongering puppets. Taking political correctness to ever-new heights, one of Strauss's defenders has written an entire book on what he calls "Straussophobia."[4] Such caricatures, from both sides, border on infantile demonology. The recent use and abuse of this long-dead professor has generated a great deal of heat—but little light.

The anti-Strauss parade began in 1985 with an essay by the English classicist Myles Burnyeat that appeared in the *New York Review of Books* under the title "Sphinx Without a Secret." It was the first in what would become a steady stream of articles over the next twenty years attempting to connect the dots between Strauss (the cultist) and neocon policy-makers in various Republican administrations (the cabal). Burnyeat there described Strauss as the "guru of American conservatism," and he claimed that "Strauss's 'ruthless anti-idealism' [leads] to a dangerously aggressive foreign policy." Two years later, Jacob Weisberg of *Newsweek* magazine published an article titled "The Cult of Leo Strauss." In it he wondered why there "are so many Straussians in the Reagan administration," and he went on to suggest that "the brotherhood is committed to no less than halting the drift of modern democracy." A few years later, Brent Staples, writing in the *New York Times*, declared that "Leo Strauss contended that the Philosopher Kings (himself included) were born to rule, servants were born to serve, and that only disaster came of letting the rabble get above its station.... This dark view of human potential is poised to become a central feature of this country's social policy." Staples assured his readers that Strauss's ideas had "survived him and crept into vogue in American politics." The anti-Strauss slurs continued into the next century and reached their pinnacle in a 2004 article by Earl Shorris that appeared in *Harper's* magazine. He claimed that Strauss's students had "methodically infected and then corrupted the government of the most powerful nation on earth." And how had the nefarious "Straussians" infiltrated and corrupted America's government? According to Shorris,

> One of the great services that Strauss and his disciples have performed for the Bush regime has been the provision of a philosophy of the noble lie, the conviction that lies, far from being simply a regrettable necessity of political life, are instead virtuous and noble instruments of wise policy. The idea's provenance could not be more elevated: Plato himself advised his nobles, men with golden souls, to tell noble lies—political fables, much like the specter of Saddam Hussein with a nuclear bomb—to keep the other levels of human society (silver, iron, brass) in their proper places, loyal to the state and willing to do its bidding. Strauss, too, advised the telling of noble lies in the service of the national interest, and he held Plato's view of aristocrats as persons so virtuous that such lies would be used only for the good, for keeping order in the state and in the world. He defined the modern method of the noble lie in the use of esoteric

messages within an exoteric text, telling the truth to the wise while at the same time conveying something quite different to the many.

Shorris's presentation of Strauss and the Straussians as philosophic mercenaries who provide philosophic "noble lies" to the highest political bidder is either cause for genuine concern or lends credence to the Straussians' counterclaim that their ideological enemies have come unglued and are flirting with conspiracy-theory nutters.[5]

The noise over Strauss reached a fever pitch in the months just before and in the year after the American invasion of Iraq. Conspiracy theories were widespread in the media. Strauss was alleged to be the sinister "brains" behind the Bush administration, despite being dead for more than thirty years. Seymour Hersh, writing for the *New Yorker,* insisted that the "Straussian movement has many adherents in and around the Bush Administration." And according to James Atlas at the *New York Times,* the "Bush administration is rife with Straussians." Then an article in the *Boston Globe* suggested that Americans "live in a world increasingly shaped by Leo Strauss."[6] And on and on it went.

At first the mainstream media was quite pleased with itself for its investigative journalism uncovering the diabolical Strauss-neocon cabal, until it was revealed in the *Wall Street Journal* that the chief source of information for many of the most high-profile articles on Strauss was none other than the Lyndon LaRouche organization. LaRouche and his followers published several gems with titles such as "Profile: Leo Strauss, Fascist Grandfather of the Neo-Cons."[7] The attempt to link Strauss to the neocons was thoroughly discredited by the hysterical rantings of that "crackpot political agitator Lyndon LaRouche," who, according to Joshua Muravchik, was responsible for kicking off the witch-hunting hysteria that attempted to link Strauss to the neocons and the Iraq War. Robert Bartley, the respected former editor of the *Wall Street Journal,* reported that Hersh and Atlas had followed LaRouche into the "fever swamps" of yellow journalism. According to Bartley, "Looking at the striking similarities in these accounts the conspiracy-minded might conclude that the *New York Times* and *New Yorker* have been reduced to recycling the insights of Lyndon LaRouche."[8] When the liberal media learned that they had been dancing their anti-Strauss waltz paired with Lyndon LaRouche, the stories came to an end rather quickly.

The response of most Straussians and neoconservatives to this seemingly co-ordinated media lynching was to "deny—deny—deny" any connection between Strauss, the Straussians, the neocons, the Bush administration, and American foreign policy.[9] In quick succession, a number of Straussians great and small responded to the claims that Strauss's ideas and his students were covertly running American government with flat denials and mocking condescension. Such conspiracy theories suppose, wrote a disdainful Peter Berkowitz, that

President Bush, Vice President Cheney, Secretary of State Powell, Secretary of Defense Rumsfeld, and National Security Adviser Rice, non-Straussians by all accounts, are stooges and dupes. It insinuates that neoconservative intellectuals—Deputy Secretary of Defense Paul Wolfowitz is at the top of everybody's list—have craftily ascended to positions of power in the federal government from which they aim to implement Strauss's teachings. And it invests Strauss, a student of political philosophy whose life's work consisted in writing learnedly about thinkers from Plato to Heidegger, and sharing his discoveries with students, with almost superhuman powers: Through the force of his ideas, we are told, this scholar and teacher is able, a generation and a half after his death, to command the respect and loyalty—and indeed, to compel the actions—of highly successful and well-placed individuals not only in politics but in the media and the academy.

The very idea that Strauss's influence had extended from beyond the grave, Berkowitz suggested, was "wildly implausible." Strauss's defenders claim that he was a "staunch friend of liberal democracy" and an opponent of tyranny.[10] They also report that Strauss's writings are thoroughly apolitical and that he almost never spoke about contemporary politics in the presence of students. According to Yale political theorist Steven Smith, "Strauss had no politics in the sense in which that term is generally meant." Summing up the Straussian position, Smith writes, "His works do not endorse any political program or party, whether of the Left or of the Right, Democratic or Republican. He was a philosopher."[11] Ironically, his students and acolytes present Strauss as a political philosopher with no ideas relevant to politics!

Some years now after the brouhaha has dissipated and the intellectual dust has settled, we are in a much better position to assess more objectively who the real Leo Strauss really was, what he thought, and how his ideas have or have not influenced the neoconservative movement. The Leo Strauss who appears in these pages is presented respectfully as a capacious and profound thinker of great depth, vision, and power, one who has many important things to say about the world in which we live, its deepest problems, and the possible solutions to our current maladies. Unlike many recent studies of Strauss and the neoconservatives, we are not interested in bearing false witness against the man, but neither are we interested in fawning obsequiousness or evasion. We aim to get at the truth of the matter. The time has come to examine more carefully Leo Strauss's political thought and its relationship to neoconservatism. Strauss deserves it, the neocons deserve it, and, most importantly, the American public deserves it.

Our method for studying Strauss and his relationship to the neocons will proceed rather differently than it has in the media or with certain scholars. Rather than beginning with the Bush administration and working backward, we begin at the beginning, with the moment when the first neoconservative first encountered Leo Strauss. Then and only then can we begin to trace Strauss's influence on neoconservative thought and contemporary American domestic and foreign policy.

From Leon to Leo

In 1952 Irving Kristol, then a young editor at *Commentary* magazine and the man who would later be known as the "godfather" of neoconservatism, wrote and published a review of Leo Strauss's book *Persecution and the Art of Writing*. This is the first known contact between the two men.[12] Remarkably, this document has never been brought to the attention of the general public until now.

Kristol's confrontation with Strauss came as an epiphany. It was, as Kristol has intimated on several occasions, the most important intellectual event of his life. Until he read Strauss, the chief influences on his intellectual development included Leon Trotsky (which means Marx) and the literary critic Lionel Trilling (which means Freud). At the time, Kristol was an up-and-comer in the avant-garde of New York City's distinctly "progressive" intellectual class. In other words, Irving Kristol was a highbrow socialist who wrote not for the working class but for the hoity-toity of the Upper West Side, the artsy-fartsy of Greenwich Village, and the namby-pamby of the Ivy League.

Leo Strauss was, by contrast, "from a different planet," according to Kristol—in almost every sense.[13] Strauss was a German Jew who, as a young man in Weimar Germany, had studied with three of the most important philosophers of the twentieth century: Ernst Cassirer, Edmund Husserl, and Martin Heidegger. In 1932 Strauss left Nazi Germany and, for the next six years, while living in Paris and then in England, worked primarily on medieval Jewish and Islamic philosophy. In 1938, at the age of thirty-eight, Strauss left Europe for good and was appointed to a teaching position at the New School for Social Research in New York City. In 1949 he moved to the University of Chicago, where he taught political science for almost twenty years.

Strauss, unlike Kristol, was neither a polemicist nor a political partisan. He was, according to Kristol, "the quintessential philosopher," living the quiet life of the scholar-recluse.[14] Strauss wrote almost nothing about American politics or public policy. Instead, he was a political philosopher who was somewhat contemptuous of "intellectuals." Strauss was an erudite, bookish man, who wrote dense and abstruse scholarly exegeses on the "Great Books" of political philosophy for the philosophically serious. In fact, it is reported that when Strauss was once asked what he taught, he responded by saying rather modestly and elliptically, "old books."[15] It was through these old and sometimes forgotten books that Strauss studied man and his place in the world and from which he resuscitated the grand questions that the certitudes of the age have forgotten or judged irrelevant.

Strauss's knowledge of political philosophy and intellectual history was as profound as it was encyclopedic. He was the scholars' scholar. By the time of his death in 1973, Professor Strauss had written some fifteen books. His primary works were commentaries on ancient political philosophers such as Thucydides, Plato, Aristophanes, Xenophon, and Aristotle; medieval Jewish and Arabic philosophers Moses Maimonides and Alfarabi; and modern political thinkers such as Machiavelli, Hobbes, Locke, Rousseau, Nietzsche, and Heidegger. Strauss wrote books with philosophically capacious titles such as *On Tyranny* (1948), *Natural Right and History* (1953), *What Is Political Philosophy?* (1959), *The City and Man* (1964), and *Liberalism Ancient and Modern* (1968).[16] In addition to the care with which he took reading the classic texts of philosophy, Strauss was also a great diagnostician and prognosticator of the most pressing philosophic and cultural trends of modern society. Palpitating from his books was a sense that the fate of Western civilization hung in the balance and that only those engaged in the task of reading and discussing the Great Books were either capable of defending the West or, alternatively, safely sheltered from its decline and fall.

Strauss's most important contribution to American intellectual life may very well have been to restore the serious study of political philosophy to America's universities just when it seemed all but dead. At a time when many young people were reading trendy philosophic lightweights such as Jean-Paul Sartre and Herbert Marcuse (who reads Sartre or Marcuse today?), Strauss introduced his students to the Great Books of political philosophy from Plato to Heidegger. His greatest ability as a teacher (and by all accounts he was a remarkable teacher) was to instruct his students in *how* to read the great texts and to inspire in them an erotic passion for ideas and the life of the mind. As Laurence Berns, one of Strauss's earliest students, has written,

> What attracted us to Strauss was no mystery.... Books we thought we had understood fairly well turned out to be far more challenging, fascinating, bold, careful, and intricate than anyone had ever led us to believe. In his teaching Strauss himself exhibited a delight and joy in learning that could not help but be catching. The first effect of all this was quite humbling: we learned that what we thought was our best was not good enough.[17]

Strauss brought to his teaching and writings a sense of urgency and drama that was utterly absent from the stale and morally neutered classrooms of the philosophers associated with the analytic philosophical tradition. As a teacher, Strauss's pedagogic method was disarmingly simple but never simpleminded: He would read the Great Books slowly, line by line, discussing with his students how the texts' ideas related to the most urgent moral and political questions of the day. He would read a passage from, say, Plato or Rousseau, and then he would ask his students to explain what the particular passage said and meant, why it was said in a particular way and in a particular place, and why something else was not said. Strauss taught his students that the great philosophers often conceal their deepest thoughts from unwary readers so that only the truly philosophic, only the most careful and diligent readers, could know the truth hidden between the lines. Ultimately, Strauss encouraged his students to read the Great Books as though each one might have some important truth to reveal.

Strauss's Talmudic-like approach to reading taught his students how to open the sometimes locked and hidden doors of the Great Books with a view to revivifying an interest in and a reconsideration of the most pressing questions—the "what is" questions—that define the human condition (e.g., What is justice and injustice? What is pious and impious? What is noble and base? What is virtue and vice? What is freedom and slavery? What is courage and cowardice? What is the best way to live?). He taught his students that a great book by a great mind is "literally full of wonders, a house of many mansions, secret rooms, labyrinthine passages." He also taught his students that a great book is also "incredibly beautiful" and that one's tastes can be elevated by exposure to such beauty. More remarkably, given the context of the time, when moral relativism was the reigning orthodoxy and the Great Books had fallen out of favor on America's college campuses, Strauss encouraged his students to read these books as if they might actually contain the final "Truth." He taught them, in the words of a former student, "to become a bit more naïve again." Another of Strauss's students has stated that "encountering Strauss at the University of Chicago in the 1950s was a liberating experience."[18] What is remarkable about the many testimonials written about Strauss is that, in most cases, they were penned by men now retired or close to retirement. Strauss still inspires in men now quite old the enthusiasm of youth.

With regard to political matters, Strauss taught his students to begin their observations and reflections from "the perspective of the common citizen." From Strauss, his students

> learned to trust the superiority of proverbs again; we learned to talk in simple words again. Instead of "values," we talked of good and bad; we discussed unhappiness rather than alienation, and things ceased to be dysfunctional—they just did not work. Gradually we realized that Hegel was right when he insisted that, contrary to opinion, it is nonphilosophers who think abstractly, while only philosophers can do justice to the world in its marvelous particulars. In teaching us to see reality—and to understand it was far richer than what so called "realism" considers—he edified us in spite of, or because of, his repeated reminder to us that Hegel had excluded edification from the tasks of philosophy.

What to some might seem a rather mundane and tired approach to teaching was for many bright students a thoroughly liberating and transformative experience that represented the philosophic equivalent of a religious conversion. Strauss taught his students "reverence" for things greater than themselves; he showed them "how to look up, and the things worthy of reverence."[19] Strauss took—and he asked his students to take—virtue seriously. He explored—and prodded his students to explore—the question of the good life for human beings as individuals and as members of a community.

As a teacher and as a commentator on the great texts, Strauss's primary rule of interpretation was that the great texts had to be read on their own terms, that is, the ancient texts should not be read through the lens of the present. He taught his students to give themselves over to the argumentative power and insight of the great philosophers. He wanted them to strip themselves bare of their contemporary prejudices and concerns and to become, in effect, disciples of each and every one of the great political philosophers that they studied. Strauss wanted his students and reading audience to become a Socratic-for-a-day, or an Aristotelian- or a Machiavellian- or a Lockean- or a Rousseauan- or a Nietzschean-for-a-day. As one of his students, Werner Dannhauser, has explained, "We were not asked to abandon ourselves, but to fulfill ourselves by contact with texts written by minds greater than ours."[20] And once immersed in all or most of the great texts, one could then participate in an ongoing (indeed, an endless) conversation—a battle of the books—where the arguments of Aristotle are pitted against those of Plato and both against Machiavelli, Hobbes, and Locke, and all against Rousseau, Nietzsche, and Heidegger. In Strauss's world, ideas and books battle ideas and books. His guiding ambition was to inspire in his students an abiding love of these great old books so that they might begin the urgent process of challenging the way modern man conceives of himself and his society.[21]

In doing this, Strauss also created an intellectual world where merit counts and where the bright and thoughtful are rewarded. He taught his students to identify and to appreciate the virtues of the philosophic aristocracy. Strauss's message was designed to appeal to those bright and ambitious students who felt trapped within the stultifying mediocrity of America's egalitarian society. For those young men and women who were brought into Strauss's intellectual orbit, it was surely heady stuff. There can be no doubt that Strauss changed the lives of many of his students. Consider, for instance, a few testimonials from some of Strauss's best students. Allan Bloom, one of Strauss's most famous students and author of the bestselling *The Closing of the American Mind*, wrote the following in tribute to his former teacher:

> Those of us who knew him saw in him such a power of mind, such a unity and purpose of life, such a rare mixture of the human elements resulting in a

harmonious expression of the virtues, moral and intellectual, that our account of him is likely to evoke disbelief or ridicule from those who have never experienced a man of this quality.[22]

Another of Strauss's students, Father Ernest Fortin, has described his teacher as a "body snatcher and a Pied Piper of souls."[23] Harry Jaffa, one of Strauss's most prolific and influential students, has written of the "blinding power of the light that emanated from Strauss himself" and has compared his encounter with Strauss "to the experience of Saul on the road to Damascus." The eminent Harvard political scientist Edward Banfield has written of Strauss that "he enabled many people to see more clearly what it means to be fully human." And yet another student has said that when he was in Strauss's presence he felt "more fully human than at any other time."[24] It is not clear whether any other professor in modern America has generated such a devoted following of students as Leo Strauss.

Paradoxically, what makes the Straussian phenomenon so perplexing is that Strauss did not bequeath to his students a formal doctrine or a system of prescriptive ideas. He did not produce an explicit political theory and left no meaningful record of his views on contemporary political issues. One did not study Leo Strauss, according to Irving Kristol, in order "to discover ready-made political opinions."[25] His written corpus is presented almost exclusively as interpretive commentaries on the great texts in the history of political philosophy. Further, his manner of writing is veiled and elusive, which leaves his readers uncertain as to his own political philosophy and view of contemporary politics. Strauss often wrote elliptically, dropping pregnant suggestions here and there that left his students and readers wondering whether they were reading Strauss's attempt to paraphrase, say, Plato or Heidegger, or whether he was actually expressing his own views. This is because his own moral and political views are often planted and wedged in a thick forest of textual commentary. Even Strauss's most skilled and serious readers have to work very hard in order to cull from his writings (usually in the form of passing asides and prophetic allusions) the faintest glimpse of his philosophic and political views. Over the course of the last thirty years, even his students have engaged in some well-known and rather schismatic debates as they attempt to determine the meaning of their teacher's legacy.[26] On the whole, however, his best and most loyal students would prefer to keep the master's ideas relatively obscure and unreachable.

On the surface at least, Strauss's distinctive pedagogic style of raising questions and posing problems did not introduce his students to a moral doctrine of do's and don'ts, but instead to a contemplative way of life defined by its *search* for knowledge rather than the acquisition of knowledge itself. Strauss's method of teaching was to make his students aware of the fundamental alternatives to the great questions that define the human condition and then to inspire in them an intransigent desire to seek out the root causes, the first principles, and the effectual truth of matters connected to the perennial problems. He attempted to induce in those who sat in his classes or read his books a skeptical and detached sense that philosophic inquiry is open-ended and that knowledge is limited, incomplete, and uncertain. Strauss's thought is characterized by a radical questioning of and, ultimately, a contempt for those who would put philosophy in the service of a political ideology or a political program. Such political ideologians were, he thought, the destroyers of philosophy properly understood. Thus the attempt by his enemies in the media and the academy to present Strauss as directing from the grave a cloak-and-dagger cabal, the purpose of which is to take over the American government by philosophic subterfuge, strikes the neutral observer as seriously misguided.

Reading Leo Strauss

Given the cultural context of the time and the very different worlds they inhabited, a meeting of the minds between Irving Kristol and Leo Strauss seems improbable. For Kristol, a grown man with an established literary career, all the important questions had been mostly answered in and revealed by the salons of the New York intellectuals. But something momentous happened to Kristol in 1952. Reading Strauss's *Persecution and the Art of Writing* unsettled and woke him from his dogmatic slumbers. It forced him to reorient his thinking about man and society in new and important ways. Many years later he wrote in an autobiographical statement that "encountering Strauss's work produced the kind of intellectual shock that is a once-in-a-lifetime experience."[27] Much has been made of Kristol's youthful Trotskyism (an image that Kristol has long fostered), but Trotsky and scientific socialism are rather barren and arid fare compared to the luminous intellectual world inhabited by Leo Strauss and his Great Books. Philosophically speaking, neoconservatism begins with Irving Kristol's confrontation with Leo Strauss. As we wrote in the introduction, Kristol's review of Strauss's book serves as a kind of philosophic Rosetta Stone that opens up and reveals the inner workings of the neoconservative mind and the deepest recesses of neoconservative thought.

So what exactly did Kristol learn from *Persecution and the Art of Writing*? Indeed, what did he learn from Strauss's larger corpus that captured his imagination and so dramatically refocused his thought? In sum, the central thesis of Strauss's book is that the truly great philosophers throughout history wrote *esoterically*, which means that they wrote on two different levels for two different audiences. Kristol learned from Strauss that political philosophers such as Plato, Xenophon, and Machiavelli hid their ultimate philosophic teaching from the masses and reserved it "for the most intelligent and perceptive." As we shall see, this rather curious and seemingly innocuous teaching contained within it a whole new way of viewing politics. The important question that immediately comes to mind is, of course, why? Why would philosophers not share their wisdom with the rest of mankind?

Strauss's theory of esoteric writing and his recovery of an esoteric philosophic tradition rest on a basic sociological assumption, namely, that an inherent and unbridgeable chasm exits between philosophy and philosophers on the one hand and the rest of society with its traditional manners and mores on the other. This gulf can never be closed entirely because the differences between the philosopher and the *demos* are wrought deeply and permanently into man's nature, which is unchanging. Kristol learned from Strauss, who in turn had learned from Plato, that there is a radical disjunction between the "realm of theoretical truth" (i.e., the realm inhabited by philosophers) and the "realm of practical moral guidance" (i.e., the realm inhabited by nonphilosophers).[28] In other words, the fundamental and defining fact of the human condition for Strauss is the necessary, permanent, and irreconcilable hostility between "philosophy" (with its reliance on wisdom and its concern for the universal and eternal) and "the city" (with its reliance on opinion and its concern for the here and now).[29] The blinding sunlight of philosophy cannot and *should not* reach the cavelike darkness of the city, at least not directly. Kristol also learned from Strauss that if philosophy were to have any role in shaping or improving the city, it must be veiled, refracted, and mediated. It must speak in the people's language and dialect, and it must be presented in the soothing tones of moderation. Strauss therefore taught Kristol a strategy and a method by which meaningful social change could occur under the veil of a new form of political rhetoric. This Straussian lesson was essential for Kristol's subsequent intellectual and political development.

Strauss and his students are beholden to Plato's famous allegory of the Cave to illustrate this point. In the *Republic,* Plato tells a story of men who are permanently chained and seated in a dark cave (i.e., the city) facing a wall on which are projected various shadows (i.e., the opinions of the city) created by puppeteers (i.e., the rulers of the city) and illuminated by a fire behind them. The cave's prisoners perceive these images as their only reality. That is to say, their perceptions are of manmade projections that reflect a shadowy, ephemeral reality, and sometimes the images represent altogether false myths or noble lies that bear no relation to reality whatsoever. Eventually, however, one of the cave dwellers (i.e., the philosopher) heroically escapes his bonds and ascends out of the cave to experience the glaring light of true reality. Freedom and virtue are thus synonymous for Plato with the philosophic ascent to knowledge and Truth. Curiously, though, Plato's philosopher returns to the cave whereupon he does *not* share his newfound knowledge with his fellow prisoners, nor does he seek to rule them.

Following Plato, Strauss believes that most men are naturally fated to live in the chained darkness of the cave, to live with images (i.e., opinions and superstitions) that reflect reality only imperfectly. Even more: to see things as they really are and to learn the true condition of one's being (e.g., that man's soul is *not* immortal) would be devastating to conventional man and civil society, so Plato-Strauss happily enables civil society to continue living by its fabricated opinions, myths, customs, and lies. Strauss's philosopher must therefore accept the natural antagonism that exists between his way of life and the folkways of the city. He must take the city as it is and live in harmony with its conventional opinions and manmade gods. The most the philosopher could hope for is to enlighten the city quietly and subtly about its conventional opinions and myths, but he must never openly challenge or try to abolish them. To do so would be simply foolish, because it endangers both the tranquility of society and, by extension, the philosopher's way of life. This is what Plato learned from the fate of Socrates. At best, the philosopher's student-statesman might hope to govern the city reasonably and prudently. He must adjudicate and sometimes elevate the competing and flawed views of justice in the city. Thus compromise is the order of the day.

Plato's allegory of the Cave also highlights for Strauss the radical dichotomy between ancient and modern enlightenment. Strauss thought the modern Enlightenment project was defined by philosophic hubris. Whereas Socrates-Plato recognized a wide and unbridgeable intellectual chasm between philosophers and nonphilosophers, the engineers of the modern world—men such as Bacon, Newton, Locke, and Jefferson—thought it possible to make all men reasonable, to bring light to a dark world through reason and science. The motive force of the Enlightenment declared that unaided reason could accept no authority above itself, and it promised to strip bare and expose the lies of throne and altar so all can see with their own eyes. The Enlightenment's success required an all-out assault on the forces of darkness and oppression, particularly on the priests and their princely surrogates. The nonrational and mystical opinions, dogmas, pieties, folkways, and faiths that had for centuries been the moral and cultural glue holding various societies together were called into doubt and ridiculed. Enlightenment was for all men, not just for the philosophers. The new philosophers were to share their wisdom with society in order to reform it. With the light of reason illuminating the world, nature's secrets would be revealed to man and then mastered and conquered in order to eliminate prejudice, poverty, and sickness. Then the progress of knowledge would usher in a new golden age of wealth, peace, and happiness.

In Strauss's view, however, the fatal conceit of the Enlightenment was its effort to span the abyss separating the wise few and the unwise many by attempting to bring the philosopher's enlightenment to all men. Following Plato, he believed that the inequality between the wise and the vulgar is an existential fact and the defining feature of human nature. The Enlightenment therefore represented for Strauss the democratization and thus the degradation of the Western mind. Modern natural science and philosophy thought it could find a way to open the bowels of Plato's cave to the sun's light, and so it brought powerful new technologies into the cave and began digging. The problem, however, according to Strauss, is that the engineers of the Enlightenment dug in the wrong direction. Rather than digging toward the surface and opening the cave to more sunlight, they dug away from the sunlight and created a cave below the cave. The result was to cut off the philosophically inclined from the possibility of genuine philosophy and the experience of transcendent truths. In Strauss's eyes, the Enlightenment cave that had been dug beneath Plato's cave created a depoliticized society and made men slaves to work, wealth, recreation, and other earthly pleasures. The modern world of science and technology alienated man from his natural consciousness and higher self, and it forced him into a world of artificial gadgetry and mechanized soullessness.[30] Strauss's philosophic project thus begins with a rejection of modern rationalism so as to launch a return to the ancient rationalism associated with Plato.

The tension between philosophy and politics is not only ineradicable for Strauss, but it is also necessary for the survival and well-being of philosophy. Indeed, without society and politics as a distant backdrop, philosophy would wither on the vine. Worse yet, the attempt by Enlightenment philosophers to bring reason, philosophy, and science into harmony with politics led, according to Strauss, to moral and social chaos, which in turn led to the rise of totalitarian regimes unknown to the ancient world. Strauss wanted to build a high wall of separation between philosophy and society, but a wall with a small door through which the philosopher may pass occasionally in order to begin the process of philosophizing, which does require exposure to the city and the multiplicity of opinions that animate its soul.

The contemplative or philosophic way of life—which Strauss identified with Plato's Socrates—is not only superior to the mundane life of the masses, but the fact of the matter is that "most men are not capable of ascending from the cave of the commonplace to the sunlight of the *vita contemplativa*."[31] The sad truth is that the vast majority of men are forever stuck in the darkness of the cave. They begin and end their lives as prisoners chained to the authoritative opinions of the world in which they live. This is the essential fact of the human condition. This unfathomable abyss between the wise few and the vulgar many is wrought into the constitution of human nature, the truth of which (and many others) no true philosopher would ever pronounce openly in public because of the unsettling effect it would have on the social order. The most important truths known by the philosopher (e.g., the meaning of death) are morally toxic, socially corrosive, and politically destructive.

What this unbridgeable chasm means in practice is that there is and can be no connection between philosophy and legislation, ideas and action. Philosophers contemplate the "transcendent" and the "eternal"—that which is "incorruptible and unchangeable"—while ordinary men are mired and encased in their immediate, necessitous, contingent, and ever-changing physical needs.[32] The great moral truths mined by philosophers are the permanent, unchanging truths that cannot and should not be applied to a corrupt and imperfect society except under the rarest conditions or with the greatest caution and moderation. In fact, the most unsettling truths must be hidden from the people. Ordinary people are simply incapable of ascending from the cave to the glaring sunlight of the "idea of the good," and for the brave few who are capable of the journey, the light of truth is too blinding to share with others and would be ultimately destructive to society. Only the philosopher, only that truly wise man who has devoted his life to the *vita contemplative*, is capable of looking at the sun, seeing the truth, and living harmoniously with it.

And what philosophic truths did Strauss-Plato assume must be hidden and locked away from the ignorant masses? First, that reason and philosophy are inherently corrosive of religion and the people's inherited folkways, which means that philosophy is a social acid that eats away at the foundation of society. Philosophy, Strauss wrote a few years before the publication of *Persecution*, is "incompatible with revelation" and is "radically atheistic."[33] Second (and most shockingly), that philosophy itself can provide no rationally demonstrable moral foundation for society. This is so for two reasons: First, because the chasm between philosophic truth and the people's need for myth, faith, and revelation is too great, and, second, because Strauss really does think that there are no rationally demonstrable moral principles to justify moral and political obligation. (We here challenge Strauss's students to explicate and defend a systematic, secular, rationally demonstrable moral code as objectively *true*.) Philosophy, according to Strauss, while critical of revelation and custom in theory, must support the people's inherited folkways in practice. Otherwise society will dissolve into chaos, thereby endangering philosophy as a result.

Ironically, then, Strauss's philosopher must master the art of dissimulation on two related fronts. First, he must assure his compatriots "that the philosophers are not atheists, that they do not desecrate everything sacred to the city, that they reverence what the city reverences, that they are not subversives, in short, that they are not irresponsible adventurers but good citizens and even the best citizens."[34] Second, he must uphold and defend when necessary the city's traditional manners and mores in order to promote good social order.

The role of the philosopher in society is therefore paradoxical: He must simultaneously respect and defend society's traditional folkways and religion at the same time that he constructively criticizes, enlarges, and improves society's prejudices. The philosopher must discreetly hide his atheism from public view, and he must not desecrate the values held most dearly by society. Irving Kristol was surely shocked and liberated from any lingering remnants of his youthful Trotskyism when he read in *Persecution and the Art of Writing* that the philosopher "may adhere in his deeds and speeches to a religion to which he does not adhere in his thoughts." In other words, the philosopher must demonstrate external conformity with the reigning religious opinions of the community in which he lives. Kristol would later write that he appreciated and learned from Strauss's view that philosophers must write in such a way "so as not, as the British would say, to 'frighten the horses.'"[35] Philosophy by this account is a private activity, a way of life in pursuit of elusive and ultimately ineffable truths.

Kristol's intellectual confrontation with Strauss in 1952 represents a turning point in his intellectual life. At the time Kristol asserted that Strauss had "accomplished nothing less than a revolution in intellectual history, and most us of will—figuratively, at least—have to go back to school to learn the wisdom of the past we thought we knew."[36] And that is precisely what Kristol did. From this point forward in his intellectual biography, we see a new Irving Kristol begin to emerge, one much more attuned to the role of ideas in society and whose analysis of society was deepened by the questions posed by Strauss and the classical political thinkers.

One of the great challenges to understanding the political thought of Leo Strauss and his student Irving Kristol is its dualistic nature.[37] The seriousness with which they took the exoteric/esoteric distinction and applied it to their own thought and policy prescriptions makes the task of unraveling and understanding their project very difficult. It is also one of the reasons why the Straussians and neoconservatives have been able to dismiss their critics so easily. The elusive, chameleonlike quality of their thought has allowed them to be all things to all people and to assume with great success a posture of perpetual plausible deniability whenever they come under attack. Kristol learned from Strauss, who learned from Plato, the Socratic lesson that one's moral fervor had to be tempered and moderated in order to adjust oneself "to the requirements of political life, or to the ways and opinions of the vulgar."[38] The dualism that defines the thought of Strauss and Kristol allows them to move back and forth between arguments of theory to those of practice as the need arises. One can only marvel at the hitherto unassailable and ever-shifting heights of their philosophic ramparts. A deeper and better understanding of Strauss's thought is, therefore, a precondition to understanding neoconservatism.

To truly understand Irving Kristol's political philosophy—and, ultimately, that of neoconservatism—we must therefore come to terms with the political philosophy of Leo Strauss and Kristol's confrontation with the Straussian world of ideas. Surprisingly, though, despite the media frenzy on the subject, the necessary—nay, the proper—connection between Strauss and Kristol is little known and rarely discussed by serious scholars. Despite the spate of recent articles and books that have been published on the alleged influence of Strauss on the neocons, no one—not one of the neocons' supporters or detractors—has identified or discussed Kristol's review of *Persecution and the Art of Writing* and its impact on his thinking.[39] This review demonstrates clearly Strauss's influence on the budding godfather of neoconservatism. More importantly, to change the metaphor, Kristol's review is the looking glass through which we can access the deepest structure and meaning of neoconservative thought. In the chapters that follow, we shall examine Leo Strauss's thought and the ways in which it has influenced neoconservative thinking about contemporary America.

CHAPTER 4
THE ROAD TO NIHILISM

To what brave new intellectual world did Leo Strauss introduce the young Irving Kristol? What did Kristol learn not only from *Persecution and the Art of Writing* but also from Strauss's larger corpus of writings that disoriented his worldview so radically? How does one go from being a Trotskyist to a Straussian?

In 1953, the year after Kristol reviewed *Persecution and the Art of Writing*, Leo Strauss published what would become his best-known and most influential work, *Natural Right and History*. The book serves as a comprehensive guide to Strauss's views on the history of political philosophy, the principal themes of which would echo in Kristol's subsequent writings over the course of the next fifty years. Written in the shadow first cast by Nazism and then by Soviet communism, the theme of *Natural Right and History* is what Strauss often called the "crisis of the West" or the "crisis of modernity." This crisis was precipitated not, however, by modern totalitarianism (a symptom), but rather by a philosophic disease that was eating away at the moral core of the liberal West.

The Occidental philosophic tradition that culminated in the writings of Nietzsche and Heidegger had imploded philosophically, Strauss argued, resulting in a profound sense of moral ennui and cultural malaise. He lamented that Europe and North America were wallowing in a spiritual and moral vacuum that was sapping the West of its cultural vitality and its ability to defend itself from philosophic and political enemies. The West had lost confidence in itself through a kind of forgetfulness or cultural amnesia: It had forgotten its defining and founding moral truths and had therefore "become uncertain of its purpose." Strauss defined the crisis of modernity as revealing itself "in the fact ... that modern western man no longer knows what he wants—that he no longer believes that he can know what is good and bad, what it right and wrong."[1] Ironically, despite having recently defeated Nazi Germany on the field of battle, American intellectuals had become seduced by German thought whilst the American people were devoting themselves increasingly to eating with Ronald McDonald and spending their leisure time with Daffy Duck. *Natural Right and History* was therefore written as a last-minute warning to the West, but its deeper goal was to revivify the question of natural right in Western culture.

Strauss identified the immediate cause of this cultural disintegration with the Nietzschean and Heideggerian doctrines of historicism, relativism, and nihilism, which he associated with the post-Kantian collapse of modern reason and "the contemporary rejection of natural right."[2] In his *Critique of Pure Reason* (1781), Kant had launched an unprecedented attack on the human mind and its ability to know reality. Kant argued that we cannot know the "things-in-themselves," that the world men perceive is not true reality "as it is" but actually the subjective creation of their consciousness, that reason is impotent to discover and acquire objective knowledge of things as they really are. This precipitated a philosophic crisis in the nineteenth century that culminated in Nietzsche's conclusion that Western man's twenty-five-century-long search for knowledge had reached a dead end.[3]

If Enlightenment reason could not ground or validate itself, then the moral and political institutions that were supposedly grounded by it could no longer stand. The moral and political upshot of Kant's denigration of reason was the conclusion that there is no way of life that is inherently worthwhile or demonstrably superior to any other. As Strauss put it (following Heidegger), "modern culture is emphatically rationalistic, believing in the power of reason; surely if such a culture loses its faith in reason's ability to validate its highest aims, it is in crisis."[4] In other words, Strauss is here saying that modern Western society, with its advanced scientific and technological culture, is grounded in Enlightenment reason, but that its intellectual class has lost its belief in reason. Consequently, American intellectuals, Strauss thought, had lost the ability or the interest to rationally and objectively distinguish good from evil, right from wrong, justice from injustice, freedom from slavery, cannibalism from civilization, and liberal democracy from tyranny. In fact, America's cultural elite promoted the idea that morality is nothing but a subjective value choice. We live, Strauss lamented, in an age of moral crisis.

With knowledge downgraded and viewed as a form of subjective social construction, the road was now open to historicism, relativism, and, ultimately, nihilism. Strauss defined historicism as the view that "all human thought is historical and hence unable ever to grasp anything eternal." It rejects the possibility that there is a way of life or a form of government that is best, and this is simply because all thought is historically conditioned and anchored to its time and place. Relativism, born of historicism and the modern social sciences, posits that all value judgments and claims to moral or cultural superiority are simply subjective prejudices that can stake no claim to absolute truth because all truth claims are, in the end, relative to their time and place. Philosophically, relativism says that all viewpoints are essentially equal, which means that any attempt to distinguish between justice and injustice is arbitrary.

Finally, nihilism takes these positions even further. It is the logical and final consequence of historicism and relativism, calling for the destruction of civilization and for the annihilation of all customary or traditional values as a virtue, as the good, and as the end. In essence, nihilism is a hatred, fear, and rejection of all morality and values as such. The uniquely German form of nihilism announced and encouraged by Nietzsche and Heidegger denied, Strauss argued, that reason was capable of establishing "any standard with reference to which we can judge of the ideals of our own as well as of any other society." German nihilism was borne of a moral nausea induced by the rise of liberal-capitalist civilization and its glorification of the bourgeois man.[5] Nihilism begins with destruction and ends with the transvaluation of all values and the will to power. Worse yet, from Strauss's perspective, historicism, relativism, and nihilism represent the death not only of Western civilization, but of philosophy itself.

Strauss's Defense of America

In response to the moral crisis he saw enveloping the West, Leo Strauss devoted much of his intellectual energy to demonstrating how the old admonition— "ideas have consequences"—works in practice. He showed how America's leading intellectuals, mindlessly following their German tutors, openly declared that there are no moral and political principles that can be shown by reason to be universally and objectively true, right, good, noble, or transcendent. According to these modern opponents of reason and natural right, "all human thought is historical and hence unable ever to grasp anything eternal." Not surprisingly, America's intellectual elite were, increasingly, treating its core principles—e.g., the doctrine of natural rights—as naïve, nondemonstrable, semimythic, and, ultimately, indefensible. Progressive American liberals, Strauss wrote, "view the abandonment of natural right not only with placidity but with relief." They view such ideas as quaint, if not reactionary. Enlightened liberalism believes "that our inability to acquire any genuine knowledge of what is intrinsically good or right compels us to be tolerant of every opinion about good or right." (Ironically, those whom he called "generous liberals" were, Strauss observed, absolutely certain that there are no moral absolutes and morally censorious of those who claim that such moral absolutes exist.) America's intellectual elite now thought of itself as somehow "beyond good and evil," a position they heralded as intrinsically good.[6]

For almost one hundred years, America's liberal intellectual elite had waged a war of attrition, Strauss noted, against the core values of American civilization. College professors regularly taught that reality is unknowable, that truth and intellectual certainty are a mirage, that there are no moral absolutes, and that all cultures are of equal worth. John Dewey, the philosophic godfather of modern American liberalism, taught that "the quest for certainty" is neurotic, that the good is determined by group consensus, and that all desires and values are legitimate.[7] As the ideas of America's progressive intelligentsia percolated down and through American culture, ordinary Americans were coming to believe that concepts such as "truth," "morality," "virtue," "the good," and "rights" are all relative or subjective. The cultural consequence of such a worldview is that ordinary, decent, and hardworking Americans had become morally permissive, culturally facile, and psychologically tolerant of all lifestyle choices.

Strauss was justifiably upset that modern man seemed to have lost the vocabulary and will to speak of good and evil, and with that loss came the inability to experience genuine shame and guilt. The blasé and easygoing acceptance of all beliefs leads to a flaccid, dull, and spiritually empty citizenry. Moral relativism, Strauss taught, led inevitably to a leveling, a sterilization, and, ultimately, a deadening of all moral attachment and nobility. Such people have no rational standards or firm moral principles by which to declare that the antebellum way of life in the North was superior to the Southern way of life, or that liberal-capitalist America was superior to Nazi Germany. In fact, it was much worse than that: American culture for Strauss was swimming in a miasma of self-loathing, and a country that hates itself cannot last. Curiously, given his critique of nihilism and liberalism, one might have thought that Strauss would have led the charge to defend Enlightenment reason, logic, objectivity, and the concept of individual rights. He did not.

In the introduction to *Natural Right and History*, Strauss goes to great lengths to present himself as a "friend" to liberal democracy and as a defender of America and the principles of the Declaration of Independence. He there suggests that Americans no longer have the intellectual or moral confidence to defend the principles on which the United States was founded, and they no longer believe those principles to be objectively true or rationally demonstrable. Further, in *The City and Man*, Strauss openly declares that the West in general and America in particular had "become uncertain of its purpose," that it had become "completely bewildered." He therefore challenged the American people to question whether they still cherish and are still willing to defend the principles on which the United States "was conceived and raised." He challenged them to rediscover and explore the difference between good and evil, to search for those principles of right and wrong that are true simply for all human beings at all times and in all places. He seemed to take very seriously the need to defend American-style liberalism from its radical critics on the Left and the Right.[8]

Strauss's immediate philosophic goal was to defend and shore up America's intellectual and political dikes against the philosophic storm that had been unleashed by Heideggerian nihilism. He saw modern man free-falling toward the abyss of nihilism, and he sought to throw him a lifeline. At first blush, readers of *Natural Right and History* are given the impression that Strauss is something of an old-fashioned conservative who will provide America's natural-rights republic with the philosophic defense that it has never had but so properly deserves. One gets the very strong sense that Strauss writes to defend natural law and an objective, permanent moral code. In fact, many conservatives in the 1960s and 1970s were attracted to Strauss precisely because he seemed to be a serious and high-minded moralist at a time and in a place that reeked of moral relativism. More recently, his defenders have worked hard to demonstrate that Strauss was "a friend of liberal democracy—one of the best friends democracy has ever had."[9]

Privately, though, Strauss had a somewhat different assessment of America and its founding principles. He did not think America represented the best or the most virtuous possible regime, although he did judge it to be a relatively decent regime that was better than the available alternatives (e.g., Nazi Germany or the Soviet Union)—not exactly a ringing endorsement! For careful readers of *Natural Right and History,* for those who read the entire book with due diligence and are not seduced by its somber and patriotic introduction, the principles on which Enlightenment liberalism and America were founded are actually brought into doubt and shown to be woefully deficient. Beneath Strauss's public defense of America is an unsparing critique of its most fundamental principles.

On a superficial political level, Strauss may very well have been a "friend" of liberal democracy, but he was something of a fair-weather friend who was certainly not a philosophic *proponent* of liberal democracy. Like Nietzsche and Heidegger before him, he was certain that "all rational liberal philosophic positions" had "lost their significance and power." Consequently, he rejected liberalism on the grounds that he could not bring himself to support "philosophic positions which have been shown to be inadequate."[10] As we shall see, Strauss was a trenchant critic of that economic system and way of life that is most uniquely American: laissez-faire capitalism and the spirit of individualism. (Milton Himmelfarb, the brother-in-law of Irving Kristol, has written that Strauss "despised" the conservatism associated with laissez-faire libertarianism.)[11]

The urgent question that we must therefore address is this: Was Leo Strauss a true friend to liberal capitalism and the principles of Americanism as his supporters claim, or was he ultimately an enemy and saboteur of those principles?

Strauss's final judgment of Western liberalism was that it contained the seeds of its own destruction, that communism, Nazism, and nihilism all represented the working out—the third and final wave—of classical liberalism's deepest premises. In other words, the differences between liberal capitalism on the one hand and those of communism or modern nihilism on the other were simply differences of degree and not of kind. In fact, lecturing at the height of the Cold War, Strauss seemed to suggest (following Heidegger) that the theoretical differences between Washington (i.e., capitalism) and Moscow (i.e., communism) were superficial, that the two are "metaphysically the same," that they both sought to establish a universal, affluent, homogenous society, characterized by freedom, equality, and entertainment.[12] Strauss believed that communism was the bastard brat or, to change the metaphor, the "somewhat impatient, wild, wayward twin" of Lockean liberalism. He argued that "communism was only a parallel movement to the Western movement" in that both stood for equality, technology, material well-being, recreation, and the withering away of the political, all of which would lead eventually to Nietzsche's "Last Man."[13]

The primary difference between communism and liberal capitalism, according to Strauss, is that they disagreed over the *means* to achieve a common end. He suggests that "liberalism seems to agree with Communism as regards the ultimate goal, while it radically disagrees with it as regards the way to the goal." Remarkably, he even goes so far as to suggest that American conservatism "has in the last analysis a common root with present-day liberalism and even with Communism."[14] It must be emphasized, however, that the question of means was no small point for Strauss. On a political level, he clearly thought that American liberal democracy was superior to Soviet communism. Time and again, Strauss indicated his unqualified preference for the American system of government.[15] Still, he considered the common goal sought by communism *and* capitalism to be morally repugnant.

In the end, even though Strauss rejected and actively opposed Heidegger's philosophical and political solutions to the problem of the modern world, he nevertheless thought that the man at whose feet he had once sat was the "only man who has an inkling of the dimensions of the problem of a world society."[16] Strauss thus leaves his readers with the very strong sense that he feels a deep and abiding sympathy for Heidegger's revulsion at the direction of the modern world while rejecting his positive philosophic and political program. Strauss's best-known student, Allan Bloom, has made his teacher's point very clear: "Liberalism has won, but it may be decisively unsatisfactory. Communism was a mad extension of liberal rationalism, and everyone has seen that it neither works nor is desirable."[17]

At the deepest level, Strauss believed that the "crisis of the West" was born with the self-devouring rationalism of the Enlightenment and the natural-rights philosophy associated with Lockean liberalism and the American founding.[18] Nihilism for Strauss is not a philosophic first cause, but is rather a symptom and consequence of a deeper malaise that has its deepest sources in early modernity. "*Liberal* relativism," Strauss declared, "has its roots in the natural rights tradition of tolerance or in the notion that everyone has a natural right to the pursuit of happiness as he understands happiness." In a nutshell, *that* is the problem. The natural-rights doctrine of John Locke and Thomas Jefferson sanctions "individualism," which in turn promotes a tolerance of "individuality," or rather the satisfaction of wants and the realization of selfhood.[19]

The modern doctrine of individuality, then, according to Strauss, is self-cannibalizing. It denatures man by denying that he belongs by nature to any whole—i.e., to a family, a tribe, a race, a city, or a nation. By Strauss's account, the idea of the self-owning, self-governing, and self-reliant rugged individual associated with America's original system of government leads over time to the self-legislating, self-defining, self-realizing, transvestite paraded daily before the American people on *The Jerry Springer Show!* Philosophically, Strauss sees a relatively straight line from John Locke to John Dewey, from Thomas Jefferson to Boy George, from the Declaration of Independence to the Port Huron Statement, from the Constitutional Convention to N.A.M.B.L.A. For Strauss, it was the principles inherent in the Enlightenment—not their corruption—that led indirectly to the N.S.D.A.P.[20]

The relativism and nihilism that Strauss identifies as destroying Western civilization were born not in the late nineteenth century, but rather in the seventeenth century when modern liberal philosophers discovered that no particular way of life has inherent worth. And a society that does not and cannot "acquire any genuine knowledge of what is *intrinsically* good or right" is compelled, Strauss wrote, "to be tolerant of every opinion about good or right."[21] Such a world would lead, Strauss thought, to boredom or to fanaticism—or to both. Thus the liberal principles of tolerance and the right to happiness are the ultimate cause of our modern maladies, and they must therefore be moderated or abandoned if Western man is to have a human future. In sum, *Natural Right and History* may very well be one of the most profound and deadly philosophic assaults on America ever written.

For Strauss, the problem is clear: Nietzschean nihilism and Heideggarian existentialism are simply a consequence rather than the cause of the moral crisis that afflicts the West. If the West is to become healthy again and regain its moral ballast, it must honestly confront the root causes of its malady and apply a restorative anodyne.[22] Strauss found his remedy in what he called the classical natural-right teaching of Plato, as we shall see in chapter 6.[23]

Neoconservatism and Nihilism

In 1888 Friedrich Nietzsche sketched a preface to his projected last book, *The Will to Power,* in which he predicted the "history of the next two centuries." The brooding philosopher warned his audience that the coming age would be defined by the *"triumph of nihilism."*[24] Fifty-six years later another Friedrich, Friedrich von Hayek, envisioned a very different future for modern man. In contrast to Nietzsche, Hayek argued that socialism (in both its communist and Nazi forms) was leading modern man down the road to serfdom and totalitarianism. Writing in the last quarter of the twentieth century, Irving Kristol and the neocons looked at the world around them and determined that it was Nietzsche and not Hayek who was right, that the nihilism ushered into the twentieth century by Nietzsche had led Western man down the road not to serfdom but to a cultural abyss.

The stale categories and formulas that Kristol learned as a young man from Trotskyist Marxism quickly gave way after his "Straussian moment" to a much deeper and a much more sophisticated philosophic analysis of Western society and its discontents. Beginning in the late 1960s, Kristol and the neocons began to write with increasing frequency and intensity on what they called, following Strauss, the "crisis of the West." They took Strauss's philosophic critique of modernity and applied it to the world around them. Their working hypothesis was that the great threat to the modern world is not, nor has it ever been, socialism or communism, fascism or Nazism (or even al-Qaeda). In fact, these modern movements are all, they argued, simply manifestations of a much deeper philosophic and cultural malady. Modern nihilism may have been given birth by Nietzsche and Heidegger, but it was first conceived during the Enlightenment.

The source of nihilism for Nietzsche, Heidegger, Strauss, Kristol, and the neocons is Enlightenment rationalism and all that flows from it: modern science, liberal individualism, and capitalist calculation. Following Strauss's archeology of nihilism's deepest source, Kristol and the neocons believe that Enlightenment rationalism and the modern scientific method turned Western man from a *supra*natural reality to nature, and from faith to reason. Enlightenment reason and science claimed that the cosmos is intelligible, that only man's mind can know it, and that the only proper method of acquiring knowledge of nature is the method of reason. Likewise, they argue, liberal capitalism turned modern man from self-sacrifice to self-interest, from duty to rights, from the community to the individual, from inequality and order to equality and freedom.[25] The result is that man and society have come unhinged from the natural order and from the religious faith that is necessary to sustain moral and political unity.

Kristol and the neocons therefore objected to Enlightenment liberalism and a free society on two broad counts. First, metaphysically and epistemologically, Enlightenment reason turned Western man's attention away from God to *this* world, to reality and nature. It taught him that reason is his only means of knowledge. Enlightenment reason gave men confidence in the power of their own minds to discover how nature really works and how it can be conquered to serve man's purposes. As a result of this newfound confidence in man's mind, faith, revelation, and mystic insight were swept aside, and with them the whole framework of the Christian dogmas, mysteries, and sacraments. In other words, according to Kristol, the light of reason destroys the sacred and the transcendental; it undermines the belief of ordinary men in the immortality of souls, of an afterlife, and of divine punishment, all of which are necessary for them to bear the drudgery, injustice, and pain associated with life in this world. Reason, argue the neocons, shatters everything that gives meaning to the lives of ordinary people; it undercuts their belief in everything that unites and brings order to society. "The more we cultivate reason," Strauss wrote in the introduction to *Natural Right and History*, "the more we cultivate nihilism: the less we are able to be loyal members of society."[26]

Furthermore, Enlightenment reason brought biblical morality into doubt and with it the only kind of moral law that served to civilize otherwise barbaric men. The neocons believe that all societies need religion—the particulars of which are secondary concerns. (If Kristol were consistent and had the courage of his convictions, he would have to believe that a resurgent but tempered Islamism is a healthy reaction to the ravages of modern Enlightenment nihilism.)[27] Finally, without a belief that their society is sanctioned by divine providence, men have lost their willingness to sacrifice themselves—to die—for their nation. The neoconservative position is simply put: The Age of Reason killed the Age of Faith, and thereby ushered in the Age of Nihilism.

Second, morally and politically, the liberal individualism that developed out of the Enlightenment destroys all sense of community (e.g., the tribe, guild, city, or nation). Lockean liberalism begins with the autonomous individual as the primary unit of political value, and it holds implicitly self-interest and egoism (i.e., the pursuit of happiness) as the moral standard of value. It espouses minimal government, as the sole purpose of which is to protect individual rights and to enlarge the sphere of individual freedom. Liberalism liberates individual self-interest and puts a premium on man's private life. The result, according to Kristol, is a society of disconnected, atomistic, and isolated individuals, all living in their own "private Idaho" and all pursuing their own petty self-interest. For the neocons, Jefferson's right to the pursuit of happiness inevitably culminates in the right to entertainment. Kristol's Enlightenment—far from heroic—leads to the liberation of the banal. The degraded symbol of American culture is captured by the image of overweight people in baggy tracksuits pushing their way through the buffet line, sipping rum punch, and dropping quarters into Las Vegas slot machines.

The problem with liberal society for the neocons is that it is devoid of some overarching, authoritative moral truth. The ideal man of this New World, the bourgeois entrepreneur, shuns the arbitrary ties and fixed hierarchy of the Old World for a New World defined by wealth creation, social mobility, and, most importantly, entertainment. Irving Kristol, Daniel Bell, and the neocons damn this world of petty shopkeepers with faint praise: They typically describe this life as doing little more than buying, selling, saving, and spending from sunrise to sunset. As a result, the American people have become happy, healthy, well-fed creatures of comfort. It is all rather dreary and banal. All nobility and heroism are lost. The serious moral life is not possible in such a world. [28] Finally, liberalism *de*politicizes society and promotes what Strauss called an "unmanly contempt for politics."[29] The idea of the community, of the public interest, of politics, and of statesmanship is downgraded to a second-class status in the liberal worldview. Men become more interested in their ever-increasingly trivial pursuits and therefore lose interest in the "public good."

Kristol's account of the Enlightenment and the growth of nihilism is not quite, however, what one might expect: It is not simply the story of European decadence and self-loathing. Instead, it is mostly a story—a very subtle story—about America and its necessary decline and fall. For Kristol and company, it turns out that America is the missing link between the Age of Enlightenment and the Age of Nihilism. The United States of America, according to the neo-conservatives, is a microcosm of the Enlightenment and everything that comes with it. The moral, political, and economic principles animating its revolutionary founding contained the seeds of America's decline and fall. As Joseph Cropsey, Leo Strauss's University of Chicago colleague and friend put it: The United States of America is an "arena in which modernity is working itself out."[30]

By this curious account, Thomas Jefferson's great Enlightenment triumvirate of Bacon, Newton, and Locke are actually the great villains of history (and one might add Adam Smith to this list of notorious thinkers). Their project to free philosophy from the community of faith, order, and duty—to use science for the "relief of man's estate,"[31] to free men from tyranny, and to liberate man's acquisitive impulse—represents the deepest philosophic source of modern nihilism. American-style "rugged individualism" is, in the end, synonymous with a rather cheap and tawdry idolatry of the self. For the neoconservatives, the same culture that produced Daniel Boone would also, inevitably, produce Liberace. What this means is that, fundamentally, the neocons see America—despite paying rhetorical lip service to the Stars and Stripes and to all the great symbols of "Americanism"—as the existential laboratory in which nihilism is being worked out in practice. The neoconservative argument may be captured in the following syllogism:

> Premise one: The Enlightenment is the cause of modern nihilism.
> Premise two: America is the nation of the Enlightenment.
> Ergo, America is the embodiment of modern nihilism.[32]

But there is more: The neoconservative critique of Enlightenment liberalism extends right down to its economic manifestation in laissez-faire capitalism.

This is all very curious given that Kristol and the neocons claim to be defenders of liberal capitalism and a free society. In fact, in the 1970s Kristol wrote *Two Cheers for Capitalism* to defend (allegedly) capitalism from the counterculture radicals of the New Left. But notice that Kristol is willing to give capitalism just two cheers. Why not three?

To the extent that Kristol and the neoconservatives support capitalism, they do so reluctantly and pragmatically—because it works, because it serves a useful utilitarian function, because it delivers the goods, and because it promotes a certain amount of political freedom. Hence the two cheers. Capitalism is marginally good for the neocons because it promotes economic growth, which is in turn what pays for the "social insurance" State to which they are so passionately devoted. In other words, capitalism is a means to semisocialist moral ends. The best thing about making lots of money is that it gives you the opportunity to share it, according to Michael Novak, particularly with one's own family—a concept that Novak refers to as "familial socialism."[33] In the context of today's vulgar and materialistically besotted world, the neoconservatives view capitalism as the worst social system—except for all the others.

But Irving Kristol's praise of capitalism is halfhearted at best. In fact, he is not a defender of capitalism at all but actually one of its most subtle and invidious critics. Following Joseph Schumpeter's theory of "creative destruction," Kristol believes that capitalism suffers from its own internal contradictions and that it will be eventually destroyed by its own successes.[34] To change the metaphor, Kristol and Daniel Bell think that capitalism suffers from what we might call an autoimmune disorder of the soul.[35] Their argument runs as follows: The problem with capitalism is that it liberates selfishness and avarice and generates great and unprecedented wealth, but such affluence has the unintended consequence of dissolving the very (bourgeois) moral virtues and habits that are necessary to sustain capitalism (i.e., industry, thrift, honesty, sobriety, probity, etc.). During the ascendancy of capitalism in the eighteenth and nineteenth centuries, so the neocon argument goes, unrestrained acquisitiveness and "dog-eat-dog" competition were held in check by the Protestant ethic and the delayed gratification of Puritan restraint. Industry, honesty, and thrift were meant to serve a higher purpose.

Eventually, however, the Protestant ethic was undermined by capitalism itself. Capitalism's virtue, paradoxically, is also its vice. The same virtues that produce wealth, luxury, and leisure eventually lead to hedonism, and hedonism leads to the gratification of the unencumbered self. A capitalist society based on nothing but selfish acquisition and the pursuit of pleasure—a society without a transcendental ethic to elevate and give it meaning—is, according to Kristol, a society rooted in nothing but infantile desires and permissive tastes. In the end, capitalist societies are self-immolating because they have no public standard and, worse yet, no concern for defining what constitutes the shameful. Eventually, argue Kristol and Bell, when capitalism is detached from its moral moorings, its moral bottom will fall out and the whole system will collapse into an enervating and squalid nihilism.

Capitalism destroys itself in other ways as well, according to Kristol and Bell. With the waning of the Protestant (or Jewish) ethos—and with it a religious justification for the wealth and inequality created by a free economy, leaving only greed, selfishness, and avarice as its foundation—capitalism lacks a self-justifying sense of distributive justice. According to Kristol, the capitalist definition of distributive justice (found in the writings of Bernard Mandeville and David Hume) is woefully deficient: "It says that, under capitalism, whatever is, is just—that all the inequalities of liberal-bourgeois society must be necessary, or else the free market would not have created them, and therefore they must be justified." But such a view is at best politically naïve and foolish, because most people demand a "metaphysical" justification that satisfies and masks their envy of those with greater wealth. Not only does Kristol reject philosophically this "*ex post facto* theory of justice," he also says that the man on the street will find it utterly deficient. Ordinary men and women will never accept or revere it, and they certainly won't defend it against its enemies. Thus envy demands and should be given a place at the neocon table. Without some kind of higher metaphysical justification for the inequalities generated by capitalism, ordinary people, Kristol argues, will "see more sense in simpleminded egalitarianism than in the discourses of Mandeville or Hume."[36] Once again, capitalism breeds its own destroyers.

Furthermore, the problems, the internal contradictions, of capitalism only get worse. Its moral foundations are not and cannot be self-sustaining. The bourgeois virtues that create wealth are rarely transferred from one generation to another. Eventually, Kristol argues, wealth creates leisure and rising expectations, which in turn creates an indolent "new class" of disaffected and alienated people (usually intellectuals and the young) who become bored with and repulsed by the bourgeois lifestyle. The children of the affluent turn against the very wealth that has given them their privileged position in life. In fact, Kristol goes so far as to suggest that it was capitalism itself that created the anticapitalist "adversary culture" of the New Left. It was capitalism that created a whole generation of feckless and frustrated young people who now have the free time, the wealth, the leisure, and the education to "experience the limitations of their social world" and then to rebel against it.[37] Capitalism, in other words, created Woodstock.

An even greater problem with a system of pure capitalism is that it is grounded on what Kristol calls "secular rationalism," which is and was, he says, incapable of producing a self-justifying moral code. Thus "the death of God," Kristol notes, "haunts bourgeois society."[38] Capitalism is *the* system of creative destruction. In addition to eliminating unsuccessful business enterprises through a system of competition, capitalism also destroys the very traditions and the higher moral virtues that are necessary for its own survival. At its best, capitalism generates the mediocre, mundane bourgeois virtues. At its worst, however, it actually liberates heinous vices: greed, selfishness, and avarice—and who, Kristol asks, could be for that? Thus he is willing to give "two cheers for capitalism," but he certainly is not willing to give any for the profit motive. "Why should anyone want to sing the praises of 'the profit motive.' And who ever has?" Kristol wondered in the *Wall Street Journal*.[39] True laissez-faire capitalism is, according to the neocons, amoral at best if not altogether immoral. "Who," Kristol asks, "wants to live in a society in which selfishness and self-seeking are celebrated as primary virtues?" Ultimately, Kristol's contempt for a truly capitalist society—i.e., a society grounded on self-interest—is simply without bounds. "Such a society," he says, "is unfit for human habitation: thus sayeth the Old Testament, the New Testament, the Koran, the Greek philosophers, the medieval theologians, all of modern moral philosophy." If capitalism, at its moral root, is about pursuing one's self-interest, "then it is doomed, and properly."[40]

With this moral trajectory in sight, and following Leo Strauss, Irving Kristol and the neocons have always argued that public *virtue* and not freedom—not the protection of individual rights nor wealth creation—is the measure of a good society. Indeed, they prefer what they call the good society over the free society. Strauss and Kristol reject the Enlightenment idea of a *free* society grounded in individual rights for a *virtuous* society grounded in duties to the community. Remarkably—nay, breathtakingly—Kristol has publicly sanctioned the anticapitalist views of the antebellum *pro*slavery writer George Fitzhugh with this very conviction in mind. Kristol, like Fitzhugh and Strauss, laments the petty and vulgar moral foundation of a free society and pines for another way of organizing society. Kristol supports Fitzhugh's contention that, in a free society

> none but the selfish virtues are in repute, because none other help a man in the race of competition. In such a society virtue loses all her loveliness, because of her selfish aims. Good men and bad men have the same end in view—self-promotion and self-evaluation.[41]

Consider what Kristol is really saying here. He has contempt for the uniquely American institutions and principles of competition, individualism, and the pursuit of happiness. In a free and open society, Kristol sees no way to distinguish between rational self-interest and criminal behavior, between Bill Gates and Bernie Madoff. More importantly, he rejects philosophically the moral principle on which America's principles and institutions rest—i.e., self-interestedness and the "selfish virtues."

But it gets worse for Kristol. A moral philosophy that begins and ends with the "self" necessarily ends in nihilism, as he states that "the pursuit of self suffers the same fate as the pursuit of happiness: he who is merely self-seeking shall find nothing but infinite emptiness."[42] This, apparently, is the legacy of the Declaration of Independence. And that is precisely what Kristol, Bell, and the neocons see in modern America. For them, liberal-capitalist society generates a new-model man whom Nietzsche described as the "Last Man"—that stupid, well-fed, sedentary, herdlike beast whose highest aspirations in life are a good meal (i.e., to be supersized at McDonalds), good entertainment (i.e., to watch Internet pornography), and a good sleep (to rest content on a Posturepedic mattress). For the neocons, such a degraded, somnambulistic creature lives without spirit, romance, and any sense of greatness or heroism.

Even at its bourgeois best, the aspirations and moral way of life associated with capitalism are low and vulgar. It has no "transcendental dimension"; it can only generate what Kristol calls a "prosaic quality of life."[43] The virtues that it celebrates (so it is said) are the petty and domestic bourgeois virtues of sobriety, thrift, industry, honesty, temperance, and self-reliance derived from the Protestant ethic. Kristol does not think it much of a moral system (it does not celebrate, for instance, aristocratic or ennobling virtues such as heroism, duty, and piety), but it is nonetheless the only one that grounds capitalism. To the extent that capitalism does or can work, according to Kristol, it must be connected to and balanced against some higher moral foundation that elevates it above its petty egoism—and that moral foundation is and must be religion. Religion is what prevents liberal capitalism from going off the rails, from becoming overly self-interested, hedonistic, and nihilistic. Capitalism without religion becomes self-cannibalizing in Kristol's view, as discussed above. Further, without religion, according to Kristol and Bell, capitalism is its own gravedigger: Because it is grounded on reason, self-interest, free will, and individual rights, capitalism liberates the individual from tradition, from religion, from the public interest, and therefore from the virtues that are necessary for the very survival and well-being of the community.

Thus Kristol's warning is dire: Capitalism worked for almost two centuries while it lived off its accumulated moral capital (e.g., the Protestant ethos). Once that capital was depleted, however, it lost its legitimacy, particularly with the young and with the intellectuals. Capitalism, in other words, needs to be saved from itself. As an economic system, it works reasonably well, but as a moral system, it fails entirely. Kristol believes that the Protestant work ethic is the necessary counterbalance to capitalist egoism, but he also assumes that the Protestant ethic creates capitalism's wealth and leisure, which in turn comes to destroy the Protestant ethic over time. In the end, unless it can find a new public philosophy to justify its moral shortcomings, capitalism is doomed. In sum, what capitalism needs is a moral philosophy of duty and sacrifice to the greater good in order to counterbalance its self-regarding vices.

Kristol believes that a healthy society must be governed and bound together by some comprehensive, overarching moral authority that provides the citizens—the ignorant many, as Plato and Strauss contend—with shared values and a common way of life. A good society is one that shares a common view of what is true and false, just and unjust, good and bad, noble and base. Religion is and always has been the traditional way that virtually all societies have ordered themselves (Kristol believes that man is by nature a "'theotropic' being, who cannot long abide the absence of a transcendental dimension to [his life.]"[44]), and so the State must assume a positive role in nurturing and protecting society's moral foundations. "The truth, which we are in danger of forgetting," Kristol warns,

> is that a "civil religion" both engenders and requires a moral endorsement of a regime, not simply a utilitarian one. It is such a moral endorsement that has always led Americans to believe that their constitutional order is not only efficient and workable, but also just. For such an endorsement to prevail, the "civil religion" must be at least minimally nourished by its religious roots.... A "covenant" is meaningless unless it is based on moral truths which, if not indisputable in the abstract, are not widely disputed in practice. The source of such moral truths has always been a religious tradition or a composite of religious traditions. Science cannot provide such moral truths, neither can philosophy; both can only offer us reasons for skepticism about them. But a "way of life" involves commitment, and only a religious attachment, however superficial, can provide that.[45]

Ultimately, the moral and cultural crisis of the modern world, according to Kristol, is inherent in the capitalist system. This is because a liberal society founded on secular, rational foundations cannot, according to the neocons, be held together by reason and mutual self-interest. Consequently, according to Kristol, capitalism can work and be self-sustaining only if it is grounded on a religious foundation—and one that requires the positive reinforcement of the State. In a free or liberal-capitalist society, he strongly endorses the idea that the State must assume a "positive responsibility to encourage established religions, because those established religions" can supply what secular-liberal political philosophy cannot, "namely, a sense of moral responsibility."[46]

And what sort of moral responsibility does Kristol envision or hope for? In lamenting attempts to modernize the Catholic church, Kristol once advised Catholic leaders—in all seriousness—to counsel its youngest members to "wear sackcloth and ashes and to walk on nails to Rome."[47] According to him, only suffering and sacrifice can prop up a free society.

The neocons believe that society must be held together by a single public orthodoxy that defines for its citizens what is true and false, good and bad, just and unjust, noble and base. Historically, religion and nationalism have been treated as the most obvious solutions to the problem of human selfishness, providing both the ends and means for the inculcation of society's necessary and salutary values. Although one has to dig rather deep in the writings of Strauss and Kristol to see their recognition of and support for the necessary concomitant to promote publicly supported virtue (i.e., the coercive force of the State), it is there. As we shall see in chapters 7, 8, and 10, the use of force is at the heart of the neoconservative project to create a virtuous and morally homogenous society. Following Strauss, Kristol and the neocons reject an open society in favor of a closed one.[48]

The neocons, following Strauss, have attempted to merge religion and nationalism into something they call "civic religion." Because Strauss and Kristol believe with Nietzsche and Heidegger that Enlightenment reason has failed, proving to be an insufficient foundation on which to establish a durable political authority, they insist that some kind of nonrational belief (e.g., myth or revelation) is required to establish a stable social and political order. The idea of a civic religion can be traced to many philosophic sources and historical examples, but the Straussianized neocons seem most influenced by Plato's discussion of civic religion in the *Republic* (see, for instance, *Republic* 377c1–3, 413b6–415e3 and the myth of Er in Book 10) and the *Laws*. In these, because ordinary people are incapable of ascending to and living by philosophic truths, they require ordering myths for two reasons: first, to help them make sense of and give meaning to the cosmos and, second, to unify them as one people. The people need to believe in something, their souls need to be nourished with some ordering system of moral and political myth or faith, and they need to *think* it's true. On some level, the neocons believe that if a nation's civic religion works, if it is salutary and does its job, it will be taken by the people as "true"—and that is what is most important.

The neocon idea of a civic religion asks Americans to turn their patriotism into a kind of automatic, unthinking faith in certain ideas, symbols, and institutions connected with "Americanism." Their idea of a civic religion, a secular religion, was born out of the mystic cords of the American past and defined by an allegiance to the symbols of nationalism—to the flag and the Pledge, or to what Strauss referred to in his 1941 lecture as an allegiance to "the flag and the oath to the flag." This is precisely why the neocons are and have been great supporters of compulsory government schooling (the high church of civic religion): They expect the schools "to play a major role in the making of public-spirited citizens." Not surprisingly, they typically think that political leaders should "take action to shape public school curriculums" in order to "provide at least the rudiments of a civic education, promoting not only patriotism but an understanding of democratic principles and the fundamentals of personal and civic morality." In fact, they go even further. Some neocons believe that it is the proper role of government to monitor and manage all education from kindergarten through the universities and graduate schools so as "to ensure that they continue to serve the interests of the state as a whole." They ask Americans to worship secular ideals connected with the "idea" of America as it is explicated, for instance, in the Declaration of Independence and the speeches of Abraham Lincoln. Democratic statesmen should therefore develop, some neocons argue, "rhetorical and symbolic measures designed to foster the 'political religion' of constitutionalism that Lincoln thought essential for the preservation of liberal democracy."[49]

State-supported religion and nationalism (via education) are necessary props for capitalist societies, but they also provide a way station for the neocons, a halfway house on the road back to their ultimate destination: classical political philosophy. To change the above metaphor, religion and nationalism provide a temporary dike against the excesses of secular liberalism and modern nihilism. The immediate goal of Leo Strauss, his students, and the neoconservatives is to arrest the development of creeping liberal modernity by reintroducing religion and nationalism back into American culture. Straussianized neoconservatives will teach the American people how to limit reason and to make room for faith—faith both in religion and in America (that is all they—the people—are capable of). By keeping the American people in a cultural holding pattern, Strauss and the neocons hope that a saving remnant can restore and reintroduce the wisdom of ancient political philosophy. Consequently, if modernity is truly on the road to nihilism, Strauss and Kristol hope to rediscover the lost road back to Plato.

Paradoxically, at the very moment when Strauss gave the neoconservatives new intellectual ammunition with which to defend America and its institutions from the assaults of the New Left, he also introduced them to a philosophic tradition that brought into doubt the virtues and viability of America's natural-rights repub-lic. In an autobiographical statement, "Confessions of a True, Self-Confessed—Perhaps the Only—Neoconservative," Kristol writes that neoconservatism draws its deepest philosophic inspiration from Leo Strauss's resurrection of classical—that is, premodern, precapitalist, preideological—political philosophy. The most urgent task for modern Americans is, according to Kristol, "to start the long trek back to pre-modern political philosophy," by which he primarily means the road to Plato via Strauss.[50] For Kristol, that's the final destination. He explicitly identifies Strauss as his guide on the road to recovering the verities and virtues of ancient political philosophy. For him, Strauss's own political teaching embodies, or is synonymous with, Kristol's unique interpretation of Plato's political teaching. It is only by examining Strauss's views on Plato, then, that we can fully understand the full scope and meaning of neoconservatism.

Part III
The Return to Plato

CHAPTER 5
THE LONG TREK BACK TO PLATO

Martin Heidegger and Leo Strauss began their philosophic investigations from the same point. They both started from an overwhelming sense that the modern world had taken a disastrously wrong turn and that nihilism was sapping the West of its moral and cultural potency. What Strauss referred to as the "crisis of the West," Heidegger characterized as a "darkening of the world"—a world where all men, particularly the creative, are reduced to "a mass" and become subject to the "mediocre."[1] Heidegger's anodyne to the impending onset of nihilism was expressed most clearly and shockingly in his 1933 *Rektoratsrede* (Rector's address), delivered at the University of Freiburg,[2] when he publicly embraced and put his mind in the service of National Socialism, a movement that he subsequently praised for its "inner truth and greatness."[3]

If Heidegger's journey out of the wilderness looked boldly and resolutely to the future and to a brave new world, Leo Strauss, by contrast, turned away from the abyss and pursued a backward-looking path that led him to rediscover a lost philosophic world. Strauss's philosophic project is synonymous with his attempt to revive Platonic political philosophy, the immediate purpose of which was to shore up (at least temporarily) the foundations of modern liberalism in the face of creeping nihilism and the ravages of modern totalitarianism.[4]

The fundamental difference between Strauss and Heidegger is that the latter dated the beginning of nihilism in the West to the very origin of philosophy itself in the person of Socrates and in the philosophy of Plato, whereas Strauss dated the origin of nihilism much later with the rise of modern philosophy in the seventeenth century. For Heidegger, it was Plato's rationalist metaphysics, his doctrine of the Forms and the Idea of the Good—with its unbridgeable chasm between the sensible and the intelligible—that set Western man down the long road to nihilism.[5] Strauss's Plato, however, is radically different from Heidegger's. As we shall see momentarily, Strauss strips Plato of his heavy metaphysical baggage, of all that for which he had been mocked and abused throughout history. For Strauss, recovering (or inventing) a new Plato is the only possible antidote to modern nihilism.

In turn, Irving Kristol's "long trek back to pre-modern political philosophy" began with Leo Strauss as his guide. It was Strauss who first challenged Kristol to see an alleged nihilism inherent in modern Enlightenment political philosophy, and it was Strauss who first introduced Kristol to the lost and forgotten world of Platonic political philosophy and classical natural right. To understand neoconservatism at the deepest level, to see it in terms of fundamental philosophic principles, we must examine closely Leo Strauss's attempt to resurrect Platonic political philosophy and classical natural right. For it was in Plato that Strauss thought he had found an alternative to the self-immolating nihilism of modernity.

Nihilism's rejection of natural right is based on a rejection of philosophy as such. Accordingly, Strauss's defense of natural right is also a defense of philosophy "in the full sense of the term." In particular, he challenged Heidegger's claim that the Western philosophic tradition had, since its beginnings in Plato, taken a disastrously wrong turn and come to a dead end in its quest for certain, metaphysical knowledge (e.g., the knowledge embodied in Plato's doctrine of the Ideas). The Heideggerian critique of the Western metaphysical tradition dating back to the ancients rejected the Platonic idea that "the whole has a permanent structure or that the whole as such is unchangeable or always the same." Strauss's former teacher rejected the possibility of natural right as little more than a dogmatic assertion that has no basis in reality—a reality that Heidegger and his students saw as defined by the "historicity of human life."[6]

Plato Old and New

In his search for a meaningful alternative to Nietzschean nihilism and Heideggerian existentialism, Strauss called for a return to and a resuscitation of classical political philosophy, especially in its original or genuine Socratic-Platonic form.[7] Strauss found in the ancients' doctrine of natural right a possible remedy to our present maladies—a remedy that might reinvigorate the spirit of the West. The purpose of *Natural Right and History* and Strauss's subsequent writings was to suggest that the classical natural-right teaching of Socrates-Plato (in contradistinction to the modern natural-rights teaching of Locke) could provide a theoretical alternative to modern nihilism and a principled foundation for modern politics and statesmanship.[8]

Strauss realized, however, that the resuscitation of classical natural right required the public rejection of the traditional Plato who had been condemned by Heidegger—i.e., the philosophically discredited Plato of "Platonism," the Plato associated with the doctrine of the Ideas, the Form of the Good, the immortality of the soul, primitive communism, and the rule of philosopher-kings.[9] Standing at the center of Strauss's new understanding of ancient political philosophy was a Plato very different from the standard, centuries-old interpretation. Strauss sought to create a non-Platonist Plato, a Plato immune to the critiques of Nietzsche and Heidegger, a Plato stripped bare of all his metaphysical baggage, a skeptical and nontotalitarian Plato. In other words, Strauss sought to re-create a Plato that could be reconciled at some level with modern liberalism.[10]

The centerpiece of Strauss's new Plato is his peculiar and controversial reading of the *Republic*. He rejected the traditional interpretation of Plato as presenting a blueprint for a communistic-like regime in which wives, children, and property are shared in common and ruled openly by philosopher-kings. Instead, he interprets the *Republic* and its theoretical construction of a collectivist regime ruled directly or indirectly by philosophers as an elaborate hoax, as a grand satire on the dangers associated with political idealism. Plato's purpose is said by Strauss to be ironic. It is meant to demonstrate the limitations associated with the real-life politics. "The *Republic*," Strauss argues, "conveys the broadest and deepest analysis of political idealism ever made," which makes it "the most magnificent cure ever devised for every form of political ambition."[11] By this account, Plato's ultimate goal was to remind his readers of the importance and necessity of moderation in political life. Rather than creating a model government ruled by philosopher-kings, Plato's purpose, Strauss maintains, is to demonstrate the impossibility of such a government and therewith the inherent and ineradicable tension between philosophy and the city.

Strauss's interpretation of the *Republic* rests on the claim that the coming-into-being of the best regime (i.e., the best regime in speech or theory) is well-nigh impossible, and this is for two reasons. First, philosophers have no desire or reason to rule because it would require the unpalatable sacrifice that they abandon philosophy, which no true philosopher could ever want to do. (Why rule when you can philosophize? Why sacrifice the higher for the lower? Why take a demotion?) The true philosopher, being "dominated by the desire, the *eros,* for knowledge as the one thing needful, or knowing that philosophy is the most pleasant and blessed possession," has no interest in or time "for looking down at human affairs, let alone for taking care of them." Instead, having "perceived the truly grand," those who have chosen to live the philosophic way of life "regard the human things as paltry." The philosopher's justice flows from contempt for the things for which the non-philosophers hotly contest. They know that the life not dedicated to philosophy and therefore even political life at its best is like life in a cave, so much so that the city can be identified with the Cave.

This prompts the question of how, if the true philosopher is loath to give up his way of life on the "island of the blessed" and to descend back into the cave to rule, could the best regime ever become a reality?[12] Moreover, as we shall see more fully below, the philosopher's quest for wisdom and truth is never finished because knowledge of the idea of justice and the final truth about the best political order is ultimately unknowable, or at least such knowledge is difficult to come by. In other words, the philosopher's claim to rule is only relative rather than absolute. Ultimately, he does not know what he would need to know in order to rule properly.

The philosopher's reluctance to return to the cave points us to Strauss's second major reason for doubting Plato's seriousness about creating the best political order or the virtuous city. Here's the dilemma: The rule of philosophers could come about only if they were forced or compelled to do so by the people or "cave dwellers," but *hoi polloi* have no reason for wanting them to rule, and even if they did, the creation of the just city would require an act of injustice. The best city in speech or theory—the truly just city—cannot be simultaneously just and unjust. Thus Strauss can state the "true reason" that makes the coming-into-being of the best city in speech "extremely *improbable*: philosophy and the city tend away from one another in opposite directions."[13] There can never be a meeting of minds between the wise few and the unwise many. The philosopher lives in the realm of moral freedom while the people must live in the realm of moral necessity. The chasm between the wise and the vulgar is inherent in human nature and it is forever built into the structure of the city.

Strauss summed up the differences between these two kinds of men and the differences between their modes of living in ontological terms: "Hence the philosophic quest for the first things is guided by that understanding of 'being' or 'to be' according to which the most fundamental distinction of manners of being is that between 'to be in truth' and 'to be by virtue of law or convention.'" Thus the philosopher's attachment to the city is partial, conditional, and ironic. His soul is, Strauss writes, "elsewhere." The rules of social conduct accepted by the philosopher "do not go beyond the minimum moral requirements of living together." He is willing to obey the philosophically defective laws of the city not because they are good, but rather because they are a "means toward an end, the ultimate end being contemplation." One might say of Strauss's Plato that he "eventually replaces the philosopher-king who rules openly in the virtuous city, by the secret kingship of the philosopher who, being 'a perfect man' precisely because he is an 'investigator,' lives privately as a member of an imperfect society which he tries to humanize within the limits of the possible."[14]

The lesson of the *Republic,* therefore, is that, wrought into man's natural constitution, there is a fundamental and an ineradicable tension between theory and practice—between philosophy and the city, freedom and necessity, wisdom and consent, the best regime in speech and the actual day-to-day politics of existing regimes. In fact, Strauss's Plato maintains "philosophy and the city tend away from one another in opposite directions." The attempt to overcome human nature, politics, coercion, necessity, injustice, and evil is not only unlikely by this account, but also dangerous. Thus, for Strauss, utopianism is a philosophic vice. He sums up his teaching on Plato in this way: "Socrates makes clear in the *Republic* of what character the city would have to be in order to satisfy the highest need of man. By letting us see that the city constructed in accordance with this requirement is not possible, he lets us see the essential limits, the nature, of the city."[15] The political conclusion that Strauss seems to draw from this permanent division between the wise few and the unwise many is that the rule of law must be harmonized with the rule of men, which means that the best regime is a "mixed regime"—a regime that brings together in the government the wise few and the unwise many. By this account, Strauss's Platonic *Republic* is history's great anti-utopian, antitotalitarian treatise.

The Zetetic Plato

In addition to rejecting the orthodox interpretation of Plato's political theory, Strauss also dismisses what most students of Plato generally agree is *the* distinguishing—if not the crucial—feature of his philosophy: the doctrine of the Forms or Ideas. Plato's famous analogy of the divided line, which he analyzes in Book 6 of the *Republic,* was said to provide the deeper metaphysical and epistemological foundation for his political theory. In essence, the traditional rendering of Plato's metaphysics held that the universe is divided into two opposed dimensions: true reality that exists independent of the reality that men experience in their day-to-day lives (i.e., a suprasensible, supernatural world of the Forms or Ideas, which are perfect, immutable, eternal, universal, and absolute), and the material world in which men actually live (i.e., an imperfect, ever-changing realm that is a shadowy reflection of the real world of the Ideas). The Plato familiar to traditional scholarship posits that the Forms or Ideas represent true reality, that they have an ontological status in some *other* realm separate from their existential manifestations in *this* world, and that knowledge of the Forms is limited to philosophers who, after years of special training, are able to grasp the Forms through some kind of intuited recollection or through some kind of ineffable mystical experience known as divination. The faculty of divination is unknown to and not possible for the common man.

Most scholars agree that Plato's theory of Ideas was intended to provide a stable, transcendent, absolute, and certain ground for man's moral and political life in the face of the apparent uncertainty, contingency, particularity, and chaos of this world. According to the traditional account, the Ideas are said to provide the metaphysical and epistemological foundation for Plato's allegedly fixed, hierarchical, and closed society governed by the philosopher-kings and the wise few. Strauss, by contrast, mocked Plato's doctrine of Ideas as exoteric exotica in order to reveal an esoteric Platonic teaching and a new Socrates who would not have to carry the discredited and rejected baggage of traditional Platonism.[16] According to Strauss, Plato was once again just being ironic or playful—this time about the doctrine of Ideas. Strauss's Plato is never seen contemplating those eternally and independently existing, unchanging beings. Instead, he is presented as contemplating and discussing the ever-changing opinions of society while privately ascending to the highest philosophic "truth" revealed to Socrates by the Delphic oracle—that Socrates is the wisest man because he knows that he does not know.

Strauss's unorthodox interpretation of Plato is remarkable if for no other reason than he is almost entirely silent and strangely evasive about Plato's doctrine of the Forms. By Strauss's own canons of interpretation, when a particularly thoughtful and careful thinker is silent about something obviously important to his argument, the careful student should sit up and take notice. Strauss's near silence on the subject of Plato's analogy of the divided line suggests that he is intentionally pretending that the 800-pound elephant in the room does not exist. He seemingly dismisses as nonsensical Plato's repeated presentation of the Ideas throughout several of the dialogues as a class of distinct, self-subsisting entities existing independently of human thought and experience. Strauss dismisses rather cavalierly several hundred years of scholarship that has held the Ideas to be at the heart of Plato's teaching, stating they are "utterly incredible" and "fantastic." At first, he considers the proposition that the Ideas are "self-subsisting, being at home as it were in an entirely different place from human beings and everything else participating in justice" as bizarre.[17] Strauss does not want his readers to take seriously the analogy of the divided line and Plato's view of reality implied therein. It would seem that he is quite consciously taking his readers on a guided detour around Plato's metaphysics. No competent student of Leo Strauss can take his deafening silence on the analogy of the divided line as having anything other than the greatest significance.

In what is surely one of the most unsatisfactory sentences Strauss ever wrote, he off-handedly rebuffs serious consideration of Plato's Ideas on the grounds that no interpreter of Plato has ever succeeded in giving a satisfactory account of the doctrine. Strauss's assertion is itself bizarre (and undocumented) in two ways. First, surely it is "utterly incredible" to suggest, despite the hundreds of articles and books written on Plato's doctrine over the course of many centuries by some of the best philosophers and scholars, that no one has ever succeeded in giving a satisfactory account of the Forms and their place in Plato's thought. Second, it is truly "fantastic" to suggest that the theory of Ideas does not play an important role in Plato's system of thought given the central role that Plato attributes to them in the *Republic* and many other dialogues.[18]

Strauss's hermeneutical goal is to dismiss, denigrate, and turn readers away from Plato's metaphysics, but the pressing question is, Why? Why does he consciously lead his readers away from the analogy of the divided line and a discussion of the Ideas? Why the misdirection?[19]

Despite his evasive dismissal of the doctrine of Ideas, Strauss does devote some small amount of space (totaling just a couple of pages scattered throughout all his writings) to presenting his own novel interpretation of the Ideas. To the extent that Strauss discusses Plato's metaphysics at all, he performs a sleight of hand: He transforms the Ideas from self-subsisting entities that exist independently of our sensory awareness of them to what he calls the "fundamental problems" that define the objects and purposes of philosophic inquiry. Strauss's attempt to save philosophy from the critique of Heidegger led him to convert Plato's "unchangeable ideas" (i.e., the "*solution* to the cosmological problem") into the "fundamental and permanent problems" (i.e., the "*quest* for cosmology").[20] The awareness of problems and the *quest* for truth replaces the *solution* or the arrival at any kind of absolute truth. For Strauss, the Platonic "Ideas" are synonymous with the fundamental problems, with the "What is" questions. Thus the universal and permanent is not the "idea" or one true conception of justice, but rather the question: "What is justice?" In other words, dialectical inquiry beginning with the "What is" questions replaces permanent knowledge and truth as the purpose of philosophy. Strauss's reconceptualization of Platonic philosophy, now stripped of its metaphysical baggage and repackaged as "quest," is ultimately intended as a response to Heideggerian nihilism. From this, Strauss becomes the philosophically playful, nondogmatic, skeptical absolutist—a position that has the virtue of appealing to liberals and conservatives alike.

Platonic philosophy by this account is not a body of thought or a system of ideas. Instead, it is synonymous with a certain way of life—the Socratic or philosophic way of life, which is a life dedicated to the relentless *pursuit* of knowledge. Strauss defines philosophy "not as a set of propositions, a teaching, or even a system, but as a way of life, a life animated by a peculiar passion, the philosophic desire, or eros." Wisdom in the "Socratic sense" means knowledge of one's own ignorance. It is a recognition that one does not know the full truth of anything absolutely nor with certainty. That is to say, it is "knowledge of what one does not know, or awareness of the fundamental problems and, therewith, of the fundamental alternatives regarding their solution that are coeval with human thought."[21] In saving philosophy from the philosophers, Strauss sought to redefine philosophy or to recapture its older, premodern meaning.

In *On Tyranny* (a work that is more revealingly personal and political than one typically sees in Strauss), Strauss presents a much clearer picture of what he means by philosophy and how he interprets Plato's doctrine of the Ideas. Philosophy for Strauss is synonymous with the Socratic way of life, which he defines as "zetetic," or skeptical "in the original sense of the term." Plato's zetetic knowledge—the knowledge that begins with Socrates's profession of ignorance in the *Apology*— provides Strauss with an alternative to and a new middle path between the Scylla of moral dogmatism (including traditional Platonist and Christian dogmatism) and the Charybdis of relativism (including Sophistic and Heideggerian). The zetetic ascent to knowledge is synonymous with Socrates's famous method of question-and-answer that exposes common beliefs as superficial, dogmatic, and contradictory. Socratic zeticism takes as its animating question, "What is the best way of life?"—a question that it asks over and over again, but must never answer in any sort of definitive way. Strauss sums up his understanding of the philosophic enterprise or the philosophic way of life this way:

> Philosophy as such is nothing but genuine awareness of the problems, i.e., of the fundamental and comprehensive problems. It is impossible to think about these problems without becoming inclined toward a solution, toward one or the other of the very few typical solutions. Yet as long as there is no wisdom but only quest for wisdom, the evidence of all solutions is necessarily smaller than the evidence of the problems. Therefore the philosopher ceases to be a philosopher at the moment at which the "*subjective certainty*" of a solution becomes stronger than his awareness of the problematic character of that solution. At that moment the sectarian is born.[22]

Thus the only attitude or posture worse than that of moral relativism for Strauss is that of moral certainty and moral absolutism, which he thinks can never be more than "subjective" claims. The moment when a "philosopher" claims certainty in answering a "What is" question is the very moment when he proves he is not a philosopher. The true philosopher, by contrast, does not promulgate a system of philosophy or a doctrine. Instead, he lives a certain way of life and asks certain kinds of questions. The best and happiest life is the philosopher's life—a life devoted to probing and searching for an answer to the question of the best way of life, a question that, ironically, must never be answered.

The philosophic way of life transcends time and place, and it is beyond conventional good and evil. The philosopher is a rare human type whose only true friends are other philosophers who speak to one another across the geographical and temporal boundaries. What this means in practice is that the true philosopher who lives in America and supports the American way of life for mere prudential reasons has more in common with a similar such philosopher living in theocratic Iran or communist Cuba than he does with his fellow Americans. Our three philosophers will sanction and may even give philosophic sustenance to the different regimes in which they live, but they long to speak directly or indirectly with each other. Likewise, a "true" philosopher whose own country undergoes several major political-ideological changes over time may very well support these different regimes on prudential grounds so that he may continue to philosophize. Not surprisingly, then, Strauss could strike up philosophic and even personal friendships with a soon-to-be Nazi (i.e., Carl Schmitt) and a Stalinist (i.e., Alexander Kojève).[23]

Strauss's brief for zetetic reasoning rejects absolutist or dogmatic assertions of the truth, which he equates with sectarianism. An attitude of moral certainty leads to dogmatism, dogmatism leads to sectarianism, and sectarianism leads to social division and strife, all of which are bad for philosophy. Strauss instead presents and praises a Socrates whose public claim to wisdom culminates in uncertainty, in the knowledge of ignorance or the limits of knowledge. The fundamental human condition for Strauss-Plato is that knowledge is always partial, incomplete, and sometimes contradictory. (What's more, Strauss's brief for zetetic reasoning is the deepest philosophic basis for the neocons' philosophy of governance and for their proclivity to describe neoconservatism as a "mood," "impulse," or "persuasion.")

In a 1948 essay titled "Reason and Revelation," Strauss fleshed out what he meant by philosophy and the philosophic way of life. "Philosophy," he wrote, "stands or falls by the possibility of suspense of judgment regarding the most fundamental questions." This state of suspended moral animation is inherently skeptical, which encourages *"looking* at things, *considering* things," but never arriving at an answer to a fundamental question or judging something as absolutely right or wrong.

> Philosophy is concerned with understanding reality in all its complexity. Its complexity may preclude demonstrative answers to the fundamental questions: the arguments in favor of the various incompatible answers may be inconclusive. This would not make the philosophic enterprise futile: for the philosopher, full understanding of a *problem* is infinitely more important than any mere answer.... Philosophy in its original sense is disputative rather than decisive. Disputation is possible only for people who are not concerned with decisions, who are not in a rush, for whom nothing is urgent except disputation.[24]

The true Straussian philosopher is distinguished from the dogmatist or ideologian by his recognition that all claims to knowledge are only "subjective certainties." The true philosopher will circle around a problem bobbing and weaving, walking one way and then the other, poking and prodding from all angles, considering and reflecting on all competing answers to the question, and then subjecting them to renewed questioning. Final knowledge or wisdom for Strauss is necessarily a phantom; indeed, as he says—and says repeatedly—"there is no wisdom but only *quest* for wisdom." Strauss's Plato is awash in the irresolvable problems and the unanswerable questions. Naturally the quest for wisdom will suggest answers to the great questions, but the philosopher is ultimately distinguished from the intellectual and the politician by his refusal to "succumb" to the siren song of real or permanent knowledge. Philosophy properly understood "is essentially not possession of the truth, but quest for the truth"; it is the uncompromising commitment to seeking the idea *of* truth. Strauss's Plato, far from knowing the final truth about virtue or justice, knows only that truth is ever "elusive." He is a skeptical and open-minded seeker of truth who rejects moral absolutism and political idealism. Strauss was, we might say, an antifoundationalist.[25]

Strauss's exoteric Plato gives the very strong impression of being a political eunuch: He eschews philosophic system-building and the institutionalization of the best city in speech. Instead, this new Plato is less concerned about the ontological principles of Being and their relationship to natural right and political organization and is more concerned with analyzing the competing opinions of his fellow citizens on issues such as the nature of justice, piety, and virtue. Strauss's Plato is tolerant, open-minded, and skeptical of reforming society with the aid of philosophic blueprints. At most, his zetetic Socrates seeks to moderate, elevate, and ennoble each one of his very different interlocutors by giving to each only what is good for him and not what is good for all in the form of a philosophic system. The philosopher's greatest contribution to the political life of the city is through his role as a gadfly. Seeing Strauss in this way will also help us to better understand how and why he could support different political ideologies at different times in his adult life (see chapter 9).[26]

In addition to his political sterility, Strauss's Platonic philosopher is also a moral eunuch, whose way of life is beyond conventional good and evil. He will deny publicly, for instance, that he is an atheist, but he will also remain ambiguous about the warp and woof of his moral beliefs. Virtue and the good life for Strauss are synonymous with contemplation and private knowledge or the pursuit of knowledge. "Philosophy," he writes, "is *the* right way of life, *the* happiness of man."[27] The quest for knowledge, inspired by mystery and philosophic desire, or *eros,* represents a pleasurable and ennobling way of life that culminates in a sublime form of happiness. The philosopher's happiness is not achieved by living according to a certain moral code or by attaining knowledge of absolute truth (which, it turns out, is unattainable), but simply in contemplating the complexity of various questions and talking about them with similarly disposed philosophers and gentlemen. For Strauss and his students, the greatest good for a man is to spend his days contemplating and talking about virtue with his friends. Philosophy, properly understood, points toward the erotic pleasure derived from the movement and progress of the soul toward the knowledge of and answers to all of the great "What is" questions. Notice also that for Strauss, true morality, the philosopher's morality, is not connected to actually following a moral code or practicing moral virtue, unless of course talking about virtue is synonymous with practicing it. "What counts" for the philosopher, according to Strauss, "is thinking and investigating and not morality."[28] The philosopher is not bound to or limited by any particular moral code other than for prudential *raisons d'état.*

In a remarkably revealing and semiautobiographical account of his life and work, Strauss wrote that he had arrived at an important conclusion that he put in the form of a syllogism:

> Philosophy is the attempt to replace opinion by knowledge; but opinion is the element of the city, hence philosophy is subversive, hence the philosopher must write in such a way that he will improve rather than subvert the city. In other words, the virtue of a philosopher's thought is a certain kind of *mania,* while the virtue of the philosopher's public speech is *sophrosyne* [moderation]. Philosophy is as such transpolitical, transreligious, and transmoral, but the city is and ought to be moral and religious.

To illustrate his point, Strauss advanced the really quite remarkable claim that the "merely moral man," or even the *kaloskagathos* (i.e., the noble gentleman—a man such as George Washington), "is not simply closer to the philosopher than a man of the dubious morality of Alcibiades."[29]

Thus for Strauss the distinction between theory and practice, knowledge and opinion, philosophy and the city, the intellectual virtues and the moral virtues, was so radical and complete that any attempt to bring them together was not only futile but also ultimately subversive and destructive of both. The man whose way of life is "transmoral" will therefore, with some reluctance and disdain, seek to elevate and gently improve the city with speech that is moderate and cleverly prudent. He will work with what he has been given—i.e., the conventional moral and religious opinions of a particular people at a particular time and place—and he will temper, elevate, and ennoble the people's opinions and institutions according to some elusive higher standard. What that standard is will be seen in the pages ahead.

Strauss's position on the nature and status of the moral is made disarmingly clear in the distinction he draws between the philosopher and the gentleman. As Strauss seems to suggest, an Alcibiades stands in closer relation to the philosopher than does a Washington, but this only serves to raise questions about the philosopher and the philosophic way of life. The truly wise man is motivated by and dedicated to the "pursuit of something which is absolutely higher in dignity than any human things—*the unchangeable truth*."[30] To that end, the philosopher wishes to be left alone in order to engage in his private speculations.[31] Thus the philosophic way of life should not be confused with the pursuit of the noble and just things, which is purely conventional. Strauss lays bare the distinction in these terms:

> If striving for knowledge of the *eternal truth* is the ultimate end of man, justice and moral virtue in general can be fully legitimated only by the fact that they are required for the sake of that ultimate end or that they are conditions of the philosophic life. From this point of view the man who is merely just or moral without being a philosopher appears as a mutilated human being. It thus becomes a question ... whether what Aristotle calls moral virtue is not, in fact, vulgar virtue.... whether by transforming opinion about morality into knowledge of morality, one does not transcend the dimension of morality in the politically relevant sense of the term.[32]

For Strauss, then, justice and moral virtue are ultimately utilitarian virtues validated and justified by the fact that they make possible a civil communal life that is a necessary precondition for philosophizing. Strauss has, in other words, transformed the Aristotelian gentleman and his pursuit of the noble things into a kind of disfigured dwarf relative to the philosopher, and he has denigrated the Aristotelian virtues to the status of "vulgar virtue."[33]

In all, Strauss's presentation of the philosopher and his way of life is curious if not troubling. The philosopher's virtue *is* knowledge for Strauss, and yet knowledge is knowledge of ignorance, which means that virtue is knowledge of ignorance. Ergo, Strauss's conception of philosophic morality is, formally speaking, *contentless*. As such, the philosophic way of life "will never go beyond the stage of discussion or disputation and will never reach the stage of decision."[34] Philosophy as a way of life is by and for the philosopher only. As such, it has no direct bearing on the lives of the ignorant and vulgar. Strauss's amoral philosopher is and must be therefore liberated from conventional moral opinion. He must question "the decisive and ultimate significance of moral criteria." In fact, the philosopher "would deny that there *is* a moral law" that applies to true philosophers. In a rather stunning statement, Strauss *de*moralizes philosophy:

> The moral life as moral life is *not* the philosophic life: for the philosopher, morality is nothing but the condition or the by-product of philosophizing, and not something valuable in itself. Philosophy is not only trans-social and trans-religious, but trans-moral as well.

That the philosophic way of life is "trans-moral," that it is beyond good and evil, is the unspeakable truth of philosophy that cannot be shared with ordinary men who require conventional morality to order and make sense of their lives. In fact, the Socratic way of life is inherently radical and dangerous. It frees those who practice it from the fear of death and from a fear of the gods and other manmade myths. This is why philosophic knowledge is subversive of society: It "dissolves," Strauss writes, "the very element of social life." Therefore, it is best left to philosophers and should not be put in the service of the city.[35] Ironically, despite all of his apparent moralizing, Strauss was an antifoundationalist when it came to morality. Likewise, apparently this is the philosophy that Irving Kristol and many of Strauss's students think is necessary to prop up the principles of the Declaration of Independence in an age of moral relativism.

This reinterpretation of the Ideas by Strauss is, in part, a response to the challenge of modern historicism, which claims that all human thought is relative to and defined by time and place. Strauss's reply is both a concession to and a rejection of Heideggerian historicism. Like the historicists he seems to despise, Strauss argues that there is nothing eternal (except for the permanent but open-ended questions), which means there are no permanent truths. By abandoning the idea or even the possibility of absolute, permanent, and universal truths, Strauss accepts the fundamental premise of historicism, but he seeks to escape its moral and social consequences by suggesting that "the fundamental problems, such as the problems of justice, persist or retain their identity in all historical change, however much they may be obscured by the temporary denial of their relevance or however variable or provisional all human solutions to these problems may be." In other words, Strauss substitutes or conflates Plato's doctrine of immutable and eternal Ideas with the "fundamental and permanent problems" as the object of philosophic inquiry—a change that is both cosmetic and substantive. Such a position allows Strauss to give the impression that he believes in absolute and permanent moral principles without appearing to be a dogmatist, or, put the other way around, it allows Strauss to be open to all ways of life without appearing to be a relativist. In short, Strauss is a zetetic absolutist.

The Straussian universe is defined by an attitude of open-minded reflection on the myriad alternative answers to the permanent questions. In the last analysis, one might say of Strauss what he himself said of Plato: "no social order and no party which ever existed or which ever will exist can rightfully claim Plato as its patron."[36] But this would be true only in the absolute sense or in the realm of truth. Strauss and his students would and do of course support different regimes at different times depending on the ever-changing facts on the ground. The philosopher might need to support fascism on one day, communism on another, Islam at a different time, and, finally, he might want to be a "friend" to liberal democracy when it is appropriate. After all, in order to preserve his way of life, the philosopher must accept and respect the values, manners, and mores of the regime under which he lives.

It is only the questions (the "What is" questions) and not the answers that are timeless and universal for Strauss. As he put it in *Natural Right and History*, "problems, such as the problem of justice, persist or retain their identity in all historical change, however much they may be obscured by the temporary denial of their relevance and however variable or provisional all human solutions to these problems may be, ... the human mind liberates itself from its historical limitations." Or, as he puts it in his essay "What Is Political Philosophy?" the foundation of Platonic political philosophy is the "quest for cosmology rather than a solution to the cosmological problem." Thus Strauss can appear to be both an advocate for and a critic of permanent moral standards. He is both dogmatist and skeptic at the same time that he is neither. In the end, Strauss's political philosophy is not so much a dead end as it is the road to nowhere.[37]

Strauss's repackaging of Plato raises an important question: Is the new Plato described by Strauss any better than the old one? Closer to home, we must also ask, can Socratic zeteticism support the principles of the Declaration of Independence as *true* in both theory and practice, or would Strauss's Socratism erode that doctrine and replace its proper defense with stale bromides and cynical sneering? Ultimately, whereas Nietzsche and Heidegger's moral relativism led to the self-overcoming of the blond brute, Strauss's Socratic relativism leads to the self-forgetting zetetic gadfly.

The Return of the Old Plato

Appearances, however, are never quite what they seem in the writings of Leo Strauss. Just when it appears that he decisively rejected the traditional Platonic theory of Ideas, Strauss drops several discreet hints that he actually *accepts* as true the very doctrine he once described as "incredible" and "fantastic." The patient and careful reader of Strauss's corpus will notice that, after some persistent digging and rereading, Strauss actually has two teachings on Plato's doctrine of the Forms: an *exoteric* teaching fit for public consumption and an *esoteric* teaching appropriate for the private consumption of the thinking few.

In *On Tyranny* and in scattered places throughout *Natural Right and History*, Strauss actually comes much closer to rendering and promoting the Platonic doctrine of Ideas in its traditional form. Philosophy as quest—as the recognition of one's ignorance, as the recognition of the permanent questions—is, it turns out, a "necessary" but "not the sufficient condition of natural right." Zeteticism is for budding or junior philosophers. Philosophic inquiry—particularly inquiry for the young—starts with and is premised on the permanence of the fundamental questions, "but there cannot be natural right if the fundamental problem of political philosophy cannot be solved in a final manner." In fact, political philosophy would be of "no practical value" if, according to Strauss, it were simply "limited to understanding the fundamental political alternative."[38] Genuine political philosophy requires something more.

Given this reformulation of his own position, how, then, does Strauss understand the nature of philosophic inquiry and its ultimate purpose? Strauss's Platonic philosopher transcends "the sphere of moral or political things" so that he can engage "in the quest for the *essence* of all beings." His philosopher ascends from and lives outside the cave of convention on "'the island of the blessed.'"[39] For the true philosopher, philosophy proper is a purely theoretical pursuit that has little bearing on life in the city. The true Socratic is concerned with the day-to-day moral and political matters of society, but only secondarily and instrumentally. His pursuit of the "essence of all beings" requires social conditions that are stable and tolerant of his peculiar way of life. In *Natural Right and History*, a rather nonzetetic Strauss writes that "Philosophizing means to ascend from the cave to the light of the sun, that is, to the truth." It also means the quest for the "all-comprehensive truth or of the eternal order"; it means the "humanizing quest for the eternal order"; it means knowing "incorruptible and unchangeable things ... with a view to which we can distinguish between right and wrong"; it means "disinterested contemplation of the eternal"; it means knowing the eternal order that "owes its validity" to "intrinsic truth"; and finally, it means the ascent "from public dogma to essentially *private* knowledge."[40] All this is more than just the "quest" for knowledge. For Strauss, private knowledge *is* knowledge of the eternal order, but such knowledge can be shared publicly only as a mere shadow of the truth.

In correspondence with his old and dear friend, the Stalinist and reputed KGB spy Alexandre Kojève (in which one assumes that he is speaking more openly and honestly than he would in print), Strauss goes even further by equating philosophy with "the escape into Logoi, ideas," which are "separate from the sensible." Referencing Plato's *Parmenides*, Strauss, speaking through Socrates, affirms the traditional Platonic two-realms distinction between "ideas" and "the sensible as meaningful and real." He then goes further to claim that "if philosophy's quest is for the knowledge of the whole, and if the whole must be understood in the light of ideas, there must be ideas of everything." For a man who once described the doctrine of Ideas as "incredible" and "fantastic," Strauss goes a very great distance in accepting the traditional Platonic doctrine. To Kojève he makes the following claim:

> There *is* a realm of ideas; hence there must be a hierarchy, an organizing principle: the idea of the good. But as the highest principle it must be the ground

not only of the ideas, but of the sensible as well. Hence the idea of the good is "the Good."[41]

In plain language, Strauss accepts and endorses the traditional two-worlds Plato for whom knowledge of the Idea of the Good is the *summum bonum* of philosophic inquiry and the ultimate standard of moral and political life.

Thus the dominant passion of the philosopher—indeed, the very definition of philosophy—according to Strauss, "is the desire for truth, i.e., for knowledge of the eternal order, or the eternal cause or causes of the whole." It turns out that all this questioning and desiring is for something tangibly real. As the philosopher "looks up in search for the eternal order, all human things and all human concerns reveal themselves to him in all clarity as paltry and ephemeral, and no one can find solid happiness in what he knows to be paltry and ephemeral." The lower world is the world of becoming and decaying, and the upper world is the world of absolute being, the world of absolute certainty and permanence. Strauss's philosopher is primarily "concerned with eternal beings, or the 'ideas,'" which should be contrasted with the paltry, ephemeral, necessitous, contingent affairs of this world. He "is as unconcerned as possible with individual and perishable human beings and hence also with his own 'individuality,' or his body, as well as with the sum total of all individual human beings and their 'historical procession.'" The philosopher therefore seeks a mind meld with the eternal beings. He must "transcend humanity (for wisdom is *divine*)" and all that is necessitous, contingent, ephemeral, and perishable. The philosopher's contemplative upward-looking search for the "eternal order is necessarily an ascent from the perishable things which as such reflect the eternal order." True philosophy, according to Strauss, "requires a radical detachment from human interests." It must point upward toward the philosophic heavens. The philosopher should encourage men "not to feel absolutely at home on earth." Rather, the citizen of the Platonic regime "ought to be a citizen of the whole." The "whole," Strauss avers, is different from ordinary, sensory beings: It is "'beyond being.'" In his most definitive statement on the subject, Strauss asserts "that there *is* an eternal and immutable order within which history takes place, and which remains entirely unaffected by history." This is to say that this order is entirely unaffected by change and ephemera.[42] This is what the A-team philosopher contemplates. (We here challenge Strauss's students to explain what precisely their teacher had in mind when he spoke of an "all-comprehensive truth," "the eternal order," "eternal beings," the "ideas," and the "whole" that is "beyond being.")

In order to keep alive Plato's doctrine of the Forms and Ideas without appearing to be doing so, Strauss employed new words and concepts to convey the old teaching. For instance, he hides his intent and the object of his study by speaking of the "eternal" or the "whole" when he is really only describing the Form of the

Good and other traditional Platonic concepts. To understand the "whole," he writes, one must understand the "unity that is revealed in the manifest articulation of the completed whole." In describing how one comes to know the "whole (i.e., the Form of the Good)," Strauss presents a rather commonsensical view of the matter: "That to which the question 'What is?' points is the *eidos* of a thing, the shape or form or character or 'idea' of a thing." Strauss's Platonism, then, is most clearly seen in his fleeting epistemological discussion of how one comes to know the *eidos* that, it turns out, mirrors Plato's discussion after all.[43]

Strauss's philosophic investigations begin with what he calls "the surface of things," because "only in the surface of things, is the heart of things." Strauss's Socrates begins with commonsense experience; he embarks on an ascent to the Form of the Good with "what is first for us, from what comes to sight first, from the phenomena." According to Strauss, that which comes to light "first" for man is the community and politics, and the most naturally occurring human phenomena in the city (and therefore the most imperfect because of their changing nature) are man's surface "opinions" about the "natures of things," particularly political things. Opinions are, according to Strauss's Socrates, what man first experiences in his relations with others. Every opinion is "based on some awareness, on some perception with the mind's eye, of something." Strauss thinks that men gain access to the ultimate nature of things via thinking about what men say about them. Opinions are therefore the basic fact of social reality and are man's "most important access to reality" because they are the "vestiges" or "fragments of the truth, soiled fragments of the pure truth" that are within man's immediate reach. In other words, man's "access to reality" (i.e., true or absolute reality) begins with opinions about what is just and good (opinions that are either false or mirror what is true), and it then ascends dialectically or zetetically "from opinions to knowledge or to the truth."[44] The philosopher's ascent and access to the true nature of things begins therefore with his contemplation of what men say about their earthly instantiation.

If unassisted reason and Strauss's Platonic "dialectics" can take man only so far up the ladder of knowledge, how, then, does man get beyond the ephemeral, trace elements of the truth to the "pure truth," to the "whole," to the "eternal order," to the Idea of the Good? By what means or intellectual processes does one know the Forms and the Idea of the Good? Once again, a close reading of Strauss suggests that he comes much closer to the traditional Platonic answer than it might at first appear. In various places in his writings, Strauss suggests that "thought" and not "sense perception" is the jumping-off point in the ascent to the Ideas. In the end, however, Strauss does *not* think that the mind—or, rather, unassisted reason—is adequate, that it has the necessary wherewithal to take the last few steps to identify and know the Form of the Good. Knowledge of the highest good cannot be known by the use of pure reason, calculation, or logic alone. Because reason can take man only so far up the ladder of knowledge before it hits a dead end, some kind of nonrational or mystical great leap forward is required for the last push to the summit of wisdom.[45]

Following Plato, Strauss understood human nature to be animated by a passionate, innate longing or need for a self-transcending union with the eternal order. Straussian-Platonic political philosophy is inspired by the assumption that the human soul has within it some kind of divine spark that ignites in man an erotic longing for ultimate knowledge of the Form of the eternal good. Man's ability and even his yearning to solve the "riddle of being" and to know the "mysterious character of the whole" is limited, though, by his imperfect, corrupt nature and by the limitations of reason. Man, even the philosopher, needs the assistance, according to Strauss, of "divine illumination" and "revelation."[46] For Strauss, man's struggle with the riddle of being and what Strauss sees as his need for self-transcendence leads him to a point where pure reason *and* divination become indistinguishable. Though Strauss himself could never walk down the path of divine revelation simply understood, he clearly muddies the differences between divination as natural and as revelatory. He makes this point clear in a talk he gave in 1962 titled "Why We Remain Jews: Can Jewish Faith and History Still Speak to Us?" In this, he addresses why "heroic delusion" is central to the Jewish experience:

> What is a delusion? We also say a "dream." No nobler dream was ever dreamt. It is surely nobler to be victim of the most noble dream than to profit from a sordid reality and to wallow in it. Dream is akin to aspiration. And aspiration is a kind of *divination* of an enigmatic vision. And an enigmatic vision in the emphatic sense is the perception of the ultimate mystery, of the truth of the ultimate mystery. The truth of the ultimate mystery—the truth that there is an ultimate mystery, that being is radically mysterious—cannot be denied even by the unbelieving Jew of our age.[47]

Ultimately, knowledge of the "self-subsistent truth" and the "eternal" is, according to Strauss, known through some kind of *a priori* "divination." For Strauss's Plato, "the opinions prove to be *solicited* by the self-subsisting truth, and the ascent to the truth proves to be guided by the *self-subsistent* truth which all men always *divine*." In other places, Strauss also writes of the "truth" that it is either known "intrinsically" or that it is itself intrinsic, which means that ultimate knowledge is acquired through the passive exposure to or intuition of revelations. Thus the eye of the philosopher's mind, once opened, is capable of receiving or accessing the higher truths. In the end, again following the traditional Plato, Strauss accepts some form or variant of innate ideas: "the souls of men have seen the ideas," he writes, "prior to birth." He also speaks of philosophers coming to know the "whole" through a "vision of the ideas"—a vision that man receives "prior to any perception of particular things."[48] In other words, Strauss's ascent to the whole or to the Form of the Good requires a great leap forward via some sort of nonrational, mystical divination. The dazzling brilliance of the philosopher's vision opens the mind's eye to things unseen, to a divine beauty, to a nonephemeral world of the permanent things and true being. This is why Strauss can write "Mysticism is one form in which philosophy can appear."[49] Furthermore and not surprisingly, the act or experience of divination is and must be private, and its revealed truths should not be made public unless wrapped rhetorically in the forms and formalities that can be understood and appreciated by those other than philosophers.

What Strauss meant by "divination" (or what he sometimes called the "faculty of divination") in *Natural Right and History* or in his correspondence with Kojève is hard to know with certainty, though his writings are sprinkled with clues that illuminate what he meant by the concept. In one of his last works, *Xenophon's Socrates,* Strauss speaks of the philosopher's need for "superhuman wisdom," which he equates with "divination" and ultimately with Socrates's famous *daimonion*—that curious little voice that occasionally spoke to Socrates.[50] Even though this topic appeared late in his oeuvre, the theme, however, is present in Strauss's writings going back at least to the 1930s. Consider, for instance, his philosophic monograph *Philosophy and Law,* published in 1935, in which he attempted to resurrect the philosophy of Moses Maimonides (1135–1204) and his medieval Arabic predecessors such as Alfarabi. Strauss's explicit purpose was to defend Maimonides's rationalism as "the truly natural model, the standard that must be carefully guarded against every counterfeit, and the touchstone that puts modern rationalism to shame." More pointedly, his purpose was to "arouse a prejudice in favor of" Maimonidean rationalism, since he considered it to be the "true rationalism." He speaks of the *"unconditional* superiority of medieval over modern philosophy."[51] Coming from the ever-moderate, ever-reserved Strauss, this is very high praise indeed. In *Philosophy and Law,* Strauss also collapses Maimonidean rationalism into Platonic rationalism. For Strauss, they should be seen as serving a common cause.

Strauss's presentation of and advocacy for Maimonides's philosophy provides a window into his own views on the nature of philosophy and the philosopher's method for accessing the most important truths. Strauss's recapitulation of Maimonides's philosophy is complex, but its relevance to the present discussion can be summed up rather briefly: Strauss considered Maimonides to be a Platonist, by which he meant two things. First, knowledge of the true or highest reality, the Form of the Good, and divine law are revealed to prophets (directly) and philosophers (indirectly) by a certain cognitive process known as divination, or revelation. Second, the divination of such knowledge is the necessary precondition for instituting the just political regime most appropriate to man's nature. The obvious question that arises, then, is, how does Strauss-Maimonides understand and explain all this hocus-pocus?

Strauss accepts Maimonides's formula for acquiring divine wisdom. This essentially states that such knowledge is, of course, not available to most men. Only a few have the innate intelligence, and even fewer have received the rigorous philosophic training necessary to access the higher truths. The problem, however, is that the philosopher-prophet's ascent to the upper world, to the world of *the* Truth, is limited by his human—all-too-human—material existence and by the natural limitations of reason. "Through reason," Strauss writes, man "becomes aware of *his* world and its dependence upon the 'upper world.'" However, reason is not capable of ascending to the most important or highest truths. The final push to the summit of Truth therefore requires something more, something *supra*rational. The philosopher-prophet's reason requires Revelation, or what Strauss sometimes calls "divination," so that he can learn "of those truths that transcend rational knowledge and that he needs for his life." The philosopher needs Revelation, according to Strauss, precisely because "he knows that his capacity for knowledge is in principle inadequate to know *the* truth." In other words, Strauss's philosopher has abandoned the volitional process of philosophic proof, which requires the validity of reason, the need for objectivity, and the method of logic. Thus he describes the final ascent to Truth as requiring a faculty that is "extrahuman" or "superhuman." Following Maimonides, he calls this faculty the "Active Intellect." Knowledge of *the* Truth comes when the philosopher-prophet's "Active Intellect" mediates an "emanation" from God or the Form of the Good.[52] Not surprisingly, Strauss's philosopher does not need to validate his highest or most important ideas, and, conveniently, he must not share these highest truths or revelations with nonphilosophers.

Because Strauss-Maimonides can provide no meaningful definition or explanation of the Active Intellect and the process of divination (we are left to guess whether this faculty is internal or external to the philosopher-prophet), they resort—as mystics often do—to a parable that mirrors closely Plato's famous Allegory of the Cave. In order for the supra*rational* faculty to see the supra*natural* realm, Strauss via Maimonides describes the human condition as though man were living in a world of everlasting darkness that is occasionally illuminated by lightning or flashes of truth. The philosopher-prophet's divination is compared to that state in which he, and only he, is exposed to continual lightning strikes that illuminate his world and allow him to see the truth of the upper world that is denied to ordinary men, to those who are forever stuck in darkness or near-darkness. The philosopher-prophet then translates and refracts these truths for orators and poets, who in turn repackage them into images (i.e., through a "noble rhetoric" or "noble lies") that can by grasped by the senses of ordinary men.[53]

Such parables do not, of course, illuminate philosophic truths or true realities, but instead they represent a psychological fantasy world. Strauss and his students cannot answer the "How do you know?" question with anything more than the all-too-easy and common refrain, "To those who understand, no explanation is necessary; those who do not, none is possible." They just know. Not surprisingly, divination is ultimately recognized by Strauss as a kind of divine madness or as a state of insobriety. Strauss's Plato even "likens philosophy to madness."[54] The burden of proof is therefore on Strauss and his students to show that the philosophers' divination of the truth is different from that of the prophet or the theologian. In the end, Strauss's zetetic Plato merges into the mystical Plato of traditional Platonism.

As we shall see in the next chapter and in chapters 7, 8, and 10, Strauss's Platonic mysticism ultimately requires coercion when translated politically. Force and/or fraud are the only means by which nonphilosophers can accept or learn to live with the philosopher's ineffable insights. Thus civic virtue for Strauss means obedience to commandments, which in turn means that it is proper to compel such obedience. Such coercion, though, is always said to be benevolent and for the good of the whole.

CHAPTER 6

CLASSICAL NATURAL RIGHT

Leo Strauss's Plato, both new and old, raises many interesting questions. What, if anything, do Plato's metaphysics and epistemology have to do with Strauss's constructive political theory? Can Strauss's two Platos be reconciled? Can the zetetic Plato be reconciled with the metaphysical Plato? What is the relationship for Strauss between philosophy (the realm of moral freedom) and politics (the realm of moral necessity)? How does Strauss's view of philosophy and the philosopher cash out politically? In light of Socrates's fate, what role, if any, should the philosopher play in the political life of the city? If the vulgar many are incapable of philosophy, how should they live their moral-political lives?

As we have seen, the starting point and defining structure of Strauss's political philosophy is the premise that a yawning chasm exists between theory and practice. He accepted as "a basic fact of human nature" that there is a "gulf separating 'the wise' and 'the vulgar.'" Such radically different men are separated not by degree, but are, in Strauss's view, actually of an entirely different order from one another.[1] Thus the Straussian philosopher will always stand at arm's length from the daily concerns of the city. His relationship to the community in which he lives is one of ironic distance and detached resignation. The city, then, for Strauss-Plato is synonymous with the cave and, as such, can never be changed or improved in any meaningful way via true philosophy unless by chance. The city is intractably and forever in darkness.

If philosophy is formally cut off from politics, if the philosopher's way of life is nonreplicable, what, then, is the "political" in Strauss's political philosophy? How should *this* world be ruled? In chapter 5, we saw how the philosopher conducts his life, so we turn now in this chapter to life in the city.

Strauss's Platonic philosopher understands that he must descend occasionally from the blinding light of the heavenly things to the darkness of the cave, that he must give something back to the city in exchange for sustenance and the freedom to philosophize. To the extent that the philosopher cares about or is willing to engage in the city's political affairs, his primary civic role is to educate future rulers either directly or indirectly. More precisely, his principal civic role is to train statesmen—i.e., those gentleman aristocrats who, "though not identical with the wise man," are his "political reflection, or imitation."[2] The gentleman statesman represented for Strauss the link between philosophy and politics. The statesman's way of life, though not strictly philosophic, has been exposed to philosophy and is the highest form of nonphilosophic life. This leads Strauss to ask some pressing questions, such as: What instruction and advice should the philosopher give the statesmen or future statesmen of the city? To what standard of excellence shall he direct their studies? How are the vulgar many to be ruled?

Strauss's zetetic philosopher has a particular interest in first knowing and then teaching his students "both the nature of political things and the right, or the good, political order." It turns out that there is, after all, a political order that is right and good, at least one that is good and right for the demos. For Strauss, the highest standard of moral and political right is what he calls *natural right*. The philosopher's goal is to teach the statesman how to "replace political opinion" with "political knowledge," which is knowledge of natural right. Natural right is synonymous, for Strauss, with that which is naturally right, just, or best for each man and for the polis as a whole. To be naturally right is to be in conformity with or to mirror nature. Classical natural right says that "man has a definite place within the whole," that "man has his place in an order which he did not originate," and that the "good life is the life according to nature, which means to stay within limits."[3] Thus natural right is hierarchical and fixed. Because it is beyond human will, it cannot be affected by it, which means that justice is defined as compliance with the natural order. This also means that natural right means stasis.

Strauss's philosophic project was to rescue the idea of ancient natural right from near philosophic extinction and to make it a living issue for the modern world once again. Premodern natural right assumes the naturalness, the givenness, and the overarching, all-consuming priority of the political, which in turn subsumes all other social modes and orders, such as the familial, the corporate, the fraternal, and the religious. The fundamental question addressed by natural right is, what is the naturally just political order? In other words, it asks, what is the best regime by nature, and this, essentially, is to ask, who should rule?[4] Strauss did not believe that the State should be neutral among the various conceptions of the good, but should instead be animated by some version of justice and the good life.

Ancient Natural Right

Classical natural right is concerned with the proper ordering of the city and is defined by three specific principles. First, the truly just political order should mirror "the hierarchic order of man's natural constitution";[5] second, natural right or the proper ordering of the city is changeable; and third, virtue and the public interest represent the end or purpose of the city. By rediscovering and resurrecting classical natural right, Leo Strauss (and through him, Irving Kristol) hoped to find "a horizon beyond liberalism."[6]

The defining principle of classical natural right is *inequality*. Classical political philosophy and its conception of the just regime is grounded in the idea that inequality is an essential characteristic of the human condition. Plato most assuredly would have characterized the claim of the Declaration of Independence that all men are created equal as a self-evident lie. There is, according to Plato and Aristotle, a teleology of the human soul. They believed that there is a hierarchy of natural human needs and aspirations that are guided toward a natural perfection that is defined by an order of rank within the human soul, ascending from desire to spiritedness to reason. According to Strauss, Plato distinguished "between pleasures which are according to nature and pleasures which are against nature, or between pleasures which are by nature higher and pleasures which are by nature lower." The truth is that some souls are nobler and some activities higher than others, while some are baser and lower. As the needs of the mind are higher than the needs of the body, the life in accordance with human reason and contemplation is the highest way of life and is that which most conforms to the hierarchic ordering of man's soul. It was Plato's view—and Strauss's—that an unhealthy society inverts and corrupts this natural hierarchy of ends by putting the low above the high. For Strauss, the good is that ordering of the soul and society according to that which is naturally right.

Strauss's understanding of classical natural right is more clearly seen by contrasting it with his view of modern natural right. Strauss argued that the modern liberalism of Locke and Jefferson had distorted the fundamental structure of human existence, that without a *summum bonum* to guide his life, modern man lacked "completely a star and compass for his life" and was therefore wrenched away from the natural ordering of society. Strauss worried that modern man is no longer concerned "by the demands of the good life." Instead, his life is "aimless" and becomes a "joyless quest for joy." In contrast to Plato's ideal man, modern Lockean man had become, according to Strauss, and paraphrasing Max Weber, a specialist "without spirit or vision" and a voluptuary "without heart."[7]

It was Leo Strauss's decided view that some men are superior to others in the "decisive respect," which means with regard to their perfection. At the heart of classical natural right is the assumption that men are fundamentally unequal in their ability to pursue wisdom, which is man's greatest good, and they are therefore unequal with regard to their contribution to the common good. Thus, by right, the best men deserve to rule the city. The command of natural justice, according to Strauss, is "that there should be a reasonable correspondence between the social hierarchy and the natural hierarchy."[8] Anything less than the rule of the wise is less than fully natural (it would represent the "natural right of folly" to rule), and the best regime is one that approximates most closely the rule of the wise, even if an absolute correspondence is not possible.[9] Knowledge rather than opinion, wisdom rather than consent, and inequality rather than equality should be, wherever possible, the organizing and animating principles of government. Natural right is a standard or benchmark for Strauss, not an absolute and actionable blueprint.

What's more, the philosopher's wisdom by definition is and must be superior to any laws made by inferior men, which means that the naturally just political order must not constrain or limit the philosopher or his philosophic statesmen to the laws or the wishes of the people. Strauss drives home the point with startling honesty:

> It would be absurd to hamper the free flow of wisdom by any regulations; hence the rule of the wise must be absolute rule. It would be equally absurd to hamper the free flow of wisdom by consideration of the unwise wishes of the unwise; hence the wise rulers ought not to be responsible to their unwise subjects.

Natural right is, then, in the purest sense, the right of the wise (i.e., the philosopher or his surrogates) to rule absolutely and unconstrained by law. That is the standard; it may be unattainable in some or all situations, but it is the standard. For one reason or another, in our imperfect world the philosopher may not be able to rule directly, and so those closest to or most influenced by the philosopher (e.g., an oligarchy of wealthy, educated, landowning gentlemen) have the next best claim to rule. But the urgent question for Strauss becomes whether the best regime is so in theory only, or whether its actualization is in any way possible. The Straussian statesman will always "wish" and "pray" for the best city, but can it actually serve as his standard?[10]

Whereas we had earlier seen that Strauss denigrated the two-millennia-old traditional interpretation of Plato's political teaching, he often equivocates and occasionally drops not-so-subtle hints that he actually accepts and approves of *The Republic*'s "exoteric" teaching. Now and again, Strauss will actually declare his real position:

> The best regime, as the classics understand it, is not only most desirable; it is also meant to be feasible or possible, i.e., possible on earth. It is both desirable

and possible because it is according to nature. Since it is according to nature, no miraculous or nonmiraculous change in human nature is required for its actualization; it does not require the abolition or extirpation of that evil or imperfection which is essential to man and to human life; it is therefore possible.[11]

The best regime may or may not be possible in any particular city and it is certainly not meant to serve on-the-ready as an actionable blueprint, but Strauss certainly thought it the standard by which all regimes should be measured and improved. As Strauss wrote in another context: "It is safer to try to understand the low in the light of the high than the high in the light of the low."[12] Strauss argues, following Aristotle, that short of being the best regime in speech and much more likely to be realized, the best practical regime is the best possible given particular circumstances. In other words, what is politically right in any given situation at some particular time and place is a part of natural right.

Natural right is also *changeable* for Strauss. Given Strauss-Plato's view of reality in *this* world and given the myriad of unpredictable situations in which man finds himself from day to day and from place to place, natural right also refers to the good decisions made by statesmen in ever-changing concrete circumstances. Strauss did not think it possible to generate an immutable moral code on the basis of a mutable society. If morality is conventional and defined by the dictates of society, then morality must be subject to continual change from time to time and place to place. Thus there can be no permanent, universal, absolute, certain, and rationally demonstrable moral principles outside the authority of society (or its statesmen), which means the authority to modify, repeal, or change at will. What is most needed, then, given man's changing social reality, is not absolute or uniform rules that may hurt rather than help society, but rather practical wisdom. What is right can be decided only at particular moments in time, and what is right cannot be overturned by immutable first principles or rules. This means that there is and can be no rule or principle that will tell man how to act in advance of actually being and acting in a concrete situation.

Moreover, such decisions require great wisdom and training in knowing how to choose between competing values in the light of necessity and justice. Sometimes, for instance, in extreme or emergency situations, the statesman may have to choose the low over the high, the base over the noble, that which is "most urgent in the circumstances." Even though the good city is defined and guided by a hierarchy of ends (i.e., by justice and virtue), there are times when "the self-preservation of society" and the "requirements of commutative and distributive justice" are in conflict. In those situations, Strauss writes, "the public safety is the highest law," which is to say that neither philosophic truth nor conventional moral rules should hamper the statesman's ability to act: He should do whatever it takes to promote the public interest. Strauss, following

Plato, does not think there is or can be a "single rule, however basic, which is not subject to exception," but for one: "the common good must be preferred to the private good." Summing up his position, Strauss writes that "Natural right must be mutable to be able to cope with the inventiveness of wickedness." Pursuing the public interest (whatever that may be) under difficult or challenging situations is the statesman's highest standard.[13]

Natural right, in other words, is synonymous with the wise decisions made by philosophically trained statesmen (which only they can know) that serve the public interest (which only they can know). Wisdom is defined as that which is thought by wise people. It is important to note at this point that Strauss was an advocate of natural right (as opposed to natural rights), but not of natural law. Like natural law, natural right is certain, universal, permanent, and transcendent, but unlike natural law, it does not set out a body of rules or laws of right conduct. Natural right is the recognition of an order of rank, but it does not provide particular rules of behavior or action. As Strauss put it, "There is a universally valid hierarchy of ends, but there are no universally valid rules of action."[14] Natural right does not establish permanent moral principles or a moral codex from which statesmen must act. Instead, it simply tells us who should rule and why such rulers should be given the maximum prerogative to train their prudential wisdom on ever-changing circumstances.

The final principle of classical natural right is the idea that *virtue,* or human excellence, is the purpose or final cause of human life. The ascent to the good life, Strauss argues, is premised on certain facts of human nature and certain conditions associated with human flourishing. The basic fact of human nature for Strauss is that "man is by nature a social being." For Strauss-Plato, the political community is *ontologically* prior and superior to the individual, though the philosopher is, of course, exempted from that rule. Man both desires and is completed by associated living, which means that the many must become one, that man's end is fulfilled through unity and social solidarity. The fact of "man's natural sociality" is, according to Strauss, "the basis of natural right in the narrow or strict sense of right," which is to say that it is naturally right for ordinary men. Man's perfection is, in other words, not possible outside of communal living, which Strauss identifies with the Greek polis. The immediate moral and political purpose of the State is therefore to foster "genuine unity." Thus Plato's conception of law, Strauss notes, requires "a unitary, total order of human life."[15] In sum, Strauss regards the political community and its common life as the primary unit of moral and political value, he takes the common good as its immediate purpose, and he sees the establishment of unity through law as the means toward that end.

For Strauss and Plato, the purpose of the city is to foster some kind of noble life defined by moral and civic virtue. Although it is the case that the city is forever cut off from the highest philosophic virtue, wisdom, it *is* capable of achieving a kind of second-class or vulgar virtue, namely, political or civic virtue. Strauss and his students believe that the inculcation of civic virtue is the responsibility of the State and is achieved through some kind of government-sponsored, compulsory moral education.[16] The most important moral and civic virtues advocated by Plato encourage a direct and robust citizen participation in political affairs and a spirit of fraternal unity. The citizen's greatest virtue is to love the city more than one's *self.* In fact, it means identifying one's entire *self* with city. Thus natural right for Strauss is, to use his language, the transformation of "parts" into the "whole." Virtue in this context means only overcoming one's petty and materialistic selfish desires and serving something greater and more complete than one's own self: the common good. Virtue means sacrifice. "All nobility consists in such rising above and beyond oneself," Strauss writes, "in such dedicating oneself to something greater than oneself." Thus the individual's identity is and must be made one with that of the city. The individual soul must be merged with the collective soul. Natural right is therefore synonymous with the common good or, as Strauss puts it, "One could say that in all cases the common good must be preferred to the private good and that this rule suffers no exception."[17] So although the common good cannot be defined in any meaningful way, it is nonetheless a moral absolute for Strauss.

Ultimately, Strauss's civic virtue means obeying. Classical natural right imposes duties on the individual to serve the greater good rather than granting him the freedom to pursue his selfish values. As such, the purpose of a government guided by natural right is to supervise the citizens' virtue and to enforce their duties rather than protecting the individual's natural rights. The great statesman's standard of success and honor is measured by the degree to which he can raise his fellow citizens "toward human perfection or virtue."[18] He will, for instance, render the right to profit subservient to the needs of common good. Duty—to the polis, the community, the State, and the "whole"—is the great moral-political virtue par excellence of Platonic republicanism. Virtue is thus the principal means to a political end—namely, the preservation, unity, and ennobling of the city.

Strauss's understanding of classical natural right is made all the more clear by contrasting it once again with his view of John Locke (the modern liberal thinker *par excellence* and the philosopher recognized by Strauss as the most important philosophic inspiration for America's revolutionary founders). For Locke, according to Strauss, "the individual, the ego, had become the center and origin of the moral world, since man—as distinguished from man's end— had become the center or origin." Strauss laments Locke's "shift of emphasis from natural duties or obligations to natural rights." He clearly prefers a world where "resigned gratitude and consciously obeying or imitating nature" is elevated over a world where "man owes almost everything valuable to his own efforts" and where "self-reliance and creativity become henceforth the marks of human nobility." Locke's natural-law teaching substituted, in Strauss's view, the ancients' and the Christians' transcendent and intrinsic ethic of duty and self-sacrifice for a subjectively materialist and hedonist foundation that is grounded on the right to self-preservation and self-expression. Locke liberated man from the constraining bonds of nature, revelation, and the force of tradition and custom. His acquisitive bourgeois man lives an agitated but aimless life in the pursuit of property, pleasure, and recreation. Strauss wondered how a regime founded on these Lockean premises could ever satisfy the highest aspirations of the human soul.

The depth and full range of Strauss's support for Platonic natural right and his contempt for Locke and the modern natural-rights teaching is summed up and contrasted rather poignantly in the following passage from *Natural Right and History*:

> Man is effectively emancipated from the bonds of nature, and therewith the individual is emancipated from those social bonds which antedate all consent or compact, by the emancipation of his productive acquisitiveness, which is necessarily, if accidentally, beneficent and hence susceptible of becoming the strongest social bond: restraint of the appetites is replaced by a mechanism whose effect is humane. And that emancipation is achieved through the intercession of the prototype of conventional things, i.e., money. The world in which human creativity seems to reign supreme is, in fact, the world which has replaced the rule of nature by the rule of convention. From now on, nature furnishes only the worthless materials as in themselves; the forms are supplied by man, by man's free creation. For there are no natural forms, no intelligible "essences": "the abstract ideas" are "the inventions and creatures of the understanding, made by it for its own use." ... There are, therefore, no natural principles of understanding: all knowledge is acquired; all knowledge depends on labor and is labor.

Notice that the modern principles and virtues identified by Strauss—reason, free will, individualism, natural rights, productiveness, creativity, money—conflict with the ancient principles and virtues of natural right, which he hopes to restore—metaphysical essences or forms, mystical intuition, duty, obeisance, dependence, self-sacrifice, community. Thus the principles that ground and define the American founding are, by Strauss's account, divorced from "natural forms," "intelligible 'essences,'" and "natural principles of understanding," and, as such, they are reduced to and ultimately synonymous with subjectivism and hedonism. Summing up his view, Strauss writes that life in a natural-rights republic is defined by "the joyless quest for joy."[19]

Following the ancients, Strauss believes that the most natural and best political society is small, closed, homogenous, and internally transparent in contradistinction to political societies, which are large, open, anonymous, and heterogeneous. Strauss and the premodern political philosophers claim "the society natural to man is the city, that is, a closed society that can well be taken in in one view or that corresponds to man's natural (macroscopic, not microscopic or telescopic) power of perception." Strauss thought there could be "order" and "unity" only in political communities that were "closed" and small, and he thought such states to be "superior to the large state or to the territorial-feudal state." By contrast, he considered the modern liberal state—with its technological complexity and its "gadgets," with its large and anonymous populations, and with its "funeral homes"—to be *contra naturam*."[20] Apparently Strauss viewed funeral homes as a symbol of conceit, a symbol of how the science and technology of modernity seeks to overcome the natural rhythms of nature.

Only in a small, closed, homogenous society is it possible for there to be "mutual trust," which in turn inspires "mutual responsibility or supervision—the supervision of actions or manners which is indispensable for a society concerned with the perfection of its members." In other words, the ignorant many must trust the civic responsibility of the wise few to mold and supervise their actions and manners in the pursuit of excellence and perfection. Sometimes, though, something more is needed than just simple trust and responsibility; sometimes the many must trust the wise few to exercise responsibly "forcible restraint"—i.e., physical force—in the pursuit of virtue. Given his view of philosophic wisdom as intrinsic, and given his assessment of the nonphilosopher's appetitive and base nature, Strauss has no compunction about giving to the State the coercive power necessary to turn men toward a more ennobling life. The small, homogenous, closed, coercive society is, according to Strauss, the best constituted for the "perfection" of man's "humanity" because it is best at "keeping down his lower impulses." In fact, he calls justice "a kind of benevolent coercion."[21]

Strauss, then, given his general view of human nature as morally base if not evil, believed that most men require some kind of comprehensive and rational guidance, control, and restraint. He held that philosophic reason and divination should govern desire and impulse. The regime must therefore regulate all aspects of men's lives. Thus the function of the regime and the statesmen who preside over it is to use the authority and coercive power of the State to habituate the citizens to virtue and, more particularly, to mold them into self-sacrificing citizens so that they might overcome their base, transient, and selfish desires in order to advance the "public interest."

Strauss's ideal statesmen will be motivated by a "serious concern for the perfection of the community," which is precisely why Strauss is willing to give political leaders much greater coercive power than ever would be permitted in the modern liberal regime. Plato and Strauss thought the "perfection" of the community both desirable and possible in some way, and that such a goal was "the properly directed activity of the statesman, legislator, or the founder."[22] Such men know what is needed for the perfection of the parts (individuals) and hence of the whole (the community). If civic virtue is to be fostered and sustained, according to Strauss, wise statesmen must design laws that will coerce ordinary people to overcome their base desires and educate them to exercise self-control.

In sum, for Strauss, natural right is binary. There is a natural right for the city and there is a natural right of the philosopher. Politically, Straussian natural right is the common good as divined by the philosopher or the philosophically trained statesman. And philosophically, Straussian natural right is synonymous with the philosopher's way of life, which is the only truly just way of life.

Classical natural right represents for Strauss that which is naturally right or best for the city and for the philosopher. It embodies man's highest goals and aspirations, and it points, ultimately, toward his perfection. That which is naturally right requires that philosophically educated statesmen have unlimited or near-unlimited power to assign to each and every man in the city that which is intrinsically good for him by nature. But there is a problem: The institutionalization of natural right and the best regime is near impossible, although Strauss often teases his readers by never saying outright that the best regime is simply or absolutely impossible. He always leaves open the possibility that the best regime in speech is more than just an exercise in political education or a flight of fancy.

Natural Right and Statesmanship

How, then, shall the city—the messy, here-and-now city of ordinary men—be governed, particularly if the philosopher's natural right is not accessible to or attainable by the general run of men? Strauss, following Plato, begins with several assumptions about the city and man that make the establishment of the best regime, or the regime that is naturally right, highly problematic. First and most fundamentally, Strauss assumes *a priori* that there is a nearly unbridgeable chasm between the perfect, unchanging world of Ideas and the imperfect, ever-changing life of *this* world. Second, the city is rent with competing factions (e.g., the wealthy few and the poor many), each of which has its own view of justice that it attempts to superimpose or force on the whole city. And third, the city is in a state of constant motion and change; it is always ascending or descending, growing or decaying. The idea of natural right is, in Platonic terms, beyond the city and man, beyond the socially constructed manners and mores that designate good and evil. Something less than natural right must govern the polis on a day-to-day basis.

The real-life political world of the polis is not one of natural right and natural justice. Prudential political practice begins not with pure natural right, but rather with the here and now; with necessity, circumstance, expediency, and force; and with the elemental "facts" of political life as they present themselves daily, which includes a diversity of competing opinions concerning justice and the good life and also the competition for power and place and the passions that drive it. It begins with *this* world, with an understanding that the reality of *this* world is contingent and in a state of constant flux and that there are massive limitations to what the ignorant many are capable of achieving.

The Straussian view of social and political reality obviously raises troubling questions for the political life of the community. If *hoi polloi* are forever cut off from true reality and natural right, and if the rule of the truly wise is unlikely, how, then—by whom and by what principles—is the city to be governed? If *this* world is governed by contingency, and if their appetites govern most men, how, if at all, can a durable and virtuous political order be established?

Strauss's answer, in short, is twofold. Presupposing any answer, of course, is Strauss's animating premise: An insuperable abyss separates theory from practice, philosophy from the city, and the wise from the unwise. Given that foundation, Strauss believes the morality that does and must govern the lives of ordinary men is different from the morality of the philosophers. The virtue of *hoi polloi* and the city "is not genuine virtue, but vulgar or political virtue only, a virtue based not on insight, but on customs or laws." Those who live in society must, in other words, organize themselves according to certain (untrue) ancestral pieties and political myths that give shape and meaning to their otherwise meaningless moral lives. Strauss thought it impossible—indeed, he thought it dangerous—for men to forget their familial, communal, or national past. He described this longing as a "necessity" of the human condition, one that must be transformed into a virtue. "The virtue in question is," according to Strauss, "fidelity, loyalty, piety in the old Latin sense of the word *pietas*." More to the point, Strauss continues, the great mass of men in any particular society must "believe" certain ordering myths or "noble lies."[23]

The philosopher is thus not above employing the gentle art of deception in order to appeal to the prevailing moral taste of the regime, temper the people's deepest fears and prejudices, and bring unity, pride, and a form of vulgar virtue to the city. The Straussian-Platonic philosopher will frequently interpret and reinterpret the traditions and values of his nation, altering them when necessary in order to make room for philosophers and their unique way of life. Thus the exoteric teachings of Straussian philosophers will be different depending on where or when they live. What Strauss calls "philosophic politics" is the effort by philosophers, regardless of the kind of regime in which they live, to win the acceptance of their particular society for their unique way of life. They do this by showing their fellow citizens that they abhor what the city abhors, that they do not desecrate the city's gods (religious or otherwise), and that they show due reverence for the things the city reveres. (This is precisely the kind of intellectual relationship that Straussians and many Straussianized neocons have established with the American people and their manners and mores.) The philosopher-prophet either creates the ordering myths of any given society through his prophecy or he honors those that already exist.

In Strauss's view, philosophy and philosophic education can thrive in a diversity of regimes. Each philosopher begins his philosophizing from the perspective of the particular cave in which he lives, but they all ascend eventually to the same place. The Straussian philosopher living in the ayatollah's Iran will establish a relationship with and develop a public philosophy for his particular regime different from the Straussian philosopher who lives in a communist, fascist, or a free nation, but they all seek to meet each other in the Elysian Fields.[24]

Sometimes, however, noble lies and the force of traditional opinions are insufficient. When push comes to shove, the laws, religion, and customs of society must be unsentimentally backed up by force and compulsion. In fact, Strauss believes that "sheer bodily (brachial) force must be recognized as having a natural title to rule, a title indeed inferior to that deriving from wisdom but not destroyed by it." Short of true natural right, for most men in most instances, the rule of might provides the basis of political right. That is what is required to control, unify, and bring order to the chaos of man's natural condition. The statesman's civic virtue thus becomes synonymous with the proper use of compulsion in pursuit of the public interest.[25]

Beyond simple force (which must always be held in reserve as an omnipresent necessity), the best that the city can hope for is to be governed by wise statesmen and magnanimous gentlemen who have been liberally trained in the Great Books and the interrogatory method of Socratic inquiry. Political knowledge in Strauss's philosophy is ceded or passed down from the philosopher to that class of aristocratic political gentlemen, of whom Strauss refers to as the magnanimous statesman—the man "who possesses political knowledge, political understanding, political wisdom, political skill in the highest degree." The wise statesman, though not himself a philosopher, is the great-souled man who has at least been exposed to philosophy and the idea of justice. Strauss's gentleman statesman "is the political reflection, or imitation, of the wise man." The spirit of the true or highest kind of statesman is "free from the narrowness of the lawyer, the brutality of the technician, the vagaries of the visionary, and the baseness of the opportunist." He is guided by the kind of "magnanimous flexibility" that "crushes the insolent and spares the vanquished."[26]

The Platonic-Straussian statesman will, furthermore, have the necessary wisdom—the *a priori* knowledge learned from his philosopher teachers—to mold society in the image of a certain *idea* of justice and of the good life. (For this reason Plato founded the Academy in order to educate correctly a new ruling class by exposing them to philosophy.) The statesman's superior wisdom, knowledge, and vision should not therefore be constrained by rules and laws made by inferior men, but instead should be given the widest possible latitude. Speaking on behalf of Xenophon's Socrates, Strauss clearly seemed to think that "The man of the highest political wisdom is superior to any law, not only because he alone can be the origin of excellent laws, but likewise because he has a flexibility which laws, however wise, necessarily lack."[27] Furthermore, the rule of law is sometimes inadequate or even a hindrance to dealing with the messiness of an ever-changing social reality, whereas the superior wisdom and prudence of the great-souled statesman is necessary and uniquely equipped for dealing with contingency.[28]

At its best and under unique, nonreplicable circumstances, the rule of gentlemen-statesmen may reflect imperfectly the rule of philosophy. Nonetheless, the statesman—given the imperfect clay that he has to work with—will necessarily be guided day-to-day by a different method and a different end. The Platonic-Straussian statesman understands just enough about philosophy to know that the philosopher's truths are most often inapplicable—even harmful—to society. He must therefore be guided by two political—i.e., nonphilosophic—virtues: moderation and prudence.[29]

Moderation for Strauss is the animating spirit of a decent political regime. Wisdom is the highest possible virtue of a truly great and philosophic statesman, but wisdom is not possible without moderation. "Moderation," Strauss wrote, "will protect us against the twin dangers of visionary expectations from politics and unmanly contempt for politics."[30] The statesman must be moderate in the sense that he must accept the reality of the city as it is and not attempt to impose on it some vision of the "good" or the "best regime." Moderation is free of moral dogmatism, political zeal, and ideological fanaticism. Strauss's philosopher-statesman is a man of modest expectations, who is "free from all fanaticism." He is attentive of "the limits set to all human action and all human planning." He also acknowledges the fact that ordinary men are by nature ignorant, corrupt, and ultimately evil (which means selfish). Furthermore, he knows that "evil cannot be eradicated" from human affairs, and so he learns to moderate his moral and political expectations for society. His spirit is one of "sublime sobriety."[31]

The Straussian statesman is not simply or solely a pessimist, though. He recognizes that selfishness must and can be transformed or enlarged by changing man's identity, so that the citizen associates his "self" and his love of self with the city as a whole. In other words, man's primary identity and self-love must become synonymous with his love of the city. For Strauss and the ancients, this is done, on some level, by accepting and supporting the "particular fundamental opinion" on which "every political society that ever has been or ever will be rests." This means that each and every society is held together and inspired by certain rituals, symbols, customs, conventions, and myths—i.e., its "particular fundamental opinion"—that define and promote the common good. Whereas the philosopher contemplates and makes sense of this world by his ascent to the idea of the good, ordinary men can make sense of their lives and their place in the world only through a form of civic piety or through the combined twin components of what we might call the *working man's philosophy*: nationalism and religion.[32] All morally healthy societies, Strauss thought, must remain closed and homogenous: Their citizens must feel inherently an "unqualified commitment" to the fatherland, a patriotic and spirited dedication to the justice and cultural superiority of their society, and they must believe that God has sanctioned their existence as a people.[33] With nationalism and religion as the two principal values also come the two cardinal virtues: self-sacrifice and piety.

Strauss was genuinely concerned with how "the unphilosophical multitude" would "conduct itself if it ceases to believe in gods who punish lack of patriotism and of filial piety" in the same way that he seemed to share Rousseau's concern that "Science must remain the preserve of a small minority" and should "be kept secret from the common man." Philosophy and science, according to Strauss, represent "the highest activity of man" because they are concerned with replacing opinion (i.e., the "element of the city") with knowledge. Strauss also recognized that philosophy and science "attempt to dissolve the element in which society breathes," which means they are a threat to society. Paraphrasing almost exactly what he had said of Rousseau in *Natural Right and History*, Strauss writes that "philosophy or science must remain the preserve of a small minority," and that philosophers and scientists have a responsibility to "respect the opinions on which society rests." As Strauss notes, however, "To respect opinions is something entirely different from accepting them as true." Philosophers must therefore walk a tightrope between seeking the truth (which often is "productive of the deepest pain") and "endangering the unqualified commitment of the many to the opinions on which society rests." Thus the philosopher must in some way support the moral and religious opinions of the city, all the while knowing that they are not true but are nonetheless "socially useful." The multitude of men in society are kept in check and "appeased by religious hopes and frightened by religious fears." Furthermore, they are more likely to obey and show deference to the commands of the ruling class. Following Machiavelli's lead, Strauss supports the idea that rulers must use the protective atmosphere provided by social folkways, ancestral pieties, divine revelation, and command as forms of social control:

> Religion as reverence for the gods breeds deference to the ruling class as a group of men especially favored by the gods and reminiscent of the gods. And vice

versa, unqualified unbelief will dispose the people not to believe in what they are told by venerable men. The ruling class will not be able in the long run to elicit this kind of deference if it does not contain men, and especially old men, who are venerable by virtue of their piety.[34]

The nation and the gods (or god) provide, he thought, a substitute for the philosopher's idea of the good. The philosopher must acknowledge, respect, and support local religious beliefs. The statesman, on the other hand, must manage, nurture, and protect the city's inherited institutions and customs, particularly its religious beliefs, or he must, as with the founders of many ancient cities, invent a civic religion that he imposes on his fellow citizens by force or fraud. The philosophic statesman knows that any such particular civic religion makes truth claims that it cannot verify rationally or demonstrate philosophically, but he also understands that such claims serve a crucial role in uniting and elevating man's baser elements and must therefore be treated with respect and even admiration. The Platonic-Straussian statesman seeks to improve the political life of his city by gradually and gently reforming the moral opinions of his fellow citizens. More selfishly, though, the philosopher also seeks to foster a stable sociopolitical environment in order to be left alone to pursue his philosophic pleasures.

Furthermore, the gentleman-statesman must also be prudent. Prudence is a cardinal virtue in the Straussian world because it is the virtue or method that guides the statesmen of the city as they deal with the fragmentary day-to-day realities of *this* world, realities that are permanently cut off from the possibilities of philosophy and the ascent to the good. Prudence, disconnected from true moral principles, begins with practical knowledge of the here and now: It takes imperfect man as he is and the teeming city as it is. Strauss understands the "sphere governed by prudence" to be "self-sufficient," by which he means that it is disconnected from theoretical knowledge.[35]

Strauss's model statesman and his conception of prudence are rather more complex—tougher and more realistic—than one might glean from a superficial reading of Plato's political dialogues. Strauss's Plato and therefore Strauss seek to reconcile "the way of Socrates with the way of Thrasymachus."[36] In fact, Socrates is not and cannot be a model for the day-to-day business of a Straussian statesmen who must govern a city of nonphilosophers. Socrates's "intransigent way" of speaking and acting "is appropriate only for the philosopher's dealing with the elite, whereas the way of Thrasymachus ... is appropriate for his dealings with the vulgar." Thrasymachus, by contrast, is a sophist and a rhetorician, which means he understands the people, how to speak to the vulgar many, and the proper use of power and coercion in the art of ruling. Thrasymachus, Strauss notes, "must be integrated into the best city because the best city is not possible without the art of Thrasymachus," which is the art of rhetoric and the art of benevolent coercion.[37] Plato's reconciliation of Socrates and Thrasymachus thus paves the way for Strauss's subtle attempt to reconcile Plato and Machiavelli.[38]

In *Natural Right and History*, Strauss presents a view of the true statesman that makes Platonic natural right compatible with Machiavellian prudence. Put slightly differently, and contrary to the common view, Machiavellian realism can and must be reconciled with Platonic idealism. When deciding what ought to be done by the statesman in the messy world of the here and now, Strauss writes that

> one has to consider not only which of the various competing objectives is higher in rank but also which is most urgent in the circumstances. What is most urgent is legitimately preferred to what is less urgent, and the most urgent is in many cases lower in rank than the less urgent. But one cannot make a universal rule that urgency is a higher consideration than rank. For it is our duty to make the highest activity, as much as we can, the most urgent or the most needful thing. And the maximum of effort which can be expected necessarily varies from individual to individual. The only universally valid standard is the hierarchy of ends. This standard is sufficient for passing judgment on the level of nobility of individuals and groups and of actions and institutions. But it is insufficient for guiding our actions.[39]

The Straussian statesman must therefore be given the widest possible latitude in dealing with the ever-changing world of the here and now. What is most urgent for particular cities in differing circumstances must take priority over the universal standard defined by natural right and the hierarchy of ends. In other words, Machiavellian prudence should rule during the active hours of the day while the Platonic standard of natural right is the faraway and sometimes unreachable standard that we longingly wish for and that rules our political dreams.

Additionally, the Straussian statesman recognizes and accepts as a fact of reality that the city is made out of competing socioideological factions and that his first responsibility is to reconcile these factions—to make one out of many. Prudence is primarily the act of balancing competing factions and their imperfect and incomplete ideas of justice. The role of the Straussian statesman is therefore that of a moderator and umpire: His job is to arbitrate between, compromise with, and elevate these competing claims by exposing them to clarifying questions that make clear their weaknesses. Strauss illuminates this point in his essay "On Classical Political Philosophy":

> In brief, the root of classical political philosophy was the fact that political life is characterized by controversies between groups struggling for power within the political community. Its purpose was to settle those political controversies which are of a fundamental and typical character in the spirit not of the partisan

but of the good citizen, and with a view to such an order as would be most in accordance with the requirements of human excellence.

With his *a priori* knowledge of justice and "human excellence," the Straussian statesman knows better than the claimants themselves what is good for them and what they truly deserve. His particular skill "consists in the right handling of individual situations," which means using the prudential art of compromise in two ways: first, to moderate between competing opinions in the city, and, second, to moderate between the demands of the city on the one hand and the demands of philosophy on the other. He thus teaches the city's leaders how "to *cope* with an individual case."[40]

Furthermore, prudence does not begin with or attempt to superimpose ideas or principles on reality. It may very well be the case that Strauss's prudent statesman will look longingly at the idea of justice and of the best regime in theory, but he must always defer to and respect the limitations of human nature and the forces of convention. Prudence is the capacity to understand and act wisely in a variety of political conditions. It is the art of being flexible and of "coping" in particular situations. The Straussian statesman recognizes that the best regime in theory is unlikely to be ever put into practice, and so he must learn to deal with what he has, which is a range of intransigent but ever-changing conditions and circumstances that require him to be intellectually nimble, flexible, moderate, tolerant, and compromising. The wise and prudent statesman therefore is not beholden to absolute or permanent first principles (except that it is just and proper that he should rule), because there are no absolute moral principles that do or should ground, guide, and govern any particular society. Nor is the Straussian statesman a party man. In fact, he is quite capable of supporting any number of platforms depending on the circumstances. He recognizes that different concrete situations call for different actions, which transcend or take precedence over moral principles. Not surprisingly, then, Strauss grants a great deal of scope to his statesman.[41]

Ultimately, though, in addition to serving as an umpire between competing and partial views of justice and teaching the city how to cope with particular problems, the magnanimous statesman must attempt to moderate, uplift, and ennoble the city by some higher, more permanent standard of human excellence. The city's competing views of justice must finally be evaluated and judged in relation to the *idea* of justice and to the *idea* of the good. All political thought and action is guided, according to Strauss, "by some thought of better and worse." But all such thought, all attempts to distinguish between "better or worse implies thought of the good." As the Straussian statesman arbitrates between competing factions in the city, he therefore does so in relation to some higher or more complete conception of the good:

Just as the partial human goods cannot be known to be goods except with reference to the highest or the whole human good, the whole human good cannot be known to be good except with reference to the good simply, the idea of the good, which comes to sight only beyond and above all other ideas.

Thus natural right and a "'blueprint' of the best polity" is what the statesman studies with his teacher, the philosopher. The vital goal of classical political philosophy is to illuminate the "highest goals or aspirations" of each and every imperfect regime in the light of the one best regime. As such, Socratic political science will gently turn the political wisdom of the city's most respected and experienced citizens and statesmen toward a more ennobling way of life. "Prudence and 'this lower world' cannot be seen properly," Strauss writes approvingly of Edmund Burke's political philosophy, "without some knowledge of 'the higher world'—without genuine *theoria*." The best city in speech is not simply, however, a "*theoretical construction*" in Strauss's view, but rather it provides statesmen and "all *decent people*" with "a *practical* ideal." In other words, it is that toward which a decent regime will incline. Strauss's practical utopianism "is the very soul of Plato's and Aristotle's political philosophy whose primary and guiding purpose is to discover that 'constitution,' that order of civil society, which is 'natural.'" Strauss's political philosopher contemplates the idea of the good and of the best regime—indeed, he takes this ideal to be "the standard of sincere, uncompromising judgments on the real." It is through this contemplation that he provides the statesman with a standard by which to judge his decisions and actions.[42]

However, although the unifying and absolute communism that defines Plato's *Republic* is achieved only in the mind of the philosopher, it is not left there simply as an object of philosophic contemplation. While it is true that Strauss's Plato rejects the "revolutionary quest for the other city [i.e., the best city in speech]," it is also true that the philosophic communism of the best city in speech is held up by Strauss-Plato as a far-off and distant model that, under the right circumstances, might be approached through slow and gentle steps. Strauss's Platonism substituted the revolutionary approach to political change with a much "more conservative way of action, namely, the *gradual replacement* of the accepted opinions by the truth or an approximation of the truth."[43] The method of Strauss's philosophic statesman is to gradually replace the accepted opinions of the city, thus moving it over time toward an approximation of the ideal city. Strauss described the relationship between the ideal and the real in these terms:

There is a common, ordinary civil justice which consists in obedience to the law of the land and just administration of that law; that justice is not concerned with the justice of the law itself; it is for this reason a very imperfect justice, for every law, every legal order is bound to be only imperfectly just; therefore, justice must be supplemented by *equity* which is the correction of *legal* justice in the direction of perfect justice; the equitable order, or, as we might prefer to say, the order of charity is the utopian order; that utopian order by itself is essentially the object of wish or *prayer*, and not of political action; equity, or charity, by themselves are not capable to subsist on this earth without solid, somewhat brutal, imperfectly just, substructure of common justice; common justice must be "completed," corrected by considerations of equity or charity—it can never be supplanted by them, although all decent men would wish, or pray, that it could.[44]

Strauss's Platonic statesman must, above all else, study the ideal of justice or equity in order to correct, improve, and elevate the imperfect justice of convention toward some approximation of the ideal. Strauss's political philosophy is therefore simultaneously radical and conservative.

In the end, as should now be evident, Strauss's Plato is all things to all people. His zetetic (exoteric) Plato provides a veil over his metaphysical (esoteric) Plato. Plato's *Republic* may very well show the limits of politics, but it still provides the standard—the "idea" of justice—by which to judge all regimes. In fact, in a 1946 letter to his friend Karl Löwith, Strauss identified what he personally regarded to be the best regime, the regime that should serve as *the* political standard of natural right. We may regard the following as the golden sentence in all of Strauss's writings: "I *really* believe, although to you this apparently appears fantastic, that the perfect political order, as Plato and Aristotle have sketched it, *is* the perfect political order.... Details can be disputed, although I myself might actually agree with everything that Plato and Aristotle demand (but that I tell only you)."[45] The "perfect political order" that Strauss took from Plato and Aristotle is the regime more in accord with the traditional reading of Plato's *Republic* than it is with Socrates's zeteticism. Strauss's modern statesman should acquire knowledge of the best regime by nature, and he should then use it as his standard (however distant) of political decision-making.

And so the secret, the riddle of the sphinx, is now revealed. Strauss's ultimate goal was to amend and modify the modern natural-rights philosophy that lay at the heart of American political practice with the classical natural-right teaching found primarily in Plato.

We have come now to the point where we can dig more deeply in our quest to identify precisely the connection between Leo Strauss, Irving Kristol, and the neocons. Let us now reconstruct the deepest layer of neoconservative thought in light of Leo Strauss's neo-Platonic influence. Let us return to Kristol and the neoconservatives and examine more closely how they apply Strauss's political thought to their "philosophy of governance."

PART IV
A NEW WORLD ORDER

Chapter 7
The World According to the Neocons

Scholars of American intellectual life have long wondered what the "neo" and what the "conservatism" are in neoconservatism. What makes neoconservatism new, and how is it different from or similar to traditional conservatism? Irving Kristol, not surprisingly, has done more than anyone else to explain how and why neoconservatism is different from traditional conservatism. In essence, neoconservatism is forward- rather than backward-looking. "What is 'neo' ('new') about this conservatism," explains Kristol, "is that it is resolutely free of nostalgia," by which he means the nostalgia of some conservatives for a return to the nineteenth-century principles of individual rights, limited government, and laissez-faire capitalism.[1] Neoconservatism claims to look to the future rather than to the past. Unlike traditional conservatives, the neocons do not long for or romanticize a pre–New Deal world. Their philosophy of governance starts from with the here and now and goes forward.[2]

Now that neoconservatism has been around for almost two generations and its newness is somewhat worn by time, a more interesting and certainly a more pressing question might be to ask what is the "-ism" in neoconservatism? Is neoconservatism simply a mode of thought, or does it rest on a comprehensive and integrated political philosophy with identifiable principles? To what class of political and intellectual phenomena does it belong? Why is it not—at least in the view of neoconservatives—an "ideology"?

As we saw in the Introduction and in chapters 1 and 2, most neoconservatives deny that neoconservatism is a systematic political philosophy, and they certainly reject the suggestion that it is an "ideology." As a general rule, Kristol frequently bemoans the all-too-frequent temptation of intellectuals to systematize their ideas into an "ideology." Systems of ideological thought, according to Kristol, lead invariably to social engineering, show trials, concentration camps, gulags, manmade famines, the Terror, and eventually to the killing fields. The disastrous consequences of national and international socialism in the twentieth century led many neoconservatives to the position that systematic political philosophy had to be abandoned, or at least publicly—hence their reluctance to identify neoconservatism even as a system of thought. Thus Kristol's old friend and fellow neoconservative, Daniel Bell, could write an entire book cheering the "end of ideology."[3]

Many of neoconservatism's best and most influential thinkers have typically described neoconservatism in strictly nonideological terms. They prefer to characterize it, as we have seen already, as a "persuasion" or as a "mood," and there certainly is some truth in describing neoconservatism in these terms. On one level, it is virtually synonymous with a psychological disposition toward "moderation" and a pragmatic mode or style of thought. As we saw in chapters 1 and 2, however, neoconservatism is more than what the neoconservatives want you to think it is. For those who have thought most self-consciously about what neoconservatism is and who have done the most to define it, they have found that it is much more than just a persuasion, mood, or state of mind. So let us return, then, to our opening question: What is the "-ism" in neoconservatism? To what does it all add up?

Neoconservatives give the very strong impression—indeed, they very much want you to believe—that neoconservatism is grounded on no systematic or consistent philosophic system or set of permanent principles. A particularly frustrating element of neoconservative thought is its claim to being nonideological and free from dogma, and on one level that is precisely what neoconservatism is or appears to be. In particular, the neocons do not think that conservatives should limit themselves by adhering to a defined set of moral principles. Instead, they profess to be pragmatic champions of a nonobjective, nondefinable, ever-changing "public interest." Hence it has been virtually impossible for many students and critics of neoconservatism to identify a fixed or underlying neoconservative philosophy because it is always changing depending on circumstances. That said, now and again Kristol will suggest that neoconservatism is more than just a tendency or an impulse, that it is indeed grounded in a comprehensive view of the world. Neoconservatism, Kristol has written, "has the kind of ideological self-consciousness and self-assurance—most of its original spokesmen, after all, had migrated from the Left—and even ideological boldness which has hitherto been regarded as the legitimate (indeed exclusive) property of the Left."[4] Kristol's claim is worth pursuing, and it prompts the following question: What is the ideology of which Kristol and the neocons are so self-conscious and self-assured?

This much we know: Neoconservatism is, as Kristol has written, a "syncretistic" intellectual movement. In other words, it is an intellectual hybrid conceived out of many different intellectual strands, which in part explains why the neo-conservatives are so hard to pin down. Neoconservatism is, however, more than just a farrago of ideas. The neocons take ideas far too seriously to not have any of their own in answer to the most important questions. Neoconservatism is, beneath the seeming intellectual schizophrenia of its syncretic, pragmatic, and zetetic "mood," a comprehensive and integrated political philosophy. Peeling away the outer layer of neoconservative thought, one can see that their ultimate goal is to forge what Kristol calls "a new synthesis" of ideas. This means that there really is an "ism" to neoconservatism. Kristol has described the neoconser-vatives' new philosophic *synthesis* as "*classical-realist* in temper and intellectual inclination."[5] Unpacking the meaning of neoconservatism's "classical-realist" synthesis is therefore the key to unlocking and exposing the deepest layer of neoconservative thought. It will also allow us to identify and reconstruct neo-conservatism as the comprehensive political philosophy that it truly is. What's more, as we shall see, built into the core of this neoconservative synthesis is a multilayered, constantly shifting *dualism* (learned from Strauss) that uses differ-ent ideas to appeal to different groups at different times and in different places. And it is precisely this dualism that makes neoconservatism appear so slippery and difficult to define.

At the intellectual core of Irving Kristol's classical-realist synthesis is Leo Strauss's political philosophy. The deeper we penetrate below the surface of neoconservative thought, the more we see the crucial importance of Kristol's initial confrontation with Strauss in 1952. In fact, as we saw in chapter 3, one is tempted to say that neoconservatism was born when Kristol read and reviewed Strauss's *Persecution and the Art of Writing*. Kristol's Straussian moment was a decisive—if not *the* decisive—event in his intellectual development.

One of the very important but subtle lessons that Kristol learned directly from *Persecution* is that genuine Platonism combines "the way of Socrates with the way of Thrasymachus"—it knows how, why, and when to use Socrates's method for contemplation of the divine things, and it knows how, why, and when to use Thrasymachus's method for governing in *this* world. The ideal relationship between philosophy and the city is described by Plato's account of the necessary relationship between Socrates and Thrasymachus. Socrates needs Thrasyma-chus and vice versa. In the context of the modern world and the developments in philosophy since Plato, Kristol would have also learned from his reading of Strauss's *Thoughts on Machiavelli* (a book that he called "by far the best book on Machiavelli yet written"[6]) that the way of Plato can be reconciled with the way of Machiavelli. It was on the basis of Strauss's reading of Plato that Kristol built his new "classical-realist" synthesis. The argument presented here is that Kristol learned from Strauss how to reconcile Plato (the "classical" thesis) with Machiavelli (the "realist" antithesis) to create the neoconservative synthesis.[7]

As we saw in chapters 3, 5, and 6, it was Strauss's reconceptualization of Platonic political philosophy and his dualistic view of philosophy and its relationship to society that radically changed Kristol's way of thinking. Most importantly, and to repeat, Kristol learned from Strauss that the "realm of theoretical truth" and the "realm of practical moral guidance" are forever cut off from one another.[8] This is the fundamental truth of philosophy for Plato and Strauss. Classical or Platonic natural right (the realm of theoretical truth) provides the end point that neoconservative statesmen should hold up as the distant standard of justice and of the good. However, the day-to-day reality of politics (the cave) suggests that a statesmanship guided by conventional morality and sometimes even Machiavellian prudence (the realm of practical moral guidance) is both necessary and salutary. In other words, in the same way that Socrates and Thrasymachus are reconciled in Strauss's Plato, so Strauss subtly presents a Plato and a Machiavelli that can be viewed in some way as complementary.[9]

The obvious question is this: How can Plato, the classical idealist, be reconciled with Machiavelli, the modern realist? At first glance, they seem to be antipodes.

Machiavelli represented, in Strauss's view, a great rebellion against classical natural right and the Platonic worldview, but Machiavelli's rebellion was against only what we might call the top half (albeit, the most important half) of Plato's philosophy. That is, Machiavelli rebelled against Platonic theorizing about the best city in speech. The Florentine did not necessarily reject, however, the bottom half or the lower realm of Platonic political philosophy. That is, he accepted Plato's recognition that the politics of *this* world is irretrievably disconnected from the world of philosophic contemplation. Or, put the other way around, Plato would not necessarily have rejected the need for Machiavellian-style politics in dealing with the realities of this-worldly politics. Philosophically, Strauss thought it possible to advocate the "shrewd 'power politics'" of Machiavelli within a larger Platonic framework that separates theory from practice, with Machiavelli representing the practice side of the equation.[10] While Strauss believed that the philosophic way of life was the best way of life, he also believed that entirely different rules apply to governing the city of nonphilosophers. In other words, Strauss took his general bearings from Platonic political philosophy, which he thought in turn occasionally made room for the necessities of Machiavellian prudence. "Machiavelli's philosophizing," writes Strauss, "remains on the whole within the limits set by the city qua closed to philosophy."[11]

If philosophy and the city are forever sundered, if the best city in speech is mostly just that, Plato and Strauss recognize that the city has to be governed in some nonphilosophic way and according to conventional principles or rules. For Strauss, Machiavelli's overall political philosophy is certainly impoverished compared to Plato's, but in the realm of this-worldly politics it does speak important truths and it certainly has a necessary role to play in the city. In the very last paragraph of Strauss's definitive essay on Machiavelli, he subtly indicates the compatibility of Plato (through Socrates) and Machiavelli:

> Toward the end of the *Nichomachean Ethics* Aristotle speaks of what one may call the political philosophy of the Sophists. His chief point is that the Sophists identified or almost identified politics with rhetoric. In other words, the Sophists believed or tended to believe in the omnipotence of speech. Machiavelli surely cannot be accused of that error.... But Xenophon, who was a pupil of Socrates, proved to be a most successful commander.... Xenophon, the pupil of Socrates, was under no delusion about the sternness and harshness of politics, about that ingredient of politics which transcends speech. In this important respect Machiavelli and Socrates make a common front against the Sophists.[12]

Strauss applauded the wisdom and moral characters of great statesmen who were devoted to and acted on behalf of the common good, but he also recognized that those very men might be required on occasion to act in ways that were less than morally honorable. He understood that the political realm will always be guided by conventional moral considerations, but he also understood that there would be times (more often than you think) when necessity and contingency would require that immoral actions, such as fraud and coercion, be used in pursuit of subphilosophic moral ends, like the "collective selfishness" of the city or nation.[13] Strauss's use of Machiavelli was not in pursuit of the vulgar low—for the acquisition and use of power for personal aggrandizement. Rather, it was in pursuit of the respectable low, the public interest, that seeks to be morally virtuous.

Politically and rhetorically, the application of Strauss's general theory works in the following way. Neoconservative intellectuals serve as surrogate philosophers who act as intermediaries between the philosopher (i.e., Strauss) and a new class of American politicians or bureaucrats (i.e., Machiavellian statesmen). Or, as Leo Strauss put the matter in a revealing letter to his communist friend, Alexander Kojève, the task of mediating between the philosopher and the city is assigned to rhetoricians:

> I do not believe in the possibility of a conversation of Socrates with the *people* (it is not clear to me what you think about this); the relation of the philosopher to the people is mediated by a certain kind of rhetoricians who arouse fear of punishment after death; the philosophers can guide these rhetoricians but can not do their work (this is the meaning of the *Gorgias*).[14]

Neoconservative thinkers such as Kristol, David Brooks, and Peter Berkowitz serve as Strauss's rhetoricians: They seek to separate and protect true philosophy from the city when necessary, and they attempt to reconcile philosophy and the city where and when appropriate.

In the pages that follow, we shall examine the ways in which the Kristol-cons have become the "rhetoricians" for Strauss's political philosophy. More generally, we shall examine how Strauss's ideas have influenced the deepest layers of neoconservative thought. More specifically, we shall reconstruct neoconservatism as a comprehensive and systematic political philosophy with a metaphysics, an epistemology, an ethics, and a political philosophy. Neoconservatism is, as we shall see, more than just a "mood."

Neoconservative Metaphysics

Irving Kristol once famously described a neoconservative "as a liberal who has been mugged by reality."[15] On one level, Kristol's point was simple: The neocons had learned from their mistakes. In the late 1960s and early 1970s, these proto-neocons were the first liberals to realize that The Great Society had been The Great Mistake. They argued that liberal wish-fulfillment should never override or conflict with social realities and pragmatic results. Kristol and his colleagues at the *Public Interest* were hardheaded realists who took the world as it is. They were anything but softheaded liberal utopians trying to force society into some prepackaged ideological system. Instead, they were reality-based and experimental. In fact, the neocons have always seemed to follow Machiavelli's admonition in *The Prince* that it is better to go to "the effectual truth of the thing than to the imagination of it," which means that one's ideas and actions should be validated as true or untrue relative to their outcome or effect and not according to some elaborate theoretical dream.[16] The effectual truth is that which advances one's cause in any given situation at any moment.

Kristol's definition of a neoconservative, memorable as it is, actually points to an important but never discussed element of neoconservative thought: their view of reality, their metaphysics, and its relationship to their political thought. The neoconservative metaphysics goes much further and much deeper, however, than simply a recognition of reality as one's pragmatic standard of action or truth. The more important question is, what do the neoconservatives view as the primary unit or standard of reality?

Following Leo Strauss, they take the "political community," the city or polis, "the public household," or what Kristol calls the "collective self" as the primary unit of social and political reality. The neocons view this "collective self" as an actual entity with ontological status. They see the polis or the political community as therefore greater than the sum of its parts, and they consider this "collective self" to be metaphysically *prior* to the individual in the same way that the oak tree is said to be prior to the acorn. According to David Brooks, "there is no self that exists before society." Americans should not see themselves as "self-made individualists," but rather as "parts of networks, webs, and communities," writes Brooks.[17] The neocons therefore accept Plato's premise that the polis is the only community adequate for the fulfillment of man's natural end, or *telos,* and the community's end or purpose is what the neocons variously call the "public interest," the "common good," the "public welfare," or the "national interest."

Reading and acting from the Straussian playbook, the neoconservatives begin with the classical view that man is by nature social and "political," which means that his nature—his *telos*—is fulfilled through the politics of the regime or the "collective self." The *telos* of the community is synonymous with the "public interest," which also has metaphysical status for the neocons, but it is never defined by them in any meaningful way. Not surprisingly, the neocons' definition of the "public interest" is open-ended and without an objective meaning. Establishing a particular or singular definition of the "public interest" is of less importance to the neocons than is the question of *who* does the defining, and this is because they assume that the "public interest" will be different from one regime to another and from one time to another. In the inaugural issue of their flagship journal, *The Public Interest,* Daniel Bell and Irving Kristol defined the public interest using Walter Lippmann's thoroughly nonobjective definition: "The public interest may be presumed to be what men would choose if they saw clearly, thought rationally, acted disinterestedly and benevolently."[18] In other words, the "public interest" is whatever wise and benevolent men say it is, which is precisely why it should never be defined once and for all. The highest task of neoconservative statesmanship is, it turns out, to superimpose ideological unity (i.e., a unity of passions, opinions, and interests) on the collective self in the name of the "public interest."

Closely related to the neocons' attribution of metaphysical status to both the political collective and the opinions that govern it is their use of the political concept "regime." Straussian-influenced neocons often refer to something they call the "American regime," and, more recently, you may have heard them speak about "regime change" in the Middle East. This notion of the regime is a central link that connects the neocons to Strauss, and, moreover, Strauss to Plato (and Aristotle to a lesser degree). The neoconservatives define the concept "regime" in the following way: The regime represents the dialectical relationship between a particular society's *formal* political institutions and the way those institutions shape and in turn are shaped by the way of life—that is, the *informal,* centuries-old, underlying habits, customs, and religion—that define a particular people. Thus it is both a cause and an effect. For Straussianized neocons, the regime represents a self-consciously chosen way of life; it embodies the idea that those institutions are meant to embody and promote. A "democratic" regime, for instance, embodies the idea of "equality," and it will consciously advance laws and policies that shape the people in a way different from an "aristocratic" or a "monarchic" regime. And in this way, politics is not only the primary unit of political value for the neocons, but, in a deeper sense, it is the primary unit of social reality. The regime and the idea it embodies is what creates a people's particular way of life. That is its purpose and function. Whoever controls the regime therefore controls the ideas and opinions that shape the regime.[19]

The neocons' metaphysical collectivism is expressed most clearly in their *nationalism*. Strauss, for instance, believed that nationalism was the best political ideology available to man in a postmodern world. He thought nationalism supplied "the best available framework for understanding the present political situation and for enlightening political action." He viewed it as a kind of "halfway house between the polis and the cosmopolis." In Strauss's view, nationalism is superior to cosmopolitanism or globalism (which, for Strauss, is the ultimate expression of liberal capitalism), but he viewed it as inferior to the polis or city (which, for him, is the most natural and purest form of the political collective). Put slightly differently, nationalism for Strauss is a suitable halfway house on the road back to the ancient polis.[20]

The neocons follow Strauss in accepting nationalism as the best political ideology available to man in a corrupted modern world. They take the "nation" as their cultural unit of political value, and the nation is somehow embodied in or a reflection of what David Brooks calls the "idea of America." By encouraging Americans to devote and sacrifice themselves to this semi-Platonic abstraction, Kristol hopes "to encourage a sense of political community, even of fraternity." This is precisely why the neocons devote so much time and energy supporting the role played by politics in controlling and shaping the public's values—"that collective self which we call public opinion and which, in a democracy, governs us collectively."[21]

The "American idea" and the "public interest" are nothing more than empty, fill-in-the-blank abstractions that can be intuited only by the wise few but that, if properly packaged rhetorically in the language of traditional patriotism, can be held up, felt, and revered by the ignorant many. The neocons want ordinary Americans to *believe* in the "idea" of the public interest or the "idea" of America so that whoever controls the "idea" controls the regime—and whoever controls the regime controls America. Politics is about attaining and controlling power so that, in turn, one has the authority to define the "idea" of the public interest and then do whatever one wants in practice. Notice, however, that the neocons' devotion to the subjectively defined "public interest" is different from an allegiance to objectively defined and certain moral principles (e.g., the doctrine of individual rights), the very idea or possibility of which they reject.

Following Strauss, neoconservatism rejects what Kristol calls the "political metaphysics of modernity."[22] Kristol and company are troubled by a political philosophy that takes the individual as the primary unit of political reality and that is grounded in the uniquely modern doctrine of natural rights, particularly the political philosophy of Thomas Jefferson and America's Founding Fathers. David Brooks vociferously rejects the view that the nation should be seen as "composed of individuals" who are "given maximum liberty to make choices." Instead, he argues, the individual should be considered as "a part of a social organism" that "thrives only within the attachments to family, community and nation that precede choice." Men are by nature "intensely social creatures," according to Brooks, "deeply interconnected with one another" in the same way as are bees and ants. Individual choice should be supplanted by obeying the commands of family, community, and nation.[23]

In a 2008 column in the *New York Times,* Brooks contrasted the moral-political systems of individualism, such as that found in the United States, and collectivism, such as as that found in China, and he clearly came down on the side of Chinese collectivism.[24] Likewise, the Catholic neoconservative thinker Michael Novak has made the same point in unequivocal terms:

> The human being is not, in fact, a solitary atom. There is not now, there never was, there never will be, a solitary autonomous self, apart from society. The human being is a social network, necessarily dependent and psychologically interrelated, a social organism, a political animal. The self is not an "I" but a "we."[25]

Metaphysically, there is no "I"; there is only "we." On this view, the polity or the nation is not simply an aggregate of individuals but rather a distinct metaphysical entity, a "collective *self*" as Kristol put it, that has priority over the interests or rights of individuals. It is hard to imagine Thomas Jefferson or John Adams declaring that the "self" in all men is "not an 'I' but a 'we.'"

The neocons' metaphysical collectivism takes a special form. Reality for the neocons begins with politics, or, put the other way around, politics is the fundamental reality. The "collective self" is political by nature. Straussianized neocons uphold politics as an autonomous realm—an irreducible reality—that is separate from and superior to the economic realm. Neoconservatism, writes Kristol, "accepts without qualm the inevitable priority of politics over economics," which means that the collective interest has priority over individual rights—the public over the private.[26] The political *is* therefore the metaphysical for the neocons; it is the fundamental irreducible unit of social reality, and it is the arena in which man's soul is elevated and perfected.

Human flourishing is only possible, Strauss and his neoconservative students argue, where men can actively participate in the cultural and political life of the city. The good Straussian citizen will take an interest in public affairs, and he will want to help shape the public ethos. For the general run of mankind, politics is the public arena in which ordinary men are inspired and sometimes even forced to overcome their private desires and needs and to deliberate on the public good. It is the vehicle by which man's selfish nature and interests (the "I") are uplifted and transformed into the concerns of the collective soul (the "we"). Furthermore, it is the means by which individuals learn to obey those who have the power to define the "public interest." Politics is also the arena in which some men (a much smaller and more exclusive group) can exercise their rational faculties as well as their moral virtues to the highest degree. Politics is the realm in which men's souls are ennobled.

Politics is the bridge to virtue and the good life for those men with more elevated souls, which is precisely why Strauss and the neocons reject the classical-liberal view of government as a Night Watchman. They scorn the Jeffersonian view of politics precisely because it elevates the realm of individual freedom and downgrades politics to a subservient role. If men are *self*-reliant and *self*-governing, if they view government as mostly a pest, the role of politics and great statesmen is diminished.

By politics, the neoconservatives do not mean institutionalizing the moral principles of a proper social system as it did for America's Founding generation, such as barring the initiation of the use of physical force against others. Instead, they mean two things: first, knowing how to rule and to be ruled, and, second, knowing how to reconcile competing views of justice in the search for the common good. For Strauss and the neocons, the private economic pursuits of selfish individuals represent the low, crass, and vulgar, whereas politics, by contrast, is a grand, ennobling affair that is necessary for the improvement—if not the perfection—of the city's collective soul.

An important corollary of the neocons' Platonic collectivism is their belief (following Strauss) that *opinions*—i.e., the various and competing opinions of the polis or the city—have metaphysical status, albeit a very low status in philosophical terms. The various and competing opinions in society about important subjects such as "justice" or "the good" are the immediate though shadowy and imperfect units of social reality with which statesmen must deal. In an important sense, ideas and opinions represent reality for the neocons in the same way that the shadows cast by Plato's puppeteers in the cave represent the prisoners' only reality. And if the polis represents the form of the "whole," and the opinions (i.e., differing opinions about justice or freedom or virtue or the good) are the "parts" that make up the city, the highest purpose of neoconservative statesmanship is to balance, adjudicate, and ennoble these competing opinions in order to make the city a unified whole. The goal is to superimpose (gently and unobtrusively) ideological unity and cohesiveness on the political community. The "I" must become a part of the "we."

A second corollary of the neocons' view that politics is the fundamental reality is their view (again following Strauss) that political reality, natural right, and one's governing philosophy are always in a state of constant flux. As we saw in the previous chapter, a central component of Platonic natural right is its contingency and changeableness. What's more, the Platonic-Straussian view shares this principle with Machiavelli, and the neocons take seriously Machiavelli's understanding of political reality—that is, that "all human things are kept in a perpetual movement, and can never remain stable." Machiavelli held the view that political states "naturally either rise or decline."[27] Human affairs are subject to what he called *fortuna*, or fortune—i.e., that men are toys of chance, indeterminacy, and accident—and this means that neoconservative statesmen must, in the words of Michael Ledeen, "be ready to change their methods, because conditions are very difficult to predict in the first place, and even if you get it right at the beginning, things are going to keep on changing." Change, according to Machiavelli and Michael Ledeen, is an unchanging fact of human history and the "first rule of human events."[28]

The principal task of neoconservative politics is, according to Kristol, knowing how to anticipate, to deal, and *cope* with change—"a changing economy, changing perceptions, changing attitudes, a constantly changing 'culture.'" Adam Wolfson, Kristol's editorial replacement at *The Public Interest*, has written that, in American politics, "almost everything is up for grabs and in continual flux." The changing nature of political opinions is embedded into the very nature of political reality; it is what first comes to sight in the city and is therefore the neocons' starting point. Neoconservatism aims to shape and guide America's ever-changing society rather than trying to fit it into some preestablished ideological pigeonhole.[29] This is one important reason why neoconservatives do not like the reliance of Goldwater conservatives on the enduring principles of the American founding. Adherence to first principles gets in the way of the neoconservative view of statesmanship, which requires ever-changing conditions on the ground and the freedom from fixed principles so as to deal with those conditions.

By way of contrast, Kristol's view of political reality is that "everything, including liberal democracy, is what it naturally becomes—is what it naturally evolves into—and our problem derives from a reluctance to revise yesteryear's beliefs in the light of today's realities."[30] In other words, as political reality changes (as it always does), principles and policies should change or evolve as well in order to remain relevant—and so that neoconservative statesmen will always have some forum in which to exercise their political judgment. As Machiavelli put it in *The Prince*: "I believe ... that he is happy who adapts his mode of proceeding to the qualities of the times; and similarly, he is unhappy whose procedure is in disaccord with the times."[31] Political reality is the here and now, but what is here today will be gone tomorrow. Thus politics is all about *coping*; it's all about anticipating, directing, and controlling future change.

In this way, as we shall see below, the neocons' view of man's nature and the nature of political reality is similar to, and has been clearly influenced by, Machiavelli's concept of "*fortuna*" and the role it plays in political affairs.[32] Thus Kristol and the neocons are, what he might approvingly call, "bold and creative pragmatists" (i.e., Machiavellians) at the same time as they are Platonic idealists. They are, in other words, classical-realists.

Neoconservative Epistemology

The neoconservatives, more than any other faction on the conservative intellectual spectrum, take ideas seriously. They know in some important way that ideas are the motor of history, which raises important questions: How do the neocons view man's mind and its role in human cognition? How do they understand the nature of knowledge and the ways in which men acquire it, particularly knowledge of political things? These seemingly abstract, epistemological questions, as ethereal as they seem, do bear directly on the neocons' philosophy of governance.

Neoconservatism's deepest and best thinkers were not academic philosophers, and none of them have ever presented a systematic theory of knowledge. Nevertheless they do have very definite views on the nature of the human mind, the way in which it acquires knowledge, and the role it plays in human affairs. To take ideas as seriously as do the neocons is to have some view about how men process those ideas. When they speak of neoconservatism as a "persuasion," a "tendency," an "impulse," or a "mode of thought," they are in fact indicating a way of *viewing* the world and a method for organizing what they observe.

Epistemologically, as we saw in chapter 2, the neocons are *pragmatists,* but they are pragmatists with a twist—they are what we might call Platonic pragmatists. Their pragmatism is defined by their dualism. Following Strauss, Kristol accepts the Platonic distinction between theory and practice, between the "realm of theoretical truth" and the "realm of practical moral guidance," between knowing and doing, between the thinking few and the unthinking many.[33] The neocons' epistemology is therefore Platonic in the sense that they believe that ordinary people, nonphilosophers, are irrational and must be guided by those who are rational. Only the men of superior wisdom, they say, have the capacity to reason to "theoretical truth" or to *the* Truth; only a small elite can have, in the words of Kristol, "an *a priori* knowledge of what constitutes happiness for other people."[34] For Socrates, Plato, Strauss, and the philosophic few, moral thinking is mostly a matter of reason and deliberation. The philosopher's *a priori* reason has it limits, though. As he ascends the ladder of knowledge to its highest rungs, the philosopher must ultimately transcend reason and rely on something more akin to a mystical intuition, a process that Strauss calls "divination." Not surprisingly, neither Strauss nor Kristol ever discusses or explains the epistemological process by which these men of superior wisdom attain their "*a priori* knowledge." We wish they would. True philosophers presumably know it, but it would be simultaneously useless and dangerous to reveal such a secret to the ignorant many. Such knowledge is, conveniently, a secret. In short, Straussianized neocons see the role of the mind in human affairs through a neo-Platonic lens: *a priori* reason and divination for the philosopher; faith, opinion, and revelation for the masses; and pragmatism disguised as prudence for the statesman.

For most men, the mind is inadequate to discover and is cut off from knowing the highest and most important truths. As we saw in chapter 4, the neocons largely have contempt for reason (Enlightenment and scientific) as such. In Kristol's view (echoing the views of Strauss), the truth of the matter is that "most men are not capable of ascending from the cave of the commonplace to the sunlight of the *vita contemplativa*."[35] The vast majority of men are forever stuck in the darkness of the cave. They live in a world of Heraclitian flux driven by their senses, appetites, and passions as their primary means of acquiring knowledge. David Brooks, for instance, rejects the Enlightenment view that held that for each individual, "reason rides the passions the way a rider sits atop a horse." Instead, he holds what he regards to be a much more sophisticated picture of human nature. According to Brooks, reason is anything but a "rider atop a horse." Instead, the human mind contains and is driven by "a panoply of instincts, strategies, intuitions, emotions, memories and habits, which vie for supremacy." Man's thinking—the thinking of nonphilosophers—is not guided by rational and logical processes subject to free will, but instead is determined by an "irregular, idiosyncratic and largely unconscious process."

Such men do reason, of course, but their thinking is limited to the ever-changing, imperfect, particular things of this world. They cannot know the most important truths about nature and man's place in it. They only know ephemera and thus cannot know the permanent things. Going even further than Kristol, David Brooks not only rejects the idea that reason is man's only means of cognition, but he has also gone so far as to suggest that individuals who rely solely on reason to guide their actions are "sociopaths."[36] This is why Strauss and the neoconservatives reject the Enlightenment, which promoted the idea that the liberation of reason would lead to an exponential growth of knowledge useful to the improvement of the human condition.[37] However, according to Strauss and the neocons, the promise of Enlightenment reason is a cruel and dangerous hoax.

The linchpin of the neoconservatives' epistemology is best seen politically through the eyes of the statesman (including judges). This is where their epistemological pragmatism comes most clearly into focus. Knowledge of the primary facts of political reality with which neoconservative statesmen or judges must deal (i.e., competing opinions of things such as the nature of justice, virtue, or the good life) and the ways in which one responds to them are gained through *experience* and one's "social emotions" or "emotional intuitions." The great challenge for statesmen and judges, however, is that the experiences, emotions, and intuitions of daily life are always changing because man's opinions, actions, and emotions are always changing. Explicitly rejecting the idea that human beings gain knowledge of the world in which they live through reason or a "cool rational process," Brooks has argued that men and women, even the most rational, ultimately gain their knowledge through their emotional intuitions, the most important of which is empathy. Judges do and *should* base their legal opinions, he writes, on their emotions rather than their reason. Ironically, Brooks's views on the nature of judicial decision-making are similar to those of scholars in the neo-Marxist, Critical Legal Studies tradition, who believe that reason and objectivity are a myth, as is the idea that America's legal system is based on the rule of law rather than the rule of men. Instead,

> Supreme Court justices, like all of us, are emotional intuitionists. They begin their decision-making processes with certain models in their heads. These are models of how the world works and should work, which have been idiosyncratically ingrained by genes, culture, education, parents, and events. These models shape the way judges perceive the world.

By Brooks's account, the rule of law—the rule of objective law—is nothing more than a "useful falsehood." Judges, he argues, perceive the world through emotional intuitions that are shaped by certain preconceived, automatic, ingrained filters. This means that concepts such as "truth" and "objectivity" are really only the products of a false consciousness. In the end, all moral, legal, and political deliberations—indeed, all the really important choices and decisions of life—are ultimately the "semiprimitive," or subjective creations of individuals whose "ideas and insights bubble up from some hidden layer of intuitions and heuristics." This is why, he argues, the "decision-making process" of judges and politicians should be a "meandering, largely unconscious process of trial and error." Judges should abandon their reason and instead tap into and "process multiple streams of emotion." And this is why Brooks thinks it is "prudent to have judges who are cautious, incrementalist and minimalist." In order to control this malleable, idiosyncratic, indeterminate, ever-changing reality, Brooks and the neoconservatives believe the opinions of the nation must be shaped, molded, and changed by those who rule, but the key is that all change must be slow and gentle. This is why they praise the virtues of moderation and prudence, which are intellectual dispositions that encourage "gradual change, small steps and modest self-restraint." It is not at all clear, however, what prudence could really mean and how Brooks could derive a concept of prudence from a view of human nature that denies the efficacy of reason and elevates man's semiprimitive emotions. If man can't really know anything through reason and the use of logic, then how can he know what would and would not be a prudent course of action in any particular context? By what standard would prudence be measured? These questions are conveniently not answered.[38]

The goal of the neoconservative statesman's thinking and actions is to subtly reconstruct and to stamp a specific character on the opinions or ideas of the city. The goal is to bring a particular social reality into existence, but the neoconservatives are not dogmatic or beholden to any one set of ideas or principles. Their thinking is *experimental, pragmatic,* and *meliorist.* They believe policy-makers should experiment with ideas and programs in order to improve the human condition. They take a wait-and-see attitude: If one of their policies fails, they go back to the drawing board and design a new policy; then if it works, it must be true—at least for now. Accepting and advancing the pragmatists' view of truth, David Frum and Richard Perle have written, "If belief in an idea leads to positive results, then the idea is true; if belief in an idea leads to negative results, then it is false."[39] The obvious question one might want to ask of Frum and Perle is, who defines what is or is not a positive or a negative result? In turn, this is to really ask, what is the common good? Ultimately, the answer for the neocons, of course, is that truth is defined by whoever is in power, either political or intellectual. Unlike Great Society liberals, the neocons are not so beholden ideologically to their policy prescriptions. If something does not work, then it should be abandoned for something that does. Neoconservative policy prescriptions are therefore constantly changing to keep up with the changing times. This is how and why neoconservative thinking, unlike that of traditional conservatives, is said to be forward- rather than backward-looking. This is how and why the neocons' thinking, unlike that of traditional conservatives, seems to be without principles.

Ironically, it is precisely because of their pragmatism that the neoconservatives take ideas seriously. As we have seen, Kristol believes that ideas rule the world. But the ideas that rule *this* world, the world of changing opinions, are different from the true ideas contemplated by the Straussian philosopher. Not surprisingly, the neocons' dualism applies to their epistemology as well. The philosopher's ambition is to contemplate moral truths that are transcendent and that have little bearing on or relationship to the way men live in *this* world. In fact, according to Kristol, Strauss rejected the "Enlightenment dogma that 'truth will make men free.'" Instead, Kristol describes Strauss as "an intellectual aristocrat who thought that the truth could make *some* minds free." Most men are incapable of ascending to or knowing the truth. Instead, Kristol argues that Strauss was "convinced"

> that there was an inherent conflict between philosophic truth and the political order, and that the popularization and vulgarization of these truths might import unease, turmoil, and the release of popular passions hitherto held in check by tradition and religion—with utterly unpredictable, but mostly negative, consequences. Strauss was respectful of the sense of the common man when this was guided by tradition, itself heir to generations of practical wisdom when it came to the art of living a humane life.[40]

In other words, what passes for philosophic reason and truth in Strauss and Kristol is restricted to the philosopher, while the common man is and must be limited to knowledge and information of a different sort: to myth, revelation, faith, tradition, custom, habit, and prejudice. The problem with the universalization of Enlightenment reason and truth, according to this view, is that it undermines everything sacred and trusted: It undermines "generations of practical wisdom" and the necessary belief systems that give structure, order, coherence, and unity to society. The "truth" will, as Strauss and Kristol have said, make only *some* men free, which means, then, that the vast majority of men are fated—indeed, they choose—to live in blissful ignorance. They prefer their comforting myths, folkways, and prejudices. Ultimately, they must be ruled by faith and, as we shall see, by faith's necessary ally: force.

Ideas are important social facts, according to Kristol, and for two related reasons: first, because ideas "define the way reality is perceived,"[41] and, second, because ordinary people must order their lives in some meaningful way and they do this through various belief systems. In Kristol's view, ideas rule the world, by which he means that people perceive and understand their reality through the ideas they hold. Reality is, in other words, what you or a group of people *think* it is or want it to be. What Kristol's neo-Kantian view means or implies is that ideas are arbitrary constructions (i.e., manmade realities that are not grounded in metaphysical reality) that serve as ordering myths, and that whoever controls the ideas controls the way in which the mass of people view *their* reality.[42] Ideas—the ideas that govern *this* world—have a power all their own to shape social reality. Simply put, consciousness is what rules the world. Reality is what people think and say, which is to say that reality is malleable—but controllable. Strauss, Kristol, and the neoconservatives believe that the vast majority of men are forever imprisoned in Plato's cave—chained to their appetites, prejudices, and constructed myths. That is the fundamental fact of human reality. It is important therefore that the wise few directly or indirectly control, regulate, and manipulate the images of the cave, that is, the ways in which the people perceive reality.

This is why the neocons have invested so much in (re)defining what David Brooks calls the "idea" of America or in redefining what Irving Kristol calls the "American grain." And this is why so many neocons advocate government censorship of pornography and obscenity—which is to say that they support the creation of special government bodies that would censor literature, music, the fine arts, the theater, the movies, radio, and the press in the name of the "public interest." In the words of Leo Strauss's student, Walter Berns, the First Amendment to the Constitution should read: "Congress shall make no law abridging the freedom of *good* speech."[43] Government censors must control bad ideas or images in order to elevate the people over and above their base desires and pleasures. In the name of the public welfare, a good and virtuous government must not allow its people to be "vicious, mean, squalid, and debased"; a meritorious polity must not "permit people capriciously to corrupt themselves" or to allow themselves to be "governed by the more infantile and irrational parts of themselves." Instead, the purpose of good government, according to Kristol, is to elevate and ennoble men toward "what used to be called 'republican virtue.'" The people must be put under "rational" control or the control of the rational. Good government is "solicitous of that *collective self* which we call public opinion and which, in a democracy, governs us collectively."[44] Once again, ideas matter—they matter so much that they must be controlled or regulated.

To control ideas is to control public opinion, which in turn is to control the regime as a whole. Power for the neocons is therefore synonymous with the control of ideas. This is why they are, at least at first blush, more concerned with gaining and holding the power to control ideas than they are with the substance or truth of those ideas. "Thinking politically" means gaining political power through a chameleonlike use of different ideas and principles in order to impose a much higher view of the good society—but one gift-wrapped in the rhetoric of the American idea. Thus it is necessary, according to Kristol, for neoconservative statesmen to impose a specific character, or *mentalité*, on the political landscape by reconstructing the intellectual terrain of society, and thereby bringing a new political reality into existence.[45] This is the domestic version of what the neocons call "regime change."

The reasoning that statesmen apply to the reality of *this* world—to political reality—begins with the here and now, with what is perceptually visible or knowable on a political level. At this point the neocons perform an epistemological bait and switch: They do not ask—indeed, they refuse to ask—if certain ideas are objectively *true* or not. Their only concern is to determine whether an idea is *good* or not, and a good idea is defined by whether it helps you politically and whether it has salutary social effects. In a certain realm—in the metaphysical realm of *this* world and of the here and now—the "truth," or the truth per se, is of no concern to the neocons. Ideas are good if they work, or rather, if they help you to attain political power and if they promote social harmony and order. In other words, the neocons apply a pragmatic test to determine whether an idea is "true" (read good) or not. The neoconservatives regard ideas as subjective tools or weapons, and they are bad when in the hands of their ideological and political enemies, but good when controlled by themselves and their ideological allies. This is how and why Kristol can write that ideas "define the way reality is perceived."[46] Ideas have the power to create particular social and political realities. This is why the neocons take ideas so seriously: Whoever controls the ideas of a particular society, they argue, controls that society. Whoever controls the ideas wields the power.

Inevitably, the neocons are *epistemological relativists* (though of an anti-egalitarian nature), which is the source, as we shall see momentarily, of their moral relativism. Because the political good in their world is mutable and always changing, the neoconservatives do not want fixed principles to which they are beholden, nor do they strive to be morally or politically consistent. Their power and authority is generated and sustained by the illusion that the world is in a state of constant change and that it is governed by what Machiavelli called *fortuna*. The truth or falsity of an idea is, according to the neocons, determined by its usefulness in a particular situation and for particular people. What is true today, they argue, may not be true tomorrow if an idea or an action fails to work in new and different situations. In such a world, there can be no certainty, no absolutes, no fixed moral principles. Truth is situational, changeable, adaptable, and relative to a hierarchy of needs. This is precisely why Kristol could say that there are

> different kinds of truth for different kinds of people. There are truths appropriate for children; truths appropriate for students; truths that are appropriate for educated adults, and *the notion that there should be one set of truths available to everyone is a modern democratic fallacy*. It doesn't work.[47]

Given Kristol's epistemological relativism, we should not be surprised that he and other neocons are opposed to what they call "Enlightenment rationalism," which sought to universalize the rule of reason and to liberate men from mysticism in order to achieve absolute and certain knowledge of this world. Strauss and the neocons, by contrast, want to liberate us from objectivity, method, logic, fact, and truth. As Strauss argues, the idea or possibility of acquiring truth is merely a mirage and thus, for Kristol and the neocons, it is a "democratic fallacy."

We should not be surprised to learn, then, that the Catholic neoconservative Richard John Neuhaus has written in support of postmodernist, subjectivist epistemology over the certainty of Enlightenment reason: "[The relativists'] rebellion against the pretentious certitudes of Enlightenment rationalism, often defined as modernity, is in large part warranted, and that is the kernel of truth in 'postmodernism.'"[48] In other words, when given a choice between Thomas Jefferson and Michel Foucault, at least one neoconservative thinker has chosen French deconstructionism over Enlightenment rationalism!

Neoconservative Ethics

Just as the neoconservatives seem to take ideas seriously, they also give the very strong impression of taking morality seriously. Prominent neoconservative scholars, such as Gertrude Himmelfarb (wife of Irving Kristol), have lamented the decline of traditional bourgeois virtues, and they have written forcefully on the rise of moral relativism and its deleterious social consequences for modern American culture.[49] Serious students of neoconservatism are left, though, with several nagging questions. Do the neocons believe that there is one rationally demonstrable, permanent moral code that is superior to all others, or do they think that morality is relative to time and place? Do the neocons have a formal ethical code to which they themselves subscribe? Or, given their metaphysical and epistemological dualism, do they advocate different moral codes at the same time—one for ordinary people and one for the philosophic elite?

To answer these questions we must recur—again—to the neoconservatives' use of the Straussian-Platonic distinction between theory and practice. If you believe, as the neocons do, that there are "different kinds of truth for different kinds of people," then you must believe that there are and must be different moral assumptions and principles for different *kinds* of people. The philosopher's morality is, as we saw with Strauss, radically different from the moral code(s) suitable to the ordinary man on the street. In brief, the true or the best moral life for Strauss and the neocons is synonymous with what they call the philosophic or Socratic way of life, which is a morally empty life of never-ending questioning and contemplation of the Good. For Socrates, as David Brooks from the *New York Times* has written, proper "moral thinking is mostly a matter of reason and deliberation."[50] For the Straussianized neoconservative, the greatest good for a man is to spend one's days talking about virtue. Indeed, contemplating and talking about virtue is synonymous with practicing it. For Kristol, who follows Strauss-Plato, the good life—the philosophic way of life—cannot be reduced to a doctrine or to a set of moral truths. The philosopher's virtue is therefore synonymous with a way of life, an attitude, a mode of thinking, an impulse, a persuasion, a mood.

Ironically, the philosopher's way of life is a moral dead end (at least in terms of conventional morality), because it's the road to nowhere. The Straussian-Platonic pursuit of wisdom never quite reaches its goal, and even if it did, it could be known and experienced only privately. The moral life turns out to be little more than the quest itself, and it is an inherently selfish, pleasurable, Epicurean enterprise. Even worse, the horrible secret is that the philosophic way of life seems to indicate that there are no *true* moral principles per se.[51] There is no particular moral code connected with the Socratic way of life, and there are no moral principles that can be accessed by ordinary men. The philosopher's quest thus ends in either mystical insight or skepticism, but neither form of knowledge is fit for human consumption.

Momentous assumptions about man and society are implicit in the Straussian-Platonic-neoconservative view of man's social reality. Despite their love of the Great Books, their interest in natural-law theory, all of their sober rhetoric praising the idea of and necessity for moral absolutes, their interest in talking about the good life, and their criticisms of moral relativism and nihilism, the Straussian-ized neocons ultimately do *not* think that there are rationally demonstrable and universally applicable moral principles—*true* moral principles. (If the neocons do in fact say that there is such a moral code, we here challenge them to state it publicly and to prove its truth claims.) The belief in such moral truths would, from their perspective, represent a form of dogmatism, or what Strauss called "subjective certainty." In the neocons' view, dedication to principle (including the natural-rights philosophy announced in the Declaration of Independence) represents an ideology—and ideology is dogmatism and dogmatism is bad. Belief in such a moral code would be evidence *prima facie* of one's dogmatism.

From a strictly philosophical perspective, Strauss, Kristol, and the necons have, on principle, dispensed with principle. They do not think that an immutably true moral code can or should be generated from man's mutable social reality. Following from their metaphysical and epistemological assumptions, Strauss and the neocons believe that moral truth (reality) is and must be flexible, the good is and must be changeable, the just is and must be contingent, and virtue is and must be relative. The neocons do not believe that there is or should be a fixed and permanent moral code that is true for all people everywhere. They do not believe that there is or should be one unchanging, absolute moral code that defines the nature of good and evil, right and wrong, just and unjust, virtue and vice. In the neoconservatives' moral universe, there are no moral absolutes, there is no moral certainty, and there is no moral objectivity.

Such a teaching, however, if ever made known to the man on the street, would be devastating, disorienting, debilitating, and socially corrosive. The philosopher's zetetic way of life cannot and must not be applied to the people. But if philosophy cannot provide a permanent moral code to guide the lives of philosophers, what about the rest of us? What sort of moral code do neoconservatives think should guide the lives of ordinary, nonphilosophic citizens, and what moral code do they think should guide the actions of Straussian-educated neoconservative statesmen?

This much is certain: The neocons believe that ordinary men and women *need* some form of conventional morality that is easily learned, followed, and transmitted from one generation to another. People need some form of an ethical code to tame, order, and transcend their "selfish" passions, which means they need some form of moral code to justify self-sacrificial behavior. Nonphilosophers need to believe that there are in fact altruistic motives and moral principles by which to live their otherwise petty and forgettable lives. Ordinary people need to believe—ironically enough—in some kind of absolute and fixed moral code. The neoconservative position on morality therefore can be summed up this way: There is no absolute moral truth; the people must have absolute moral truth.

So what kind of morality do the neocons peddle for nonphilosophers? Recently, David Brooks has enlisted the help of psychobiology and the cognitive neurosciences in order to claim that man is naturally constituted to pursue "proactive moral behavior, such as helping other people." Brooks wants ordinary Americans to believe that they are hardwired, "like bees," to be "successful cooperators" who are linked "together into communities and networks of mutual influence." Man's natural "moral intuition[s]" lead him, according to Brooks, to be "cooperative, empathetic and altruistic creatures," and they lead him (in ways still unexplained by the cognitive sciences) to having "feelings of awe, transcendence, patriotism, joy and self-sacrifice." This, of course, is where religion comes back in. In addition to their moral intuitions, the neocons believe that the vulgar many need their religion, their traditional cultural norms, and their loyalty to the nation to serve as the ordering myths by which to live moderately successful lives.[52]

Still, the people need more. Most importantly, they need to be ruled (apparently their "moral intuitions" are insufficient to live truly moral lives without auxiliary aids), but the relevant questions are, how and by whom? If, following Strauss's reading of Plato, man's social reality is dualistic—if there is a radical disjunction between philosophy and politics—the central question for the statesman becomes, how is *this* world—the world of necessity, contingency, indeterminateness, and variability—to be governed morally and politically? Plato's answer via Strauss is that the politics of *this* world must be governed by very different standards than would be the case if all men were open to or capable of philosophy. And here is the point when Strauss's neoconservative students turn to Machiavelli and his political ethics for guidance. Over the years, they have frequently looked to the Florentine statesman for inspiration and direction on *how* to rule. Despite Strauss's exoteric presentation of Machiavelli as a "teacher of evil," Kristol and other Straussianized neoconservatives believe that there are nonetheless important lessons that modern statesmen can and should learn from Machiavelli.[53]

Three recent neoconservative authors who are directly or indirectly indebted to Strauss and Kristol have explicitly called anew for the application of

Machiavellian principles to American government and politics. The well-known neoconservative Michael Ledeen, in his *Machiavelli on Modern Leadership: Why Machiavelli's Iron Rules Are as Timely and Important Today as Five Centuries Ago,* has written that Machiavelli's rules for leadership "are as valid for us as they were for the leaders he counseled five hundred years ago." Ledeen declares that what America needs most is a strong dose of "Machiavellian wisdom and leadership." However, Ledeen's book is no dispassionate, scholarly study of Machiavelli: His purpose is to publish a guidebook that presents "the basic principles of the proper and successful use of power in language that contemporary leaders can understand."[54]

Likewise, the journalist Robert D. Kaplan, in his *Warrior Politics: Why Leadership Demands a Pagan Ethos,* has written a book for a popular audience not about "what to think" as a political leader, but rather about "*how* to think," which means primarily *how to think* like a Machiavellian (and, secondarily, as a Hobbesian). Drawing explicitly on the writings of Leo Strauss and his students, Kaplan seeks to restore "Machiavelli's self-evident truths," by which he means Machiavelli's pagan ethic and, more particularly, his conception of moral and political *virtù.* Kaplan advises Americans to accept and support leaders who have a certain view of reality, particularly that it's always in flux and subject to the goddess Fortuna, and a certain view of human nature, specifically that "men are naturally wicked," factious, and rapacious. This also means that they should abandon abstract principles of justice ("what to think") for a view of politics that elevates a certain mode of thinking ("how to think"). Ultimately, he suggests, they must learn *how* to be "ruthless"; "to be bad"; to employ "tactics" that use "violence" as the "circumstances require"; to achieve their long-range goals by "hurting others"; to use "mischievous evasions of truth," "fraud," the "'art of deceit,'" and the "utmost cunning"; to use the "Leviathan [a]s a monopolizer of force"; and, finally, to live by a "morality of results rather than of good intentions." Furthermore, they must learn all this in the name of the "public good." Kaplan advises American leaders to learn a simple Machiavellian lesson: "projecting power comes first; values come second," particularly the "'power to hurt.'"[55]

Finally, Carnes Lord, in his *The Modern Prince: What Leaders Ought to Know Now,* has written a somewhat more sophisticated, academic version of Ledeen's book, but one that nevertheless counsels many of the same conclusions. Lord claims that his book "does not necessarily endorse all of Machiavelli's ideas," which is to say that he endorses a good many of them. And let us not forget, of course, Irving Kristol's call to the Republican Party to adopt a "strong dose of Machiavellian shrewdness" in their search for political power.[56]

But what are the principal lessons that the more thoughtful neocons have taken from Machiavelli? Most importantly, it turns out that Machiavelli (the realist) can be reconciled with Plato (the idealist) in one very important way. Straussianized neocons accept Plato's dichotomy between philosophy and the city. This means that the ordinary men who live in *this* world are to be governed in a very practical way that takes into account a certain view of human nature (e.g., that man is irrational and driven by low desires and selfishness, and is therefore essentially evil by nature) and a view of how men really do live in the here and now. As a consequence, wise rulers must rely, when necessary, on auxiliary means in the pursuit of the public interest—namely, *force* and *fraud*.

"Truth" and ideas of justice, certainly as they apply to day-to-day social and political realities, must be seen and treated as flexible, adaptable, and relative in order to give philosophically trained statesmen the elbow room they need to exercise their prudence (aka pragmatism). The statesman's end is the ever-changing "public interest," and expediency is the ever-changing means to that end. Natural right is that which works in promoting the ever-elusive "public good," which is defined and redefined by the wise few and to which everyone else must submit. More to the point, what this really means is that, as Strauss makes very clear in *Natural Right and History,* wise statesmen must learn to use "forcible restraint" and "benevolent coercion" in order to keep down the irrational, selfish, and base desires of ordinary men so as to direct them toward some higher ideal of sacrifice and service to the common good. Making Strauss's lessons more accessible to twenty-first-century leaders, the neo-conservative public intellectual Michael Ledeen has suggested that ordinary men and women "must not be left to [their] own devices." Instead, they "must be forced or, under ideal circumstances, convinced or inspired to do good," which is what Strauss means by "benevolent coercion." In fact, the neoconservative statesman, "in order to achieve the most noble accomplishments," must sometimes "have to 'enter into evil.'"[57] Hence Kristol's willingness to use the coercive power of the State to redistribute wealth and to enforce laws that censor thought and speech. It's all for the "public good."

Kristol, following Strauss, recognizes that Machiavelli "*can* be a dangerous teacher," but he also believes that Machiavelli may also "be a useful [teacher]."[58] Given that Kristol has brought Machiavelli to the Republican cause, it might be helpful to know what "useful" lessons Kristol thinks Machiavelli teaches. Kristol is, for instance, quite taken with Machiavelli's "most candid statement of 'Machiavellianism'" that is drawn from his *Florentine History*. Machiavelli there puts into the mouth of one of his protagonists the following political advice that Kristol finds "useful" (and that we find useful to quote at length):

> If we had now to decide whether we should take up arms, burn and pillage the houses of the citizens, and rob the churches, I should be the first among you to suggest caution, and perhaps to approve of your preference for humble poverty

rather than risking all on chance of a gain. But as you have already had recourse to arms, and have committed much havoc, it appears to me the point you have now to consider is, not how shall we desist from this destruction, but how we shall commit more in order to secure ourselves.... It is necessary to commit new offenses by multiplying the plunderings and burnings and redoubling the disturbances ... because, where small faults are chastised, great crimes are rewarded.... It grieves me to hear that some of you repent for consciences' sake of what you have already done and wish to go no further with us. If this be true you are not the sort of men I thought you were, *for neither conscience nor shame ought to have any influence upon you.* Remember that those men who conquer never incur any reproach.... *If you watch the ways of men, you will see that those who obtain great wealth and power do so either by force or fraud, and having got them they conceal under some honest name foulness of their deeds.* Whilst those who through lack of wisdom, or from simplicity, do not employ these methods are always stifled in slavery or poverty. Faithful slaves always remain slaves, and good men are always poor men. Men will never escape from slavery unless they are *unfaithful* and *bold,* nor from poverty unless they are *rapacious* and *fraudulent,* because both God and Nature have placed the fortunes of men in such a position that they are reached rather by robbery than industry, and by evil rather than by honest skill.

According to Kristol's "Straussian" reading of Machiavelli, the Florentine philosopher puts this teaching in the service of a new kind of patriotism that serves the fatherland or nation. According to Kristol, if the new statesman that he is promoting "cares dearly for his country, it does not matter what else he cares for." In other words, love of the nation and the need to defend it in any and all ways necessary trumps all other moral considerations. This is precisely why Kristol advocates injecting a "strong dose of Machiavellian shrewdness" into conservative politics, and this is also why he endorses the Machiavellian principle that "it is *right* for political knowledge to be divorced from moral knowledge." This is, of course, precisely the lesson that Kristol learned from Strauss's *Persecution and the Art of Writing.*[59] It all adds up.

Man's metaphysical condition and his social reality therefore dictate how rulers should rule and how the ruled are to be governed. The neoconservatives' ethical-political views begin with Strauss's assessment of human nature. Strauss had argued in *The City and Man* that man is by nature inherently evil, that "as long as there will be men, there will be malice, envy and hatred, and hence there cannot be a society which does not have to employ coercive restraint."[60] Necessity and man's natural condition is such that, following Machiavelli's advice, neocon rulers are compelled to be good *and* bad, virtuous *and* vicious, just *and* unjust, and all so that ordinary men can be made to be good, virtuous, and just. Because society is continually changing, because man is constantly subject to *fortuna,* and because most men are governed by their passions and are inherently evil, the wise ruler must tame *fortuna* by deceiving and coercing her. Thus the moral code decreed by prudent neoconservative statesmen must change with and stay ahead of the times, and it must be enforced by coercion, fraud, and violence if necessary.

Strauss, Kristol, and the neoconservatives very much believe that ordinary men and women desperately need a common, authoritative moral code by which to live, but the particulars of which they are not so fussy. In fact, with regard to the man on the street, the neocons' public ethics is formally *contentless.* Morality for the neocons—the morality for *this* world and for ordinary men—is a social construction, one that will be different for each and every society. In this way, despite all of their public rhetoric about "timeless values" and "permanent truths," the neoconservatives are moral and cultural relativists.

Because ordinary people cannot ascend to true philosophic virtue, because they cannot escape the cave of their own prejudices, customs, and habits, the neocons accept—indeed, they praise—the people's traditional manners and mores as both necessary and salutary. (This is why neocons seem to be defenders of traditional American principles and institutions, and this is why they would no doubt praise traditional Arab and Islamic virtues if they lived in Saudi Arabia.) For the neocons, the moral is strictly conventional; it is that which is created and accepted over the *longue durée* by particular societies. And a society's ethical customs are judged to be good if they "work," which is largely demonstrated by their ancientness. The moral is the practical, and the practical is what has worked from time immemorial. Thus social expediency is the neocons' public standard of the good. In the end, what counts is results.

In ethics as in epistemology, the neocons are relativists, social utilitarians, and pragmatists despite the fact that they *appear* to support and sometimes publicly advocate natural law, natural right, and an absolute, traditional moral code. Their frequent but tepid advocacy of the bourgeois virtues (e.g., chastity, sobriety, thrift, honesty, hard work, diligence, cleanliness, piety, etc.) is grounded, for instance, not on the fact that they regard such virtues to be necessarily true, good, or representative of the best way of ordering one's moral life, but simply because they happen to be the virtues that worked historically in capitalist societies. From a Socratic perspective, they regard the bourgeois virtues to be thoroughly prosaic and utterly lacking in heroism, grandeur, or transcendence. "The attitude of neoconservatives to bourgeois society and the bourgeois ethos is one of detached attachment," observes Kristol.[61] This means that they praise the bourgeois virtues because they provide capitalism with some kind—any kind—of moral foundation that helps to regulate and order the private lives of individuals in a free society. Without such moral order, free and capitalist societies are quickly reduced to bread and circuses.

The neocons' relativistic ethics is a variation on the social version of pragmatism. Because they regard the polis, the city, the community, or the nation as the primary unit of political value, and because they elevate the "public interest" as the highest purpose of government, they regard moral good and virtue to be that which works—not for the individual, but for society as a whole. The right and the good, they hold, is that which promotes the welfare of the community. Individual morality is therefore defined as overcoming one's low and petty self-interest so as to sacrifice one's individual interests to the greater good of the community. Morality for ordinary men must be connected to the "public interest," which means that a life of self-sacrificial service is the neocons' highest moral standard. Given that different communities will generate different definitions of the good, moral codes and forms of sacrifice will differ from society to society.

David Brooks is constantly and effusively praising those politicians (liberal and conservative alike) who call on all Americans to "serve a cause greater than self-interest" and who encourage young people to participate actively in politics as "the means to a meaningful, purpose-driven life." Brooks even sees the residue of some self-sacrificial good coming from the tragedy of September 11: America's young people now have, he gushes, "an unconsummated desire for sacrifice and service." If the collective is the primary unit of moral and political value, then one's highest actions should be directed toward promoting the collective good. Not surprisingly, the neocons (following Strauss) regard "selflessness," "duty," and "military valor" among the "ennobling" and "higher virtues," and this is why they support establishing "an ambitious national service program to demystify the military for the next generation of Americans."[62]

Readers should not be surprised to learn that most neoconservatives believe that religion is necessary and salutary for a healthy society despite the fact that most neocons are themselves not particularly devout. Indeed, many are charitably described as *a*religious or as "pro-religion atheists." Irving Kristol has written that the neoconservatives are "pro-religion even though they themselves may not be believers." According to Kristol, the neocons learned directly from Strauss that "whether you believe or not is not the issue—that's between you and God— whether you are a member of a community that holds certain truths sacred, that is the issue." Going further, Kristol has ambiguously described himself as a "neo-orthodox Jew," by which he means that he is "a non-practicing—or nonobservant as we say—but in principle, very sympathetic to the spirit of orthodoxy."[63] In other words, religion is a very good thing—politically—but mostly for other people. Neoconservatives typically view a liberal, Great Books education as providing the necessary moral training for gentlemen and statesmen, and they see religious education as the one thing that is most needed for the masses.

The neocons learned from Machiavelli that statesmen must be adept at using religious belief and opinion to their advantage. The neoconservative statesman who has taken his lessons from Machiavelli may not be "a regular churchgoer himself," but "he knows that a good state must rest on a religious foundation." The Straussian neoconservative Carnes Lord has, for instance, explicitly sanctioned Machiavelli's advice to rulers that they must learn how to deceive the many with regard to religious matters in order to advance revolutionary policies under the cover of darkness, stating that "A prince should thus take great care that, to see him and hear him, he should *appear* all mercy, all faith, all honest, all humanity, all religion. And nothing is more necessary to appear to have than this last quality."[64] Straussian and neoconservative statesmanship is thus about projecting certain appearances, particularly the apprearance that one is religious or at least a "friend" to the people's religion.

The neocons are public religionists who think that ordinary people need religion—and this is for two reasons. First, ordinary folk need religion, according to Kristol, in order to justify their otherwise miserable lives. Only a transcendental morality grounded in religion, he believes, can help people cope with tragedy and the cosmic unfairness of life.[65] Second, the preservation of society and political order, particularly a liberal-capitalist society, requires the support of tradition, myth, and religion in order to restrain man's lower impulses—his selfishness—and to sustain social and political order. Without religion as its moral ballast, a free society inevitably succumbs to its dark side: Freedom eventually leads to vice and viciousness; openness gives way to the democratization of vulgarity and banality; tolerance collapses into philistinism and spiritual malaise; and all eventually degenerate into a deadening nihilism. The unthinking masses need religion, any religion, because it gives a necessary order to their lives by teaching them to submit to and obey some higher authority. Religion forces man to live for something other than himself, for something higher, grander, and beyond his selfish desires. If the neocons thought Islam could be tamed and reconciled with democracy, they would be for Islam, too.[66] This is because without religion, a free society will disintegrate into moral and social chaos. Religion, they argue, encourages and sometimes forces ordinary people to obey the laws and to live justly, but such people will do so only if they think that the laws are ultimately a reflection of divine decree and are sanctioned by divine punishments. This is the ground on which neocons defend religion as the basis for capitalism. Without religion, they argue, capitalism degenerates into selfishness and the liberation of man's base desires.

The neocon position on religion is not therefore dissimilar to Karl Marx's—but with a twist. Whereas Marx contemptuously said that "religion is the opiate of the masses" and must be therefore purged, the neocons partially agree and say, "yes, religion is the opiate of the masses, and it's a good thing too." Religion is the vehicle by which traditional values reign supreme over society; otherwise, they say, nihilism reigns. In a cultural battle between religion and nihilism, the neocons side with the religionists (most of the time), but their preferred position is to support a "morality that is neither absolutist nor nihilistic."⁶⁷ As long as the religionists do not become too religious, the neocons think that traditional religion is the only means by which ordinary Americans can be moral in a conventional sense. Thus Kristol and the neocons regard religion as a noble lie that is a necessary precondition for social cohesion. Kristol's position on this is crystal clear and should be read with care:

> If God does not exist, and if religion is an illusion that the majority of men cannot live without ... let men believe in the lies of religion since they cannot do without them, and let the handful of sages, who know the truth and can live with it, keep it among themselves. Men are then divided into the wise and the foolish, the philosophers and the common men, and atheism becomes a guarded, esoteric doctrine—for if the illusions of religion were to be discredited, there is no telling with what madness men would be seized, with what uncontrollable anguish. It would indeed become the duty of the wise publicly to defend and support religion, *even to call the police power to its aid,* while reserving the truth for themselves and their chosen disciples.⁶⁸

What this means in contemporary political terms is that neoconservative statesmen should defend and support publicly society's traditional manners and mores even if, at the deepest philosophic level, they think those principles untrue. The laws made by wise neoconservative statesmen must cultivate and enforce moral virtue through the "police power" of the State, or what Strauss called "forcible restraint." Thus Kristol has no qualms in arguing that "if you want to prevent pornography and/or obscenity from becoming a problem, you have to be for censorship," which is just one form of Strauss's "benevolent coercion."⁶⁹

Neoconservative Politics

Let us conclude this chapter by returning, once again, to the neoconservatives' view of politics. This much is certain: The necocons love politics. Indeed, they romanticize and ultimately glorify what they call "the political." (This is particularly true of the Strauss-influenced neocons.) They want—they *need*—a citizenry agitated by politics, one that is consumed by the *res publica* and prepared to sacrifice private values for public values, and they want a citizenry that thinks and talks incessantly about the "public good." They also want—they *need*—ordinary Americans to live in the political here and now and to stay at the concrete-bound, perceptual level of politics. What the neocons don't want (or need), however, is for American citizens to take their political *principles* too seriously, particularly if they are moral principles that support limited government and laissez-faire capitalism. Ultimately, the neocons want—they *need*—a politicized citizenry that looks to politics, government, and great statesmen to solve all of society's problems. Neocons have what we might refer to as an unmanly love of politics.

The great threat to the neocon view of reality is, as it was for Leo Strauss, a *de*politicized world, or a world where the role and status of politics in society is downgraded from that of an all-encompassing, paternalistic, Bismarckian State to that of a limited Night Watchman state. What the neocons do not want— what they do not need—is a free and independent citizenry that governs itself without the caring help of wise and prudent statesmen. Whereas self-government for Jefferson meant individuals living largely free of government control and interference, self-government for the neocons means a political community that is independent of all others. They view the *self* in self-government not as the self-governing individual, but rather as the individual merged with a collectivized "self"—the community and the public interest.[70] In their view, a self-governing community is one that is ultimately governed by rulers who are recognized as wise and just by a citizenry enlightened just enough to know that the wise and just should rule. A thoroughly politicized citizenry is one that can recognize and appreciate the virtues of great statesmen.

If the neoconservatives do not think there are true and permanent moral principles on which to ground one's political actions, how, then, and by what standard are rulers to rule? Kristol and the other neocons are, as we saw in chapter 2, openly and explicitly *pragmatists,* but they are pragmatists of a peculiar sort. They are not simply your garden-variety John Dewey–inspired, liberal pragmatists. Instead, their pragmatism is, as we have seen, at the deepest level defined by a "classical-realist" synthesis that combines Plato and Machiavelli, by which we mean that Machiavellian means (i.e., Machiavellian *virtù*) are put in the service of Platonic ends (i.e., Platonic natural right).[71]

Central to the neoconservative governing philosophy is their attention to the idea of statesmanship and its attendant virtue: prudence. Their debt to Strauss here is obvious. Furthermore, as with almost everything else touched by the neocons, there are two levels to their understanding of statesmanship and prudence. As we have seen already, Strauss and Kristol believe that there is a natural tension between theory and practice that is built into the very nature of man's social reality. To the extent that perfect "ideas" of justice and the good life can be applied to the lives of ordinary people in an imperfect world, these ideas must be negotiated, tempered, compromised, and sometimes abandoned. The neocon art of compromise claims to know how the world actually works; it is a recognition of the near-unbridgeable gulf between pure ideas and the instability and flux of this world. Thus, there is a neoconservative statesmanship that is appropriate for the day-to-day politics of contemporary America (and presumably one for modern Iran or Cuba), and then there is a statesmanship that points longingly to an undefined, higher ideal, but rarely ever do theory and practice meet as one.

The deeper one probes into the neocons' use and glorification of prudence, the more clearly we see how they perform a sleight of hand. Kristol and the Strauss-influenced neocons covertly transform *faux* Aristotelian prudence into Machiavellian prudence.[72] Machiavellian prudence is how one deals with the world of necessity, contingency, and *fortuna*, the world of constant change. The Straussian statesman knows that chance particulars are an ever-present reality of the human condition. He also believes that necessity, contingency, and emergency situations can never be fully known or predicted by the modern scientific method, nor can they be controlled or regulated by laws, institutions, or constitutions. Something more is needed than just controlling, limiting, directing, and regulating power through constitutional structures. Politics is not a science, but an art. The statesman's prudence therefore requires flexibility in dealing with changing times and situations. Straussian prudence—and by extension neoconservative prudence—is thus concerned with the ability to anticipate the necessities and contingencies of the future and with knowing when and how to adapt one's principles to changing circumstances.[73]

From Machiavelli (and Plato), neocons learned that the modern prince should have a relatively wide latitude for the exercise of his prudential judgment. They also believe that if government is in the hands of the wise and good, it ought not to be limited too much by constitutional rules and boundaries. The neocons do not object to using the coercive power of the State against individuals so long as it is used for the "right" purposes. In other words, the neoconservatives are much more concerned about "who rules" than they are about the limits of political rule. In *The Modern Prince*, Carnes Lord has denigrated the rule of law and constitutional restraints on statesmen and advocated the "need for a single will to command ... in all states at all times." Lord notes that it would be "foolish" for ambitious statesmen to think that they cannot "topple" political constitutions that most people think are "hewn out of a kind of political granite."[74] The neocons advocate slowly eroding the permanence and objectivity of America's constitutional republic in order to make room for politics and a more expanded and active role for wise statesmen. Their view of statesmanship promotes statesmen who act without the guidance of fixed principles and who pursue a mystical, nonobjective "public interest" that cannot be defined except by those in power.

Prudence as understood by Machiavelli also requires shrewdness and deception. It requires knowing how to be a "great pretender and dissembler," and it means *appearing* to have certain virtues but to actually practice other less-appealing vices that have been disguised as virtues. The neoconservative understanding of political prudence is summed up best by Machiavelli in *The Prince*, where the Florentine statesman advised present and future rulers "to *appear* merciful, faithful, humane, honest, and religious, and to be so; but to remain with a spirit built so that, if you need not to be those things, you are able and know how to change to the contrary." In a world defined by flux and contingency, it is important that the neoconservative statesman "have a spirit disposed to change as the winds of fortune and variations of things command him, and as I said above, not depart from good, when possible, but know how to enter into evil, when forced by necessity."[75] Prudence for Machiavelli and the neoconservatives means, for instance, covering one's atheism with the appearance of religiosity or appearing to be patriotic while secretly changing or undermining the principles of the regime. Ultimately, Machiavellian prudence means the prudent acquisition of political power and the prudent use of force in achieving one's political aims. Simply put, in neoconservative terms, it means "thinking politically."[76]

The classic, unadulterated neoconservative view of statesmanship—the view stripped bare of all its pseudo-Aristotelian pretensions—is presented by Michael Ledeen in his *Machiavelli on Modern Leadership*, where he presents "Machiavelli's standards" of political rule—rules that Ledeen hopes Americans and their political leaders will adopt:

> Only a strong, resolute, and virtuous leader can save the enterprise from ruin. Paradoxically, preserving liberty may require the rule of a single leader—a dictator—willing to use those dreaded "extraordinary measures, which few know how, or are willing, to employ." ... His call for a brief period of iron rule is a choice of the lesser of two evils: if the corruption continued, a real tyranny would be just a matter of time (making it even harder to restore free institutions), whereas freedom can be preserved if a good man can be found to put the state back in order. Just as it is sometimes necessary temporarily to resort to evil actions to achieve worthy objectives, so a period of dictatorship is sometimes the only hope for freedom.... We should not be outraged by Machiavelli's call for a temporary dictatorship as an effective means to either revivify or restore freedom.

It gets worse. Among the kinds of dictators that Ledeen singles out and praises for their success in gaining power are "the great mass murderers of this century ... Hitler, Stalin, and Mao."[77] Since it is not clear that any meaningful analysis can be added to Ledeen's breathtaking comments, we shall simply leave the reader to ponder his words on their own.

There is a second, deeper level to neoconservative statesmanship, one that goes beyond the cave of opinion and points to something much grander and more "ennobling." In addition to having physical and material "needs" that can be satisfied only by the neocons' redistributive-regulatory State, it turns out that the people also have spiritual and moral "preferences" that they are more than willing to turn over to those who understand their preferences better than they themselves do.

Central to the neoconservatives' philosophy of governance and statesmanship (and revealing of their true intentions) is the conceit that it is possible, in the words of Kristol, for a small elite "to have an *a priori* knowledge of what constitutes happiness for other people." Indeed, such knowledge, he says, is "the property" of the wise few. The implication here is of course that ordinary, everyday Americans do not and cannot know their own happiness. Drawing his inspiration from Strauss's neo-Platonism, Kristol believes that "such uncommon knowledge could not be expected to be found among common men." The philosopher's privileged knowledge presents itself as a "superior wisdom about the spiritual dimensions of a good life." Kristol's philosopher views "material production" as uninspiring and the "material consumption of commodities" as low and base and, therefore, deserving of philosophic regulation.[78]

In a truly stunning and revealing statement, Kristol avers that if the philosophic few "believe that man's spiritual life is infinitely more important than his trivial and transient adventures in the marketplace, then you may tolerate a free market for practical reasons, within narrow limits, but you certainly will have no compunctions about overriding it if you think the free market is interfering with more important things."[79] This means that, first, ordinary men need and want spiritual fulfillment and they are more than happy to turn over their "preferences" to the State for moral guidance. Then, because the common people cannot possibly know what they really want or what constitutes their true happiness (such knowledge is cut off from ordinary men), it is entirely appropriate for the philosophical-political elite to guide them to their true happiness, and with Machiavellian force and fraud if necessary.

All of this is a necessary political consequence of the neoconservative view of human nature. The neocons treat ordinary Americans as though they are children in need of nurturing parental guidance. Ultimately, Irving Kristol, David Brooks, and Michael Ledeen want government officials to prevent individuals from making bad decisions. The neocons advocate using government force to make "good" choices for America's nonphilosophers in order to nudge them in certain directions—that is, toward choosing a life of responsibility, virtue, and duty. In other words, only government controls can save men from themselves. The neocons have assumed the role of paternal guardians for America's vulgar many, and they are more than willing to use the coercive power of the State to force individuals to act for their own good. David Brooks makes the neocon case with unusual clarity: "If you start thinking about our faulty perceptions, the first thing you realize is that markets are not perfectly efficient, people are not always good guardians of their own self-interest and there might be *limited circumstances* when government could usefully slant the decision-making architecture." One wonders, how does Brooks define the "limited circumstances" when government force might be used to "usefully slant the decision-making architecture"?[80]

We get a clearer picture of precisely what the neocons really mean by all this from Michael Ledeen, who contends that "we" Americans cannot and should "*not* be left to our own devices." Instead, he goes on, "we must be *forced* or, under ideal circumstances, convinced or inspired to do good." The problem of course is that ordinary men are governed by and "will do anything to satisfy" their "ruinous impulses." This is why wise and prudent leaders, according to Ledeen, will have to use "*all manner of nastiness ... to keep*" ordinary men and women "*under control.*" There is more. According to Ledeen, it may be necessary for wise neoconservative statesmen to "enter into evil" so that "we" might be able to "achieve the most noble accomplishments." Invoking the royal "we," Ledeen sums up the neoconservative position by saying that we Americans can achieve "greatness" and "glory" "if, and only if, we are properly led." For Strauss, Kristol, Brooks, and Ledeen, statecraft is ultimately about "soul-craft"—the crafting of souls. It's about the State assuming the role of moral guardian over the regime. The purpose of government, according to the neoconservatives, is to suppress man's "rottenness" and to promote his "nobility," "greatness," and "glory."[81]

The inability of common people to know what constitutes their own true happiness is particularly acute in a free society, according to Kristol. The freedom to choose can lead only to the common man's frustration or, worse yet, to his self-degradation. If left free to choose, Kristol and the other neoconservatives think that John Q. Public will always choose the Sex Pistols over Bach, *Penthouse* over *Crime and Punishment*, or Howard Stern over Masterpiece Theater. The problem with a free society, according to the neocons, is that individuals will choose things that are bad for them (e.g., drugs) or bad for society (e.g., pornography). It is precisely because capitalism is not "guided by the wisdom of the elite," Kristol writes, that it "was bound to be ultimately frustrating, since the common people could not possibly know what they *really* wanted or what would really yield them 'true happiness.'"[82] Irving Kristol, David Brooks, Peter Berkowitz, Michael Ledeen, and the other neoconservatives presumably know what we "really" want and can teach us what our true happiness is—and apparently what we most "need" today is "Machiavellian wisdom and leadership."[83]

The neocons are advocates therefore of what we might call "regulated choice," which is the golden mean, that "precise point" between that which is morally and socially good and bad. We saw in chapter 2 how the neocons applied their theory of "regulated choice" to the realm of economics, but it is also important to note that they apply it to the spiritual realm as well. But of course this notion of "regulated choice" is a sham. In some future neoconservative state, the people's choices might work like this: In music, they might be free to choose between Bach and Mozart, but not Snoop Dog. In literature, they might be free to choose between Jane Austen or Anthony Trollope, but not the Marquis de Sade. In philosophy, they might be free to choose between Plato and Locke, but not Marcuse. In other words, the American people should be free to choose the good but not free to choose the bad.

The problem with the people's moral choices in a free, capitalist society is that they too often choose that which is morally unhealthy for them. Culturally, they are more likely to choose the low instead of the high. Morally, they are more likely to choose vice over virtue. Thus, in a neoconservative world, it is both possible and necessary for prudent statesmen to identify and institutionalize the proper balance between freedom and unfreedom, virtue and vice, good and bad. According to David Brooks, this "sort of conservatism measures its success not by how big or small government is but by the habits it encourages in its citizens."[84] The neocons believe that the people would lead spiritually corrupted and meaningless lives but for the moral guidance of "good" government and wise statesmen.

The neoconservative believes that social change must be watched, managed, nurtured, and supervised by the authority of some higher wisdom that understands what is truly best for man and society. The highest purpose of neoconservative statesmanship is therefore to shape preferences, form habits, cultivate virtues, and create the "good" society, a society that is known a priori to those of superior philosophic wisdom. Straussianized neocons do not object to the use of government coercion against defenseless citizens so long as it is used to promote the "public interest." This is one of the reasons why the neocons detest the Jeffersonian conception of limited government: It leaves people alone to order their own lives, and it does not carve out a large enough role for the superior wisdom and prerogative of great statesmen. A free and self-governing citizenry has little need to be ruled by the wise and good.

For the neoconservatives, there is and should be no area of human life that is off-limits from government regulation, which means that neoconservative statesmen should have an unlimited prerogative power to pursue the "common good." This is why they support, in the words of Kristol, "the propriety of governmental intervention and regulation in the area of public taste and public morality."[85] The neocons are happy to regulate man's material pursuits and his spiritual pursuits. They want less regulation of the economy than do the liberals but a good deal more than conservatives, and they want less regulation of man's spiritual life than does the Moral Majority but a good deal more than the

ACLU. Their twin policies of regulating both the economic and spiritual realms are fundamentally complementary: Each involves a growth in the power of the central government, and each rests on appeals to the ethics of the public good and the ethics of sacrifice.

The neocons, like those on the secular Left, want to control man's temporal life, and like those on the religious Right, they want to control man's spiritual life as well. Thus the neocons are what we might call "moderate totalists": They want to regulate moderately (and they think they can) all aspects of human life. (The reason they're *moderate* totalists is because they do not think they could get away with total control and regulation and because they promote moderation as a virtue.) Or, to put it in terms that the neoconservatives will certainly understand, their political philosophy advances a unique form of what Tocqueville called "soft despotism."[86] Neoconservatism thus represents the worst elements of both liberalism and conservatism.

CHAPTER 8
BENEVOLENT HEGEMONY

Since September 11, 2001, the neoconservatives have gained notoriety as the intellectual force responsible for the Bush administration's response to the first attacks on American soil since Pearl Harbor. In particular, they are credited with establishing the intellectual framework for the invasion of Iraq. Indeed, much of the neoconservatives' legacy is now tied up, justifiably or not, with the Iraq War.

It was not obvious, in the immediate aftermath of September 11, that President Bush would embrace the neoconservative foreign policy strategy focused on regime change and "nation-building." When asked during the 2000 presidential campaign about his foreign policy convictions, Bush said that a president's "guiding question" should be, "what's in the best interests of the United States? What's in the best interests of our people?"[1] A president focused on American interests, he made clear, would not risk troops' lives in "nation-building" missions overseas:

> I don't think our troops ought to be used for what's called nation-building. I think our troops ought to be used to fight and win war. I think our troops ought to be used to help overthrow the dictator when it's in our best interests. But in [Somalia] it was a nation-building exercise, and same with Haiti. I wouldn't have supported either.[2]

In denouncing "nation-building," Bush stood alongside a long-standing animus of Americans and traditional conservatives who are against using our military to try to fix the endless problems of other nations.[3]

And yet by 2003, Bush had launched a war against Iraq, not simply to "overthrow the dictator," but to build Iraq into a "democratic," peaceful, and prosperous nation. This "Operation Iraqi Freedom," he explained, was only the first step of a larger "forward strategy of freedom," whose ultimate goal was no less than "the end of tyranny in our world"[4]—a prescription for ongoing, *worldwide* military intervention and nation-building. All of this, he now stressed, was necessary for America's "national interest."

President Bush's pronounced shift in foreign policy views reflects the profound impact that September 11 had on him and on the American public at large. It also reflects the important role played by neoconservative intellectuals and policy-makers in shaping the administration's foreign policy objectives in the months and years following September 11.

How did the neocons gain such influence? What were the results? What basic principles animate their foreign policy objectives and policies? What connection, if any, is there between Leo Strauss's thought and neoconservative foreign policy? What is the relationship between neoconservative foreign and domestic policy? And what does their foreign policy reveal about neoconservatism in general? These are some of the questions we will try to answer in the remaining chapters of this book.

More notably, we also present a radically new interpretation of neoconservative foreign policy in the pages that follow. Our guiding premise is that we view neoconservative foreign policy as one component of their overall attempt to develop a "governing philosophy" for the GOP, and, more particularly, we view their foreign policy as a branch of their domestic policy. In the very same way they developed a new governing philosophy for domestic policy, the neocons developed a new governing philosophy for foreign policy. "Conservatives will not be able to govern America over the long term," William Kristol and Robert Kagan argued, "if they fail to offer a more elevated vision of America's international role."[5]

September 11 and the Rise of Neoconservative Foreign Policy

Before September 11, most Americans were basically satisfied with the existing foreign policy. They had little desire to make significant changes—certainly not in the direction of more nation-building. The status quo seemed to be working; Americans seemed essentially safe. The Soviet Union had fallen and America had become the world's lone superpower. To be sure, we faced occasional aggression, including Islamic terrorist attacks against Americans overseas, but these did not seem sufficiently threatening nor close enough for most to lose sleep over, let alone demand fundamental changes in foreign policy.

All this changed on September 11, 2001, and Americans, including President Bush, sought out a meaningful alternative to the foreign policy that was now seen as somehow responsible for the unprecedented attack on the United States. The "hear no evil, see no evil" attitude of most Americans disappeared overnight. The only prominent group of intellectuals who offered a seemingly compelling alternative claiming to be able to protect America in the modern, dangerous world (a standard by which neither pacifists nor Buchananite xenophobes qualify) were the neoconservatives.

Neoconservatives had not only been critics of America's pre–September 11 foreign policy, they had spent the previous decade—a period in which most Americans ignored foreign policy issues—working out an alternative foreign policy strategy. On the pages of *The Weekly Standard, The National Interest, Commentary,* and the journal *Foreign Affairs,* as well as in numerous books, a new generation of neoconservative theoreticians and policy-makers sought to redefine and remake American foreign policy.[6] They were not simply critics, though. They offered a new, theoretically sophisticated and comprehensive strategy. Their goal was to build for the GOP a comprehensive "governing philosophy" in the realm of foreign policy that would complement and serve their domestic policy.

This new generation was led by William Kristol (son of Irving), Robert Kagan (son of Donald), and John Podhoretz (son of Norman). They challenged the notion that the world had entered a new era of peace and that America no longer faced any enemies. They chastised Americans and, above all, conservatives for being complacent and lacking a compelling and comprehensive foreign policy vision. They warned against "an American public that is indifferent, if not hostile, to foreign policy and commitments abroad, more interested in balancing the budget than in leading the world, and more intent on cashing in the 'peace dividend' than on spending to deter and fight future wars. Most conservatives have chosen to acquiesce rather than challenge this public mood."[7]

This criticism focused on the 1990s, which were dominated by foreign policy "realism." This is what neoconservatives criticized for having a narrow view of the "national interest," in which only tangible, immediate threats to American security warranted military action. The neoconservatives rightly pointed out that "realism" was a shortsighted prescription for long-range disaster—a policy of inaction and appeasement in the face of very real threats, and thus a guarantor that those threats would grow bolder and stronger over time. An almost prophetic neoconservative essay published in 2000 expresses this viewpoint:

> The United States, both at the level of elite opinion and popular sentiment, appears to have become the Alfred E. Newman of superpowers—its national motto: "What, me worry?".... [T]here is today a "present danger." It has no name. It is not to be found in any single strategic adversary.... Our present

danger is one of declining military strength, flagging will and confusion about our role in the world. It is a danger, to be sure, of our own devising. Yet, if neglected, it is likely to yield very real external dangers, as threatening in their way as the Soviet Union was a quarter century ago.[8]

In place of "realism," neoconservatives developed a new foreign policy strategy that they variously called "benevolent hegemony," "hard Wilsonianism," or "democratic internationalism." This theory of republican empire, or what we might call "bighearted imperialism," advanced a policy in which America would accept its rightful role as leader of the world. The objectives of benevolent hegemony are twofold: first, to provide America with security (a realist policy motivated by self-interest), and, second, to spread democracy to the rest of the world (an idealist policy motivated by altruism). Such a policy would have as its "first objective ... to preserve and enhance that [U.S.] predominance by strengthening America's security, supporting its friends, advancing its interests, and standing up to its principles around the world."[9] America was to be the world's leader—"a leader with preponderant influence and authority over all others in its domain."[10] The neoconservative foreign policy was devised quite intentionally as a unique blend of realism and idealism.

Led by Kristol and Kagan, the neoconservatives went on to articulate what such a leadership role would require of the United States. As early as the mid-1990s, they elevated the foreign policy debate above all other concerns. They proposed significant increases in defense spending in order to enhance the United States' ability to meet its challenges as the world's leading hegemonic power. While begrudgingly rejecting the idea of a draft (a concession to popular sentiment rather than a matter of principle), they advocated increased citizen involvement in America's military service. They called for "educating the citizenry to the responsibilities of global hegemony." And, above all, they called for greater moral clarity in American foreign policy: "American foreign policy should be informed with a clear moral purpose, based on the understanding that its moral goals and its fundamental national interests are almost always in harmony."[11] By insisting on and using a direct and forceful moral language, the Strauss-influenced neocons distinguished their foreign policy statesmanship from the language of moral equivalency that was often associated with the realists' foreign policy.

This idea, that what is moral is consistent with what is in America's national interest, is a theme that the neoconservatives return to repeatedly, and one that we shall discuss in greater depth later in this chapter.

Throughout the 1990s, the neoconservatives advocated a strong and aggressive U.S. foreign policy that would seek to proactively overthrow threatening (and nonthreatening) regimes and to replace them with peaceful "democracies." They were strong proponents of U.S. involvement in the Balkans, and once such involvement occurred, they were very critical of its limited scope—they wanted the Milosevic regime purged and replaced, and by American ground troops if necessary. Furthermore, since the end of the first Gulf war, the neoconservatives had loudly championed the need to overthrow the regime of Saddam Hussein in Iraq. Bad regimes, they asserted, created instability and anarchy and were therefore responsible for potential domestic threats like terrorism. Such threats, by contrast, could never emerge from "democracies." By dealing with threats before they metastasized into catastrophes, and by actively replacing threatening governments with "democracies" that would become our allies, the United States both advanced its interests as a nation and fulfilled its moral responsibility as a benevolent hegemon or as a "behemoth with a conscience."[12] In place of a series of "realist" responses to the crisis of the moment, the neoconservatives were offering a long-range foreign policy to protect America now and in the future.

Then, just when it seemed that few people were listening, disaster struck. September 11 proved to be a kind of redemption day for the neoconservatives. Their diagnosis of America's foreign policy maladies appeared prescient and their prescriptions for a post–September 11 world seemed timely. After September 11, the neoconservatives felt intellectually vindicated, and they viewed it as an opportunity to implement their foreign policy strategy in full. An editorial in the leading neoconservative publication, *The Weekly Standard*, called for a "war to replace the government of each nation on earth that allows terrorists to live and operate within its borders."[13] The replacement governments would be "democracies" that would allegedly ensure that new threatening regimes would not take the place of old ones. Politically, the neocons' rhetoric was calibrated perfectly to take advantage of the moment. (Of course, they never quite addressed the problem of what to do if one of those terrorist-sponsoring nations was a "democracy" or if it were big and powerful, perhaps possessing nuclear weapons, like China, Iran, or Pakistan.)

Given the extent of the work that neoconservatives had done in foreign policy and the fact that they were armed with a strategic long-term vision as well as an explicit plan for dealing with the crisis at hand, they faced little opposition as they began filling America's foreign policy vacuum. Indeed, virtually no one on the Right challenged their approach. Thus, their ideas exerted a major influence on President Bush and his administration immediately after September 11, an influence that grew in the coming years.

On September 20, 2001, influenced by neoconservative colleagues and speechwriters, Bush proclaimed a desire to end state sponsorship of terrorism, stating that "Every nation, in every region, now has a decision to make: either you are with us, or you are with the terrorists.... From this day forward, any nation that continues to harbor or support terrorism will be regarded by the

United States as a hostile regime."[14] His neoconservative deputy secretary of defense, Paul Wolfowitz, publicly called for "ending states who sponsor terrorism" (though the "realists" in the State Department caused the administration to partially recant).[15]

Soon thereafter, President Bush made clear that he wanted to replace the state sponsors of terrorism with "democracies," beginning with Afghanistan. When he dropped bombs on that country, he supplemented them with food packages and a tripling of foreign aid. He declared that the Afghan people were America's "friend" and said that we would "liberate" them and help them establish a "democracy" to replace the terrorist-sponsoring Taliban.

The full influence of neoconservatism was evident by the time of the Iraq War. Prior to September 11, the idea of democratic "regime change" in Iraq with the ultimate aim of "spreading democracy" throughout the Arab-Islamic world was unpopular outside neoconservative circles. It was dismissed as a "nation-building" boondoggle waiting to happen. After September 11, however, President George W. Bush became convinced—and he subsequently convinced a majority of the American people—that such a quest was necessary in today's dangerous world and that it could and would succeed. "Iraqi democracy will succeed," he said in 2003, "and that success will send forth the news, from Damascus to Teheran—that freedom can be the future of every nation. The establishment of a free Iraq at the heart of the Middle East will be a watershed event in the global democratic revolution."[16]

Thus, the neoconservative foreign policy of benevolent hegemony, with the United States actively engaging in "regime change" and in the "spreading of democracy," had become *America's* foreign policy—and the hope of many Americans for protecting the nation. Led by the neocons' vision, the goal of American foreign policy was to assume the leadership role in fomenting democratic revolution around the world. This new role was subsequently described as integral to America's vision of itself and to its historic mission.

Since then, some neoconservatives, seeking to avoid blame for the failures of the Iraq War, have stated that many within the administration who have been characterized as neoconservatives were not and that the neoconservative influence has been exaggerated. But even to the extent that Rumsfeld, Cheney, and Bush were not, strictly speaking, neoconservatives, they and their staffs were clearly influenced by neoconservative ideas. And that's the critical point. The truth of the matter, however, is that Cheney and Rumsfeld had allied and worked closely with the neoconservatives throughout the 1990s. Furthermore, even if they had rejected neoconservative ideas, they had no coherent alternative with which to challenge them.

Ultimately, as neoconservative columnist Charles Krauthammer wrote in 2005:

What neoconservatives have long been advocating is now being articulated and practiced at the highest levels of government by a war cabinet composed of individuals who, coming from a very different place, have joined ... the neoconservative camp and are carrying the neoconservative idea throughout the world.[17]

Influenced by the neoconservatives and their vision for a new, democratic Middle East as a solution to the menace made real by September 11, the Bush administration launched America into war in Iraq. At first, Operation Iraqi Freedom—and thus our new neoconservative foreign policy—seemed to most observers to be a success. The war's architects had expected that by ousting a tyrant, "liberating" Iraqis, and allowing them to set up a "democracy" in Iraq, we would at once be deterring future threats from Iran and Syria; setting up a friendly, allied regime in Iraq; and empowering pro-American influences throughout the Middle East. So when the American military easily took Baghdad, when we witnessed Kodak moments of grateful Iraqis hugging American soldiers or razing a statue of Saddam Hussein, when President Bush declared "major combat operations in Iraq have ended,"[18] neoconservatives in particular were confident that everything was working according to plan.

Their feeling of triumph was captured on the back cover of *The Weekly Standard* on April 21, 2003, in which the magazine parodied prominent Iraq War critics by printing a fake apology admitting that their opposition to Operation Iraqi Freedom reflected stupidity and ignorance. "We're Idiots. We Admit It," the parody read. "We, the Undersigned, Agree that We Got this Whole War in Iraq Business Spectacularly Wrong. We didn't see that it was a war of liberation, not a war of colonization.... We thought the Iraqi people would resent American troops. We thought the war would drag on and on.... We wanted to preserve the status quo."[19] Future cover stories of *The Weekly Standard* featured inspiring titles such as "Victory: The Restoration of American Awe and the Opening of the Arab Mind" and "The Commander: How Tommy Franks Won the Iraq War."

But the luster of the Iraq War quickly wore off as American troops faced an insurgency that the Bush team had not anticipated. It turned out that many of the lovable, freedom-loving Iraqis we had heard about before the war were in fact recalcitrant, dictatorship-seeking Iraqis. Still, even through 2005, many viewed the Iraq War as a partial success due to the capture of Saddam Hussein and such alleged milestones as a "transfer of power" in 2004, an election in January 2005, the passage of a constitution in January 2005, and a ratified constitution in December 2005. These events were heralded even by many of the president's most dependable critics, such as the *New York Times*.

By mid-2007, however, the Iraq War was rightly regarded by most as a disaster that utterly failed to live up to its promise. The Bush-neoconservative vision of deterred enemies, a friendly Iraq, and the inspiration of potential allies around the world did not materialize. Instead, for the price of more than 4,000 American soldiers' lives, we got an Iraq in a state of civil war, whose government not only follows a constitution avowedly ruled by Islamic law, but is also allied with Iran. We got regimes in Iran and Syria that are more confident and less deterred. We got a resurgent Taliban in Afghanistan. And we got the increasing power and prestige of Islamic totalitarians around the world—in Egypt, the Palestinian territories, Saudi Arabia, and Lebanon. And all of this from a policy that was supposed to provide us with a clear-eyed, farsighted view of our "national interest"—as against the blindness and short-range mentality of our former "realist" policies.

Even today, despite the success of the "surge" in curbing domestic violence in Iraq, the war cannot be viewed as a success. The Iraqi government insists that U.S. troops exit the country, leaving either the Iraqi Shiite government to solidify its control or the country to reignite into civil war. Furthermore, if one examines this government carefully, it is clear that it is not America's friend—it is a friend of Islamic Totalitarianism, the ideology with which we are at war. Once we leave Iraq, it is likely to be a worse threat to America than it was under Saddam Hussein. If a Shiite government survives, it will be an ally to Iran, which is the greatest threat today to the United States.

In the face of such facts, neither the neoconservatives nor their would-be and now-failed presidential candidate, John McCain, regrets the Iraq War. Instead, they say it was necessary, that it must be won, and that we are winning. And once we win? Then we must continue our military adventures elsewhere—endlessly spreading democracy throughout the Middle East and around the globe until the threat of terrorism is ended.

How exactly did the United States get itself lost in this quagmire? How are we to make sense of all this? What exactly happened? What is it about the neoconservative philosophy that drove them to advocate war in Iraq? And why, in the face of failure, do they continue to advocate for a policy of global intervention? What motivates the neoconservatives in foreign policy?

The Case for the Iraq War

As we have discussed and illustrated in previous chapters, neoconservative ideas appear and function in multiple layers. Their animating philosophy is split between its *exoteric* ideas—those made available for public consumption—and its *esoteric* ideas—the real motivations and deeper purposes behind their policy proposals, which are largely hidden from the general public. In the next few sections, we shall identify both aspects of the neoconservative foreign policy, peeling away layer after layer in order to reveal their deepest motivations and purposes.

Let us start with the exoteric. In the months leading up to the war with Iraq, President Bush and the neoconservatives tried to emphasize the threat posed by the Hussein regime. Much was made of the existence of weapons of mass destruction (and we have no reason to doubt the sincerity of these claims), of links between Hussein and Islamic terrorist groups, and of the threatening nature of the regime to American interests in the Middle East. In all these claims there were elements of truth. This was the argument from self-interest, and it was an argument designed for immediate political purposes.

However, a real post–September 11 risk assessment of the threats faced by America would not have resulted in finding that Iraq was at the top of the list of potential targets. Iran's links to Islamic totalitarian groups, for instance, were far more significant than Iraq's. While Iraq was run by a secular thug, Iran is a theocracy, whose ideology was and is aligned with bin Laden's (even though one is Shiite and the other Sunni). It was Iran that had directed major terrorist attacks against the United States, possessed weapons of mass destruction, and was developing nuclear capabilities. Clearly, the Iranians were the greater threat. Even more, there was Saudi Arabia, a regime that turned a blind eye (and still does) to its prominent citizens' funding of bin Laden; a regime that is dedicated to exporting its anti-American, anti-Western, radical form of Wahhabi Islam that motivated the September 11 terrorists; and a regime that, in spite of its appearance of being an ally of the United States, was harboring al-Qaeda operatives, financiers, and spiritual leaders.

So, why Iraq?

Iraq presented the neoconservatives with a unique opportunity. Here was a country led by a man universally despised, who not only posed a threat to the United States, but who had also murdered thousands of his own people, started two wars, and was under UN sanctions. Saddam Hussein was, in other words, an easy target. Here was a war—so the neocons thought—that could easily be justified to the American people, and possibly to the international community, as both practical and moral. Iraq, the neoconservatives believed, could be the start of a democratic revolution in the Middle East. It was a domino theory applied to the Middle East. Indeed, the neocons believed Iraq was uniquely situated for this role.

We see here, then, the first two layers of the neoconservative argument: Emphasize the Iraqi threat to American security, but combine it with the greater goal of using America's military might to fight tyranny and to bring democracy to the Middle East in order to begin the process of establishing America's benevolent hegemony. Supposed self-interest and altruism, realism, and idealism were all united into one.

It must be stressed that, from day one, the mission in Iraq was *not* victory over a dangerous enemy, but the liberation of the Iraqi people from a monstrous dictator. Thus the name "Operation Iraqi Freedom." As Kagan and Kristol wrote in *The Weekly Standard* in February 2004: "It is fashionable to sneer at the moral case for liberating the Iraqi people long brutalized by Saddam's rule.... In fact, of course, it was one of Bush's reasons, and the moral humanitarian purpose provided a compelling reason for a war to remove Saddam.... In our view ... liberating the people of Iraq from Saddam's brutal, totalitarian dictatorship would by itself have been sufficient reason to remove Saddam."[20]

Our mission in Iraq, according to the neoconservatives and President Bush, required us to "sacrifice for the freedom of strangers." Later that year, in a landmark speech at the National Endowment for Democracy, Bush expanded on this point:

> Are the peoples of the Middle East somehow beyond the reach of liberty? Are millions of men and women and children condemned by history or culture to live in despotism?... I, for one, do not believe it. I believe every person has the ability and the right to be free.... Securing democracy in Iraq is the work of many hands. American and coalition forces are sacrificing for the peace of Iraq....[21]

Why must America "sacrifice for the freedom of strangers"? Neoconservatives have a twofold answer: It is *morally right* and *practically necessary*.

The moral component of this is straightforward. As we have seen, the neo-conservatives' ethical prescription for ordinary citizens consists in a life of selfless service to others, in which the individual puts the needs and well-being of others above his own. This is also the premise underlying the neocons' support of the welfare state at home. Neoconservative Max Boot applies this premise logically to the peoples of other nations: "Why not use some of the awesome power of the U.S. government to help the downtrodden of the world, just as it is used to help the needy at home?"[22]

This is a logical extension of the neoconservative idea that "need' is something to which one is morally entitled (see chapter 2). Why should this moral entitlement stop at the nation's border? Iraqis, after all, needed freedom—and schools, roads, health care, and more. The neocons believe that we have a moral responsibility to bring these things to the oppressed peoples of the world.

Although this moral argument is powerful in a culture awash in altruism, it is not and was not sufficient to convince Americans to go to war. Imagine if neoconservatives openly said: "We believe that Americans should be sent to die for the sake of other nations, even though it will achieve no significant American in-terest." Ordinary Americans—the ones who actually fight the wars—would have rebelled against the demand for naked self-sacrifice. Thus, a crucial component of the neoconservative call for international self-sacrifice is the argument that it is ultimately a practical necessity—that it is ultimately in *our* self-interest—that the sacrifice is ultimately not really a sacrifice.

Nearly every moral or political doctrine in history that has called on individuals to sacrifice their well-being for some "higher" cause has claimed that those sacrifices are practical necessities and will lead to some wonderful long-term benefit, either for the sacrificers or for their fellow citizens or descendants.

For example, calls to sacrifice one's desires for the sake of the supernatural are coupled with the threat of burning in hell and promises of eternal bliss in heaven. (In its militant Muslim form, calls to sacrifice one's life along with as many others as possible are coupled with promises of seventy-two virgins.) Environmentalist calls to sacrifice development and industrial civilization for nature are coupled with promises to stave off some ecological apocalypse (currently "global warming") and to reach some future ecological paradise. Calls to sacrifice for the socialist dictatorship of the proletariat were coupled with claims about the inevitable collapse of capitalism and promises that the sacrificers' children and grandchildren would live in a utopia where the state had withered away.

The argument always takes the same form. Our well-being depends on "higher cause" X—"God," "Allah," nature, the proletariat—and therefore we must sacrifice for its sake if we are to avoid disaster and/or procure some necessary benefit. The "higher cause" is always viewed as *metaphysically* superior to the individuals being sacrificed: Religionists view man as helpless in comparison to their supernatural being of choice; environmentalists view man in relation to "Mother Nature" in much the same way; and collectivists view man as metaphysically inferior to the collective as a whole. If we refuse to subordinate ourselves to this cause, they believe, only disaster can result. And if we do subordinate ourselves, something positive must follow.

Fittingly, neoconservatism promises an ultimate, self-interested payoff to Americans for their acts of international sacrifice: a level of security that is unachievable by any other means. It promises that when we toil and bleed to create a "democratic international order," we will ultimately bring about a world in which we achieve new heights of peace and security, in which the collective will of the various "democracies" will make war or terrorism virtually impossible. Thus self-sacrifice is packaged as self-interest.

Instead of the dangerous, threatening world we live in today, the argument goes, which is a world in which aggressors are willing to threaten us without hesitation, the "international order" would soon feature an array of friendly, peace-loving "democracies" that would not even think of starting wars, that would inspire backward people of the world to set up similar governments, and that would eagerly act collectively, when necessary, to halt any threats to the "international order." This was the basic argument behind Bush's deployment of soldiers in order to set up voting booths in Iraq, a sacrifice that was ultimately supposed to lead to "the end of tyranny"—including international aggression—"in our world."

What if, instead, we refuse to sacrifice for foreign peoples and resolve to use our military only to protect our own security? We will fail, the neoconservatives say, because our security depends on the well-being of other nations and on "international order." If we let other peoples remain miserable and unfree on the grounds that it is not our problem, they argue, that will give comfort to dictators and breed hatred in populations, and this will ultimately lead to attacks on the United States.

In their essay "National Interest and Global Responsibility," William Kristol and Robert Kagan write that America should

> act as if instability in important regions of the world, and the flouting of civilized rules of conduct in those regions, are threats that affect us with almost the same immediacy as if they were occurring on our doorstep. To act otherwise would ... erode both American pre-eminence and the international order ... on which U.S. security depends. Eventually, the crises would appear at our doorstep.[23]

After September 11, neoconservatives argued that the case of Afghanistan proved the necessity of "interventions" to resolve foreign crises and to spread "democracy." Max Boot writes that many thought that after Afghanistan was abandoned as an ally to fight the Soviets, we could

> let the Afghans resolve their own affairs ... if the consequence was the rise of the Taliban—homicidal mullahs driven by a hatred of modernity itself—so what? Who cares who rules this flyspeck in Central Asia? So said the wise elder statesmen. The "so what" question has now been answered definitively; the answer lies in the rubble of the World Trade Center.[24]

What should we have done in Afghanistan? Boot says that, in the case of Afghanistan, we should have kept troops there throughout the 1980s and 1990s:

> It has been said, with the benefit of faulty hindsight, that America erred in providing the [mujahedeen] with weapons and training that some of them now turn against us. But this was amply justified by the exigencies of the Cold War. The real problem is that we pulled out of Afghanistan after 1989.... We had better sense when it came to the Balkans.[25]

The Balkans are where American troops have been acting as peacekeepers for more than a decade, helping to prevent Muslims and Christians from slaughtering each other. The neoconservatives were vocal advocates of U.S. involvement in Bosnia and Kosovo during the 1990s. While American troops have been in the region, peace has been maintained. But what American interest has been served? And has our involvement really changed the centuries-long hostility between the warring factions?

In President Bush's second inaugural address, he clearly summarized his agreement with the neoconservatives' position regarding the threat of Islamic terrorism, that American security requires us to bring "democracy" to all corners of the earth. He stated that,

> We have seen our vulnerability—and we have seen its deepest source. For as long as whole regions of the world simmer in resentment and tyranny—prone to ideologies that feed hatred and excuse murder—violence will gather, and multiply in destructive power, and cross the most defended borders, and raise a mortal threat. There is only one force of history that can break the reign of hatred and resentment, and expose the pretensions of tyrants, and reward the hopes of the decent and tolerant, and that is the force of human freedom.
>
> We are led, by events and common sense, to one conclusion: The survival of liberty in our land increasingly depends on the success of liberty in other lands. The best hope for peace in our world is the expansion of freedom in all the world.[26]

Thus, the neoconservatives argued that the Iraq War was necessary, both morally and practically. Morally because America has an obligation to "sacrifice for strangers"; and practically because only by spreading "democracy" could we protect ourselves from outside threats.

In developing their new and comprehensive governing philosophy (i.e., a philosophy for gaining power), the rhetorical message of the neocons—a message of realism and idealism, of self-interest and self-sacrifice—was meant to forge a new political coalition, a new governing majority made up of conservative hawks and social democrats.

Democratic Vistas

The neoconservative foreign policy depends on the view that by spreading "democracy" around the globe—and *only* by spreading "democracy" around the globe—can the United States achieve security. But this was never a reasonable premise. In fact, it's as dangerous as it is illogical and historically false.

The alleged practical justification for "spreading democracy" is that "democracies don't start wars." Thus to promote "democracy" around the globe is to promote our long-term security. But that idea is a dangerous half-truth. "Democracies," in the literal sense, *do* attack other countries. To take a modern example, observe the elected Hamas government whose fundamental goal is to exterminate Israel. Or observe the triumph of the Supreme Council for the Islamic Revolution in Iraq and the influence Moqtada al Sadr has had in Iraq's "democratic" political process.

The idea that our security depends on the well-being, democracy, and freedom of other nations—or, more specifically, that "the survival of liberty in our land increasingly depends on the success of liberty in other lands"—is given seeming plausibility by the fact that truly free nations do not start wars and are not a threat to other free nations, including America.[27] But a free society is not simply one that holds elections (as is implied by the neocons in their emphasis on elections and their simultaneous willingness to accept little to no protections of individual liberties in places like Iraq). It is one that holds elections as *a delimited function* to select officials who must carry out—and cannot contradict—a constitution whose purpose is the protection of individual rights. And this idea evades the fact that innumerable unfree nations are in no way, shape, or form a threat to America (e.g., most of the nations of Africa) because their peoples and leaders have no ideological animus against us or, crucially, because their leaders and peoples *fear* initiating aggression against us.

By the necessary logic of the neoconservative position, the United States should spend the next several decades (or centuries) sending its military around the world "liberating" the peoples in scores of nations from East Timor to China, from Burkina Faso to Syria, from Burma to Zimbabwe. In other words, the neoconservatives are consciously advocating a policy of perpetual war in the name of peace and freedom.

Consider the Orwellian nature of this idea: America's national security is best achieved by launching a series of military campaigns in the name of universal freedom against countries large and small (usually small) that may or may not have ever initiated force against the United States. The neoconservatives give new meaning to the old sporting adage that the best defense is a good offense. In their view, peace is achieved through launching war after war in the name of freedom.

But America does not require the freedom of the whole world to survive and thrive. It is not a mere appendage or parasite of an international organism that cannot live without its host. America is an *independent nation* whose safety and well-being requires not that all nations be free, prosperous, and happy, but simply that they be *nonthreatening*. And this can be readily achieved by instilling in them fear of the consequences of any aggression whatsoever against America.[28]

More to the point, the notion that we could end the threat of Islamic totalitarianism by spreading democracy throughout the Middle East was absurd on its face. If one knows anything about those to whom we are bringing about "the end of tyranny in our world"; if one looks at the endless warring tribes and religious factions raised on a philosophy of faith, mindless obedience, and coercion; and if one knows anything about the meaning and preconditions of freedom, then one sees that the neoconservatives' policy is a prescription for endless welfare wars and countless American casualties.

When commentators criticized the viability of Bush's plan to "democratize" Iraq, the Middle East, and ultimately the whole world, the president pointed to the example of Japan, which previous generations of commentators once said was unfit for proper government. Max Boot invokes this same example when he writes that "we need to liberalize the Middle East.... And if this requires occupying Iraq for an extended period, so be it; we did it with Germany, Japan and Italy, and we can do it again."[29] In fact, the examples of Germany and Japan do not vindicate the neoconservative foreign policy. Note that these occupations were entirely different than the Iraq "liberation" occupation—the type prescribed by neoconservatism—both in ends and means. Their purpose was *to render nonthreatening the hostile populations of those countries.* Additionally, the way in which those occupations produced their desired result was through the *utter destruction and resulting demoralization* that the Allies brought on the Germans and Japanese.[30] Interestingly, even Paul Wolfowitz, one of the architects of the Iraq War and a prominent neoconservative foreign policy expert, once understood this:

> post–World War II experiences with Germany and Japan offer misleading guides to what is possible now, even in a period of American primacy. What was possible following total victory and prolonged occupation—in societies that were economically advanced but, at the same time, had profoundly lost faith in their own institutions—does not offer a model that applies in other circumstances.[31]

But even this knowledge could not withstand the opportunity Wolfowitz and other neoconservatives believed existed to promote their foreign policy after September 11.

In the Iraq War, none of the lessons of World War II were practiced: We treated hostile Iraqis with kid gloves and made it our mission to let them elect whatever government they so chose, no matter how hostile to America or how friendly to Islamic totalitarians they were. To try transforming an enemy nation without first defeating and demoralizing its complicit inhabitants is to invite those inhabitants both to rise up and rebel against America and to feel no fear in empowering even more anti-American leaders. Despite their claims that their policy for Iraq was a practical necessity, there were no grounds for thinking it could be anything except a disaster.[32]

How were the neoconservatives so deluded about Iraq? To understand this, consider a central component of their political philosophy. For neoconservatives (particularly those influenced by Strauss), politics is the primary force influencing and guiding any and every culture. Moreover, the neoconservatives attribute enormous explanatory power to what is, for them, the architectonic political concept: the idea of the "regime."[33] The concept "regime" is defined, loosely, as the defining political forms and formalities that govern each nation. Regime analysis, beginning with the traditional taxonomy of regimes (e.g., democracy, aristocracy, and kingship), studies how each political form is defined by an animating principle (e.g., democracy by equality, aristocracy by virtue, and kingship by honor), which in turn percolates down and through the particular society over which it governs. Thus, a country's culture is first and foremost determined by its politics—by its regime. Neoconservatives believe that the individual is necessarily an ineffectual product of the regime in which he is brought up. Bad regimes, they argue, inculcate in people bad behavior and norms. If you take the same people and place them under a good regime (i.e., a "democracy"), they will become radically better people. The regime changes the culture. Thus, it is the governing elite, not the people, who ultimately determine the regime and the culture in a given country. If we replace the elite through regime change and help to establish a better elite that is pro-"democracy," then a new, better culture will be born.

Ultimately, according to the neoconservatives, the foundations for any good culture, the sort that a regime must strive to foster, lie in a respect for tradition and a strong role for religion. These are the forces that restrain individuals in every society from pursuing their own "selfish" passions and thus from immorality and anarchy.[34]

By this standard, Iraq was a promising yet troubled country in need of assistance. It was a tradition-based, religion-oriented society that for decades had been ruled by a cruel, inhumane, secular elite—the Ba'ath Party and Saddam Hussein—who had not been chosen by the people. Do away with that elite, cultivate the local traditions and the religious leaders, and Iraq was ripe for "democracy." Once Iraqis experienced the wonders of electing their own leaders, once they participated in writing their own constitution, the neoconservatives postulated, Iraq would be transformed. The euphoria they expressed after the January 2005 Iraqi elections and the subsequent approval of a new constitution expressed their sincere belief that Iraq had fundamentally changed for the better. The new regime and the new practices in "democracy" would bring out miraculously the best in the Iraqis. This approach would not only lead to political freedom in Iraq, but also to economic prosperity through the adoption of free markets and to the peaceful coexistence of Iraq with its neighbors. Even more—in the ultimate payoff for America—this new Iraq would become our ally in the Middle East; it would help us reshape the region and destroy the threat of terrorism forever.

The neoconservative view of the relationship between individuals and regimes is one that ex-President Bush implicitly holds in an even stronger form, believing that freedom is "written on the soul of every human being." This view also explains the plausibility of the idea that bringing "democracy" militarily to one country will likely set off a chain reaction of creating "democracies" in other countries due to overwhelming civilian demand. This, in turn, would then lessen the need for future military "interventions." As Bush put it, to raucous applause at the National Endowment for Democracy in late 2003: "Iraqi democracy will succeed—and that success will send forth the news, from Damascus to Teheran—that freedom can be the future of every nation. The establishment of a free Iraq at the heart of the Middle East will be a watershed event in the global democratic revolution."[35]

As a result of the neoconservatives' view of regimes, they take lightly the colossal task of replacing a barbaric nation with a civilized one—in fact, they do not even acknowledge that some nations are barbaric. The pitiful peoples of oppressed nations are lionized as mere victims of bad actors, victims who must merely be "liberated" in order to transform from members of terrorist states to good neighbors.

Let us now examine more closely the political system most neoconservatives want to export to the rest of the world: "democracy."

When ex-President Bush and the neoconservatives used the term "democracy," they acted as if the term refers more or less to the type of government we have in the United States. Thus, the term "Iraqi democracy," at least prior to its implementation, conjures up images of a nation with civilized courts; rule of law; respect for individual rights (including those of ethnic and religious minorities); a prosperous, free-market economy; separation of church and state; and so on.

But the literal meaning of "democracy"—and the meaning applied in the actual implementation of "Iraqi democracy"—is *unlimited majority rule*. "Democracy" refers to the system by which ancient Athenians voted to kill Socrates for voicing unpopular ideas. In 1932 the German people "democratically" elected the Nazi Party, including future chancellor Adolph Hitler. "Democracy" and liberty are not interchangeable terms, but are in fact antithetical. The distinctively American, pro-liberty principle of government is the principle of *individual rights*, which, to be upheld in a given society, requires a constitution that specifically protects these rights *against* the tyranny of the majority.[36]

Neoconservatives are unabashed promoters of "democracy," all the while knowing that it is not America's founding system of government and that it was actually opposed by the Founding Fathers of this country. As Joshua Muravchik, a neoconservative, writes, "This is the enthusiasm for democracy. Traditional conservatives are more likely to display an ambivalence towards this form of government, an ambivalence expressed centuries ago by the American founders. Neoconservatives tend to harbor no such doubts."[37]

Because the neoconservatives do not believe in individual rights, because they do not believe in any first principles of freedom, politically they advocate

for democracy. They like the messiness and the never-ending change built into
the system, which of course requires compromise, coalition-building, politics,
a balance of power, and wise statesmen who can magnanimously rise above and
sort out the competing claims. They also know that majority rule, as unstable
as it is, provides opportunity for the strong—both intellectually and, in the case
of the United States, militarily—to exert significant impact.

Thus they were not concerned about the specifics of an Iraqi constitution or
the messy process of Iraqi democracy. To the neoconservatives, this is the very
essence of politics. Since Iraq was weak, it would rely more strongly on the United
States, thus providing more opportunities for wise American administrators to
help guide Iraq toward prosperity and toward becoming an example of what
benefits American hegemony could bring to others in the Middle East.

But of course Iraq did not turn out the way the neoconservatives had
hoped.

Because the neocons and President Bush lacked an understanding of the
relationship between voting, freedom, and aggression, we have been treated to
the spectacle of an Iraqi "democracy" in which "Islam is a fundamental source
of legislation" and "No law may contradict the undisputed principles of Islam."[38]
We have a "democracy" that is dangerously close to being a puppet or ally of the
theocracy of Iran, which is an enemy we will have created on the grounds that
"democracies don't start wars."

Holding the false view that freedom equals "democracy" and clinging to the
fiction that regime change alone can completely change a culture and a people's
character, we have abetted and applauded the freedom-haters in Iraq as they have
voted themselves toward terrorist theocracy. Furthermore, we have promoted
elections around the Middle East as the solution to the threats these nations
pose, as if the people are civilized and friendly toward America but just "happen"
to be under despotic rule. The results of these elections, which have empowered
Islamic totalitarians or their close allies in the Palestinian territories, Egypt, and
Lebanon, is testament to the extent of the neoconservative's delusion about the
advocacy of "spreading democracy."

But this advocacy is deluded only by the standard of U.S. national security.
As we shall see, however, U.S. national security was never the neoconservatives'
primary goal.

"Hard Wilsonianism"

The neoconservatives argued that bringing democracy to the world was necessary
for the United States to achieve its "national interest." Given the Iraq debacle,
given that it clearly *had* to be a debacle, and given that neoconservatives *continue*

to support exporting democracy to Iraq and around the world, it is painfully obvious that by achieving America's "national interest," they do not mean "securing the lives and freedom of Americans."

What, then, do they mean?

As we have seen, neoconservatives believe that America should not conduct its foreign policy by focusing its military energies on decisively defeating genuine threats to its security and thus otherwise staying out of the affairs of other nations. Instead, they believe that America has a "duty" to, as William Kristol and Robert Kagan put it, "advance civilization and improve the world's condition."[39] Just as neoconservatives hold that the individual should live in service to the American collective, so they also hold that America should live in service to an unspecified international collective, that America should take on the duty of policing the world, and thereby creating American hegemony.

To understand the nature of this goal and the ways in which it is distinct from, if not opposed to, the goal of U.S. security, it is helpful to compare neoconservatism's foreign policy goals with the nearly identical goals of the foreign policy school of which President Woodrow Wilson was the most prominent member. This school is known in modern terms as "Liberal Internationalism" or just "Wilsonianism." Recall that some neoconservative intellectuals such as Max Boot have referred to their foreign policy as "Hard Wilsonianism."

According to Wilsonianism, America must not restrict itself to going to war when direct threats exist. It must not "isolate" itself from the rest of the world's troubles, but must instead "engage" itself and work with others to create a world of peace and security, a world that alleviates suffering, collectively opposes "rogue nations" that threaten the security of the world as a whole, and brings "democracy" and "self-determination" to various oppressed peoples around the world. It was on this premise that both the League of Nations and its successor, the United Nations, were formed—and on which America entered World War I ("The world," Wilson said, "must be made safe for democracy"). In many ways and on many levels, neoconservative foreign policy seemingly shares many principles with liberal Wilsonianism. This is why, after September 11, many liberals, from the Liberal Internationalist school of foreign policy, like Christopher Hitchens and Tony Blair, as well as so many Democratic politicians, expressed strong agreement with the neoconservative strategic goals and supported the war in Iraq, even as they quibbled with some of the tactics.

The Wilsonian-neoconservative view of America's "national interest" is, it should be noted, in stark contrast to the traditional, individualistic American view of America's national interest in foreign policy. Angelo Codevilla, an expert on the intellectual history of American foreign policy, summarizes the difference. Before the twentieth century,

Americans, generally speaking, wished the rest of the world well, demanded that it keep its troubles out of our hemisphere, and hoped that it would learn from us.

By the turn of the 20th century, however, this hope led some Americans to begin to think of themselves as the world's teachers, its chosen instructors. This twist of the founders' views led to a new and enduring quarrel over American foreign policy—between those who see the forceful safeguarding of our own unique way of life as the purpose of foreign relations, and those who believe that securing the world by improving it is the test of what [Iraqi "democracy" champion] Larry Diamond has called "our purpose and fiber as a nation."[40]

As to *how* one might "secure the world by improving it," Wilsonianism and neoconservatism have substantial differences. Wilsonianism favors American subordination to international institutions and "diplomacy," whereas neoconservatism favors American leadership and more often advocates force in conjunction with diplomacy. Traditional Wilsonians are not pacifists (Wilson, after all, brought America into World War I), but they do tend to believe that almost all problems can be solved by peaceful "cooperation" among members of world bodies to paper over potential conflicts or "isolate" aggressive nations that go against the "international community." Neoconservatives, on the other hand, openly state that their ambitious foreign policy goals require the use of unilateral force, regardless of whether that means removing a direct threat or stopping a tribal war in a faraway land.

Some neoconservatives, such as Max Boot, embrace the term "Hard Wilsonianism," not only to capture their affinity with Woodrow Wilson's liberal international collectivism, but also to highlight their differences in tactics:

> [A] more accurate term [than "neoconservatism"] might be "hard Wilsonianism." Advocates of this view embrace Woodrow Wilson's championing of American ideals but reject his reliance on international organizations and treaties to accomplish our objectives. ("Soft Wilsonians," aka liberals, place their reliance, in Charles Krauthammer's trenchant phrase, on paper, not power.)[41]

Not only must "power, not paper" (to reverse Krauthammer's expression) be used more often in achieving the desired "international order" than the Wilsonians think, say neoconservatives, but America must lead that order. It must not subordinate its decision-making authority to an organization such as the United Nations, nor cede to other countries the "responsibilities" for solving international problems.

America must lead, they say, because it is both militarily *and* morally the preeminent nation in the world. America, they observe, has on many occasions come to the rescue of other nations, even at its own expense (such as in World

War I or Vietnam), and this is the ultimate proof of altruistic virtue. (According to the neoconservatives, "Americans had nothing to gain from entering Vietnam—not land, not money, not power.... [T]he American effort in Vietnam was a product of one of the noblest traits of the American character—altruism in service of principles.")[42] By contrast, they observe, other nations, including many in Europe, have not even shown a willingness to defend themselves, let alone others.

The cornerstone policy of the neoconservatives' American-led, "hard Wilsonian" foreign policy is the U.S.-led military "intervention," which means using the American military or some military coalition to correct some perceived evil, give "humanitarian" aid, provide "peacekeeping," and, ideally, enact "regime change" and establish a new, beneficial "democracy" for the formerly oppressed.

Given the desired "international order" and America's "responsibility" to "improve the world's condition," the obligation to "intervene" goes far beyond nations that threaten the United States. Furthermore, when America *is* "intervening" in a threatening nation, the "intervention" cannot simply defeat the nation and render it nonthreatening, but rather it must seek, as we have seen, to benefit the nation's inhabitants, preferably by furnishing them with a new "democracy" and the extended benefits of the American welfare state.

Throughout the past decade and a half, neoconservatives have called for major "interventions" in remote tribal wars in Bosnia, Somalia, Kosovo, Darfur, and Liberia—none of which entailed a threat to the United States. And when neocons have called for responses to real threats, their focus has been on "liberating" the Afghans, Iraqis, and Iranians—not on breaking the hostile inhabitants' will to keep supporting and sponsoring Islamist, anti-American causes.

Endorsing this broad mandate for "intervention," William Kristol and Robert Kagan write in their seminal neoconservative essay "National Interest and Global Responsibility" that America must be "more rather than less inclined to weigh in when crises erupt, and preferably before they erupt." They argue that we must be willing to go to war "even when we cannot prove that a narrowly construed 'vital interest' of the United States is at stake." In other words, to use a common phrase, America must be the "world's policeman"—and not just any policeman, either: It must be a highly active one. In the words of Kristol and Kagan: "America cannot be a reluctant sheriff."[43] Kagan has even encouraged Americans to "see themselves in heroic terms—as Gary Cooper at high noon."[44] But there's more: America must not only be the "world's policeman," but it should also be the "world's social services' worker." If we drop bombs, they argue, we should also drop food packages.

Despite the differences between Wilsonianism and "Hard Wilsonianism," they agree entirely on a key aspect of the means to their goals: Any mission must involve substantial American *sacrifice*—the surrender of American life, liberty, and property. Observe, for instance, the nature of the neoconservative military response to September 11. In response to the attacks, America could have used its unequaled firepower not to "democratize" but to *defeat* the threatening countries, which would be those countries that continue to support the cause of Islamic Totalitarianism, and then to make an example of them in order to *deter* other countries. America could have made clear to the rest of the world that our government does not care what kind of government they adopt, so long as those governments do not threaten us.

There was and is no practical obstacle to such a policy. America's military and technological prowess relative to the rest of the world, let alone to the economically and militarily weak Middle East, has never been greater. Nor is there any obstacle in terms of knowledge. America's ability to destroy enemy regimes is not some secret of history; everyone knows how we got Japan to surrender and then covet our friendship for sixty-three years and counting. America could have responded to September 11 by calling for devastating retaliation against the state sponsors of terrorism, and this would demoralize the Islamists and deter any future threats from thinking they can get away with attacking America.[45] But the neoconservatives never considered a ruthless war as an option because they believe that going all-out to defeat America's enemies would be viewed as immoral.

Consider this typical neoconservative response to September 11 in the editorial from *The Weekly Standard* immediately following the attacks: "There is a task to which President Bush should call us. It is the long, expensive, and arduous war to replace the government of each nation on earth that allows terrorists to live and operate within its borders."[46] There is no practical reason why a war between superpower America and piddling dictatorships need be "long, expensive, and arduous." Terrorist nations should feel terrified to threaten us—but they do not. Why? Because, per the neoconservatives' prescriptions, America has placed the full use of its military capabilities off-limits. The neoconservatives have taken all-out war—real war—off the table.

The right to self-defense rests on the idea that individuals—and nations by extension—have a moral prerogative to act on their own judgment for their own sake. In other words, it rests on the morality of *rational egoism*. Egoism, rightly understood, holds that a nation against which force is initiated has a right to kill whomever and to destroy whatever in the aggressor nation as necessary in order to achieve victory.[47] The neoconservatives, true to their embrace of altruism, reject all-out war in favor of self-sacrificial means of combat that inhibit—or even render impossible—the defeat of our enemies. They advocate crippling rules of engagement that place the lives of civilians in enemy territory above the lives of American soldiers—and, by rendering victory impossible, above the lives of *all* Americans.

In Afghanistan, for instance, we refused to bomb the known hideouts of many top Taliban and al-Qaeda leaders for fear of civilian casualties. As a result, these men were left free to continue killing American soldiers. In Iraq, our hamstrung soldiers were not allowed to smash a militarily puny insurgency. Instead, they suffered hundreds of casualties at the hand of an enemy who operated at the discretion of America. Neoconservatives are avid supporters of such restrictions and of the altruistic theory on which they are based: "Just War Theory." To act otherwise would have been to contradict the duty of selfless service to others that is allegedly the *justification and purpose* of America using its military might.[48]

Following the invasion of Iraq—in which American soldiers were forced to resort to the half-measures that eventually enabled pitifully armed Iraqis to take over cities and kill thousands of our soldiers, neoconservative Stephen Hayes wrote glowingly of the just war tactics of our military.

> A war plan that sought to spare the lives not only of Iraqi civilians, but of Iraqi soldiers. Then, liberation. Scenes of jubilant Iraqis in the streets—praising President Bush as "The Hero of the Peace." A rush to repair the damage—most of it caused not by American bombs, but by more than three decades of tyranny.[49]

But no practical benefits for American self-defense can materialize from a policy whose central pursuit is American self-sacrifice. Given this goal, it should be no surprise that, by the standard of the interests of individual Americans, a war conceived on a self-sacrificial philosophy turned out to be a failure. The key notion to understand, however, is that by the standard of neoconservatism, the war has been a success.

Guided by neoconservative altruist-collectivist values, the Bush administration sought and fought *a war of self-sacrifice*. This is a war that necessarily failed to accomplish the only thing that can end threats to America: the thorough defeat of the enemies who threaten us.

In the run-up to the war, President Bush stated not one but three goals driving the invasion of Iraq: (1) ending the threat to the United States posed by Saddam Hussein's support of terrorists, his apparent possession of chemical and biological weapons, and his apparent pursuit of nuclear weapons; (2) "restoring" the "integrity of the U.N.," which Saddam Hussein had allegedly tarnished by violating seventeen U.N. resolutions; and (3) "liberating" Iraq from the evil tyrant Hussein and furnishing the Iraqi people with a peaceful, prosperous new "democracy."

In the view of President Bush and the neoconservatives, this combination of self-interested and altruistic goals was ideal. It was an act of selfless service to the world that would also supposedly protect America. But in fact, it was disastrous because it did not focus America on identifying and eliminating the actual threat in Iraq. Instead, it tore us between the contradictory goals of ending a threat and empowering Iraqis to do whatever they want. Combined with tactics designed to protect Iraqis at the expense of American lives, this contradictory combination guaranteed the fiasco that we are witnessing today.

This same mistake was committed in Afghanistan, where we focused on establishing a "democratic" government, building infrastructure, and cultivating a coalition of NATO nations with various agendas, but all the while neglected to defeat the enemy. As a result, our enemies, al-Qaeda and the Taliban, have gained strength in the region (including in Pakistan) and pose an ever-greater threat to U.S. troops in Afghanistan as well as to U.S. interests in the region. Bin-Laden and his deputy are, of course, still alive, and while we have selectively killed al-Qaeda leadership with missiles from drones, we have not dealt a death blow to the forces of al-Qaeda.

It is interesting that, in spite of being an advocate of "change," President Obama's policy toward Afghanistan is very much consistent with the neocons' views. He is sending in more troops, but their purpose is primarily to help safeguard the Afghans and help solidify their floundering "democracy." In addition to troops, the Obama administration is sending civilians to help the Afghan people build infrastructure and improve their political processes. This is right out of the neocon handbook. So, even out of power, the neocons' ideas are still, to a large extent, alive and well because there are seemingly no effective alternatives. Obama has diverted from neocon foreign policy in tone, in his insistence to withdraw all troops from Iraq as soon as possible and his changed emphasis away from democratizing the Middle East. But in many respects, we expect the changes that this administration will bring will move us more toward traditional Wilsonian foreign policy instead of the "hard Wilsonianism" of the neocons. A change, yes, but not as dramatic as many would seem to think.

And indeed, we expect many of the trends that the neocon foreign policy facilitated to continue and possibly intensify. Our sacrificial objectives and sacrificial tactics have not and will not deter our enemies, nor will they inspire freedom-seeking allies. Instead, they inspire large populations to elect our enemies into political power and ultimately to strike at America. We have seen a definite trend in the growth of Islamic Totalitarianism, the ideology that motivates Islamic terrorists and their strongest supporters—for example, the rise of Hamas in the Palestinian territories, Hezbollah in Lebanon, Ahmadinejad in Iran, and the Muslim Brotherhood in Egypt. Our enemies who were militant before September 11 are now even more so. Iran and Syria, for instance, continued to support the slaughter of American soldiers in Iraq without fear of consequence, and Iran pursues nuclear weapons to bolster its policy of worldwide Islamic terror.

The explanation for all this is clear: The goal directing our foreign policy was never (and is not today) American security or an end to war, but rather it was a "national mission," one that took precedence over any concern about defending American lives. Such a goal was rooted in the neoconservatives' basic philosophy of collectivism, and in its political expression, nationalism. In chapter 10, we shall examine how the neocons' foreign policy actually serves as an arm of their "National Greatness" domestic agenda.

PART V
SOFT DESPOTISM

CHAPTER 9
LEO STRAUSS AND THE FASCIST TEMPTATION

In light of the recent attacks on Leo Strauss and his alleged influence on the neoconservatives, the Bush administration, and the Iraq War,[1] several of his students and defenders have gone to great lengths to remind us that their teacher was a "friend" to liberal *democracy*.[2] Yale political theorist Steven Smith has even gone so far as to suggest that Strauss was not only "a friend of liberal democracy" but even "one of the best friends democracy has ever had."[3] However, the real question that needs to be asked is not whether Strauss was a "friend" to liberal democracy but, rather, what kind of a friend was he—genuine or two-faced? Furthermore, to change the terms of the question: Was Strauss a friend or a foe to liberal *capitalism*? The difference between liberal democracy and liberal capitalism is real, and it may force Strauss's defenders to answer the question rather differently.[4]

In order to answer these important questions, we need to examine the career and thought of Leo Strauss at a time when his "friendship" with liberal democracy was being tested: the period during and surrounding the Weimar Republic. Readers may wonder, though, why we include a discussion of the early Strauss after several chapters on Strauss's mature thought. This penultimate chapter returns to the early Strauss for three reasons. First, because newly discovered material regarding Strauss's political views in the 1930s has become available only recently to scholars and to the general public. Second, because the somewhat enigmatic political views of the later Strauss are more easily understood in light of his early views. Third and finally, because Strauss's early political views provide a window, we think, to the ultimate meaning and direction of neoconservative thought with which we conclude this book.

The broader questions examined by this chapter are as follows. First, if we peek behind the esoteric veil of Strauss's interpretive commentaries on the Great Books of Western thought, will we find that he held political views on the immediate issues of the day. Secondly, which form of government did he think best for the time in which he lived? To answer these questions, this chapter must be read in the context of chapters 3, 4, 5, and 6. Or, put the other way around, our earlier chapters on Strauss must be read in the context of this chapter in order to fully understand what Strauss was up to. While we do not address directly the issue of whether Strauss's thought changed from the 1930s to the 1960s, our earlier chapters on Strauss might be reread in the light of the analysis presented in this chapter.[5]

As a philosopher, Strauss viewed the Weimar era through a philosophic lens, which means that he viewed it, not only at the time but also in subsequent decades, through the ideas of the two philosophers who had the greatest impact on his early career: Nietzsche and Heidegger. In fact, Strauss's view not only of the Weimar republic but of modernity itself can be read as a response to these two preeminent German philosophers.

At first blush, Nietzsche and Heidegger appear in *Natural Right and History* as ominous background figures against whom Strauss is writing (Heidegger is not even mentioned by name and Nietzsche only a few times), but his connection to the midwives of modern nihilism is rather more complicated than it might first appear. We shall leave it to others to determine whether Strauss was ultimately a philosophic enemy of Nietzsche and Heidegger, but it is indisputably the case that Strauss was indebted intellectually to Germany's two greatest philosophers of the post-Hegelian period. He was, as it were, a student who learned from and took away a great deal from both.

Strauss's connection to Nietzsche and Heidegger is reasonably well known. Like many young men of his generation, Strauss was smitten first by Nietzsche and then by Heidegger. He once wrote privately that "Nietzsche so dominated and bewitched me between my 22nd and 30th years, that I literally believed everything that I understood of him."[6] So, throughout most of the 1920s, Strauss was enthralled by Nietzsche. His relationship with Heidegger, however, is somewhat more complicated because Strauss knew the man personally. Early on, his early enthusiasm for Heidegger was no less passionate or decisive than was his attraction to Nietzsche. Strauss, who audited several of Heidegger's courses during the early 1920s, credited the German philosopher with "revolutionizing all thought in Germany and continental Europe." Recalling the first impression that Heidegger made on him, Strauss writes, "I had never seen before such seriousness, profundity, and concentration in the interpretation of philosophic texts." Strauss and others of his generation saw in Heidegger a "phenomenon," a philosophic hurricane, the likes of which had not been "seen in the world since Hegel." The philosopher from the Black Forest was, for Strauss, the greatest thinker of the twentieth century. Heidegger was the only philosopher in Strauss's world who fully understood the crisis of the modern world. Over time, the young Strauss gradually came to see "the breadth of the revolution of thought" that Heidegger was preparing. Initially, Strauss also sympathized with several fundamental components of Heidegger's revolution, causing Strauss to radically reorient his view of the world. He even goes on to describe Max Weber (whom Strauss and his generation once considered to be the great intellectual oracle of Weimer liberalism) as an "orphan child" compared to Heidegger's luminous genius.

These, then, were the two men—Nietzsche and Heidegger—who most profoundly influenced Strauss's early intellectual development and who laid the foundation for his deepest philosophic principles. Strauss's indebtedness to Nietzsche and Heidegger does raise obvious questions concerning their potential influence on his political views that we shall address in the pages that follow. To his credit, Strauss acknowledged the connection between his two philosophic mentors on the one hand and the rise of Nazism on the other. Strauss was the first to recognize an "undeniable kinship between Nietzsche's thought and fascism," and anyone who read Heidegger's *Being and Time* during the 1920s could see, he wrote, "the kinship in temper and direction between Heidegger's thought and the Nazis."[7] Leo Strauss saw as far and as deeply into the substance and meaning of these two German philosophers' thought as anyone of his generation. He was no innocent.

So what exactly did Strauss learn from Nietzsche and Heidegger? What ideas and principles did he accept and reject from these two major influences on his thinking?[8] What we know with certainty is that Strauss's philosophic project began, following Nietzsche and Heidegger, as a moral protest against the developments of modern Western civilization, and he seems to have accepted their diagnosis of and prognosis for it. That Strauss would later show great personal disdain for Heidegger (at the same time that he was granting him a high degree of begrudging intellectual respect) does not change the fact that his lifelong distaste for modernity draws its inspiration from his former teacher. Ultimately, we cannot know Strauss's final judgment on America (and therewith that of the neoconservatives) until we examine his deepest reflections on the Enlightenment as they first emerged from his confrontation with Heidegger (and others).[9] We must therefore probe more deeply into Strauss's antiliberalism to see where it came from and where it led him politically. Thus the archeology of Strauss's mature thought must begin with the development of his thought as a young man. It is from that vantage that we can see the birth, genesis, and purity of views that motivated Strauss to seek new (or forgotten) moral and political continents.

German Nihilism and the Rise of Nazism

A full decade before he published *Natural Right and History,* Strauss delivered in 1941 at the New School for Social Research a remarkably revealing, semiautobiographical lecture titled "German Nihilism."[10] Speaking to a distinguished group of scholars and fellow refugees, Strauss's purpose was to show the connection between German philosophic nihilism and the rise of Nazism. To listeners then and readers today, Strauss describes how and why the young men who came to maturity during World War I and the 1920s—young men just like himself whom scholars of Weimar Germany would later describe as the generation of "Conservative Revolutionaries"—were initially attracted to the ideas of Nietzsche and Heidegger and ultimately to fascism and/or Nazism.[11]

What is most remarkable about Strauss's lecture is its open sympathy with the Weimar nihilists' diagnosis of the Enlightenment and modern capitalist civilization. This comes through by the way in which Strauss largely speaks in his own voice when describing the young nihilists' critique of liberal capitalism. "I take it for granted," he claimed, "that not everything to which the young nihilists objected, was unobjectionable," and he goes on to argue that their critique of Western, liberal-capitalist civilization was "not entirely unsound."[12] The "young nihilists" described by Strauss were those young men who, like himself, had studied with or been influenced by Martin Heidegger (among others) during the 1920s. (In addition to Heidegger, Strauss lists Oswald Spengler, Moeller van den Bruck, Carl Schmitt, and Ernst Jünger as the intellectuals who most influenced the "young nihilists" and "who knowingly or ignorantly paved the way for Hitler."[13])

Strauss and the conservative revolutionaries of the World War I generation were contemptuous of liberal capitalism and hoped for its destruction. They were repulsed by the average, mediocre, vulgar, routinized, humdrum, formless, everyday quality of liberal-bourgeois life, and they rebelled against the self-satisfied but hollow culture of the merchant and the moneymaker. In Strauss's view, the soul of liberal man had atrophied and was facing its final indignity as a homogenous mass indistinguishable from a huge herd of cattle safely grazing in comfort and peace. The conservative revolutionaries viewed bourgeois normalcy, contentment, and decency with utter disdain. It was their philosophic *bête noire.* They were increasingly frustrated and disgusted with Weimar liberalism and were therefore open to radical change. Life was without meaning unless it was dedicated, proclaimed the conservative revolutionaries, to something higher than the self and its petty pleasures. Strauss and his generation thought men were made for higher, nobler, and more heroic things—for a greatness that transcends the individual and his sordid interests. The problem, of course, is that when men of such grand ambition are denied access to greatness, they often become villains bent on destruction. One senses in Strauss a very strong sympathy for the motives of the young men of his generation who were, in his view, legitimately repulsed by the moral ethos of liberal-capitalist society.

As the collectivism of the Left and Right gained influence in the first four decades of the twentieth century, it became intellectually fashionable to mock the principles and practices of a free and liberal society. Strauss was no exception to this trend. In that 1941 lecture and in subsequent writings through the 1960s, he showed a genuine moral and political contempt for the "*moral* meaning" of modern liberal capitalism. The young Strauss and those who sat with him in Heidegger's lectures launched what Strauss called a "moral protest" against "the spirit of the West, and in particular of the Anglo-Saxon West." Truth be told, he was repulsed and motivated by a nightmare vision that liberal capitalism—i.e., the world of production, consumption, and recreation—might win the battle of ideas and inherit the world, and he was contemptuous of a depoliticized culture that lived for nothing but work and play. Strauss and his friends objected to a moral-political philosophy that "safeguard[ed] the rights of man" in order to "relieve man's estate." They believed that capitalism's goal to conquer nature had alienated man from his natural state or true being. Strauss clearly agrees with the Heideggerian-educated nihilists of Weimer Germany, for whom the tendency of modern capitalist society is to "lower the moral standards, the moral claims, which previously had been made by all responsible teachers, but to take better care than those earlier teachers had done, for the putting into ... political and legal practice, the rules of human conduct." The nihilists associated the lowering— indeed, the collapse and degradation—of all moral standards with the classical liberal "identification of morality with an attitude of claiming one's *rights*, or with enlightened self-interest, or reduction of honesty to the best policy; or the solution of the conflict between common interest and private interest by means of industry and trade."[14] (Notice here and above Strauss's contempt for the moral core of liberal individualism: the doctrine of individual rights and enlightened self-interest. The full scope and consequences of that contempt will be seen at the end of this chapter.) Strauss accepted the all-too-common view of most German philosophers that self-interest is base, but self-sacrifice is noble; that natural rights promote selfishness, but duty promotes fraternity. He therefore joined them in rejecting capitalism and an individualist ethics grounded in rational self-interest or self-interest rightly understood as immoral.

Leo Strauss, like Heidegger, objected to the idea of an "*open* society" (or what he also called the "mechanic society") based on the rights of man and economic laissez-faire, a society characterized by production, competition, and consumption and inspired by the pursuit of wealth and happiness. Strauss and his generation were morally repulsed by the bourgeois life defined by comfortable self-preservation, one that strangled the soul out of the serious few who sought higher and nobler values. For Strauss and the generation of young nihilists, the triumph of liberalism meant the decline and fall of a morally serious life and the rise of a culture defined by entertainment, amusement, and fun. Heidegger and Strauss regarded the open and depoliticized nature of laissez-faire liberalism as inherently amoral, if not simply immoral. They demonized the moral-political vision identified with John Locke, Adam Smith, and Thomas Jefferson and the way of life associated with Cornelius Vanderbilt, Andrew Carnegie, and John D. Rockefeller. Weimar's thinkers and their students opposed, Strauss noted, "the identification of the morally good with the object of enlightened self-interest however enlightened." A society founded on rational self-interest and individualism is defined by an easygoing pursuit of happiness, particularly the pursuit of material gain and the petty pleasures that come with acquisition. A life of comfortable preservation—i.e., the bovinelike existence synonymous with bourgeois life—was thought by Strauss and the young men of Weimar to be vulgar, trivial, and ignoble.

Thus the modern way of life, according to Strauss, is demeaning and stunting to the morally serious and ambitious man, and it runs counter to the necessary requirements of a truly moral life defined by noble virtue and suprahuman excellence. Modern life, notes Strauss, was thought to be "irreconcilable with the basic demands of *moral life.*" Morality is, in other words, inconsistent with enlightened self-interest. The "moral life," by contrast, is connected in some way with accepting one's social duties and submitting oneself to the unity of the whole, while the vulgar moral ideal connected with American liberal capitalism was one of *self*-ownership, *self*-governance, and *self*-reliance. It was therefore "to the lasting honor of Germany" that its philosophers, according to Strauss, stood up to and against the "debasement of morality" associated with English and American morality, which they saw as a moral doctrine grounded in the modern natural-rights teaching and the liberal capitalism associated with Locke and the American founding. In a different context, Strauss referred to English utilitarianism, with its promotion of "egoism as the basis of morality," as "disgusting, boring, naïve."[15]

The "moral protest" launched by Nietzsche and Heidegger against liberal-capitalist society that inspired so many young Germans (including Strauss) in the decade after World War I was not simply nihilistic in that it only hoped to destroy values without creating new ones. Rather, the young nihilists sought to replace the petty life of bourgeois man with what Strauss called a morally serious life. In place of the "open" or "mechanic" society envisioned by Enlightenment liberalism, Strauss and his fellow Heideggerians longed for a return to or the creation of a *"closed* society" and an "organic community." Strauss stated his positive political vision clearly and forcefully: "the root of all moral life is essentially and therefore eternally the *closed* society."[16]

Liberal individualism led to a fracturing of community and man's collective identity. Only in the closed society did the conservative revolutionaries think it possible to live a natural and morally serious life, the distinctive features of which are symbolized, Strauss wrote, in "the flag and the oath to the flag." But the morally serious life means more than just patriotism. It aspires to something higher and more bracing. It also means a belief in the purifying and transformative power of violence. It means to seek out and to live a romantically mystical and dangerous life, a life that inevitably points toward the noblest causes of all: war, sacrifice, death. War, sacrifice, and death elevate and ennoble life by introducing a kind of sublime intensity to man's otherwise humdrum existence. Strauss and the conservative revolutionaries valorized political and military conflict as the mechanism by which bourgeois man might be transported out of his petty and hollow life. The morally serious society is naturally and "constantly confronted with, and basically oriented toward ... the serious moment, M-Day, *war*."

Thus the essence of virtue, according to Strauss, is self-sacrifice and selfless duty to something greater than the self, to the greater good, to the public interest, and to the nation. In drawing a hard distinction between "the noble and the useful, between duty and self-interest," the Weimar philosophers and their young followers carried out the logic of their argument to its climax: They promoted "warlike virtues" and, more particularly, adopted "one virtue, courage, military virtue," the actions of which can lead only to one result: "death on the field of honour, death for one's country." Martial courage is the ultimate Kantian virtue because it has no admixture of self-interest: It "is *never* rewarded. Instead, it is the flower of self-sacrifice," which is the cardinal virtue. For Strauss and his generation, only "life in such a *tense* atmosphere, only a life which is based on constant awareness of the *sacrifices* to which it owes its existence, and of the necessity, the *duty* of sacrifice of life and all worldly good, is truly human." In other words, duty, sacrifice, and death embody the highest, most noble way of life for man. He views the good life, at least the good life for the common man, as one of self-abnegation, renunciation, and sacrifice. Only in the closed, organic community can ordinary men overcome their petty, self-interested desires and instead aspire to a life of moral nobility, social discipline, and heroic glory, which means a life of sacrifice and the duty to sacrifice. This is why the "open society is morally inferior to the closed society."[17]

Strauss's overt sympathy with the young nihilists' critique of the open society and their idealization of the closed society did not, however, go the whole way. He broke with the Heideggerian nihilists only insofar as he thought they went *too* far in demanding "self-*sacrifice* and self-*denial*" as the primary virtues of a moral society; that they went *too* far in stressing "the dignity of military virtue"; that they went *too* far in glorifying courage as the only "unutilitarian virtue" left to modern man with which to combat that which is truly morally degrading—

self-interest; and, finally, that they went *too* far in eventually advocating Nazism. Their sin was in having gone *too* far. This is why Strauss did express some modicum of respect for the English, who at least had the "very un-German prudence and moderation not to throw out the baby with the bath, i.e., the prudence to conceive of the modern ideals as a reasonable adaptation of the old and eternal ideal of decency, of rule of law, and of that liberty which is not license, to changed circumstances." Strauss and those like him who read Nietzsche and studied with Heidegger were contemptuous of Hitler and the National Socialists, whom they regarded to be "contemptible *tool*[s] of 'History.'"[18] Hitler and the Nazis were a kind of evil twin, a bastard brat, to what was an otherwise understandable if not a laudable movement on the German nationalist Right.

It is also important to note that the young nihilists' critique of the open society and their advocacy of the closed society eventually pushed Strauss toward a radical—indeed, the ultimate—response to the problem of modern nihilism. Strauss accepted the critique of modern liberal society launched by Nietzsche and Heidegger, and he followed the path they beat back to ancient philosophy. However, Strauss would ultimately break from his teachers by accepting as true and attempting to recover the teachings of Platonic political philosophy.

Strauss was never an active member of the conservative revolutionary movement, but he was influenced by many of their leading voices and he often sang their tune. He was a fellow traveler to that generation of influential German thinkers whose assault on classical-liberal theory and practice in the post–World War I period helped turn the tide of national opinion against the defenseless Weimar republic. Philosophers such as Nietzsche, Heidegger, and lesser lights such as Oswald Spengler, Moeller van den Bruck, Ernest Jünger, and Carl Schmitt softened the culture and prepared it for the National Socialist revolution.[19]

The World War Between Merchants and Heroes

Let us digress for a moment to identify an aspect of the larger culture of opinion in which the young Strauss developed his critique of liberalism and his later political views. Strauss's critique of the "open" society and his defense of the "closed" one bear a remarkable resemblance to the views of Werner Sombart, the well-known German Marxist who later became a defender of Hitler and Nazism. In 1915 Sombart published a small book with the provocative title *Merchants and Heroes*. His theme was as simple as it was powerful. He argued that World War I was, at root, a battle between two different and antagonistic worldviews, a struggle between the moral culture of the merchant (i.e., England) and the moral culture of the warrior (i.e., Germany). The shopkeeper's morality consisted of the petty bourgeois or utilitarian virtues such as calculation, frugality, industry, temperance, honesty, productiveness, and selfishness, and his highest values included money, trade, comfort, and respectability. The warrior's morality, by contrast, consisted of the aristocratic virtues of courage, daring, endurance, loyalty, magnanimity, obedience, and self-sacrifice, and his highest values included honor, glory, and pride. "The trader," Sombart wrote, in condemning language that surely would have appealed to Strauss, "approaches life with the question: what can you give me" and he "speaks only of 'rights.'" The hero, by contrast, "approaches life with the question: what can I give you?" and he speaks "only of his duties." Not surprisingly, the German conception of the State was as a "super-individual," with a "life outside us," and, like Strauss (as we shall see momentarily), Sombart compared this conception of the State to "the spirit of the ancients; and Plato's Republic," which is the "model after which all the German ideal conceptions of the State have been formed." (As we saw in chapters 5 and 6, Strauss too found his alternative to English morality in the philosophy of Plato's *Republic*.) The merchant does not see beyond himself while the warrior looks to the *Volk*. Sombart's theme and conclusion spoke of the "incomparable superiority" of the German heroic spirit over the spirit of the English shopkeeper.[20] Sombart helped to shape the climate of opinion that influenced the primary thinkers, who in turn influenced Strauss and the generation of young nihilists in the decade immediately after the end of the First World War.

It is here that our plot now thickens. One of Sombart's closest friends and intellectual allies was the future Nazi scholar Carl Schmitt.[21] By the early 1930s Schmitt, a professor of law at the University of Cologne, was one of Germany's most influential jurists and legal theorists. On May 1, 1933, he joined the Nazi party and was subsequently promoted to a distinguished professorship at the University of Berlin and then to the position of chief counselor of Prussia under the Nazi regime. Schmitt was philosophically committed to the principles of National Socialism and was a high official in the Nazi regime.[22]

In 1932 Leo Strauss wrote an extended review and critique of Schmitt's best-known book, *The Concept of the Political* (first published in 1927). The purpose of Schmitt's book was to undermine classical-liberal theory and practice in order to recover and restore the essence of what he called "the political." The world of liberal individualism had, according to Schmitt, "depoliticized" modern society, alienated man from his true being, and ushered in an artificial and repellent world of play and recreation. Schmitt denied the claim of liberal theorists that politics is just one cultural realm among many equal, codependent realms (e.g., economics, religion, education, the arts) and that there could and should be a separation between church and State, economy and State, and education and State. He also rejected the liberal hope that the State could and should be neutral between competing moral-religious-political claims over the right way to live. Finally, he regarded Kant's brief for perpetual peace as a dangerous fantasy that would necessarily lead to a world lacking moral seriousness and commitment. Liberal depoliticization would, Schmitt argued, strip man of his humanity. A depoliticized world is a morally neutered world, a pacified world that stands for nothing but the pursuit of amusement, a world in which man has nothing to die for—which likewise means he has nothing to live for.

For Schmitt, then, "the political" represents not just an autonomous sphere but *the* fundamental, comprehensive sphere of human action. Man is a herding or tribal being in Schmitt's view, and "the political" is the primary unit of moral value and the realm in which he most fully realizes his humanity. "The political" represents "the most intense and extreme antagonism," wrote Schmitt, "and every concrete antagonism becomes that much more political the closer it approaches the most extreme point, that of the friend-enemy grouping."[23] For him, the defining characteristic of the human condition and the essence of the political was the natural tendency of men everywhere to divide into groups of "friends" and "enemies." More fundamentally, "the political" is the ultimate realm in which men pursue and battle over that which is most fully human: competing views of right and wrong, just and unjust, noble and ignoble. "The political" represents the ultimate expression of the human condition, particularly the manner in which societies are naturally set against one another in a state of war or war-readiness. Confrontation, struggle, war, and the possibility of death heighten, intensify, and ennoble the human experience. To put one's life on the line against "the other" is the apex of human seriousness. This was precisely Sombart's point in differentiating England and Germany in *Merchants and Heroes.*

Strauss's review of Schmitt provided the younger man with the perfect opportunity to defend liberal democracy at the very moment when it was under assault and most vulnerable. Strauss was, after all, a "friend" to liberal democracy—indeed, "one of the best friends democracy has ever had"![24] Here was an opportunity for Strauss to defend freedom, individual rights, limited government, and laissez-faire capitalism. Here was the opportunity to denounce Schmitt as the enemy of freedom and justice. This was the kind of moment that defines a man's intellectual character and moral fiber. Shockingly, though, this "friend" to liberal democracy chose not to defend his best friend. In fact, on the eve of Weimar's collapse, he took this opportunity to stab his friend in the back and twist the knife. Worse yet, Strauss wrote to deepen and improve Schmitt's argument. Leo Strauss was, it turns out, a friend to Carl Schmitt—maybe the best friend Schmitt ever had.[25]

Ironically, one might say of Strauss precisely what he wrote of Edmund Burke's somewhat neutered reaction to the French Revolution (at least on Strauss's account):

Burke comes close to suggesting that to oppose a thoroughly evil current in human affairs is perverse if that current is sufficiently powerful; he is oblivious of the nobility of last-ditch resistance. He does not consider that, in a way which no man can foresee, resistance in a forlorn position to the enemies of mankind, "going down with guns blazing and flag waving," may contribute greatly toward keeping awake the recollection of the immense loss sustained by mankind, may inspire and strengthen the desire and the hope for its recovery, and may become a beacon for those who humbly carry on the works of humanity in a seemingly endless valley of darkness and destruction.... It is only a short step from this thought of Burke to the supersession of the distinction between good and bad by the distinction between the progressive and the retrograde, or between what is and what is not in harmony with the historical process. We are here certainly at the pole opposite to Cato, who dared to espouse a lost cause.

It is surely true to say that Strauss in 1933 was "at the pole opposite to Cato," that his defense of Weimar was more in the tradition of Judas than Cato. He would not defend the "lost cause" that was Weimar; he would not keep "awake the recollection" of nineteenth-century liberalism precisely because he did not "hope for its recovery."[26] Strauss, it would seem, was just as happy to let Weimar liberalism die an ignominious death.

Strauss's primary purpose in "Notes on Carl Schmitt, *The Concept of the Political*," was to assist Schmitt in advancing, strengthening, and deepening his "radical critique of liberalism"—to aid Schmitt in the "urgent task" of overcoming, or killing, liberalism.[27] Strauss and Schmitt began with the present, with the world in which they lived. It was a world for which neither man had any respect: It was the world of liberal-bourgeois man; the world of comfort and ease and of universal peace and security; a world without politics, a meaningful State, moral seriousness, or sacrifice—it was the world of the Last Man. Or, as Strauss put it recapitulating Schmitt's central point: In the "politics-free" world of bourgeois liberalism, there will be "culture, civilization, economy, morals, law, art, *entertainment*, etc., but there will be neither politics nor state."[28] What a pity! Strauss was forced to live in a country with too much "culture, civilization, economy, morals, law, art," and, worst of all, too much "*entertainment*." Apparently the Western Front would be preferable to the Las Vegas strip. The import and tendency of liberal individualism (i.e., the politics of the Night Watchman state and the culture of entertainment) was to impoverish the meaning of human life. This was Strauss's greatest worry. By creating a political world that was officially neutral on the most important and pressing moral issues, the philosophy of liberal individualism had denatured man. A year later, Strauss's theoretical aspiration became reality: Germany was awash in politics and under the thumb of the State.

Strauss's engagement with Schmitt's critique of liberalism goes beyond the merely negative. It also lays the groundwork for an alternative to liberalism and the construction of a positive political theory grounded in a new understanding of the "political." The "political" for Strauss is not just one autonomous realm among many or even the most important domain. It is the *"fundamental,"* "authoritative," and architectonic realm.[29] Summing up Schmitt's argument as his own, Strauss lays the groundwork for a radically new politics:

> Agreement at all costs is possible only as agreement at the cost of the meaning of human life; for agreement at all costs is possible only if man has relinquished asking the question of what is right; and if man relinquishes that question, he relinquishes being a man. But if he seriously asks the question of what is right, the quarrel will be ignited … the life-and-death quarrel: the political—the grouping of humanity into friends and enemies—owes its legitimacy to the seriousness of the question of what is right.[30]

Strauss hoped to reinvigorate the political—the quarrel—by restoring for public discussion and debate the question of what is right. "The affirmation of the political is ultimately," Strauss contended, "nothing other than the affirmation of the moral," which in turn is the affirmation of the truly human.[31] He knew, however, that to elevate the question of right to the center of public debate was to reignite the friend-enemy distinction in politics and to therefore reassert the need for the magnanimous statesman to moderate and adjudicate these debates.

Strauss's posture in his "Notes" is to challenge Schmitt to probe ever more deeply into his understanding of the "political" and ultimately to radicalize that understanding. Strauss's critique of Schmitt can be summed up in just a few sentences. Schmitt failed in his illiberal attempt to kill liberalism because he shares liberalism's deepest premises. He remained, Strauss wrote, bound to "the horizon of liberalism."[32] The linchpin of Schmitt's error, according to Strauss, was that he sought to restore "the political" by returning to Hobbes's absolute sovereign and authoritarian politics without realizing that Hobbes rested his political Leviathan on a liberal moral foundation (the individual as the primary unit of moral value). In fact, Strauss argued that Hobbes was the source of the liberal idea of rights and was therefore the father of liberal individualism. To return to Hobbes was only to return to the source of liberalism. Just as Rousseau claimed that Locke and Hobbes had not gone back far enough in looking for the state of nature, so Strauss argued that Schmitt had not gone back far enough in search of "the political." Strauss therefore hoped to assist Schmitt "in gaining a horizon beyond liberalism."[33] His confrontation with Schmitt provided a philosophic way station on the road to that horizon beyond liberalism.

As we saw in chapters 5 and 6, Leo Strauss found that horizon in Platonic po-litical philosophy (via Alfarabi and Maimonides). Furthermore, by deepening and improving Schmitt's broadside against liberalism, by aiding and abetting the work of a Nazi theorist, Strauss ultimately sided with those who worked for Weimar's defeat. And as Weimar stood tottering, he stood in line with the likes of Schmitt and the conservative revolutionaries to give it the final push into the abyss.

Schmitt and Strauss drew very different political prescriptions from their mutual hatred of liberalism and their understanding of "the political." Schmitt would very shortly enlist his career and ideas with the Nazi cause. Strauss's poli-tics at this time, however, are more difficult to discern, but recently published private letters do indicate where Strauss was headed in 1933. We now turn to two such letters.

Flirting with Fascism

Given that Strauss shared the nihilists' critique of modern Enlightenment civilization but rejected Nazism, what positive or constructive vision for a new, post-Enlightenment epoch did Strauss advance or take seriously in the early 1930s? What kind of "closed" society did Strauss stand for? The answers to these questions are complicated, to say the least. We are, however, given some indica-tion of Strauss's views in two fascinating letters that he wrote over the course of eight months during the traumatic period between September 1932 and May 1933. The first of these two letters Strauss wrote to Carl Schmitt on September 4, 1932, as a kind of appendix or supplement to his review of *The Concept of the Political*, which had just been published in the *Archiv für Sozialwissenschaft und Sozialpolitik*. As Strauss continued to reflect on Schmitt's book and his review of it, he decided that he had not fully or satisfactorily aided Schmitt in developing his "polemic against the Left." More importantly, Strauss sought to assist Schmitt in developing principles of and for the "Right." Strauss reported to Schmitt that the

> ultimate foundation of the Right is the principle of the natural evil of man; be-cause man is by nature evil, he therefore needs *dominion*. But dominion can be established, that is, men can be unified, only in a unity *against*—against other men. Every association of men is *necessarily* a separation from other men. The *tendency* to separate (and therewith the grouping of humanity into friends and enemies) is given with human nature; it is in this sense destiny, period. But the political thus understood is not the constitutive principle of the state, of "order," but only the condition of the state. Now this relationship of rank between the political and the state does not emerge sufficiently, I believe, in your text.[34]

Strauss's letter to Schmitt provides some important guidance as to where Strauss's philosophic and political views were headed in the early 1930s. The letter clearly indicates Strauss's view of human nature as evil, which therefore requires authoritarian control or dominion in order to create the corporate or State unity that is necessary to tame it. The political dominion necessary to create unity is, for Strauss, both a cause and a consequence of unity: Dominion is the political cause that creates unity, but unity is also a consequence of man's natural inclination to join with a group in opposition to other groups. In other words, man, for Strauss, is naturally disposed to live in groups, but he also requires the force of dominion to keep the group together. The coercive power of the State and corporate unity are therefore mutually reinforcing. And there's more. By logical inference, Strauss seems to indicate in the Schmitt letter that unity is best created and perpetuated in the face of an "enemy," which suggests that if you do not have an enemy perpetually knocking on your door that you should go in search of one. In sum, Strauss's nationalist politics seem to promote the politics of authoritarianism and imperialism.[35] (The principles that Strauss enunciates in 1932 will, as we saw in chapter 8 and shall demonstrate in chapter 10, reemerge seventy years later in the neoconservative foreign policy prescriptions of William Kristol, David Brooks, and Robert Kagan.)

Our second letter, which Strauss wrote and sent from Paris to his friend Karl Löwith in May 1933, concerns the Nazi takeover of power in Germany. It was a desperate and disconcerting time for both men. As Germans, as Jews, and as philosophers, how should they respond to the rise of a vicious tyranny in their homeland? Picking up where he left off in the letter to Schmitt, Strauss told his old friend and fellow Heidegger student that he preferred the principles of the Right—particularly the principles of fascism—as the best antidote to the rise of Nazis:

> the fact that the new right-wing Germany does not tolerate us [i.e., Jews] says nothing against the principles of the Right. To the contrary: only from the principles of the Right, that is from fascist, authoritarian and *imperial* principles, is it possible with seemliness, that is, without resort to the ludicrous and despicable appeal to the *droits imprescriptibles de l'homme* [rights of man] to protest against the shabby abomination.... There is no reason to crawl to the cross, neither to the cross of liberalism, as long as somewhere in the world there is a glimmer of the spark of the *Roman* thought. And even then: rather than any cross, I'll take the ghetto.[36]

What are we to make of this extraordinary letter?[37] While it is difficult to know exactly Strauss's intent and meaning in the letter to Löwith, it does tell us something, and possibly something important. At the very least, particularly when read in the light of the 1932 letter to Schmitt just examined, it provides a window into Strauss's thought at the time. The great challenge is to determine whether the sentiments expressed in this letter indicate something fleeting or something fundamental and enduring about Strauss's philosophic project.[38]

Serious scholars of Leo Strauss must take the Löwith letter seriously. To do otherwise would be dishonest or cowardly; it would be to evade scholarly responsibility and to replace philosophic inquiry with the partisanship of a sect. It simply will not do to pretend that Strauss did not write this letter or to explain it away with tendentious rationalizations. Strauss's students have attempted, for instance, to deflect criticism away from their teacher by conflating fascism with Nazism and then arguing that because he was not a Nazi he could not have been a fascist. Strauss was obviously not a Nazi, but that is a different thing from being a fascist. (Strictly speaking, all Nazis are fascists, but not all fascists are Nazis.) Nor will it do from the other side of the fence to hurl hysterical accusations at Strauss that he was some kind of Nazi sympathizer. Unlike many of Strauss's critics, we do not and will not argue by innuendo. The charge is much too serious to be taken lightly, whether cheaply or dismissively by either Strauss's critics or his defenders. It is, however, a subject worthy of serious investigation, and we must follow the evidence wherever it leads us. The real challenge is to figure out how Strauss understood fascism as distinct from Nazism.

To begin with, the 1933 letter to Löwith is unique in Strauss's corpus because it represents one of the very few times that Strauss ever indicated his views on contemporary politics. That means something. The letter tells us, for instance, that Strauss preferred to live in a ghetto than crawl to "the cross of liberalism." It also means something that he appeals openly and unreservedly to the principles of Italian fascism, principles that he clearly distinguishes from and uses against those of National Socialism. In fact, Strauss is suggesting that fascism is the best antidote to the repulsive barbarism of Nazism. We have every reason to believe that, as a German Jew, Hitler's National Socialist party sickened Strauss. Nazism was, as Strauss wrote to Löwith, a "shabby abomination." Those who want to claim, however, that because Strauss was opposed to the Nazis he could not therefore be sympathetic to the broader principles of fascism are committing the same elementary and irresponsible error as those who argue that he was a Nazi sympathizer because he was opposed to liberal capitalism. It simply does not follow that a rejection of Nazism necessarily leads to a rejection of fascism in the same way that a Trotskyist rejection of Stalinism does not make one an anticommunist. Pro-Strauss and anti-Strauss partisans view him as they want to see him, oblivious to the facts of the case.

To understand Strauss's deeper meaning in the Löwith letter, we must raise a series of important questions. What exactly did Strauss mean by the principles of the Right? To which Right was he referring? What kinds of fascism were known by and available to Germans of Strauss's generation? To which principles of fascism might Strauss have been attracted? Why did he think that fascism might provide an antidote to Nazism? Does his understanding of fascism comport in any way with his later political views? How, for instance, should we understand his apparent support for fascism in 1937 with his later support (twice) for Adlai Stevenson in the 1950s and his support for Richard Nixon in 1972?[39] These are difficult questions that do not admit of obvious or easy answers, particularly given that Strauss's full meaning is surely lost in the sloppy grammar and muddied syntax of the translation. Still, they are questions that must be asked and answered. That Strauss's students have evaded raising and answering these questions only deepens the mystery.[40]

In order to clear the air and bring light to this important subject, one of the first things that an objective observer must do is to understand exactly what fascism stood *for* and *against* during this period. The obvious place to seek an answer to this question is the source itself. In 1932, the year before Strauss's letter to Löwith, Benito Mussolini (with Giovanni Gentile, the philosopher of Italian fascism) published the "Doctrine of Fascism," a fascinating document that lays out the core principles of fascism. A close reading of the text shows a remarkable similarity in language and substance between Mussolini's philosophy of fascism and the views expressed in Strauss's critique of Schmitt and in his speech on "German Nihilism."[41] A comparison between Strauss's views and the words of Mussolini will help us to make sense of the Löwith letter and its meaning.

Let us begin by summing up what we know about Strauss's basic philosophic principles during the early 1930s (particularly when read in the context of his lecture on "German Nihilism"), and then compare them directly with the principles of Mussolini's fascism.[42] First, Strauss was sympathetic to the nihilist-fascist critique of modern Enlightenment liberalism;[43] second, he rejected the liberal-bourgeois view of life's purpose and meaning;[44] third, he promoted an "organic" view of government and society over and against a "mechanistic" one;[45] fourth, he preferred a community-oriented to an individual-oriented public ethos;[46] fifth, he agreed with the young nihilists' call for a return to the closed society and a duty-based ethics;[47] sixth, he considered sacrifice (particularly during war) as the ultimate virtue;[48] seventh, he opposed a depoliticization of the community and instead favored some kind of paternalistic State;[49] eighth, he supported an omnipotent, corporatist State that actively controlled both the economic and the spiritual realms;[50] ninth, Strauss believed that the State has an obligation to positively shape and nurture man's spiritual place in the community,[51] and this should be done through State-mandated education[52] and a State-supported civil religion;[53] and finally, he (like Heidegger) sought a model of the closed society in ancient political thought and practice. This much, then, is clear: first, that Strauss's views in 1933 were much closer to those of Mussolini and Gentile than they were to those of John Locke or Thomas

Jefferson; and, second, that he preferred fascism to natural-rights individualism as the antidote to Nazism.

It should also be noted that Strauss's views during this period were not out of the ordinary; indeed, they were quite common. Given the ideological maelstrom of the time, many young intellectuals in the 1920s and '30s were experimenting with ideas from across the political spectrum. It should be recalled that many Western intellectuals prior to 1933—including many liberal, socialist, and "progressive" thinkers—were attracted to the principles and practices of Italian fascism.[54] Strauss was, apparently, one of those thinkers who studied and was influenced at some level by Mussolini during the early 1930s. According to his old friend and fellow Heidegger student Hans Jonas, Strauss "had a first-class philosophical mind" and was "an early supporter of Mussolini, before he turned anti-Semitic."[55]

There is more. We also now have concrete evidence that Strauss actually read and was influenced at some level by Mussolini. In a 1933 letter to Gerhard Krüger, written just two months after the letter to Löwith, Strauss indicates his familiarity with Mussolini's work: "We have seen how the entire modern world is creaking in all its joints. The enemies of *this* modern world, I mean the active ones, put forth solutions that are no less modern and thus fundamentally lead to the same negative result (see, for example, Mussolini's article on the state)."[56] The article that Strauss refers to here is none other than Mussolini's (with Giovanni Gentile) "The Doctrine of Fascism," which first appeared in the 1932 *Enciclopedia Italiana di scienze, lettere ed arti*. Strauss's meaning in the Krüger letter is rather ambiguous and open to two interpretations. The first would suggest that Strauss is lumping Mussolini in with those active enemies of the modern world who have not fully liberated themselves from modernity to be true or decisive critics. This reading would suggest that Strauss groups Mussolini with Carl Schmitt. A second possible reading would suggest that Strauss has learned from Mussolini that the enemies of modernity have not gone far enough in their critique of modernity. Either way, at the very least, Strauss was in fundamental agreement with Mussolini's critique of modernity, at least as far as it went. The only question is whether Strauss thought Mussolini went far enough.

As we bring this chapter to a close, let us briefly consider an interesting public lecture that Leo Strauss delivered in 1943 at the New School for Social Research in New York City on "The Re-Education of Axis Countries Concerning the Jews." Despite the lecture's title, Strauss limits his theme to Germany and to a discussion of any future reeducation of the German people in anticipation of an Allied victory. Curiously, this professor of political philosophy redirects his audience away from searching for a philosophic explanation for the rise of Nazism. Strauss did not think the "root of the difficulties" was to be found in "Nazi indoctrination," and he did not think that his American audience should

take the Nazi ideas "too seriously." Instead, he argues that the real meaning
of the Nazis' ascent to power will be found in their political actions, or, rather,
by "the prospect opened up by Nazi rearmament, by Nazi diplomacy, and by
Nazi arms." In other words, Strauss argues that the German people believed
that the expression of Nazi militarism through a "a short and decisive war" was
the "solution" to "*all* German problems," which means that the ultimate form
of reeducation for the German people would be the complete destruction of
its military. To the extent that Strauss is willing to consider the deeper philosophic ideas that led to the Nazi takeover of power in Germany, he does so in
a peculiar way. First, he assumes that the appeal of Nazism to most Germans
extended beyond the movement's anti-Semitism. In fact, he seems to suggest
that it was only a minority of Germans, in particular the "German Oberlehrer
[senior high school teacher] and the German Lutheran pastor," who were "the
most important carriers of the anti-Jewish virus." Strauss therefore seeks to
explain why the vast majority of ordinary Germans were attracted to Nazism,
which means that he looks for the deeper philosophic cause of Nazism shorn of
its anti-Semitic elements. What "guided" the "outlook, and hence [the] actions"
of most Germans was the

> crucial *implication* of the Nazi doctrine, viz. the implication that the needs
> of the German people as interpreted by the most efficient man in the land are
> the supreme law, not subject to any higher consideration. To put it bluntly,
> the Nazi education consisted in this: that they convinced a substantial part of
> the German people that large scale and efficiently prepared and perpetrated
> crime pays. I remember the argument of German students in the early 1920s:
> a country whose policies are *not* fettered by moral considerations is, other
> things being equal, twice as strong as a country whose policies are fettered by
> moral considerations. For 50% of all possible ways and means are rejected, as
> immoral, by the moralistic countries, whereas *all* ways and means are open to
> the unscrupulous country.[57]

What is most interesting about this statement is its compatibility with the "way
of Thrasymachus" (which Strauss says is a necessary component of any regime
and of the Platonic regime in particular) and its compatibility with those elements of Machiavellian prudence, of which Strauss seems to approve. Although
the complementary ways of Thrasymachus and Machiavelli are necessary, they
are insufficient ingredients for the life of Strauss's city. Standing alone, the
doctrines of Thrasymachus and/or Machiavelli are incomplete and maybe even
erroneous (just as Strauss thought the Nazi doctrine was "erroneous"), but they
are nonetheless necessary components of any regime.

In the face of an overwhelming Axis defeat, Strauss argues that "*the* refutation
of the Nazi doctrine," and with it the "re-education of Germany will not take

place in classrooms: it is, he argues, taking place right now in the open air on the banks of the Dnjepr [Dnieper] and among the ruins of the German cities." A crushing defeat is the most salutary form of instruction. But if such classroom re-education were to become necessary and possible, what should it teach? Strauss's answer, not surprising given his audience, is that the "true doctrine" is "liberal democracy," but he then goes on to list all the reasons why liberal democracy can have no "roots" in "German soil." Instead, Strauss suggests—with faint echoes of his May 1933 letter to Löwith—that his former countrymen might adopt something quite different: a "German form of collectivism," that is, "an authoritarian regime of bureaucracy based on a resuscitated authoritarian interpretation of Christianity."[58] In other words, a defeated Germany might overcome its Nazi past by adapting something like the broad principles and structures of fascist theory to the particular conditions on the ground in Germany, though purged of its anti-Semitism.

When charges were first leveled at Strauss that he was or might be a closet fascist, his partisan defenders demanded that such an irresponsible allegation be supported with real evidence beyond the tenuous connections linking Strauss to Nietzsche, Heidegger, and Schmitt.[59] Some such evidence is clearly now available. Strauss's recently published letters from this period do offer some incriminating evidence suggesting that Strauss was not only familiar with Mussolini's writings, but also that he had actually studied them and may have even been sympathetic to them. And then, of course, there is the Löwith letter. There is now compelling evidence to suggest that Leo Strauss did in fact flirt with fascism in the early 1930s. Readers thus must now judge for themselves whether Strauss was or was not a "friend" to liberalism.

In the light of the evidence provided in this chapter and previous chapters on Leo Strauss's Platonism, how are we to understand his seemingly elusive political thought? Did Strauss actually stand for anything beyond the politics of moderation and prudence? Should we accept Steven Smith's claim that Strauss was a "friend" to liberal democracy?

In sum, we think Smith was partially right, but for the wrong reasons. Strauss *was* a friend to liberal democracy when the times called for it, but he could also be a friend to fascism when he needed to be. Strauss could be all this and more, and he could do so without contradiction. Let us explain. Strauss could be a friend to fascism in 1933 for the same reasons that he would later become a friend to liberal democracy and for the same reason that he would be a friend to an Islamic theocracy if he were to live in Iran today or a friend to communism if he had moved to the Soviet Union instead of the United States. Politically, in the here and now, Strauss's philosopher is whatever he needs to be, which explains the chameleonlike quality of his thought. The true Platonic philosopher will befriend and improve whatever regime he lives under in order to protect his way of life. In the end, however, the evidence clearly suggests that Strauss's private and preferred political views came much closer to Mussolini's "Doctrine of Fascism" than to Jefferson's Declaration of Independence and First Inaugural, and this is for many of the same reasons that he secretly harbored admiration for Plato's best city in speech. Thus Leo Strauss must surely bear (indirectly) some small degree of responsibility for hastening the collapse of liberal capitalism and for helping to usher in the age of political collectivism and statism.

In our next chapter and in the Conclusion, we shall examine how and why Strauss's neoconservative followers have begun to think through and to work out the implications of Strauss's positive philosophic prescriptions and then apply them to American political life.

CHAPTER 10
NATIONAL-GREATNESS CONSERVATISM

Inspired by Leo Strauss's diagnosis of Western culture, neoconservatism has always found its most forceful and compelling voice in assessing and judging the state of contemporary American culture. Time and again, the neocons have argued that America is culturally sick, and the primary symptoms of which are decadence and moral flaccidity. The central problem with bourgeois American culture is that it is too concerned, according to Irving Kristol, with promoting a "healthy and happy life-style."[1] The pursuit of such values, according to the neocons, is an obvious sign of cultural decline. A free society, they contend, means the abolition of decency, community, and virtue.

Though the neocons would never admit this publicly, the philosophic source of the cultural decadence they loathe so much is inspired by the promise of the Declaration of Independence, or rather, a government that protects the rights of individuals, including the right to the pursuit of happiness (both material and spiritual). A secular capitalist society that frees its citizens to pursue their self-interest and happiness is, according to the neocons, one that leads to untrammeled individualism, an amiable philistinism, an easygoing nihilism, a vulgar commercialism, and a spiritual emptiness. Liberal capitalism, writes Adam Myerson, has "low aspirations," which ultimately lead to "dehumanizing tendencies." In their pursuit of health and happiness, Americans have become soft and lazy, so much so that they are unable to defend America at a time when it most needs defending. "In short," writes Irving Kristol, "millions of spiritually sick people are shopping around for a patent medicine of the soul."[2]

The neoconservatives are more than just nattering nabobs of negativity, however, and they are more than just feckless critics of modern American culture and politics. The neocons also offer real solutions to our current maladies. And "what medicine," what moral and cultural antivenin does Kristol "prescribe for a social order that is sick because it has lost its soul"?[3] Kristol and the neocons offer a two-step antidote for this cultural malaise: the inculcation of public *virtue* and the promotion of *nationalism*. Specifically, they support the public inculcation of those virtues (the means) that promote nationalism (the end). Consider, for instance, Kristol's seminal essay "'When Virtue Loses All Her Loveliness,'—Some Reflections on Capitalism and the 'Free Society,'" which is a classic neoconservative exercise in Straussian rhetoric and cultural analysis. The essay's title is taken of course from George Fitzhugh's 1854 proslavery tract, *Sociology for the South, or the Failure of Free Society*, an essay in which Kristol openly sanctions Fitzhugh's call for the creation of a society in which virtue regains "her lost loveliness." The comprehensive, all-consuming virtue that Kristol, David Brooks, and their fellow neocons seek to restore is the classical-republican virtue of sacrifice, or, more specifically, the sacrifice of one's petty self-interest for the good of the whole. Ultimately, this means rejecting the "political metaphysics of modernity" and following Leo Strauss on "the long trek back to pre-modern political philosophy—Plato, Aristotle, Thomas Aquinas, Hooker, Calvin, etc."[4] The question, though, is, how does one get back to Plato?

During the early 1970s, Kristol, following Leo Strauss's lead, began to flirt with "the secular myth of nationalism" as an antidote to the internal contradictions inherent in bourgeois capitalism. As Kristol would have learned from Strauss, nationalism can serve as a kind of halfway house on the road back to premodern political philosophy. As religion waned in the late twentieth century, Kristol went in search of a new theory of political obligation that could unite a secular liberal society barely held together by the nonadhesive social glue of individual self-interest. The major weakness of a capitalist society, according to Kristol, is its supposed immorality—"the self-interested nature of commercial activity." In this, a market economy promotes a society in which individuals care more about the pursuit of their individual self-interest and happiness than the collective or national interest. The real problem with liberal-capitalist society for Strauss, Kristol, and Brooks, then, is that individuals do not sacrifice themselves to anything higher than themselves and their petty self-interest. More to the point, the deeper problem is that individuals are not willing in a liberal-capitalist society, as Leo Strauss noted, to make the ultimate sacrifice—to die *for* the State. Following Strauss, Kristol does not think that liberal utilitarianism has a compelling theory of civic loyalty that "will convince anyone that it makes sense for him to die for his country."[5] According to Kristol, however, nationalism, by contrast, provides that rationale. Promoting the idea and practice of *sacrifice*—sacrificing for something greater than the self—is therefore the neocons' great moral antidote for all that ails

America. Nationalism will inspire Americans to pursue the virtuous life and to practice the ultimate virtue.

By 1983 Kristol was prepared to argue publicly, following Strauss's lead, that neoconservatism was "not merely patriotic ... but also nationalist" in orientation. A decade later, he declared that the "three pillars of modern conservatism [by which he means neoconservatism] are religion, nationalism and economic growth."[6] In these modern times, even as the large nation-state replaces the small polis as the primary unit of political value, it is, as Strauss said, a halfway house between the polis and the cosmopolis. Nationalism will provide modern man with a shelter from the moral and cultural storm that Strauss and Kristol associate with a free society.

National-Greatness Conservatism

After Irving Kristol's conversion to nationalism, neoconservatism's ideological and journalistic redoubt, *The Weekly Standard*, began to formulate a new public philosophy or political theology for America, something they variously call "one-nation conservatism," "national-greatness conservatism," or "courageous conservatism."[7] Following Kristol and Strauss before them, David Brooks, William Kristol, and a new generation of neocons rediscovered the "nation" as the fundamental unit of political reality, "nationalism" as the rallying cry for a new public morality, and the "national interest" as the moral standard of political decision-making. This new nationalism, according to Brooks, "marries community goodness with national greatness." In general terms, the goal of this new political theology is to promote "American unity" and "national cohesion," thereby culminating in a "manifest American glory."[8]

The primary political vehicle by which the neocons hope to promote this new social "unity," "cohesion," and "American glory" is not through churches, but rather through their control of the government schools, which they insist must "serve the interests of the state as a whole." As the Straussianized neocon Walter Berns has written, Americans should "follow the advice of ancient wisdom and so educate our citizens that suppression and persecution become unnecessary and, since moral education requires some censorship, to avoid rulers who appoint censors like Herr Goebbels the tyrant and John Winthrop the bigot." In other words, we should elect rulers who will select the good kind of censor rather than the bad. Ironically, the neoconservatives are willing to use "suppression and persecution" through a system of government-run schools in order to avoid the suppression and persecution associated with public censorship of the bad kind. The good news, however, is that their censorship will find the golden mean between the tyranny of Herr Goebbels and the bigotry of John Winthrop![9]

The true character of neoconservatism's new political theology is best seen in the views of David Brooks, a commentator on the PBS *NewsHour with Jim Lehrer*, a regular columnist with the *New York Times*, and, in our view, the journalistic heir to Irving Kristol. In the late 1990s, Brooks began to lay out the principles of this new national-greatness conservatism. Like Strauss and Kristol before him, Brooks is contemptuous of the moral ethos associated with America's liberal-capitalist society. "American society," he writes, mimicking Strauss, "may now be too bourgeois," too animated by a "small-scale morality," too "prosaic and mundane," too "obsessed with risk avoidance and safety," and too concerned with "nothing but making money." The neocons scorn material comfort and security for ordinary Americans, and they instead extol some un-defined sort of spiritual duty and service. Drawing inspiration from Theodore Roosevelt's speech on "The Strenuous Life" (1899), Brooks is disdainful of a society that is "sunk in a scrambling commercialism, heedless of the higher life, the life of aspiration, of toil and risk." Something higher, something nobler, is needed in order to elevate Americans above their petty selfishness. Brooks warns Americans that if they "think of nothing but their narrow self-interest, of their commercial activities, they lose a sense of grand aspiration and noble purpose." What America needs therefore is a new public morality, a new moral vocabulary, a new "American idealism," and a new patriotism that will "act as a counter-vailing force to excessive individualism" and as an "antidote to the temptations of affluence."[10]

The grand moral purpose of national-greatness conservatism, or one-nation conservatism, is to energize the American spirit; to fire the imagination with something noble, majestic, and sublime; to advance a "unifying American creed"; to "make manifest American glory"; and to inspire Americans to look beyond their narrow self-interest to some larger national mission—to some mystically Hegelian "national destiny." The new American citizen must be animated by a moral ethos devoted to public service, which will inculcate new "nationalist virtues" such as "duty, loyalty, honesty, discretion, and self-sacrifice." The duty to self-sacrifice is, in particular, the heart and soul of the new moral ethos pro-moted by Brooks and the neoconservatives.[11] Their basic moral-political principle is as clear as it is simple: the subordination and sacrifice of the individual to the nation-state.

The role of government in the neocons' world of national greatness is not to protect our individual rights as it was for Jefferson and the Founding Fathers, but rather to "protect" Americans against what Brooks calls "embourgeoisement" and the miniaturization of the soul. In other words, the role of government is to protect us from the consequences of living in a free society. Ordinary Americans therefore need a government that will turn them away from "the easy comforts of private life" and nudge them toward "higher, more demanding principles and virtues." They need a government that will "inculcate virtue in the young" and guide them toward "grand causes" and "transcendent glories." They need a Platonic Guardian looking over them rather than a Night Watchman.[12]

Politically, Brooks's new nationalism (reminiscent of the nationalistic conservatism that arose in Germany in the 1920s and to which Leo Strauss's generation was so attracted) would use the federal government to pursue great "nationalistic public projects" and to build grand monuments in order to unify the nation spiritually and to prevent America's "slide" into what he calls "nihilistic mediocrity." The American people, he writes, need something grand, noble, and awe-inspiring around which to rally. They need to be "inspired by some larger national goal." It is important that the American people conform, swear allegiance to, and obey some grand central purpose defined for them by the federal government. Ultimately, Brooks proclaims, "American purpose can find its voice only in Washington." In fact, he goes so far as to say that the mental health of the American people depends on the government in Washington developing a purpose for the people: "Without a vigorous national vision, we are plagued by anxiety and disquiet."[13] If it was not for the philosophic vision of neoconservative statesmen, ordinary Americans would surely sink into the abyss of cultural neuroses.

Not surprisingly, David Brooks and his colleagues at *The Weekly Standard* viewed the twentieth-century *fin-de-siècle* as the nadir of American civilization. They were appalled by Bill Clinton's narcissism and by the response of the American people to Clinton's various infidelities, but they were even more dissatisfied with the narrowness and feckless impotence of Newt Gingrich's "Republican Revolution." As the Republican Party fiddled during the Clinton years, Brooks openly longed for politicians who might "dare to make great plans" and "issue large challenges to themselves and their country," but his pessimism turned to optimism—if not glee—after September 11, when he saw that America might be "entering an era of epic legislation" and an "age of government activism."[14]

Brooks and various Straussianized neocons believe that the federal government can and should play an active role in shaping American culture or the American regime. "The national-greatness ideal assigns the government," according to Brooks, the role of accomplishing great "national missions" and thereby setting the "national tone." It stands as a welcome relief to a modern American culture that "no longer speaks of a unified and coherent order." National-greatness conservatism therefore supports "great projects designed to physically and spiritually unify the nation."[15] Brooks therefore applauds what he calls an "activist" and "energetic" government that takes on big projects and builds great monuments—and the bigger the better. He wants the American people to aspire to "grand projects," to "greatness," and to "transcendent glories." Brooks praises almost giddily the great national projects undertaken by the federal government at the end of the nineteenth century that helped to forge a national culture. These projects included constructing a transcontinental railroad, instituting land-grant colleges, and, best of all, building the Library of Congress. (Brooks conveniently forgets to tell his readers two important lessons about the building of America's transcontinental railroads in the nineteenth century: First, three of the transcontinental railroads built with government assistance went bankrupt; and, second, that one railroad man in the nineteenth century, James J. Hill, built a successful transcontinental railroad without government assistance in the form of cash or land grants.[16]) However, for Brooks, building railroads, colleges, and libraries is not primarily about transportation and book-learning, but instead it serves a larger moral-political end, which is to forge a collective national identity and purpose and to liberate the ambitions of great American statesmen. Brooks euphorically described the construction of the Library of Congress in purely Hegelian terms: It symbolized, he wrote, the emergence of America as "a world-historical force." Likewise, Michael Ledeen, following his teacher, Machiavelli, "wants leaders to make the state spectacular."[17]

At its core, though, the neocons' national-greatness conservatism is more than just a political doctrine: It is—to repeat—a moral doctrine meant to serve, in the words of the pragmatist philosopher William James, as the "moral equivalent of war."[18] The idea is that neoconservative social planners will engineer a collective national purpose for decadent and nihilistic Americans. The moral goal of all this monument-building is to turn the individual away from his mere selfish interests and to redirect those interests toward some higher collective good. Brooks's national-greatness ideal will be "based on iron discipline," and its ideal citizen will extol virtues such "public service," "duty," and "self-sacrifice"—all of which must serve what Brooks calls "the greater good." Americans must learn to serve, he writes, "the public good, not merely private interest."[19] He goes on to argue that the highest and most ennobling form of life is self-sacrifice and devotion "to public service." In the eyes of the neoconservatives, the good life and the moral ideal for ordinary men is essentially one of discipline, obedience, renunciation, and selflessness. That which is right—naturally right—advances the public interest, not private interest; it is that which promotes the nation and its vision of greatness and not the pursuit of individual happiness. In Brooks's view, it is the duty of the individual to subordinate his petty personal ambition in order to serve larger national ideals. It is his duty, above all else, to sacrifice.

Brooks's ultimate message is: sacrifice yourself to the greatness, to the glory, to the grandeur of some mystical American mission, to some transcendent American destiny. The ideal American man, he argues, should negate and forego his individual values and interests and merge his "self" into some mystical union with the collective soul. In the end, Brooks wants to "remoralize" America by creating a new patriotic civil religion around the idea of "Americanism"—an

Americanism that will essentially redefine the "American grain."[20] In the neo-conservative universe, nationalism is the political end and sacrifice is the primary moral virtue.

The political embodiment of neoconservatism, the electoral standard-bearer of national-greatness conservatism is—or was—John McCain, whom the neo-conservatives promoted as the next Teddy Roosevelt. Consider, for instance, Brooks's support of McCain's 2000 and 2008 presidential campaigns. In a series of essays and op-eds, Brooks effectively developed a platform and a governing philosophy for the Arizona senator. He took McCain's straight-talk and feel-good patriotism and rewrote it for the senator by turning it into a new civil religion—the religion of the "American idea." According to Brooks, McCain is an "agent of creative destruction": His "brand of conservatism rejects the notion that the highest end of government is to leave us alone." Brooks applauds McCain for replacing "the old mostly libertarian attitudes toward government that characterized the 'Leave Us Alone' coalition" with an appeal to a public philosophy that says "public service is the noblest calling."[21]

At the heart of Brooks's rhetorical campaign to repackage McCain's public philosophy was his development of a new political theology for the senator. Brooks encouraged McCain's attempt to "redirect a religiously based moral conservatism into a patriotically grounded moral appeal." Under Brooks's tutelage, McCain's philosophy of governance conflates religion and patriotism, and thus it converts patriotism into a secular religion. We are told by his ghost-writing supporter at the *New York Times* that the Arizona senator's "faith-based institution is America." For Brooks, the religious becomes the patriotic and the patriotic becomes the religious. The two are and must be inextricably connected. Religion, when connected to politics, is the moral glue that unites people and gives them the inspiration necessary to lay down their lives for the collective good. Brooks likes McCain precisely because the senator urges Americans to "serve a cause greater than themselves," because he urges Americans to "serve the public good, not merely private interest."[22] This new civil religion advocated by Brooks and many neoconservatives will induce in the masses a kind of God-fearing, unthinking filiopietistic devotion to America's Founding Fathers and their religious heritage. Put differently, the virtue to sacrifice means the virtue to obey.

So how has John McCain promoted the neoconservative agenda? How is it that Americans, particularly America's youth, are to expend their patriotic desire to sacrifice and serve the nation? In a *Washington Monthly* essay published in 2001, McCain laid out his plan to expand Bill Clinton's signature AmeriCorps program—a domestic national service program that would enlist America's youth in programs to help their fellow Americans who are most in need. McCain, lisping the sentiments of Leo Strauss, Irving Kristol, and David Brooks, sets the ultimate moral meaning of his program in these terms:

Success, wealth, celebrity gained and kept for private interest—these are small things. They make us comfortable, ease the way for our children, and purchase a fleeting regard for our lives, but not the self-respect that, in the end, matters most. Sacrifice for a cause greater than self-interest, however, and you invest your life with the eminence of that cause.

Enlistees in McCain's National Civilian Community Corps program would be "'detailed' to work for organizations like Habitat for Humanity, the Red Cross, or Big Brothers/Big Sisters." But there is more. Eerily similar to militarized youth programs in pre–World War II Germany, the "McCain Youth" would "wear uniforms," "work in teams," "gather together for daily calisthenics, often in highly public places such as in front of city hall," and "live together in barracks on former military bases." The stated goals of this militarized program are to promote the idea of sacrifice for the common good, to foster "group cohesion and a sense of mission," to narrow the "gap between our nation's military and civilian cultures," and to promote the idea of the "citizen-soldier."[23]

The neoconservative vision of a good America is one in which ordinary people work hard, read the Bible, go to church on Sunday, recite the Pledge of Allegiance, practice homespun virtues, sacrifice themselves to the "common good," obey the commands of the government, fight wars, and die for the State. But of course they expect the people to leave the governing up to the neoconservatives. It is one thing for the American people to recite the Pledge of Allegiance and get all teary-eyed, but it is an altogether different thing to truly believe and support the idea that the actual purpose of their government is to protect the rights of American citizens and to otherwise leave them alone. The problem, of course, is that the neocons do not actually believe that the principles of the Declaration are philosophically true or socially desirable. The distance between the neoconservatives' view of government and that of the Founders is ably summed up by Walter Berns: "the formation of character is the principal duty of government."[24] By contrast, the purpose of government for America's Revolutionary Founders was not to make men virtuous, moral, or religious, nor was it to ensure that everyone has food, clothing, shelter, health care, education, and old-age pensions, and neither was it to regulate production and trade—all things, by the way, that are supported in one way or another by the neocons. The Founders, by contrast, instituted governments whose purpose was, in the words of the Declaration of Independence, to "secure these rights." The Founders' principles may be rhetorically useful for the neocons in their search for power, but these principles certainly cannot and should not be followed in practice.

In summary, the neoconservatives are the advocates of a new managerial State—a State controlled and regulated by a new mandarin class of conservative virtucrats who think the American people are incapable of governing themselves without the help of the neocons' special, *a priori* wisdom. They are the conservative version of FDR's brain trust, or rather, an elitist group of Platonic Guardians who want to regulate virtually all areas of human thought and action. In the end, they do not like and certainly do not trust the market because it undermines the idea that human action can and should be controlled and regulated by some central intelligence agency that has special knowledge of man's deepest spiritual needs and requirements. The only real difference between FDR's and the neocon brain trust is that both want to regulate slightly different areas of human action and thought in slightly different ways.

The neoconservative position may be summed up in a phrase: Platonic ends achieved by Machiavellian means. This is how they combine moralism and amoralism, idealism and realism. Their idealism elevates the nation to some abstract mystical entity, while their amoral realism (disguised as prudence) translates the abstraction into a practical course of action. This is how they reconcile the seemingly irreconcilable: the idea of sacrifice as an absolute duty with the principle that there are no absolutes. In other words, neoconservative idealism declares that there are no moral absolutes to guide individual action, but only morally absolute demands and commands in the name of the public interest. What this means in practice is that the nation is above or superior to individual moral principles. This is precisely what Irving Kristol meant when he described neoconservatives as "classical-realists."

The neocons thus combine the worst elements of the Left and of the Right. They actively support a government that regulates body and soul, the public and the private. As we have already seen, they support government control and regulation of the economy, as well as government control of people's moral and spiritual lives. The neocons want all aspects of human life to be brought into the public square and put up for examination and regulation. They want to regulate the bedroom as much as they want to regulate the boardroom.

Foreign Policy and the "National Interest"

National-greatness conservatism is not simply or solely a form of domestic policy, although that's its primary focus. It is also the animating force behind the neoconservatives' foreign policy. But what of their claim that their ultimate goal in foreign policy is to promote America's "national interest"? How can this be reconciled with their calls for international sacrifice? How do they reconcile their seemingly contradictory calls for self-interest (realism) and self-sacrifice (idealism)?

The neoconservatives are not simply prevaricating or speaking out of both sides of the mouth when they speak in the same breath of pursuing America's national interest and spreading democracy around the globe: They *are* committed to both. Explaining the paradox of their embrace of America's "national interest" and their demand for self-sacrifice globally will help reveal what is really behind the neoconservative foreign policy—and its Iraq policy in particular.

When most Americans hear the term "national interest" in foreign policy discussions, they think of our government protecting our lives, liberty, and property from foreign aggressors, both today and in the future. Thus when neoconservatives use the term "national interest," most Americans assume that they mean the protection of American lives and rights. But this assumption is wrong. To neoconservatives, the "national interest" means something entirely different than the protection of the lives and property of American citizens.

As we have seen already throughout this book, the neoconservatives have no real use for individual rights or, for that matter, the individual. For them the "national interest" is not about individuals and their rights, but about an abstraction: the nation. The neoconservatives are collectivists of a certain type—they are *nationalists*. Individuals' lives are only truly meaningful, say the neoconservatives, if they sacrifice for some collective, "higher" purpose that "transcends" their unimportant, petty, finite, ephemeral selves. That "higher" purpose is the *nation*. For neoconservatives, the *nationalistic* pursuit of "national greatness" *is* the "national interest." This is the interest not of an individualistic nation whose purpose it is to protect the rights of individual citizens, but rather of an *organic* nation whose "greatness" is found in the subjugation of the individuals it comprises.

The short-term goal of neoconservatism is to defeat modern progressive liberalism. Its long-term goal is to overcome the world created by the classical-liberal tradition, which means the world created by the American Revolution. Enlightenment liberalism is responsible, they believe, for the decadence, materialism, and selfishness that is prevalent in America today, and so the neocons seek to transcend it. To save us, we need to unite around a goal "greater than ourselves." We need to abandon our selfish concerns with our life, wealth, and happiness, and we must sacrifice for a great cause—for America. According to David Brooks, "Patriotism can serve as an antidote to the temptations of affluence."[25] But how does one encourage patriotism? Surely one way is to seek out a long-term foreign policy adventure, and do so all in the name of national defense and national greatness.

As we have seen already, the call to "national greatness" during the late 1990s became the rallying cry of leading neoconservatives. In their influential 1997 *Wall Street Journal* op-ed, William Kristol and David Brooks called directly for a new national-greatness conservatism that would have consequences for both domestic and foreign policy. They pined for leaders who would call America "forward to a grand destiny."[26] What kind of "grand destiny"? Brooks explains:

> It almost doesn't matter what great task government sets for itself, as long
> as it does some tangible thing with energy and effectiveness.... [E]nergetic
> government is good for its own sake. It raises the sights of the individual. It
> strengthens common bonds. It boosts national pride. It continues the great
> national project.[27]

Brooks and Kristol bemoaned America's lack of some grand mission with which
to achieve "national greatness." The lives of ordinary Americans were too full
of mundane pleasure-seeking, and as such, the pursuit of individual happiness is
not ennobling or heroic enough for the neoconservatives. The American people
need something larger than themselves to live for, pursuits above and beyond
their trivial pursuits. They need sacrifice—they need war.

The transcendent purpose of national-greatness conservatism is national
regeneration. Its immediate purpose is to rouse Americans from the dogmatic
slumbers of their petty bourgeois lifestyles and give them something grand and
noble to strive for both at home and abroad. A national-greatness agenda is the
neoconservative antidote not only to the narcissism of Clinton-era liberalism,
but also to the rugged individualism of Goldwater conservatism. The moral
goal of a national-greatness foreign policy is to inspire the American people to
transcend their vulgar, mundane, infantilized, and selfish interests for national
projects that promote a new moral and political culture of selfless service to the
nation. The neoconservatives' policy of bighearted imperialism will "relish the
opportunity for national engagement, embrace the possibility of national greatness, and *restore a sense of the heroic*."[28]

One of the major problems with pre–September 11 America, according
to Kristol and Kagan, is that the United States lacked a "visible threat" to its
"vital interests." This meant that the American people have been tempted "to
absentmindedly dismantle the material and spiritual foundations on which their
national well-being has been based." In other words, American foreign policy
should be constantly on alert and ready to fight in order to combat creeping
nihilism. Simply put, the American people need dragons to slay in order to prevent their slide into self-absorption and decadence. For Kristol and Kagan, the
main *foreign* policy threat to the United States comes not from any particular
foreign nation or force, but rather from "its own weakness"—particularly its
own internal moral weakness.[29]

The hornetlike use of American military power around the globe and the
exporting of American democratic hegemony is one important means by which
American moral confidence can be restored and maintained. Kristol and Kagan
lament the fact that the "overwhelming majority" of Americans "neither understands nor is involved, in any real way, with its mission." In order to combat this
moral and political lethargy, Kristol and Kagan advocate militarizing American

culture by narrowing the traditional "separation of civilian and military cultures." To do that, they support lowering "the barriers between civilian and military life" by involving "more citizens in military service." In doing so, they hope it will then give ordinary Americans a greater "appreciation of military virtues," not to mention an appreciation for "national greatness" and a "sense of the heroic." They also support a policy of domestic moral regeneration by "actively promoting American principles of governance abroad."[30] Good soldiers make good citizens.

Kristol and Kagan believe that if Americans do not have a "broad, sustaining foreign policy vision"—i.e., if they do not have a constant and "visible threat" to inspire their willingness to sacrifice, promote national unity, and pursue the "heroic"—they will be "inclined to withdraw from the world and will lose sight of their abiding interest in vigorous world leadership." The neocons hope that a reinvigorated foreign policy of aggressive confrontation with tyranny will inculcate both the virtue of self-sacrifice among the people as well as the virtues associated with statesmanship for the country's natural aristocracy.[31]

Not surprisingly, the neoconservatives are great fans of the most nationalist president in American history, Theodore Roosevelt. As Brooks points out, "One way to promote a sense of national unity, TR recognized, was to conduct an energetic foreign policy that demonstrates America's distinct national character and reminds a heterogeneous American population of its common role in the world."[32] Roosevelt, like the neoconservatives, worried that Americans were too inclined to focus on their own narrow self-interest, economic well-being, commercial interests, and, ultimately, individual lives. The American people need, the neocons believe, a common, inspirational goal. As Brooks writes, "Roosevelt urged an increase in military spending and called upon the United States to take a greater role in the Philippines. But his real concern was the moral health of the nation."[33] In urging that the United States play a greater role internationally, and in particular in China, Roosevelt said, "We cannot ... be content to rot by inches in ignoble ease within our borders, taking no interest in what goes on beyond them, sunk in a scrambling commercialism, heedless of the higher life, the life of aspiration, of toil and risk."[34] Max Boot praises Roosevelt for thinking that "only warfare could restore the 'barbarian' virtues," which he clearly thinks is a good idea. With faint echoes of the young Leo Strauss's antiliberalism and prowar views, Boot praises Roosevelt for restoring the "great manly virtues, the power to strive and fight and conquer" and for believing that it is only "through strife, or the readiness for strife, that a nation must win greatness."[35] In sum, foreign policy, according to Roosevelt and Brooks, serves a fundamental domestic purpose, which is to remind us who we are and to unite America around its destiny as a nation.

An aggressive, proactive foreign policy therefore serves a greater purpose—to raise Americans above their daily, selfish concerns and to provide them with a "higher life." As Brooks writes, "[Teddy Roosevelt] saw foreign policy activism and patriotism as remedies for cultural threats he perceived at home."[36] Thus in the same way that one-nation conservatism promotes an energetic domestic policy at home, it also promotes an energetic foreign policy abroad—and in both instances for the same reason. In fact, Brooks has equated the moral effects of an activist foreign policy to the effect of the frontier in promoting the pioneer spirit of eighteenth- and nineteenth-century America. In both instances, it promotes what Brooks calls—quoting Roosevelt—"the strenuous life" and what Boot calls the "'barbarian' virtues," which is precisely what hedonistic and soft Americans need. Neoconservatism therefore promotes an energetic foreign policy and an expanding "republican empire" precisely because "Americans will never devote themselves to democratic self-government at home if they do not see themselves ardently championing democratic self-government abroad."[37]

Americans sacrificing for the "higher" good of the nation and its "greatness" is what the neoconservatives mean by the "national interest." And in foreign policy, this is the sort of "national interest" they strive to achieve. But national greatness requires a mission—it requires real sacrifice for a higher purpose. What could be a more worthy mission for a great country than to be the world's policeman and liberator? How grand and ennobling is that? Going to war, sacrificing both treasure and blood in order to bring "democracy" and stability to strangers—this is a worthy mission for a nation like America, pronounce the neoconservatives. Their brand of nationalism is thus unique. Kristol and Kagan come out for "a nationalism ... of a uniquely American variety: not an insular, blood-and-soil nationalism, but one that derived its meaning and coherence from being rooted in universal principles first enunciated in the Declaration of Independence."[38] In other words, they advocate a nationalism that rallies around the "idea of America." They interpret the Declaration of Independence as a document promoting American imperialism.

While most nationalists in history have been imperialists, expanding their dominance over other nations by force, the neoconservatives are a different kind of nationalist. They are not imperialists in the conventional fascist or Roman sense. They do not advocate war for territorial expansion or to colonize other nations or to rule them directly or permanently. They do not advocate total war and absolute submission of the enemy. Why? Because this would not be "great" according to their notion of greatness. It would be too self-interested. To be great requires the self-sacrificial ethics of altruism. Furthermore, domination—or rather, establishing a benevolent hegemony in the world—does not require as much brute force as others think. Through the messiness of the democratic process in the countries America "liberates," we will be able to exert control over them.

So while the neocons do not actively support permanent occupation, they do want American forces stationed all over the world. Is this to protect us? Not really. They want to exercise the necessary statesmanship required to respond to that ever-changing *fortuna* associated with foreign affairs, to a world that is forever in flux and forever in conflict. A state of perpetual peace is not regarded by the neocons as either possible or even desirable—the world is never peaceful nor should it be. Nor would it be good for the world to be at peace, for if it were, where would the moral adventure come from? What of the great sacrifices gained through war? What of the nobility of battle? Max Boot seems positively light-headed and giddy at the thought that countries such as Afghanistan or Iraq might "cry out for the sort of enlightened foreign administration once provided by self-confident Englishmen in jodhpurs and pith helmets." (Boot clearly seems to delight at the thought of American statesmen strutting around Kabul in their jodhpurs and with pith helmets.) It is also interesting to note he supports establishing what he calls a "regency" government in Baghdad to match our regency government in Kabul.[39]

Permanent War as Constant Vigilance

We should not be surprised to learn by now that the neocons support a foreign policy of perpetual or permanent war (both ideological and military), the purpose of which is to serve the moral goals associated with their domestic policy. Why? Because they believe that an energetic and muscular foreign policy—one that includes military intervention abroad, war, regime change, and imperial governance—will keep the American people politicized and therefore virtuous. By keeping America on alert and in a state of semipermanent war, ordinary Americans will overcome their nihilistic and individually selfish tendencies and learn to serve a cause greater than themselves. This is one important reason why, for instance, the neocons have supported over the last twenty years wars or American military intervention in Panama, the Persian Gulf, Somalia, Haiti, Bosnia, Kosovo, Afghanistan, Iraq, and, more recently, Sudan. They seek grand and ennobling missions so that the American people can restore some semblance of their original virtues—or acquire new ones. By saving the world from tyranny, America would save itself from itself.

Following Machiavelli and Carl Schmitt, Leo Strauss and his neoconservative students believe that a critically important means of establishing internal political order, social cohesion, and public virtue is through the fear or reality of an external threat. As the Straussianized Carnes Lord has made very clear: "statecraft is the art of using wars and other instruments available to political leaders to attain national goals."[40] The perceived menace of a common enemy serves the salutary function of uniting otherwise selfishly individualistic and hedonistic people. Machiavelli once argued that healthy republics must frequently return to their first principles and restore their founding virtues, chief amongst which was the virtue of self-sacrifice. This was particularly true of commercial republics, which liberated the individual's concern for his own interest. War, or a state of semipermanent war, is the best recipe for maintaining a state of constant vigilance and virtue in the republic. In this way, the neocons surely seem to follow the lessons of Machiavelli.

Furthermore, by keeping America involved in perpetual democratic nation-building around the world, America's intellectual and political elite will be given the opportunity to exercise statesmanlike virtues. As we have seen already, the Straussianized neocons are great proponents of the nobility of statesmanship and its public and private rewards, and so they are deeply concerned about promoting the conditions that make it possible. There is and can be no statesmanship without politics, and there can be no great or truly magnanimous statesmanship without war, so the neocons fear and loathe moral and political principles that delegitimize or depoliticize the realm of politics. "Paradoxically," writes Michael Ledeen, "peace increases our peril, by making discipline less urgent, encouraging, encouraging some of our worst instincts, and depriving us of some of our best leaders." By contrast, war and "military preparation provides a real test of character, and in the best circumstances creates a pool of leaders for the nation."[41] A condition of permanent war, a policy of benevolent hegemony, and the creation of a republican empire means (with its various regency governments) that there will always be a need for politics and statesmanship.

The causes and consequences of the Iraq War should now be of no surprise to us. It was a war not dedicated to protecting individual Americans' interests or to furthering any rational, individualistic meaning of America's national interest. Rather, it was a war devoted to the "national greatness" of endless "sacrifice[s] for the [alleged] freedom of strangers," motivated by the idea that America needs a moral, noble adventure.[42] Here, then, is the real reason for the Iraq War. It presented an opportunity for Americans to forget their daily selfish routines, to take on a grand cause, and to reignite their primal patriotism. And what kind of cause would the Iraq War inspire? A strenuous one, a cause requiring sacrifice of treasure and blood; a noble cause that would better the lives of "strangers"; and a cause that would reinvigorate America and unite her around a common purpose. The neocons found the ultimate antidote to nihilism: war and imperialism.[43]

Nihilism and Perpetual War

As we conclude this chapter, we can now identify the deeper purposes of neo-conservative foreign policy, purposes that are often hidden from public view.

Our central thesis is that neoconservative foreign policy is a special branch of its domestic policy. The purpose of neoconservative foreign policy is *not*, in the words of Irving Kristol, to serve "a myopic national security." Instead, its ultimate purpose is twofold: first, to *re*moralize the citizens of the United States, and second, to advance America's "national destiny." These two purposes are, of course, connected. By advancing our destiny through sacrifice and hardship, we remoralize our citizens. In the revealing words of William Kristol and Robert Kagan, "The remoralization of America at home ultimately requires the remoralization of American foreign policy."[44]

This explains why the neocons were bursting with ambition at the horror of September 11, 2001. Here, finally, was an epochal event and a defining moment, something they could turn into a national mission. It was a tragedy they could use to save America from its moral descent into nihilism, to give Americans a mission, one that is disguised as a war to end the Islamist threat. However, it really aims to give the American people a higher purpose, a goal that is a vehicle for them to not only forget their daily, material, and insignificant concerns, but to elevate them to greatness. With September 11, the neoconservatives finally got their "serious moment, M-Day, war," as Leo Strauss put it in his speech on "German Nihilism."[45] They got the ultimate excuse to pursue a "national-greatness" agenda through foreign policy.

Consider the following passage from the lead editorial of *The Weekly Standard* the week after September 11, the deadliest foreign attack ever on American soil. Before you read it, though, recall how *you* felt at that time and how much you wished you could return to the seemingly peaceful state of September 10, and also recall Strauss's thoughts on post–World War I Germany:

> We have been called out of our trivial concerns. We have resigned our parts in the casual comedy of everyday existence. We live, for the first time since World War II, with a horizon once again.... [There now exists] the potential of Americans to join in common purpose—the potential that is the definition of a nation.... There is a task to which President Bush should call us ... [a] long, expensive, and arduous war.
> ... It will prove long and difficult. American soldiers will lose their lives in the course of it, and American civilians will suffer hardships. But that ... is what real war looks like.[46]

The Weekly Standard practically celebrated the slaughter of thousands of Americans. Why? Because the slaughter created "the potential of Americans to join in common purpose—the potential that is the definition of a nation." Even if a "long, expensive, and arduous war" were necessary to defeat the enemy that struck on September 11—which it is not—it is profoundly un-American and morally obscene to treat such a war as a positive turn of events because it generates a collective purpose or "horizon." (Note here the subtle allusion to Strauss's language in his review of Carl Schmitt's *The Concept of the Political.* The neoconservatives turned September 11 into a positive good because they saw it as a catalyst that could help Americans to discover a "horizon beyond liberalism" and to recapture the loveliness of virtue.)

Observe also the scorn with which this editorial treats the day-to-day lives of individuals in a free nation. Pursuing our careers and creative projects, building skyscrapers, making money, participating in rewarding hobbies, enjoying the company of friends, raising beloved children—these are desecrated as "trivial concerns" and "parts in the casual comedy of everyday existence." The editorial makes clear that its signers think the exalted thing in life is "the potential of Americans to join in common purpose"—not the potential of individual Americans to lead their own lives and pursue their own happiness. This is the language of those who believe that each American is merely a cog in some grand collective machine, to be directed or discarded as the goal of "national greatness" dictates—a goal, of course, that is not determined by you or me, but instead by our national leaders. By contrast, in an individualistic view of the "national interest," a war is a *negative necessity*; it is something that *gets in the way* of what individuals in a society should be doing, which is living their lives and pursuing their values and happiness in freedom. Not so for the neoconservatives.

And there's more. In the immediate aftermath of the attacks, David Brooks praised President Bush's leadership not because he was preparing to eliminate America's enemy (that, after all, would be the "myopic" concern with "national security"), but rather because his rhetoric was "infused with moral purpose" and he encouraged Americans to join him in a "great moral struggle" in the war on terrorism.

Not surprisingly, September 11 saw a significant increase in external expressions of patriotism (a crucial virtue for molding a "good" society), and the neoconservatives loved it. September 11 and the subsequent invasion of Iraq provided them with an opportunity to restore American virtue at home. They saw an indefinable and potentially never-ending "war on terror" as an opportunity for Americans to restore a sense of shared purpose and to sacrifice for the common good—and sacrifice they have. As Herbert Croly, one of the neoconservatives' favorite political theorists and the intellectual guru to Theodore Roosevelt, once put it: "The American nation needs the tonic of a serious moral adventure."[47] September 11 was the neocons' tonic.

In January 2001, eight months before three passenger jetliners slammed into the towers of the World Trade Center and the Pentagon, causing the gruesome deaths of several thousand innocent individuals, Michael Ledeen, a leading neoconservative thinker, published what is surely the most stunning, the most revealing, and the most repulsive neoconservative statement on the relationship between foreign and domestic policy, between war and virtue. In a book explicitly extolling Machiavelli's virtues and their relevance for us today, Ledeen writes:

> Of course, we can always get lucky. Stunning events from outside can providentially awaken the enterprise from its growing torpor, and demonstrate the need for renewal, as the devastating Japanese attack on Pearl Harbor in 1941 so effectively aroused the United States from its soothing dreams of permanent neutrality.

America got "lucky," in Mr. Ledeen's words, and the neoconservatives got the war they wanted—a war not intended to defend America, but rather to help it overcome its devotion to individualism, capitalism, and prosperity and to renew its Spartanlike virtues of sacrifice and duty. But there is more. Consider Ledeen's Machiavellian praise, with its echoes of Strauss's lecture on German nihilism, for the salutary effects of war:

> Preparing for war makes you tough, and reminds you of the qualities necessary for victory: cold, prudent judgment, alertness to changing conditions, bravery under fire, courage when challenged, solidarity with your comrades-at-arms, and total commitment to mission. Such preparation is physically and mentally taxing, leaving little time or energy for the enjoyment of luxury. Furthermore, the good warrior is dedicated to advancing the common cause ... not his own personal situation.[48]

In the end, *this* is what neoconservatism is all about, and this is precisely why neoconservatism must be defeated on the battlefield of ideas. This is precisely the kind of rhetoric that Strauss ascribed to himself and to the "young nihilists" of the 1920s as they prepared to eradicate classical-liberal principles and institutions from Europe so as to replace them with some form of fascism. In the simplest moral and political terms, neoconservatism is about sacrificing one's "personal situation" to the "common cause," which must, of necessity, mean employing benevolent coercion over time, not only abroad but also within America's borders and on the American people.

Surely this is *not* what the American spirit of liberty is all about. Surely this is *not* what it means to be "in the 'American grain.'"

CONCLUSION
IN THE AMERICAN GRAIN

The United States of America was the first nation in history to build its constitutional, political, social, and economic institutions on the basis of an explicit philosophy and moral law. In the first essay of *The Federalist,* Alexander Hamilton identified the significance of the American Revolution and its unique place in world history. Hamilton wrote that it had been reserved to the American people "to decide *the* important question, whether societies of men are really capable or not of establishing good government from reflection and choice, or whether they are forever destined to depend for their political constitutions on accident and force."[1] Hamilton's view—that America was founded consciously on the basis of reason (i.e., "reflection") and free will ("choice"), on philosophic principles and on the consent of the people—was shared by the entire Revolutionary generation, and it goes to the core of America's singularity.

Hamilton and his fellow Revolutionaries delineated a necessary relationship between reason and liberty. They understood that reason requires freedom in order to function—to explore, experiment, and create. In his *Notes on the State of Virginia,* Jefferson self-confidently expressed the ambition and hope of the Enlightenment: "Reason and free inquiry are the only effectual agents against error.... They are the natural enemies of error, and of error only.... Reason and experiment have been indulged, and error has fled before them. Truth can stand by itself."[2] America's unique political culture was defined originally by a rational commitment to certain moral and political values considered to be self-evidently true rather than defined by blind loyalty to blood, tribe, and custom. The Founders' view of man as rational and free led them to believe that man was capable of self-government in the full sense of the term, which in turn led them to claim that individuals are the primary unit of moral and political value. In other words, they elevated the sovereignty of the individual to the center of American life.

The great accomplishment of America's revolutionary founding, then, was to translate theory into practice. The American Founders' appeal to reason led ultimately to the idea that men can and should deal with one another voluntarily as free agents and that they are capable of settling their disputes through a process of rational persuasion and public deliberation. Thus did America's founding statesmen accomplish, in the words of James Madison, "a revolution which has no parallel in the annals of human society."[3] America was founded as a philosophic experiment, as a *Novus Ordo Seclorum* (a new order of the ages). It was the first nation to recognize publicly man's nature as a rational and volitional being, and it was the first to ground its political, social, and economic institutions on an absolute moral law: the rights of man. The founding of America's revolutionary republic was the high point of the Enlightenment.

The Founding Fathers' genius was to subordinate society and government to this overarching moral law. The Founders believed that human happiness requires freedom, and that freedom is impossible without a limited government that protects rights. At the heart of their experiment was a recognition that the moral law begins with the individual's freedom to think and to act on his own judgment; to pursue property and happiness in accord with one's ability, vision and effort; to live free of the burdens, demands, and constraints of Old World traditions, laws, and hierarchies; and to build new communities on the basis of voluntary association and new governments on the basis of consent. James Wilson, a leading framer of the Constitution of 1787, summed up quite admirably the new American view of the individual and his relation to government: "Does man exist for the sake of government," he asked, "[o]r is government instituted for the sake of man?"[4] The American people infused their various social-constitutional-political systems with a moral code that dramatically limited the coercive power of the State and greatly expanded the sphere of individual freedom. They established a system of government that limited power by dividing, separating, checking, and balancing its grasping tendencies.

America's founding generation understood that government is defined by one fundamental fact: its monopoly on coercive force, or, rather, the power of government officials to bend the will of a man against his consent to the wishes and commands of the government. Throughout history, government coercion had been used to demand obeisance and obedience from its citizens and to command people in what they might think and how they might act. In America, by contrast, the Founding Fathers sought to limit if not eliminate the ability of governments to *initiate* force against innocent citizens. James Madison, father of the Constitution, summed up succinctly the Founders' general view of government in the following terms: "That Government is instituted and ought to be exercised for the benefit of the people; which consists in the enjoyment of life and liberty, with the right of acquiring and using property, and generally of pursuing and obtaining happiness and safety."[5] The Founders' liberalism stripped the traditional State of its power to dictate what men may believe and how they might live, and it denied the State the authority to mold its citizens into a prefabricated model of the just and good citizen. The American Founders expanded the realm of individual freedom by contracting both the ends and the means of government. In some fundamental sense, these are the principles that define the distinctive way of life known as Americanism.

Neoconservatism Versus Americanism

Given what we now know of neoconservatism, it seems fitting that we return one last time to Irving Kristol's declaration that neoconservatism is the only "ism"—certainly the only conservatism—that is "*in* the 'American grain.'" This is a remarkable claim, but it is one that should be taken seriously and subjected to critical analysis. We therefore conclude this book by summing up the nature and meaning of neoconservatism and considering whether neoconservative ideas and policies are "in" or "outside" the 'American grain.'"

How do the neocons evaluate the philosophy of Americanism sketched ever so briefly in the preceeding pages? Pointedly, Leo Strauss and the neoconservatives are, at a deep and unseen level, opponents of all that is unique about the American experiment in free government. America's fatal flaw is, they argue, connected directly to the Founders' moral and political vision. The neocons reject the two defining characteristics of man's nature on which America's Founding Fathers established their Revolutionary governments (i.e., reason and choice), which means that they also reject the core moral-political principles of the American Revolution derived from reason and choice (the pursuit of individual happiness, individual rights, limited government, and laissez-faire capitalism). They seek to replace the Founders' view of man and society with something more "ennobling."

Strauss-influenced neocons reject Enlightenment reason as the modern god that failed. Following his teacher, Leo Strauss, Irving Kristol has abandoned the Enlightenment's "faith in the ability of reason to solve all our problems, including our human need for moral guidance." In his clearest statement rejecting the ideas and principles on which America was founded, Kristol, clearly following Strauss, claims that:

> *Secular rationalism has been unable to produce a compelling, self-justifying moral code.* Philosophical analysis can analyze moral codes in interesting ways, but it cannot create them. And with this failure, the whole enterprise of secular

humanism—the idea that man can define his humanity and shape the human future by reason and will alone—begins to lose its legitimacy. Over the past thirty years, all the major philosophical as well as cultural trends began to repudiate secular rationalism and secular humanism in favor of an intellectual and moral relativism and/or nihilism.[6]

Consider what Kristol is really saying here. The fact that modern philosophers have abandoned Enlightenment reason seems to be all the evidence he needs to *know* that reason is indefensible—and with it the moral principles associated with Enlightenment liberalism. Consequently, man's only choice today is to accept traditional modes of belief (religion and inherited manners and mores) on the one hand or postmodern subjectivism on the other. In any such contest, the neocons come down invariably on the side of religion—not because they think it is *true*, but rather because it has salutary or utilitarian effects for society as a whole. This, however, is a false alternative.[7]

Directly connected to the neocons' rejection of Enlightenment reason is their rejection of the Enlightenment idea of free will or "choice," or, rather, the right, responsibility, and freedom to choose how to live one's life. They do not deny that man has free will as such, but, given their view of human nature, they tend to view human volition as ultimately driven by what they see as man's lowest desires, impulses, and passions rather than by his higher faculties. Following Plato, Machiavelli, and Strauss, the neocons typically view human nature as fundamentally low and base, or at least they view most men as living lives guided deterministically by their basest desires. They believe therefore that most men will naturally run to the gutter and stay there if their moral choices are not guided daily by the moral precepts of religion and/or the political regulation of enlightened statesmen. They believe that most men cannot and should not be left free to pursue their own individual happiness or to use their own judgment to make their own choices about what values and forms of happiness to pursue and how to pursue them. The problem is that most men will make bad choices. This is precisely why they emphasize duties over rights. Rights imply the freedom to choose and act, but duties imply control and command. The neocons believe that we all have enforceable moral obligations to our "collective self"—the nation. The duty to obey implies a right to command, and the right to command implies the force necessary to make one's duty to obey meaningful.

William Kristol has made the neoconservative position on reason and free will very clear: "[neo]conservatism's more fundamental mandate is to take on the sacred cow of liberalism—choice." Kristol is not simply rejecting the modern liberal's subjectivist theory of choice, but also the classical-liberal theory of choice. Kristol's friend and sometimes coauthor David Brooks opined approvingly during the 2008 Bejing summer Olympics that the "Western idea of individual choice is an illusion." He went on to praise the Chinese communists for putting much more emphasis on the collective good and what he calls the harmony of "social contexts."[8] For the neocons, "choice" is synonymous with the liberation from all "natural" standards and norms (e.g., birth control), and liberation is synonymous with moral nihilism. The neocons' solution to the very real problem of subjectivism and nihilism is to throw out the idea of choice altogether and, with it, the idea of individual rights. Having rejected reason and choice, at least as it applies to ordinary men and women, the neocons have therefore concluded that the only way in which ordinary citizens can be brought to virtue is through controlling and manipulating the incentive mechanisms of the State by a specially trained intellectual elite who have "*a priori* knowledge" or a "divination" of what is good for the people.

This is obviously not a position that the neocons can advocate openly, so they have developed policies and use a rhetoric that speaks in an American idiom. The neocons are thus advocates for a kind of *faux* "choice" that presents the common man with a limited and proscribed range of "choices" predetermined by government officials. Put another way, they promote what we have described in chapter 2 as *regulated choice*. Thus the neocons *appear* to be for "choice" when they are seeking the political support of free-market conservatives on issues such as education or health care, but against "choice" when they are seeking the political support of social conservatives on issues such as pornography or abortion. Occasionally, they claim to be for "choice" in the following way: If the American people want (i.e., choose) Social Security or Medicare, then we should give it to them because that is what they want and it's a good choice. However, if they choose or want liberal drug laws or stem-cell research, we should not give it to them because sometimes they want things that are not good for them. In other words, the neocons approve of "choice" when ordinary Americans make choices of which the neocons approve, and they oppose "choice" when the people make choices of which they do not approve.

Either way, the neocons claim to have an *a priori* knowledge of what is good for the American people, and they are willing to use the government to control man's material and spiritual choices in order to superimpose *their* view of the good life on the people. Michael Ledeen makes the neocons' Machiavellian point with unusual clarity: Machiavelli saw—and so should modern Americans—that "compulsion ... makes men noble, and enables them to remain free, while abundant choice is dangerous, leads to chaos, and leaves men at the mercy of their enemies."[9] In other words, government compulsion should be used against ordinary American citizens and their choices should be restricted so that America can remain the land of the free!

Politically, the neocons combine the worst vices of both liberalism and conservatism. Whereas American conservatives want to regulate man's spiritual or moral concerns (e.g., abortion, pornography, drugs, education) and liberals want to regulate man's material concerns (e.g., property, production, trade), the neocons want to regulate both—but moderately so. Neoconservatism is, to use two rather old-fashioned terms, collectivist and statist in nature. The neocons differ from various enemies of a free market with regard to particulars and specific programs, but they share with them all a belief that they have a *natural* right to control the lives, property, and happiness of others; that selfishness and the profit motive are morally tainted; that those who have achieved owe a moral debt to those who have not; and that freedom and those who work and produce in a market society should be controlled by those who have divined the public interest. For Strauss and the neocons, the pursuit of wealth and pornography are both elements of the same evil: base selfishness. The neoconservatives therefore seek to impose their moral code on the rest of the country by force of law, which means promoting policies that regulate what goes on in the boardroom as well as in the bedroom.

Not surprisingly, the neocons support the concentration of power in a comprehensive State—one that regulates man's material and spiritual concerns—albeit one governed by moderate and prudent statesmen. When viewing the neocons' political goals in the context of the *purpose* of government, we can see that they view the management of the economy, the regulation of business, the redistribution of wealth, the censorship of art and literature, the indoctrination of children with government-approved ideas in government-run schools, the inculcation of public virtue, the regulation of what people do in the privacy of their homes, and the self-sacrificial exportation of democracy to foreigners as legitimate purposes of government. The neocons are, we fear, laying the groundwork for a new kind of soft despotism that will surely pave the way one day for despotism of the hard variety.[10]

What this really means, of course, is that the neocons are opposed to the moral conditions of a free and truly virtuous society. In a free and virtuous society, physical force is prohibited from social relationships, but individuals in such a society also require a strict moral code based on an absolute standard of right and wrong.[11] The neocons reject both freedom and virtue rightly understood. They want to create a society no less regulated—indeed, in many ways more regulated—than the modern liberal-socialist state. More fundamentally, however, they want to create a society in which the rational and independent judgment of ordinary men is dulled, restricted, denied, and ultimately replaced by unthinking obedience. The neocons understand that in order to advance their political agenda, they must first prepare men epistemologically and morally; they must undercut a man's confidence in his ability to think, judge, and act independently. Their willingness to use force to control and regulate the images of the cave is a negation of the mind and a precondition for compliance. There is no place for the virtues of rationality, honesty, justice, and independence in the neoconservatives' moral lexicon. Virtue in their world means to sacrifice one's interests to a "higher cause" and to obey one's unchosen duties in the name of the "public interest."

The neocons do, however, get one thing right: It is true, as they often say, that we live in an age of moral crisis. Their message appeals to many Americans precisely because it appeals to that very sense of moral crisis that many Americans experience—and also because it comes gift-wrapped in the unique language of Americanism. Whereas the Old and New Left have always criticized openly America's founding principles, the neoconservatives have assumed a different approach to changing America. They are idiomatic experts at feigning verbal fealty to America's founding ideals as they simultaneously denounce them in private. Their exoteric rhetoric is calculated to appeal specifically to an American audience. The neocons typically adopt the traditional terminology and values associated with the American Founding Fathers and great American statesmen such as Abraham Lincoln; they are masters at using patriotic slogans and value-laden principles that trigger in most Americans a sentimental attachment to the neoconservative message—and they do all this at the same time that they sublty debunk and defame those very same principles. Thus neocons keep up the exoteric charade that they are the champions of ideas that their esoteric philosophy systematically undermines. Many Americans have been seduced by the neoconservative message because they see in the neocons (mistakenly) allies in their effort to restore the original code of Americanism.[12] Little do they know, however, that neoconservatism is an ideological pied piper marching them in the opposite direction, and that by joining the neocons they support their own philosophic enemies.[13]

What fundamental truths and core American values do the Straussianized neoconservatives struggle to evade, hide, or annihilate? Once one peels away the outer layers of their sentimental but disingenuous patriotic rhetoric, the answer can be summed up quiet easily: They reject the idea of *America* itself. And if there are two principles that describe what makes America unique and irreplaceable and that sets it apart from all other nations, they are the mutually reinforcing principles of *freedom* and *individualism*. But the idea of a truly free society makes the neocons very nervous. Indeed, they find it morally repulsive. They rarely ever write about freedom except to minimize, criticize, or to change its unique American meaning. They typically present themselves rhetorically as great defenders of freedom, but what they hide is their thoroughly collectivized understanding of the term. Freedom for Strauss, Kristol, and Brooks is synonymous with political or communal self-government (not individual freedom). Furthermore, self-government for Strauss, Kristol, and Brooks is synonymous with nationalist self-assertion and obedience to the commands of the government.

The "self" in the neocons' understanding of self-government refers not to the individual, but to a collective political entity: the nation-state. Obedience to the State is freedom for neocons like David Brooks, precisely because it is obedience to one's own self-legislating commands.

Not surprisingly, then, the neocons reject America's individualist heritage and its capitalist system. Brooks has, for instance, openly and explicitly mocked the rugged individualism of traditional Americanism and, more particularly, Barry Goldwater's vision and celebration of a "certain sort of person—that individualistic stout pioneer crossing the West, the risk-taking entrepreneur with a vision, the stalwart hero fighting the collectivist foe."[14] The neocons do not want an America where individuals are given a sphere of freedom and autonomy to solve their own problems and to improve their own lives as they think best. They have made that very clear. Instead, their goal is to diminish rather than to expand the sphere of freedom for ordinary Americans.

Although it is certainly true that the self-governing institutions and mores of ordinary Americans have eroded over the course of the last century, it is also true that some spark of that original spirit of liberty still burns in the American soul. Deep down, the American people respect business, entrepreneurship, and material wealth. The neocons, by contrast, dismiss such values as vulgar, hedonistic, and, worst of all, selfish. The American people applaud technological innovations while the neocons question technology because it corrupts man's proper relationship to nature. The American people admire rugged individualism and self-reliance as the neocons say these values destroy a sense of community and promote selfish virtues. The American people think the American dream is connected to pursuing one's own happiness, and the neocons think the pursuit of happiness is synonymous with hedonism. The American people respect virtues such as rationality, honesty, justice, integrity, productiveness, and well-deserved pride, but the neocons reject virtues that promote individual achievement for virtues that promote self-sacrifice in the name of the collective good. The American people think government should keep its nose out of religion and men's private affairs, while the neocons think government should use its coercive force to promote religion and public virtue. The American people want less government interference in their lives, and the neocons want more. Many Americans are suspicious of or reject the welfare state, as the neocons are proponents of an expanded welfare state. The American people believe that America is a great nation because it leaves them free to pursue great things, but the neocons believe that the federal government should design programs that would force the American people to do "great" things. Most Americans just want to be left alone from a hectoring "nanny" State. The neocons, however, want the State to inspire Americans to a higher calling and to national greatness. The American people love their United States. The neocons secretly sneer at America as low and vulgar.

A great nation does not need a government-sponsored philosophy of "national greatness." It does not have to tell itself or anyone else that it is great. It certainly does not export its greatness to other nations by force. Nor does a great nation build monuments to itself. The skyline of any American city, built as they all are with private monies for private purposes, trumps any "public" palace and monument of Europe, Asia, or Washington, D.C. The greatness of America is captured in a computer chip smaller than your baby-finger nail, in Amazon's Kindle reader, or in an iPod—not in the behemoth Library of Congress. American greatness is seen every day in the entrepreneurial genius of tens of thousands of ordinary Americans who improve the quality of our lives on a daily basis. It is defined by energy, resourcefulness, moxie, and the get-up-and-go attitude of private Americans pursuing personal profit—not in the commands of Washington central planners.

Ultimately, what makes America great is the implicit belief system that allows everyday Americans to pursue their own *selfish* values. America was made great by a moral and political system that left individuals free to pursue their goals and values—to be inventive, imaginative, and hardworking. America was made great precisely because the "Leave Us Alone" philosophy rejected by the neocons liberated ordinary Americans to achieve great things individually or through voluntary associations. The neocons, by contrast, believe that America's individualist heritage and "Leave Us Alone" mentality should be abandoned for a command-and-obey system of governance. They insist that the American people sacrifice their own narrow and petty goals, purposes, plans, and dreams for some grand and noble ideal (discerned through some kind of divination or intuitive insight that is conveniently unavailable to ordinary men and women). What this means in practice is that they will command obedience to *their* particular vision of national greatness. The Straussianized neocons are bothered by the fact that America's free and seemingly chaotic society is not governed by some overarching plan devised by some some magnanimous statesman.

The neocons are the conservative version of central planners: They hope to bring some kind of philosophic order and structure to the world. They believe that wise statesmen can best determine what the American people want or should want. These magnanimous leaders will gently and moderately (so they say) guide the nonrational and pleasure-loving mass of men and women toward some higher spiritual purpose that transcends the fanciful and sensual whims of the "self." However, they will, of course, use force (this they don't tell you) when their reason or myth-making is unable to convince the people to sacrifice their individual values in the name of the common good. In sum, the neocons' vision for America would deny individuals the right and responsibility to think, choose, and act for themselves. Instead, the American people must sacrifice their individual plans and purposes in order to obey the commands of their leaders in the service of some mystically intuited hierarchy of ends. There is no other way to assure that the actions of all the people will become one and move in a direction that fulfills the nation's call to greatness. This is what the neoconservatives mean by one-nation conservatism.

America, however, was not made great by the social engineers and collectivists of the Left, and it will certainly not be made great by the social engineers and collectivists of the Right. The mentality of all social planners—whether they be socialists, fascists, or neoconservatives—is the same: to impose on society an ideological blueprint to which all men will be expected and, when necessary, forced to conform. The "Leave Us Alone" creed that was emblematic of the Founders' liberalism stands in striking contrast to the neocons' view. The Founders were more modest in their view of government and the "wisdom" of government officials. They were much more optimistic in their assessment of the self-governing abilities of ordinary people than are the neoconservatives, who really do believe that the American people should be led by great statesmen. The neocons do not want to leave you alone. Straussianized neoconservatives would deny to individuals their right and their ability to pursue values of their own choice for better or worse, which has the ultimate result of actually denying to every man the right to act as an ethical agent.

Our position is, by contrast, crystal clear: We view neoconservatism as not only *outside* the American grain, but actually as a threat to the principles, institutions, and accomplishments that are America's unique contribution to Western civilization.

Could It Happen Here?

As we conclude this study of neoconservative thought and practice, let us return one last time to our animating question: To what does it all add up? More to the point: In which direction is the neoconservative "persuasion" taking America?

A central purpose of this book has been to demonstrate that neoconservatism *is* a comprehensive political philosophy. The neoconservatives want you to believe, of course, that neoconservatism does not add up to much at all, that it is just a "persuasion," an "impulse," or a pragmatic mode of thinking. More recently, the neocons have presented themselves as advocating a new politics of "moderation."[15] The burden of our argument throughout this book has been to suggest that the neocons' exoteric self-presentation is no more than a veil that masks a much more comprehensive and ominous political philosophy. All their talk about moderation and prudence is really only meant to disarm intellectually their competitors in the conservative movement who want to defend the Founders' principles of individual rights and limited government. The neocons preach moderation as a virtue so that ordinary people will accept compromise as inevitable. But a political philosophy that advocates "moderation" and "prudence" as its defining principles is either dishonestly hiding its true principles or it represents a transition stage on the way to some more authoritarian regime—or both.

Our deepest fear is that the neoconservatives are preparing this nation philosophically and culturally (whether they know it or not) for a soft, American-style fascism—a fascism purged of its ugliest features and gussied up for an American audience. This is a serious charge and not one that we take lightly. Let us be clear: We will not pursue this line of analysis, as have others, through insinuation or smear. Instead, the charge must be proved, or at least a reasonable case must be made based on real evidence. It is also important to note that our claim must be qualified in important respects. There can be no doubt that there is much about fascism, for instance, that the neocons would reject and oppose. In fact, any such association will no doubt appall them. Once again we want to emphasize that we are not suggesting that the neoconservatives are fascists. We argue instead that neoconservatism shares some common principles and features with fascism, that neoconservatism is outside the American grain, and that neoconservatism is paving the road for some kind of soft despotism that may in the end point toward some variant of fascism. An historical analogy may be useful here. Neither Bismarck nor Nietzsche were fascists, but most respectable historians think they certainly played some role in preparing Germans politically and intellectually for its introduction and acceptance. So too, we argue, with Strauss and the neocons. It is of course true that no neoconservative would admit publicly that what he supports leads to fascism. In fact, they would all, to a man, say they are opposed to it. How, then, are we to reconcile our fear with their denial?

Let us begin, then, by defining our terms. Because the term "fascism" has been so badly used and abused over the course of the last seventy-five years, it is important that we know more precisely what it really is. Given its ugly history and connection to Nazism, it is near impossible to have an intelligent conversation about the "F-word" in politics. The word as it is used today has little relationship to its original meaning. Let us therefore examine fascism more closely by clearing up three of the most common misconceptions about it. First, one can support fascistic ideas without being a Nazi. (Strictly speaking, as we stated before, all Nazis are fascists but not all fascists are Nazis.) Nazism is just one particular form of fascism, of which there have been many varieties. Second, fascism is not necessarily synonymous with anti-Semitism, although they are often found together. It is entirely possible for one to be fascist without being anti-Semitic. The idea or possibility of an Israeli fascism is not an oxymoron. Finally, one can also be a fascist without necessarily supporting violence and brutal aggression at home or abroad (at least in theory, though almost certainly not in practice). We might call this *naïve* or *soft fascism*. This kind of fascism is the preserve of certain intellectuals who naïvely assume that it is possible to create fascism's corporatist society without explicit indoctrination and authoritarianism, without coercion and violence, and without militarism and imperialism. We must always remember that fascism was born not on the streets with marauding youth gangs or in beer hall putsch's, but as an ideology, as a system of ideas, as the political stepchild of philosophers and intellectuals.

Fascism, because it is a nationalist movement and because every nation is different from every other, comes in many shapes and forms. Each fascist nation will be built on the manners, mores, and forms and formalities that arise in and are unique to particular localities. There can be fascist states, for instance, that are grounded in religion and fascist states grounded in secularism, just as there can be fascist states that are anti-Semitic and those that are not. Italian fascism was different from Spanish fascism, and both were different from German fascism. Fascism always begins as a localist movement based on an allegiance to one's nation, community, culture, religion, ethnicity, or race. If fascism were ever to come to the United States, it would no doubt take a unique form different from all the others.

At this point, a working definition of fascism—one that isolates its essential ingredients—would be helpful. The definition used by Jonah Goldberg in his recent book, *Liberal Fascism: The Secret History of the American Left from Mussolini to the Politics of Meaning,* is as good as any:

> Fascism is a religion of the state. It assumes the organic unity of the body politic and longs for a national leader attuned to the will of the people. It is totalitarian in that it views everything as political and holds that any action by the state is justified to achieve the common good. It takes responsibility for all aspects of life, including our health and well-being, and seeks to impose uniformity of thought and action, whether by force or through regulation and social pressure. Everything, including the economy and religion, must be aligned with its objectives. Any rival identity is part of the "problem" and therefore defined as the enemy.[16]

It should be obvious by now that Goldberg's definition of fascism bears a striking resemblance to neoconservative thought and practice. Like the fascists described by Goldberg, the neocons accept some of fascism's essential ingredients. Intellectual honesty and probity require of us that we examine the parallels more closely.

Let us begin with the intellectual doyen of neoconservatism, Leo Strauss. This much we know with certainty: In 1933 Leo Strauss was apparently sympathetic to certain fascist principles, and he seemed to think that fascism was the best possible option at the time. (Ten years later, he argued that liberal democracy was the best possible political option given the circumstances.) We also know that his anti-Enlightenment, antiliberal views were deeply influenced by those who clearly were or would become fascists and Nazis in the 1930s. Most importantly, we know that Strauss held views that could be described objectively only as fascistlike or in sympathy with many of fascism's basic tenets. That Strauss thought Hitler a barbarian does not change the fact, however, that he was nonetheless clearly attracted to a cluster of ideas that were fundamental to the fascist impulse. In the end, we might say of Strauss's politics precisely what he once said of Nietzsche's politics, namely, that what "Nietzsche says in regard to political action" is "indefinite and vague," and that "all political use of Nietzsche is a perversion of his teaching." Still, Strauss's books, like those of Nietzsche, were "read by political men and inspired them." Thus, he is "as little responsible for fascism as Rousseau is responsible for Jacobinism. This means, however, that he is as much responsible for fascism as Rousseau was for Jacobinism."[17] And so it is with Leo Strauss.

The neoconservative synthesis that grows out of Strauss's thought bears striking similarities to fascism. Like the fascists, Strauss and the neoconservatives reject the values and principles associated with Enlightenment liberalism—namely, reason, free will, egoism, individual rights, material acquisition and wealth, limited government, freedom, capitalism, science, and technology. In all, they are repulsed by the moral ethos associated with liberal-capitalism, individualism, and the "open society." Furthermore, they denigrate the bourgeois virtues as low and praise the nobility of the "barbarian" virtues such as discipline, courage, daring, endurance, loyalty, renunciation, obedience, and sacrifice.

Like the fascists, Strauss and the neocons are metaphysical collectivists: They take the nation as the primary unit of political value; they view the body politic as an organic whole; they support a closed over an open society; they prefer a community-oriented to an individual-oriented public ethos; they elevate the public and "the political" over the private and the economic; they glory in the mystical unity of the nation-state; they promote social duties over individual rights; they support using the coercive power of the State to promote order, unity, and cohesion; they demand that individuals subordinate themselves to the "public interest" and serve some fuzzy notion of "national greatness"; and they want Americans to pursue a morally serious life dedicated to a selfless service to the nation that culminates in the ultimate form of heroic sacrifice: death in battle.

Like the fascists, Strauss and the neocons are statists who strongly oppose a depoliticized—i.e., a Jeffersonian, "Leave Us Alone," Night Watchman—theory of government in favor of an all-embracing, paternalistic, corporatist, omnipotent State. They advocate using the coercive power of the State to regulate man's material life (the economy) and his spiritual life (the culture); they support a Bismarkian-inspired social-insurance state; they support government control of private property and the means of production; they advocate coordinating and harmonizing the nation into a unified whole through a system of government education, national service, and the building of great public monuments; they advocate restoring authority and order to society; they support the creation of a state-sponsored civil religion, the purpose of which is to turn the American people toward worshipping America's national destiny; they support using the State's police power to promote the virtuous society; and they believe that the people's ideas and values must be controlled by State censors.

Like the fascists, Straussianzed neocons downplay the importance of constitutional rules and boundaries, and they glamorize the virtues of great statesmen. They support transferring power to the exective branch of government and creating a "temporary dictatorship" as an "emergency" measure during times of imminent danger or "crisis"; they believe that life is or should be defined by conflict and that a state of ongoing peace and prosperity is morally degrading; they advocate keeping the American people in an agitated state of permanent fear and loathing against internal and external threats; they want to militarize American culture; they romanticize the virtues of war and empire as regenerative; and they support a foreign policy of hornetlike militarism and perpetual war in order to restore America's national destiny and sense of greatness.

In sum and point of fact, Strauss and the neocons share important core values with the principles of fascism. They make us feel comfortable with certain fascist principles by Americanizing them without our ever knowing it. They have seduced the American people into believing that a free and virtuous society is somehow compatible with government controls over all aspects of man's economic and spiritual endeavors. This is not the fascism of Nazi Germany or fascist Italy, but instead something rather different. It points toward what we might call *fascism-lite*—a fascism that is moderate, defanged, and well-suited to the smiley-face optimism of America's Ronald McDonald culture. It is a moderate fascism that is less filling but tastes great when packaged in the various rhetorical tropes of the "American grain." The neocons' nationalism is not, for instance, the "blood and iron" or the "blood and soil" or the "race and Volk" nationalism of Nazi Germany, and it is not the nationalism of racism and anti-Semitism. Instead, it is a nationalism wrapped in the symbols and rhetoric of American patriotism—the Declaration of Independence, Lincoln's Gettysburg Address, and the Pledge of Allegiance. The fascist impulse buried deep within neoconservatism is draped in American manners and mores, in its culture and institutions, and in its traditions and national symbols. It hides its fascistlike principles behind the rhetoric of Lincoln and Teddy Roosevelt.

To repeat: This is a serious charge and not one we make lightly. We do not mean to paint the neocons as cartoonish, goose-stepping, stormtrooping villains as do many on the Left. The fact of the matter is, however, that the neocons are opposed to America's traditional individual-rights republic and the foreign policy that goes with it, and they clearly want to move the United States toward something very different. Of this much we can be certain: The neoconservatives' deepest moral and political principles share more in common with Mussolini's "The Doctrine of Fascism" than they do with the principles of Jefferson's "First Inaugural." The modern social system that comes closest to their core principles is fascism, and the unintended consequence of their political and cultural policies is to move the United States of America quietly and gently in the direction of what we might call a Platonic fascism. In fact, it is probably truer to say that the sort of fascism advocated by the neocons is a means and not an end. It is meant to be, as Leo Strauss and Irving Kristol have intimated, a halfway house on the road back to Platonic political philosophy.

As we know, fascism comes in many forms, and it is not something that pops up over night. The transition from one social system to another takes place slowly and over the course of many decades and sometimes even centuries. It happens most often when ordinarily decent people come to accept and tolerate through ignorance, neglect, blindness, and moral cowardice ideas that have been slowly injected into the lifeblood of a nation through ideological and political subterfuge. The American spirit of liberty is not yet dead, but the neoconservatives have very subtly undermined its animating philosophy and political institutions. Following Strauss, the neocons have played an integral role in helping to deconstruct America's moral infrastructure.

Freedom has almost never been abolished at a single sudden stroke. It has always been lost slowly over a period of time and through a series of gradual steps. The neoconservatives have, through stealth and by imperceptible degrees, corrupted and softened America's individualistic culture and prepared its people to journey down the road toward some kind of *de facto* fascism.

Leo Strauss and the neoconservative intellectuals who follow him question and denigrate America's basic philosophic foundations, and they are at odds with the essential character of its culture, institutions, and individualistic people. The neoconservative intellectual movement has demonstrated repeatedly its unwillingness and inability to defend the political principles of a free society. Not only do its intellectual leaders refuse to validate philosophically the principles on which this country was founded, they see in those principles everything that is wrong with contemporary America.

In conclusion, the neoconservatives are the false prophets of Americanism, and neoconservatism is America's Trojan horse. Those who wish to defend America's Enlightenment values and the individual-rights republic created by its revolutionary Founders must therefore recapture from the neocons the intellectual and moral high ground that once defined the promise of American life.

NOTES

Introduction

1. See, for instance, David Brooks, "The Neocon Cabal and Other Fantasies," in *The Neocon Reader,* ed. Irwin Stelzer (New York: Grove Press, 2004), 41–42.

2. Irving Kristol, *Reflections of a Neoconservative: Looking Back, Looking Ahead* (New York: Basic Books, 1983), 74–75.

3. Norman Podhoretz, "Neoconservatism: A Eulogy," *Commentary* 101, no. 3 (March 1996): 19–27; Seymour Martin Lipset, "Neoconservatism: Myth and Reality," *Society* 25, no. 5 (July/August, 1988): 29–37.

4. David Brooks, quoted in Sam Tanenhaus, "When Left Turns Right, It Leaves the Middle Muddled," *New York Times,* September 16, 2000.

5. Brooks, "The Neocon Cabal and Other Fantasies," 41–42.

6. See Joseph Dorman, *Arguing the World: New York Intellectuals in Their Own Words* (Chicago: University of Chicago Press, 2001). On the differences between certain first-generation "neocons" and the second and third generations, see Michael Lind, "Intellectual Conservatism, RIP," *Salon,* September 22, 2009, www.salon.com/opinion/feature/2009/09/22/neoconservatism/print.html.

7. James Q. Wilson, contribution to "Neoconservatism: Pro and Con," *Partisan Review* 4 (1980): 509.

8. Daniel Bell, *The Cultural Contradictions of Capitalism* (New York: Basic Books Colophon Book, 1978), xi.

9. Among the academic attempts to draw a connection between Strauss and the neoconservatives, see Shadia Drury, *Leo Strauss and the American Right* (New York: St. Martin's Press, 1997); Anne Norton, *Leo Strauss and the Politics of American Empire* (New Haven: Yale University Press, 2004); and Francis Fukuyama, *America at the Crossroads: Democracy, Power, and the Neoconservative Legacy* (New Haven: Yale University Press, 2006).

10. See, for instance, David Brooks, "National Greatness: Teddy Roosevelt's Vision for the Twenty-First Century," *American Experiment Quarterly* (Winter 1998–99), www.americanexperiment.org/uploaded/files/aeqv1n4brooks.pdf; Irving Kristol, "The

Neoconservative Persuasion," *Weekly Standard,* August 25, 2003; David Gelernter, *Americanism: The Fourth Great Western Religion* (New York: Doubleday, 2007); Robert Kagan, "Neocon Nation: Neoconservatism, c. 1776," *World Affairs: A Journal of Ideas and Debate* (Spring 2008), www.worldaffairsjournal.org/2008%20-%20Spring/full-neocon.html.

11. See James Nuechterlein, "Neoconservatism & Irving Kristol," *Commentary* 78, no. 2 (August 1984), 43–52.

Chapter I

1. Sidney Blumenthal, *The Rise of the Counter-Establishment: The Conservative Ascent to Political Power* (New York: Times Books, 1986); Patrick Buchanan, *Where the Right Went Wrong: How Neoconservatives Subverted the Reagan Revolution and Hijacked the Bush Presidency* (New York: St. Martin's Griffin, 2005); Shadia Drury, *Leo Strauss and the American Right* (New York: St. Martin's Press, 1997); Claes G. Ryn, *America the Virtuous: The Crisis of Democracy and the Quest for Empire* (New Brunswick, NJ: Transaction Publishers, 2003).

2. Quoted in Joshua Muravchik, "The Neoconservative Cabal," in *The Neocon Reader,* ed. Irwin Stelzer (New York: Grove Press, 2004), 243–44.

3. Catherine and Michael Zuckert have ably shown the relationship between LaRouche's various publications on Leo Strauss and the neocons and the way in which they were repackaged by and for the mainstream press. See Zuckert's *The Truth about Leo Strauss: Political Philosophy and American Democracy* (Chicago: The University of Chicago Press, 2006), 1–20.

4. David Brooks, "The Neoconservative Cabal and Other Fantasies," in *The Neocon Reader,* 42.

5. Irwin Stelzer, ed., *The Neocon Reader* (New York: Grove Press, 2004), 41, 245, 42, 250–52. See also Peter Berkowitz, "What Hath Strauss Wrought?" *Weekly Standard,* June 2, 2003; and Clifford Orwin, "The Straussians Are Coming!" *Claremont Review of Books* (Spring 2005), www.claremont.org/publications/crb/id.982/article_detail.asp.

6. James Nuechterlein, "Neoconservatism and Irving Kristol, *Commentary* 78, no. 2 (August 1984): 43.

7. Quoted in Sam Tanenhaus, "When Left Turns Right, It Leaves the Middle Muddled," *New York Times,* September 16, 2000, www.nytimes.com/2000/09/16/arts/when-left-turns-right-it-leaves-the-middle-muddled.html?pagewanted=1.

8. Abraham Lincoln, "House Divided Speech," June 16, 1858.

9. See also the accompanying book by Joseph Dorman, *Arguing the World: New York Intellectuals in Their Own Words* (Chicago: University of Chicago Press, 2001). Books of varying quality on neoconservatism include: Mark Gerson, *The Neoconservative Vision: From the Cold War to the Culture Wars* (Lanham, MD: Madison Books, 1997); Peter Steinfels, *The Neoconservatives: The Men Who Are Changing America's Politics* (New York: Simon & Schuster, 1979); Gary Dorrien, *The Neoconservative Mind: Politics, Culture, and the War of Ideology* (Philadelphia: Temple University Press, 1993); John Ehrman, *The Rise of Neoconservatism: Intellectual and Foreign Affairs, 1945–1994* (New Haven: Yale University Press, 1995); Murray Friedman, *The Neoconservative Revolution: Jewish Intellectuals and the Shaping of Public Policy* (Cambridge, UK: Cambridge University Press, 2005); Douglas Murray, *Neoconservatism: Why We Need It* (New York: Encounter

Books, 2006); Francis Fukuyama, *America at the Crossroads: Democracy, Power, and the Neoconservative Legacy* (New Haven: Yale University Press, 2006); Jacob Heilbrunn, *They Knew They Were Right: The Rise of the Neocons* (New York: Doubleday, 2008); Ben J. Wattenberg, *Fighting Words: A Tale of How Liberals Created Neo-Conservatism* (New York: St. Martin's Press, 2008).

10. For an attempt to whitewash the communist commitments of these proto-neocons, see Francis Fukuyama, *America at the Crossroads: Democracy, Power, and the Neoconservative Legacy* (New Haven: Yale University Press, 2006), 15–17.

11. Nathan Glazer, "Neoconservative from the Start," *Public Interest* no. 159 (Spring 2005): 15; Irving Kristol, *Neoconservatism: The Autobiography of an Idea* (New York: Free Press, 1995), 486. See also Kristol, "Why I Am For Humphrey," *The New Republic,* June 8, 1968.

12. The Editors, "C'mon In, the Water's Fine," *National Review,* March 9, 1971.

13. Richard Perle quoted at: www.csmonitor.com/specials/neocon/neoconQuotes .html; Elizabeth Drew, "The Neocons in Power," *New York Review of Books,* June 12, 2003; Howard Dean quoted in *U.S. News & World Report,* August 11, 2003, 14.

14. Irving Kristol, *Two Cheers for Capitalism* (New York: Basic Books, 1978), 138.

15. Irving Kristol, "Forty Good Years," *Public Interest* no. 159 (Spring 2005): 9.

16. Kristol, *Two Cheers for Capitalism,* 129.

17. Daniel Bell, *The Coming of the Post-Industrial Society* (New York: Basic Books, 1973), 433.

18. Irving Kristol, *Two Cheers for Capitalism,* 158. As we shall see in chapter 4, Kristol's understanding of what he calls "the crisis of modernity"—and his solution to it—follows directly from the writings of Leo Strauss.

19. See Irving Kristol, "Skepticism, Meliorism, and *The Public Interest,*" *Public Interest* no. 77 (Fall 1985): 31–41. See also Adam Wolfson, "About the Public Interest," *Public Interest* no. 159 (Spring 2005): 18–21.

20. See Michael Walzer, *Radical Principles: Reflections of an Unreconstructed Democrat* (New York: Basic Books, 1980), 92–106.

21. Not all neoconservatives, maybe not even most, have been opposed to Johnson's Great Society programs. Ben Wattenberg, for instance, has come out recently in support of Johnson's massive expansion of the welfare state. Wattenberg blames the failure of many of the Great Society programs on bureaucratic overreach. See Wattenberg, *Fighting Words,* 27–28.

22. James Q. Wilson, foreword to *The Essential Neoconservative Reader,* by Mark Gerson (Reading, MA: Addison-Wesley Publishing Company, 1996), ix; Irving Kristol, *Reflections of a Neoconservative: Looking Back, Looking Ahead* (New York: Basic Books, 1983), xiv–xv.

23. Irving Kristol, "The Neoconservative Persuasion," *Weekly Standard,* August 25, 2003.

24. Irving Kristol, *Two Cheers for Capitalism,* 121–25.

25. Irving Kristol, "The Neoconservative Persuasion," *Weekly Standard,* August 25, 2003 (emphasis added), www.weeklystandard.com/Content/Public/Articles/000/000/003/000tzmlw.asp.

26. David Brooks and William Kristol, "What Ails the Right," *Wall Street Journal,* September 15, 1997; David Brooks, "The Era of Small Government Is Over," *Weekly Standard,* October 2, 2000; "How to Reinvent the GOP, *New York Times,* August 29, 2004, www.nytimes.com/2004/08/29/magazine/29REPUBLICANS.html?pagewanted=all;

Brooks quoted in Sheldon Richman, "Four Cheers for Capitalism," *The Future of Freedom Foundation*, March 1997, www.fff.org/freedom/0697c.asp.
    27. Fred Barnes, "Big-Government Conservatism," *Wall Street Journal*, August 15, 2003.
    28. Peter Berkowitz, "Moderation is No Vice, and Extremism is No Virtue in Politics," *Weekly Standard*, July 27, 2009, www.weeklystandard.com/Content/Public/Articles/000/000/016/747thgnk.asp?pg=1. Berkowitz is a political philosopher who formerly taught at George Mason University School of Law. He is now a Visiting Fellow at the Hoover Institution and widely published in a variety of magazines and journals.
    29. We shall have more to say about the neocons' intellectual method in chapter 2. The philosophic source of the neocons' use and abuse of "prudence" and "moderation" as political virtues is Leo Strauss, whose views on the subject we discuss in chapter 6.
    30. Berkowitz, "Moderation is No Vice, and Extremism is No Virtue in Politics."
    31. David Brooks, "Fresh Start Conservatism," *New York Times*, February 15, 2008, www.nytimes.com/2008/02/15/opinion/15brooks.html; Irving Kristol, *Two Cheers for Capitalism*, 222.
    32. As unrepentant New Deal liberals, first-generation neoconservatives have always supported Franklin Delano Roosevelt's introduction of socialist principles into American intellectual and political life. In more recent years, the second generation of neoconservatives has embraced the writings and policies of Theodore Roosevelt. However, the deeper one digs, the more one sees the role played by Herbert Croly in turning the Republican Roosevelt toward a new socialist ideal wrapped in the language of a manly conservatism. Teddy Roosevelt's New Nationalism was inspired directly by Croly's view that it was the government's job to solve society's social, economic, and political problems. Croly is best known as the author of *The Promise of American Life* (1909) and as cofounder of the *New Republic* magazine. For neoconservative support of their intellectual triumvirate, see Kristol, *Reflections of a Neoconservative*, 110–11, 112; *Neoconservatism: The Autobiography of an Idea*, xi, 379, 473; David Brooks and William Kristol, "What Ails Conservatism," *Wall Street Journal*, September 15, 1997, A22; David Brooks, "A Return to National Greatness: A Manifesto for a Lost Creed," *Weekly Standard*, March 3, 1997, 16; David Brooks, "Bully for America," *Weekly Standard*, June 23, 1997, 14; Brooks, "Politics and Patriotism: From Teddy Roosevelt to John McCain, *Weekly Standard*, April 26, 1999, 16. As with virtually all things in the neoconservative world, it all goes back to Irving Kristol, who first praised Croly in *Two Cheers for Capitalism*, 252.
    33. Herbert Croly, *The Promise of American Life* (New York: Dutton, 1963), 209; Theodore Roosevelt, "The New Nationalism," chap. in *The New Nationalism*, with an Introduction by William Leuchtenburg (Englewood Cliffs, NJ: Prentice-Hall, 1961), 33–34; Franklin Delano Roosevelt, "First Inaugural," March 4, 1933.
    34. Wattenberg, *Fighting Words*, 10; Irving Kristol, "The Neoconservative Persuasion," *Weekly Standard*, August 25, 2003 (emphasis added).
    35. David Brooks, "Bully for America," 14; Herbert Croly, *Promise of American Life*, 152.
    36. David Brooks, "Pabulum with a Purpose," *Weekly Standard*, August 14, 2000.
    37. Kristol, *Two Cheers for Capitalism*, 27, 230, ix. In chapter 7, we shall see how Kristol's rejection of the politics of principle was derived from his teacher Leo Strauss.
    38. Kristol, *Reflections of a Neoconservative*, 116–17.
    39. Kristol, *Two Cheers for Capitalism*, 237–38.
    40. David Brooks, "Revolt of the Nihilists" and "The Establishment Lives," *New York*

Times, September 30, www.nytimes.com/2008/09/30/opinion/30brooks.html; and September 22, 2008, www.nytimes.com/2008/09/23/opinion/23brooks.html.

41. David Brooks, "From Freedom to Authority," *New York Times,* May 14, 2006, http://select.nytimes.com/2006/05/14/opinion/14brooks.html; "The Establishment Lives," *New York Times,* September 22, 2008.

42. Irving Kristol, *Two Cheers for Capitalism,* 118.

43. In recent years, the neocons have become big fans of Bismarck, the German chancellor who first invented the idea of a "conservative welfare state" and who laid the groundwork for the collective-authoritarian politics of the twentieth century. See, for instance, the views of on-again–off-again neoconservative Francis Fukuyama. Of Bismarck, Fukuyama has said: "the other person I like actually is Bismarck, the great non-democratic German chancellor because he also had a theory about how to use power. He had a very powerful state and he realized that the best way to use it in a sense was through indirection and so . . . the policy I would recommend is actually one in which . . . we actually may have to detach ourselves from the overt and very loud promotion of democracy because I think at this stage in world history that may not be the best thing." (Francis Fukuyama, "Has Neoconservatism Failed or Succeeded? Part Two: A Conversation with Francis Fukuyama," interview by Ben Wattenberg, *Think Tank with Ben Wattenberg,* www.pbs .org/thinktank/transcript1234.html.) See also Fukuyama, *America at the Crossroads: Democracy, Power, and the Neoconservative Legacy* (New Haven: Yale University Press, 2006), 189.

Chapter 2

1. Irving Kristol and David Brooks are the two leading neoconservative thinkers to explicitly call on Republicans to develop a "philosophy of governance."

2. David Brooks, "Bully for America," *Weekly Standard,* June 23, 1997; "One Nation Conservatism; How George W. Bush and John McCain—Without Quite Realizing It—Are Creating a New Republican Philosophy," *Weekly Standard,* September 13, 1999, www.jewishworldreview.com/weekly/standard091099.asp.

3. David Brooks, "Waiting to Be Wooed," *New York Times,* November 30, 2006, http://query.nytimes.com/gst/fullpage.html?res=9F0CE0D9113EF933A05752C1A9 609C8B63.

4. See Irving Kristol, *Two Cheers for Capitalism* (New York: Basic Books, 1978), 116–20.

5. Irving Kristol, "The End Game of the Welfare State," *Wall Street Journal,* September 11, 1989, and "The Trouble with Republicans," *Wall Street Journal,* April 22, 1988 (emphasis added). Kristol's call for "shrewdness" may very well have been inspired by his reading of Leo Strauss's *Thoughts on Machiavelli* (Glencoe, IL: The Free Press, 1958), 43. In chapter 7, we shall explore in some depth the neoconservatives' adoption and use of Machiavelli's philosophy for governance.

6. Not surprisingly, it was neoconservative intellectuals such as Myron Magnet and Michael Knox Beran who played a pivotal role in developing compassionate conservatism as a pseudopolitical philosophy. See C. Bradley Thompson, "The Decline and Fall of American Conservatism," *Objective Standard* 1, no. 3 (Fall 2006): 15–51.

7. Irving Kristol, "When It's Wrong to Be Right," *Wall Street Journal,* March 24, 1993 (emphasis added).

8. Irving Kristol, "When It's Wrong to Be Right" (emphasis added).

9. Michael Ledeen, *Machiavelli on Modern Leadership* (New York: St. Martin's Press, 1999), 58–59.

10. William James, "What Pragmatism Means," in *Essays in Pragmatism*, ed. and with an Introduction by Alburey Castell (New York: Hafner Publishing, 1948), 144–46.

11. Peter Berkowitz, "Pragmatism Obama Style," *Weekly Standard*, May 4, 2009, www.weeklystandard.com/Content/Public/Articles/000/000/016/425yustu.asp.

12. James, "What Pragmatism Means," 144–46. David Frum and Richard Perle have openly and explicitly hitched the neocon wagon to pragmatism in "Beware the Soft-Line Ideologues," *Wall Street Journal*, January 7, 2004.

13. See, for instance, Leo Strauss, *Liberalism Ancient and Modern* (Chicago: University of Chicago Press, 1968), 205–08; and Carnes Lord, *The Modern Prince: What Leaders Need to Know Now* (New Haven: Yale University Press, 2003), 27–28. Also see Peter Berkowitz, "Moderation is No Vice, and Extremism is No Virtue in Politics," *Weekly Standard*, July 27, 2009.

14. Kristol quoted in Geoffrey Norman, "The Godfather of Neoconservatism," *Esquire*, February 13, 1979 (emphasis added).

15. Lord, *The Modern Prince*, 24 (emphasis added). The reader will notice that the neocons' idea of politics as the art of coping was first learned from Leo Strauss (see chapter 6). Also see Leo Strauss, *What Is Political Philosophy?* (Chicago: University of Chicago Press, 1959), 83. In this he writes: "'Political science' as the skill of the excellent politician or statesman consists in the right handling of individual situations; its immediate 'products' are commands or decrees or advices effectively expressed, which are intended to cope with an individual case." Interestingly, the Kristol-Strauss view of prudence as "coping" bears a striking resemblance to the views of the liberal-socialist philosopher Richard Rorty. In *Philosophy and Social Hope*, Rorty, the leading American pragmatist philosopher, writes that pragmatists "start with a Darwinian account of human beings as animals doing their best to cope with the environment—doing their best to develop tools which will enable them to enjoy more pleasure and less pain." See Rorty, *Philosophy and Social Hope* (New York: Penguin Books, 1999), xxii–xxiii.

16. David Brooks, "Why Experience Matters," *New York Times*, September 16, 2008, www.nytimes.com/2008/09/16/opinion/16brooks.html.

17. Kristol, *Two Cheers for Capitalism*, 217.

18. Ben J. Wattenberg, *Fighting Words: A Tale of How Liberals Created Neo-Conservatism* (New York: St. Martin's Press, 2008), 3.

19. Kristol, *Two Cheers for Capitalism*, 174.

20. For the fullest Straussian/neocon explication of the idea of statecraft and statesmanship, see Lord, *The Modern Prince*.

21. As Carnes Lord has written, "All societies need some mechanism for arbitrating disputes among powerful interests and distributing scarce resources." *The Modern Prince*, 20. In Anglo-liberal societies based on the rule of law, the mechanism for resolving disputes is common law adjudication. For the neocons, however, something more is needed, something that gives greater authority to the wisdom, prudence, discretion, and judgment of statesmen.

22. David Brooks, "Big-Spending Conservative," *New York Times*, April 21, 2009, www.nytimes.com/2009/04/21/opinion/21brooks.html; Norman Podhoretz, "Neoconservatism: A Eulogy," *Commentary* (March 1996), 21.

23. Paul Mirengoff, "Trading Places: Have Republicans Replaced Democrats as the Party of Pragmatism?" *Weekly Standard*, March 21, 2005, www.weeklystandard.com/Content/Public/Articles/000%5C000%5C005%5C384xkuik.asp; Irwin M. Stelzer, "A Conservative Case for Regulation," *The Public Interest* (Summer 1997), 85–97.

24. Carnes Lord, *The Modern Prince*, 107. One might say of the neoconservatives what their philosophic doyen, Leo Strauss, used to say about modern social scientists, namely, that they are "specialists without spirit and voluptuaries without heart." See Strauss, *Natural Right and History* (Chicago: University of Chicago Press, 1953), 42.

25. Lord, *The Modern Prince*, 31.

26. Irving Kristol, "What Is a Neo-Conservative?" *Newsweek*, January 19, 1976, 87 (emphasis added).

27. Kristol, *Two Cheers for Capitalism*, 20–21.

28. Irving Kristol, *Neoconservatism: The Autobiography of an Idea* (New York: Free Press, 1995), 368.

29. Kristol, *Two Cheers for Capitalism*, 20–21.

30. The neocons agree with much of the Catholic critique of American culture, but they thought it imprudent to state such things publicly. For an insightful discussion of the neocon-theocon relationship, see Damon Linker, *The Theocons: Secular America Under Siege* (New York: Anchor Books, 2006), 54–62.

31. William Kristol, "The Majority Party," *Weekly Standard*, September 13, 2004, www.weeklystandard.com/Content/Public/Articles/000/000/004/569uofdm.asp.

32. Kristol, "The End Game of the Welfare State."

33. David Brooks, "No U-Turns," *New York Times*, March 29, 2007, http://select .nytimes.com/2007/03/29/opinion/29brooks.html.

34. Ibid.

35. Ibid.

36. Norman Podhoretz, "Neoconservatism: A Eulogy," *Commentary* (March 1996): 21. See also Peter Berkowitz, "Moderation is No Vice, and Extremism is No Virtue in Politics."

37. Irving Kristol, "A Conservative Welfare State," *Wall Street Journal*, June 14, 1993; Nathan Glazer, *The Limits of Social Policy* (Cambridge: Harvard University Press, 1988), 58; Ben Wattenberg, "Response to George Gilder's 'Why I Am Not a Neo-Conservative,'" *National Review*, March 5, 1982; Wattenberg, *Fighting Words*, 101.

38. Kristol, *Two Cheers for Capitalism*, 123–24.

39. Irving Kristol, "American Conservatism 1945–1995," *Public Interest* no. 121 (Fall 1995): 88; Kristol, "Skepticism, Meliorism, and *The Public Interest*," *Public Interest* no. 121 (Fall 1985): 40.

40. Irving Kristol, *Reflections of a Neoconservative: Looking Back, Looking Ahead* (New York: Basic Books, 1983), 116.

41. We shall have more to say in chapters 7, 8, and 10 about the neoconservatives' fascination with national-service programs.

42. See Mark Gerson, *The Neoconservative Vision: From the Cold War to the Culture War* (New York: Madison Books, 1997), 201.

43. Nathan Glazer, contribution to "Neoconservatism: Pro and Con," *Partisan Review* 4 (1980): 499.

44. Kristol, *Two Cheers for Capitalism*, 118 (emphasis added).

45. Berkowitz, "Moderation is No Vice, and Extremism is No Virtue in Politics."

46. Kristol, "A Conservative Welfare State."

47. See David Brooks, "The Empathy Issue," *New York Times,* May 29, 2009, www
.nytimes.com/2009/05/29/opinion/29brooks.html.
48. Kristol, *Two Cheers for Capitalism,* 119 (emphasis added).
49. Richard H. Thaler and Cass R. Sunstein, *Nudge: Improving Decisions about Health, Wealth, and Happiness* (New York: Penguin, 2009).
50. Kristol, *Two Cheers for Capitalism,* 180–209.

Chapter 3

1. Richard Hofstadter, *The Paranoid Style in American Politics* (New York: Knopf, 1966).
2. From among the following representative books, readers can decide for themselves what is good sense and what is nonsense: Shadia B. Drury, *Leo Strauss and the American Right* (New York: St. Martin's Press, 1997); Kenneth Deutsch and John A. Murley, eds., *Leo Strauss, the Straussians, and the American Regime* (Lanham, MD: Rowman & Littlefield, 1999); Anne Norton, *Leo Strauss and the Politics of American Empire* (New Haven: Yale University Press, 2004); Francis Fukuyama, *America at the Crossroads: Democracy, Power, and the Neoconservative Legacy* (New Haven: Yale University Press, 2006); Catherine H. Zuckert and Michael Zuckert, *The Truth about Leo Strauss: Political Philosophy and American Democracy* (Chicago: University of Chicago Press, 2006). The credibility of Drury's sometimes thoughtful and insightful book on Strauss and the neoconservatives is often undercut and diminished by her relentless hostility to Strauss and his students.
3. See Zuckert and Zuckert, *The Truth about Leo Strauss,* 228–59.
4. Peter Minowitz, *Straussophobia: Defending Leo Strauss and Straussians Against Shadia Drury and Other Accusers* (Lanham, MD: Lexington Books, 2009).
5. Myles Burnyeat, "Sphinx Without a Secret," *New York Review of Books,* May 30, 1985, 30–36; Jacob Weisberg, "The Cult of Leo Strauss," *Newsweek,* August 3, 1987, 61; Brent Staples, "Undemocratic Vistas: The Sinister Vogue of Leo Strauss," *New York Times,* November 28, 1994, A16; Earl Shorris, "Ignoble Liars: Leo Strauss, George Bush, and the philosophy of mass deception," *Harper's,* June 2004, 65–71. See also Richard Lacayo, "You've Read About Who's Influential, But Who Has the Power?" *Time,* June 17, 1996, 43. A much more serious and powerful criticism of Strauss can be found in Stephen Holmes, "Strauss: Truths for Philosophers Alone," chap. in *The Anatomy of Antiliberalism* (Cambridge: Harvard University Press, 1993), 61–87.
6. Seymour Hersh, "Selective Intelligence," *New Yorker,* May 12, 2003, www
.newyorker.com/archive/2003/05/12/030512fa_fact; James Atlas, "Leo-Cons: A Classicist's Legacy," *New York Times,* May 4, 2003, www.nytimes.com/2003/05/04/weekinreview/the-nation-leo-cons-a-classicist-s-legacy-new-empire-builders.html?pagewanted=1; Jeet Heer, "The Mind of the Administration," *Boston Globe,* May 11, 2003, www.boston.com/news/globe/ideas/articles/2003/05/11/the_philosopher/.
7. See, for instance, Jeffrey Steinberg, "Profile: Leo Strauss, Fascist Grandfather of the Neo-Cons," *Executive Intelligence Review,* March 21, 2003, http://larouchepub.com/other/2003/3011profile_strauss.html. For a fuller discussion of how Lyndon LaRouche's essays and press releases on the relationship between Strauss and the neocons influenced the mainstream media, see Zuckert and Zuckert, *The Truth About Leo Strauss,* 8–15.
8. Robert Bartley, "Joining LaRouche in the Fever Swamps," *Wall Street Journal,*

June 9, 2003, www.opinionjournal.com/columnists/rbartley/?id=110003602; Joshua Muravchik, "The Neoconservative Cabal" in *The Neocon Reader,* ed. Irwin Stelzer (New York: Grove Press, 2004), 245.

9. Jenny Strauss Clay, "The Real Leo Strauss," *New York Times,* June 7, 2003, www.nytimes.com/2003/06/07/opinion/the-real-leo-strauss.html?pagewanted=1. For defenses of Strauss by his students and supporters, see Robert Locke, "Leo Strauss, Conservative Mastermind," FrontPageMagazine.com, May 31, 2002; Robert J. Lieber, "The Neoconservative-Conspiracy Theory: Pure Myth," *Chronicle of Higher Education,* May 2, 2003; Daniel Drezner, "Et Tu, Kristol?" *New Republic Online,* May 14, 2003; Peter Berkowitz, "What Hath Strauss Wrought," *Weekly Standard,* June 2, 2003; Steven Lenzner and William Kristol, "What Was Leo Strauss Up To?" *Public Interest* no. 153 (Fall 2003): 19–39; Mark Blitz, "Leo Strauss, the Straussians and American Foreign Policy," openDemocracy.com, November 14, 2003, www.opendemocracy.net/democracy-americanpower/article_1577.jsp; Nathan Tarcov, "Will the Real Leo Strauss Please Stand Up?" American Interest Online, www.the-american-interest.com/ai2/article.cfm?Id=166&MId=5; Thomas G. West, "Leo Strauss and American Foreign Policy," *Claremont Review of Books* (Summer 2004), www.claremont.org/publications/crb/id.1075/article_detail.asp; Adam Kirsch, "The Demonization of Leo Strauss," *New York Sun,* May 17, 2006.

10. Berkowitz, "What Hath Strauss Wrought." See also Clifford Orwin, "Leo Strauss, Moralist or Machiavellian?" *Vital Nexus* 1, no. 1 (May 1990): 107.

11. Steven B. Smith, *Reading Leo Strauss* (Chicago: University of Chicago Press, 2006), 12.

12. Irving Kristol, review of *Persecution and the Art of Writing,* by Leo Strauss, in *Commentary* (October 1952): 392–97. Interestingly, Strauss's ideas and influence actually entered the Kristol home two years earlier than Kristol's review of *Persecution and the Art of Writing.* Kristol's wife, Gertrude Himmelfarb, discussed Strauss's ideas at some length in two review essays published in *Commentary* in 1950 and 1951. In a 1950 review that included an examination of Strauss's *On Tyranny,* Himmelfarb wrote of Strauss's "brilliant exposition of Xenophon's 'Hiero.'" She is clearly impressed with Strauss's "misology," which she defines as a "distrust of free, democratic inquiry." Strauss's doctrine, according to Himmelfarb, implies by extension "the existence of an esoteric truth which it would be dangerous or unwise to circulate in society. A truth, an objective truth about the nature of social reality, may become, when it escapes from the sanctum of philosophy, a political 'falsehood.' The philosopher might know it to be the truth, for example, that social institutions have their origin in a struggle for power, in force rather than justice, but he is morally and politically obliged to act as if they had their origin in justice rather than force. The truths of philosophy, the misologist would say, are not necessarily the truths of politics and morality." Himmelfarb goes on to suggest that Strauss's misology, or esoteric teaching, "can help clarify the character of conservative thought." (Himmelfarb, "The Prophets of a New Conservatism," *Commentary* [January 1950]: 85–86.) A year later, Himmelfarb ranked Strauss amongst the "wisest and most penetrating ... contemporary political philosophers." She also had this to say about Strauss's philosophic method: "Strauss has found that one of the obligations of the philosophical enterprise is the occasional veiling, often at critical points, of the real meaning or significance of an idea. There appears to be a body of private, esoteric teachings in most great philosophers that is available only to the prudent disciple and that is concealed from the irresponsible public.... The assumption is that nothing in the text

is said or left unsaid heedlessly. Strauss himself, in the style of great philosophy, writes deliberately and precisely, so deliberately that one must read him as carefully as he would have us read others. (So deliberately, too, that one might almost suspect him of harboring esoteric theories of his own. . . .)" (Gertrude Himmelfarb, "Political Thinking: Ancients vs. Moderns, The New Battle of the Books," *Commentary* [July 1951]: 76–83).

13. Irving Kristol, *Neoconservatism: The Autobiography of an Idea* (New York: The Free Press, 1995), 7.

14. Kristol, *Neoconservatism*, 7.

15. Quoted in Smith, *Reading Leo Strauss*, 6.

16. For a good brief introduction to Strauss's thought, see two essays by Mark Lilla, "Leo Strauss: The European," *New York Review of Books*, October 21, 2004, and "The Closing of the Straussian Mind," *New York Review of Books*, November 4, 2004. See also Dinesh D'Souza, "The Legacy of Leo Strauss," *Policy Review* (Spring 1987): 36–43; Steven Lenzner and William Kristol, "What Was Leo Strauss Up To?" *Public Interest* no. 153 (Fall 2003): 19–39. For a critical look at Strauss and the Straussians and their influence on American foreign policy, see Norton, *Leo Strauss and the Politics of American Empire*.

17. Laurence Berns, "Correcting the Record on Leo Strauss," *PS: Political Science and Politics* 28, no. 4 (December 1995): 659–60.

18. Werner Dannhauser, "Leo Strauss: Becoming Naïve Again," *American Scholar* 44 (Autumn 1975): 640; Hilail Gildin, "Leo Strauss on the Understanding of the Politically Better and Worse," *Interpretation* 35 (2007): 3.

19. Dannhauser, "Leo Strauss: Becoming Naïve Again," 640, 641–42. See also George Anastaplo, "Leo Strauss at the University of Chicago," and Joseph Cropsey, "Leo Strauss at the University of Chicago," in *Leo Strauss, the Straussians, and the American Regime*, eds. Kenneth L. Deutsch and John A. Murley (Lanham, MD; Rowman & Littlefield, 1999), 3–30, 39–40; and Hadley Arkes, "Strauss and the Religion of Reason," *National Review* (June 26, 1995), http://findarticles.com/p/articles/mi_m1282/is_n12_v47/ai_17108642/.

20. Letter from Werner J. Dannhauser to the editors, *New York Review of Books*, October 24, 1985.

21. For Strauss's impact as a teacher and a scholar, see Milton Himmelfarb, "On Leo Strauss," *Commentary* (August 1974): 60–66; Dannhauser, "Leo Strauss: Becoming Naïve Again," 636–42; and Stanley Rosen, "Leo Strauss in Chicago," *Daedalus* 135 (Summer 2006): 104–13.

22. Allan Bloom, "Leo Strauss," *Political Theory* 2, no. 4 (1974): 372.

23. Ernest Fortin, "Dead Masters and Their Living Thought: Leo Strauss and His Friendly Critics," *Vital Nexus* 1, no. 1 (May 1990): 70.

24. Harry V. Jaffa, "Strauss at One Hundred," in *Leo Strauss, the Straussians, and the American Regime*, eds. Deutsch and Murley (Lanham, MD: Rowman & Littlefield, 1999), 41; Edward Banfield, "Leo Strauss," in *Remembering the University of Chicago*, ed. Edward Shils (Chicago: University of Chicago Press, 1991), 501; Ted A. Blanton's eulogy for Leo Strauss quoted in Laurence Berns with Eva Brann, "Leo Strauss at St. John's College (Annapolis)," in *Leo Strauss, the Straussians, and the American Regime*, 36–37.

25. Kristol, *Neoconservatism*, 9.

26. See, for instance, the acrimonious debate in the pages of *The Claremont Review of Books* between Harry Jaffa and Thomas Pangle, two of Strauss's most influential

students. The exchange began with Jaffa's review essay of Pangle's "Introduction," to *Leo Strauss: Studies in Platonic Political Philosophy* (Chicago: University of Chicago Press, 1983), which was published as "The Legacy of Leo Strauss," *Claremont Review of Books* 3 (1984): 409–13. A subsequent exchange between Pangle and Jaffa followed in volume 4, pages 18–24.

27. Kristol, *Neoconservatism*, 7.

28. Kristol, review of *Persecution and the Art of Writing*, 394.

29. Strauss and his students often use the term "city" generically to represent political units of various kinds or sizes, but he most often used the term in the ancient sense to represent the small city-state.

30. Leo Strauss, *Persecution and the Art of Writing* (Chicago: University of Chicago Press, 1952), 155.

31. Kristol, review of *Persecution and the Art of Writing*, 394.

32. Leo Strauss, *Liberalism Ancient and Modern* (Chicago: University of Chicago Press, 1968), 13.

33. Leo Strauss, "Reason and Revelation," in *Leo Strauss and the Theologico-Political Problem*, by Heinrich Meier (Cambridge, UK: Cambridge University Press, 2006), 141, 146. Strauss's own students have debated whether their teacher thought the claims of religion to be true or not and whether he was or was not a believer himself. Stanley Rosen, a former Strauss student, has said this of Strauss and the Straussians: "He was an atheist. They [Straussians] all are. They are epicureans and atheists." Rosen is quoted in Jeet Heer, "The Mind of the Administration," *Boston Globe*, May 11, 2003.

34. Leo Strauss, *On Tyranny. Including the Strauss-Kojève Correspondence*, ed. Victor Gourevitch and Michael Roth (Chicago: University of Chicago Press, 1991), 205–06.

35. Strauss, *Persecution and the Art of Writing*, 139; Kristol, *Neoconservatism*, 8.

36. Kristol, review of *Persecution and the Art of Writing*, 397.

37. The dualism in Strauss's thought is confirmed by his supporters and detractors. Among Strauss's supporters, see Zuckert and Zuckert, *The Truth about Leo Strauss*, 21. Two of Strauss's best and most influential students, Michael Zuckert and Harry Jaffa, have both written that Leo Strauss "was a thinker of dualities (see Zuckert, "Jaffa's New Birth: Harry Jaffa at Ninety," and Jaffa, "A Reply to Michael Zuckert's 'Jaffa's New Birth: Harry Jaffa at Ninety,'" *The Review of Politics* 71 [2009]: 210, 241). Among Strauss's detractors who also see the dualities in his thought, consider Shadia B. Drury, *The Political Ideas of Leo Strauss*, 2d ed. (New York: Palgrave, 2005), 1–17; and Drury, *Leo Strauss and the American Right*, 144–47. We shall have more to say on Strauss's dualism in chapters 5 and 6 and on the influence of Strauss's dualism on the neoconservatives in chapter 7.

38. Leo Strauss, "Farabi's Plato," in *Louis Ginzberg Jubilee Volume* (New York: American Academy for Jewish Research, 1945), 383.

39. The Canadian scholar Shadia B. Drury has written an entire book on the relationship between Strauss and the neoconservatives, but she makes no mention of Kristol's review of *Persecution and the Art of Writing*.

Chapter 4

1. Leo Strauss, *The City and Man* (Chicago: University of Chicago Press, 1964), 3; Strauss, "The Three Waves of Modernity," chap. in *An Introduction to Political Philosophy: Ten Essays by Leo Strauss*, ed. and with an Introduction by Hilail Gildin (Detroit: Wayne

State University Press, 1989), 81. A helpful introduction to Strauss's view on "modernity" can be found in Robert Pippin, "The Modern World of Leo Strauss," *Political Theory* 20 (August 1992): 448–72.

2. Leo Strauss, *Natural Right and History* (Chicago: University of Chicago Press, 1953), 5. Strauss's clearest statement of the decline and fall of modern reason is contained in his essay "The Three Waves of Modernity," chap. in *An Introduction to Political Philosophy*, 81–98. What makes Strauss's "Three Waves" essay so interesting is the degree to which he seems to support Nietzsche's critique of Enlightenment reason. Also see Allan Bloom, *The Closing of the American Mind: How Higher Education Has Failed Democracy and Impoverished the Souls of Today's Students* (New York: Simon & Schuster, 1987), 256–68.

3. See, for instance, Nietzsche's effusive praise of Kant's "extraordinary courage and wisdom" in winning the "most difficult victory, that over the optimistic foundations of logic, which form the underpinnings of our culture." Kant, according to Nietzsche, smashed the "optimistic" Enlightenment view that "treated the universe as knowable, in the presumption of eternal truths, and space, time, and causality as absolute and universally valid laws." Nietzsche praises Kant for showing "how these supposed laws serve only to raise appearance ... to the status of true reality, thereby rendering impossible a genuine understanding of that reality." (Friedrich Nietzsche, *The Birth of Tragedy and the Genealogy of Morals*, trans. Francis Golffing [Garden City, NY: Doubleday & Company, 1956], 111.)

4. Strauss, "The Three Waves of Modernity," 82. Two intellectual histories that trace the status of reason in the nineteenth century include Karl Löwith, *From Hegel to Nietzsche: The Revolution in Nineteenth-Century Thought*, trans. David E. Green (New York: Doubleday & Company, 1967); and Leonard Peikoff, *The Ominous Parallels: The End of Freedom in America* (New York: Penguin, 1982). Catherine Zuckert's *Postmodern Platos: Nietzsche, Heidegger, Gadamer, Strauss, Derrida* (Chicago: University of Chicago Press, 1996) examines how Nietzsche's twentieth-century students responded to the nineteenth-century crisis of reason.

5. Leo Strauss, *Natural Right and History*, 6, 12, 5. See also Strauss's lecture on "German Nihilism" delivered on February 26, 1941, at the New School For Social Research. The lecture was posthumously published in *Interpretation* 26 (Spring 1999): 353–78.

6. Strauss, *Natural Right and History*, 12, 5.

7. See John Dewey, *The Quest for Certainty: A Study of the Relation of Knowledge and Action* (New York: Minton, Balch and Company, 1929).

8. Strauss, *The City and Man*, 3; *Natural Right and History*, 1. At this point, we must define more precisely the way in which Strauss uses the term "liberalism." Liberalism, for Strauss, is a political philosophy that has its origin in the Enlightenment ideas of John Locke, Adam Smith, and America's Founding Fathers. This is the liberalism of natural rights, limited government, constitutionalism, and laissez-faire capitalism. For Strauss, however, there is a direct connection between the "classical liberalism" of the seventeenth, eighteenth, and nineteenth centuries and the modern liberalism associated with John Dewey, Herbert Croly, Woodrow Wilson, Franklin Delano Roosevelt, Adlai Stevenson, and Hillary Clinton. The latter liberalism openly, explicitly, and systematically rejects the entire philosophy associated with classical liberalism. (See, for instance, Dewey's *Liberalism and Social Action*, Great Books in Philosophy Series [Amherst, NY: Prometheus Books, 2000].) We reject Strauss's conflation of the two liberalisms. In our

view, the "liberalism" of John Dewey and his twentieth-century students represents a complete break with and rejection of classical liberalism.

9. Steven B. Smith, *Reading Leo Strauss: Politics, Philosophy, Judaism* (Chicago: University of Chicago Press, 2006), ix.

10. Strauss, "An Introduction to Heideggerian Existentialism," in *The Rebirth of Classical Political Rationalism,* ed. Thomas L. Pangle (Chicago: University of Chicago Press, 1989), 29.

11. See Milton Himmelfarb, "On Leo Strauss," *Commentary* 58 (August 1974): 62.

12. Strauss, "An Introduction to Heideggerian Existentialism," 42.

13. Strauss, *The City and Man,* 4–5. For Nietzsche's discussion of the "last man," see *Thus Spoke Zarathustra,* trans. R. J. Hollingdale (New York: Penguin Books, 1969), 39–53.

14. Strauss, *Liberalism Ancient and Modern,* vii–ix.

15. For a particularly powerful defense of Strauss's loyalty to American liberal democracy as superior to Soviet communism, see Catherine H. Zuckert and Michael Zuckert, *The Truth About Leo Strauss: Political Philosophy and American Democracy* (Chicago: University of Chicago Press, 2006), 74–75.

16. Strauss, "An Introduction to Heideggerian Existentialism," 43.

17. Allan Bloom, in "Responses to Fukuyama," *National Interest* (Summer 1989): 19–21. Bloom's response is available online: www.wesjones.com/eoh_response.htm#Title.

18. As we shall see, Kristol adopted Strauss's critique of Western liberalism and applied it more specifically to modern capitalism. In 1979 Jeanne Kirkpatrick, America's neoconservative ambassador to the United Nations, published a now-famous article that applied Strauss's fundamental claim to American post–WWII foreign policy: "Because socialism of the Soviet/Chinese/Cuban variety is an ideology rooted in a version of the same values that sparked the Enlightenment and the democratic revolutions of the eighteenth century; because it is modern and not traditional; because it postulates goals that appeal to Christian as well as to secular values (brotherhood of man, elimination of power as a mode of human relations), it is highly congenial to many Americans at the symbolic level. Marxist revolutionaries speak the language of a hopeful future while traditional autocrats speak the language of an unattractive past. Because left-wing revolutionaries invoke the symbols and values of democracy—emphasizing egalitarianism rather than hierarchy and privilege, liberty rather than order, activity, rather than passivity—they are again and again accepted as partisans in the cause of freedom and democracy." (Jeanne Kirkpatrick, "Dictatorships and Double Standards," *Commentary* (November 1979); repr. in Mark Gerson, ed., *The Essential Neoconservative Reader* [New York: Basic Books, 1997], 182.)

19. Strauss, *Natural Right and History,* 1–8.

20. N.A.M.B.L.A. is the acronym for the North American Man/Boy Love Association. The N.S.D.A.P stands for the National Socialist German Workers' Party, otherwise known as the Nazi party. Neoconservatives typically lump the advocates of a free society and capitalism with the cultural policies of the New Left. Andrew Peyton Thomas, for instance, blames most of America's social maladies on the "moral laissez-faire disorder of libertarianism" and on America's "rights-happy radical individualism." See Thomas, "The Death of Jeffersonian America," *Weekly Standard,* August 26, 1996.

21. *Natural Right and History,* 6, 5 (emphasis added).

22. My understanding of Strauss's thought has been greatly improved by the recent publication of six works on Strauss that have appeared in recent years: Thomas L. Pangle,

Leo Strauss: An Introduction to His Thought and Intellectual Legacy (Baltimore: Johns Hopkins University Press, 2006); Steven B. Smith, *Reading Leo Strauss: Politics, Philosophy, Judaism* (Chicago: University of Chicago Press, 2006); Zuckert and Zuckert, *The Truth About Leo Strauss*; Heinrich Meier, *Leo Strauss and the Theologico-Political Problem* (Cambridge, UK: Cambridge University Press, 2006); Daniel Tanguay, *Leo Strauss: An Intellectual Biography*, trans. Christopher Nadon (New Haven: Yale University Press, 2007); and David Janssens, *Between Athens and Jerusalem: Philosophy, Prophecy, and Politics in Leo Strauss's Early Thought* (Albany: State University of New York Press, 2008).

23. Readers should be alerted to the fact that Strauss draws a major distinction between what he calls ancient natural right and modern natural rights. Ancient natural right, in sum, is the right ordering of society according to that which is naturally right or in accord with nature. Modern natural rights are those rights that all individuals are said to have, that make the individual the primary unit of moral and political value, and that create a sphere of freedom between individuals. Strauss's conception of ancient natural right will be explained in much greater detail in chapter 6. Our own understanding of individual rights will be discussed in the conclusion.

24. Friedrich Nietzsche, *The Will to Power*, trans. Anthony M. Ludovic, with an introduction by David Taffel (New York: Barnes & Noble, 2006), xix.

25. Strictly speaking, Strauss traces the conception of modern political philosophy and, with it, nihilism to Machiavelli. See Strauss, *Thoughts on Machiavelli* (Glencoe, IL: The Free Press, 1958). Kristol, in turn, follows Strauss. Machiavelli, writes Kristol, "is the first of the nihilists." Kristol has described Strauss's *Thoughts on Machiavelli* as "by far the best book on Machiavelli yet written." See Kristol, "Machiavelli and the Profanation of Politics," chap. in *Reflections of a Neoconservative: Looking Back, Looking Ahead* (New York: Basic Books, 1983), 126, 130.

26. Strauss, *Natural Right and History*, 6.

27. Some neoconservatives have taken exactly this position. They believe that a tamed and moderate Islam can play an important role in countering the single greatest threat to the world: secularization. See Michael Novak, *The Universal Hunger for Liberty: Why the Clash of Civilizations Is Not Inevitable* (New York: Basic Books, 2004).

28. As a testament to his contempt for such a society, David Brooks refers to the man of bourgeois society as "Patio Man." See Brooks, "Patio Man Revisited," *New York Times*, October 20, 2008.

29. Strauss, *Liberalism Ancient and Modern* (New York: Basic Books, 1968), 24.

30. See Joseph Cropsey, "The United States as Regime and the Sources of the American Way of Life," in *The Moral Foundations of the American Republic*, ed. Robert Horowitz (Charlottesville: University Press of Virginia, 1977), 92.

31. Sir Francis Bacon, *The Advancement of Learning* in *The Works of Francis Bacon*, ed. Basil Montagu, vol. 1 (Philadelphia: Carey & Hart, 1852), 174.

32. Catherine and Michael Zuckert draw, by implication, very different conclusions than I do on the relationship between Strauss and the neocons and the philosophic status of the United States. The Zuckerts identify three propositions as "comprising the core of Strauss's approach to American liberal democracy: 1. America is modern. 2. Modernity is bad. 3. America is good." The syllogism that I have constructed obviously draws a very different conclusion. I shall argue that for Strauss and the neocons "America is bad." Zuckert and Zuckert, *The Truth About Leo Strauss*, 21.

33. Michael Novak, "In Praise of Bourgeois Virtues," *Society* 18, no. 2 (January/February 1981): 62.

34. See Joseph Schumpeter, *Capitalism, Socialism and Democracy,* 5th ed. (New York: Harper and Brothers; London: George Allen and Unwin, 1976).

35. See Daniel Bell, *The Cultural Contradictions of Capitalism* (New York: Basic Books, 1976).

36. Irving Kristol, *Neoconservatism: The Autobiography of an Idea* (New York: The Free Press, 1995), 100–01.

37. Irving Kristol, *Two Cheers for Capitalism* (New York: New American Library, 1978), xi.

38. Irving Kristol, "The Capitalist Future," a speech delivered as the 1991 Francis Boyer Lecture at the American Enterprise Institute, December 4, 1991; Kristol, *Two Cheers for Capitalism,* 174.

39. Irving Kristol, "No Cheers for the Profit Motive," *Wall Street Journal,* February 20, 1979, 16.

40. Kristol, *Two Cheers for Capitalism,* 80.

41. Kristol, *Two Cheers for Capitalism,* 245.

42. Kristol, *Two Cheers for Capitalism,* 237–38.

43. Kristol, *Two Cheers for Capitalism,* x.

44. Kristol, *Neoconservatism,* 143.

45. Irving Kristol, "The Spirit of '87," *Public Interest* no. 86 (Winter 1987): 8–9.

46. Irving Kristol, "The Disaffection of Capitalism," in *Capitalism and Socialism: A Theological Inquiry,* ed. Michael Novak (Washington, DC: AEI Press, 1988), 31.

47. Kristol, *Neoconservatism,* 441.

48. We shall examine Strauss's distinction between and his moral evaluation of the "open" and "closed" society in chapter 9.

49. See Walter Berns, *Making Patriots* (Chicago: University of Chicago Press, 2001), 79; Carnes Lord, *The Modern Prince: What Leaders Need to Know Now* (New Haven: Yale University Press, 2003), 138–39, 140, 229–30.

50. Kristol, *Reflections of a Neoconservative,* 76; Kristol, *Two Cheers for Capitalism,* 253.

Chapter 5

1. Martin Heidegger, *Introduction to Metaphysics,* trans. Gregory Fried and Richard Polt (New Haven: Yale University Press, 2000), 40, 47. The connection between Heidegger and Strauss is ably discussed in Steven Smith, *Reading Leo Strauss* (Chicago: University of Chicago Press, 2006), 108–30, and Zuckert and Zuckert, *The Truth About Leo Strauss,* 27–35, 91–102.

2. The subject of Heidegger's address was "The Self-Assertion of the German University."

3. Heidegger, *Introduction to Metaphysics,* 152. On the relationship between Heidegger's philosophy and his politics, see Richard Wolin, *The Politics of Being: The Political Thought of Martin Heidegger* (New York: Columbia University Press, 1980); Victor Farías, *Heidegger and Nazism,* with a foreword by Joseph Margolis and Tom Rockmore (Philadelphia: Temple University Press, 1987); Wolin, ed., *The Heidegger Controversy: A Critical Reader,* 2nd ed. (Cambridge: MIT Press, 1993); Wolin, *Heidegger's Children: Hannah Arendt, Karl Löwith, Hans Jonas, and Herbert Marcuse* (Princeton: Princeton University Press, 2001).

4. The purposes of Strauss's philosophic project are summed up elegantly in Harry Jaffa, "A Reply to Michael Zuckert's 'Jaffa's New Birth: Harry Jaffa at Ninety,'" *The Review of Politics* 71 (2009): 241–50.

5. See Martin Heidegger, "Plato's Doctrine of Truth," in *Pathmarks*, ed. William McNeill (Cambridge, UK: Cambridge University Press, 1998), 155–82. For an especially illuminating discussion of Heidegger's critique of Plato, see William Galston, "Heidegger's Plato: A Critique of 'Plato's Doctrine of the Truth,'" *Philosophical Forum* 13 (1982): 371–84.

6. Leo Strauss, *Natural Right and History* (Chicago: University of Chicago Press, 1950), 35, 30–31. See also Catherine H. Zuckert, *Postmodern Platos: Nietzsche, Heidegger, Gadamer, Strauss, Derrida* (Chicago: University of Chicago Press, 1996), 33–69.

7. The best recent discussions of Strauss's Socratic turn can be found in Zuckert, *Postmodern Platos*, 104–200; Steven Smith, *Reading Leo Strauss: Politics, Philosophy, Judaism* (Chicago: University of Chicago Press, 2006), 87–107; and Daniel Tanguay, *Leo Strauss: An Intellectual Biography* (New Haven: Yale University Press, 2007), 49–143.

8. The best overview and analysis of *Natural Right and History* is Richard Kennington's essay "Strauss's *Natural Right and History*," in *Leo Strauss's Political Thought: Toward a Critical Engagement*, ed. Alan Udoff (Boulder, CO: Lynne Rienner Publishers, 1991), 227–52.

9. The traditional view of Plato that Strauss was reacting against can be seen in John Dewey, *Reconstruction in Philosophy* (Boston: Beacon Press, 1920); and Karl Popper, *The Open Society and Its Enemies,* vol. 1, *The Spell of Plato* (Princeton: Princeton University Press, 1962).

10. This seems to be the thesis of Steven Smith's *Reading Leo Strauss: Politics, Philosophy, Judaism* (Chicago: University of Chicago Press, 2006). See also Robert Kagan, "I Am Not a Straussian, at Least I Don't Think I Am," *Weekly Standard,* February 6, 2006.

11. Leo Strauss, *The City and Man* (Chicago: University of Chicago Press, 1964), 127, 65.

12. Leo Strauss, *The Rebirth of Classical Political Rationalism* (Chicago: University of Chicago Press, 1989), 68.

13. Strauss, *The City and Man*, 124–25 (emphasis added). Note that for Strauss, the coming-into-being of the best regime is improbable rather than simply impossible. Put otherwise, the coming-into-being of the best regime is possible, but not likely.

14. Strauss, *Natural Right and History,* 91; Strauss, *Persecution and the Art of Writing* (Chicago: University of Chicago Press, 1952), 139, 17.

15. Strauss, *The Rebirth of Classical Political Rationalism*, 68; Strauss, *The City and Man,* 125, 138.

16. Curiously, Strauss's students have also been almost entirely silent on the question of Plato's idealism. In one of his later writings, though, Strauss could mention, in passing, Plato's recognition of Socrates's "crucial turn toward the 'ideas.'" See Strauss, *Socrates and Aristophanes* (New York: Basic Books, Inc., 1966), 4.

17. Strauss, *The City and Man,* 119.

18. The doctrine of Ideas and Forms is mentioned either directly or in passing in most Platonic dialogues (e.g., the *Meno,* the *Parmenides,* the *Cratylus,* the *Philebus,* the *Sophist,* the *Theaetetus,* the *Phaedo,* the *Phaedrus,* the *Symposium,* the *Timaeus*), including and

mostly famously in Book 6 of the *Republic*. See J. A. Stewart, *Plato's Doctrine of Ideas* (Oxford: Clarendon Press, 1909); Sir David Ross, *Plato's Theory of Ideas* (Oxford: Oxford University Press, 1951); and R. M. Dancy, *Plato's Introduction of Forms* (Cambridge, UK: Cambridge University Press, 2007).

19. The same questions can be asked of Strauss's students who, for the most part, follow their teacher in neglecting any serious discussion of the ideas. Partial but inadequate exceptions to the general rule include: Seth Benardete, *Socrates' Second Sailing: On Plato's Republic* (Chicago: University of Chicago Press, 1989), 157–76; Stanley Rosen, *Plato's Republic: A Study* (New Haven: Yale University Press, 2005), 255–301. Also see Rosen, *The Ancients and the Moderns: Rethinking Modernity* (New Haven: Yale University Press, 1989), 37–64.

20. Strauss, *What Is Political Philosophy?* (Chicago: University of Chicago Press, 1959), 38–39 (emphasis added).

21. Strauss, *The Rebirth of Classical Political Realism*, 259; *Natural Right and History*, 32.

22. Strauss, *On Tyranny. Including the Strauss-Kojève Correspondence*, ed. Victor Gourevitch and Michael Roth (Chicago: University of Chicago Press, 1991), 196 (emphasis added).

23. For Strauss's view on the philosopher and his relationship to the city, see Leo Strauss, *On Tyranny: Including the Strauss-Kojève Correspondence*, 205–06 (page references are to the revised edition). Interestingly, Gourevitch and Roth in their introduction to *On Tyranny* suggest that the political differences between Strauss and the Stalinist Kojève were "comparatively superficial" (ix). It is not unimportant to note that Kojève was, it is now believed, a KGB spy for the Soviet Union. On Kojève, see Mark Lilla, *The Reckless Mind: Intellectuals in Politics* (New York: New York Review of Books, 2001), 113–36. Also see this from the *New Criterion*: http://evans-experientialism.freewebspace .com/kojeve03.htm, and this from *Lingua Franca*: http://linguafranca.mirror.theinfo .org/0003/kojeve.html.

24. Leo Strauss, "Reason and Revelation," in *Leo Strauss and the Theologico-Political Problem*, by Heinrich Meier (Cambridge, UK: Cambridge University Press), 147–48.

25. Strauss, *On Tyranny*, 196; *What Is Political Philosophy?* 11, 38. In his correspondence with Kojève, Strauss indirectly mocks Aristotle's criticism of Plato's Ideas. The fact that Aristotle wrote treatises instead of dialogues suggests to Strauss that the Peripatetic mistakenly assumed that actual "wisdom" was possible rather than just philosophy as a way of life (Strauss to Kojève, May 28, 1957, *On Tyranny*, 276–80). Strauss goes on to suggest that Aristotle misunderstood Plato's doctrine of the Ideas because he did not understand (as Strauss apparently does) that Plato wrote ironically. Surely, though, it is utterly incredible to suggest that one of history's two or three greatest philosophers who was himself a student of Plato did not understand the irony of Plato's dialogical method. The suggestion is too absurd to take seriously.

26. Strauss's political amoralism provides the ground on which he could be, as we shall see in chapter 9, a "friend" to fascism at one time and place, and a "friend" to liberal democracy at another time and place.

27. Strauss, "Reason and Revelation," 147.

28. Leo Strauss, *Jewish Philosophy and the Crisis of Modernity: Essays and Lectures in Modern Jewish Thought*, ed. Kenneth Hart Green (Albany: State University of New York Press, 1997), 464–65.

29. Strauss, "A Giving of Accounts," 463.

30. Strauss, *Natural Right and History*, 151–52 (emphasis added).

31. Obviously David Brooks's condemnation of the "Leave Us Alone" philosophy applies only to ordinary people who might try to live free of the government and not to philosophers who really do want to be left alone by government!

32. Strauss, *Natural Right and History*, 151–52 (emphasis added).

33. Readers interested in exploring Strauss's thoughts on this subject should consult Victor Gourevitch, "The Problem of Natural Right and the Fundamental Alternatives in Natural Right and History," in *The Crisis of Liberal Democracy: A Straussian Perspective*, ed. Kenneth Deutsch and Walter Soffer (Albany: State University of New York Press, 1987), 30–47; and Marc D. Guera, "The Ambivalence of Classic Natural Right: Leo Strauss on Philosophy, Morality, and Statesmanship," *Perspectives on Political Science* 28 (Spring 1999): 69–74.

34. Leo Strauss, *Liberalism Ancient and Modern* (Chicago: University of Chicago Press, 1968), 6; *The City and Man*, 20; *What Is Political Philosophy?* 11.

35. Strauss, "Reason and Revelation," 162, 147, 146. At first blush, Strauss seems to present classical natural right as a unified or single doctrine that unites Socrates-Plato and Aristotle around a common view of nature. A close reading of chapter 6 on "Classical Natural Right" in *Natural Right and History* shows instead that Strauss equates classical teleology (as least as it relates to the human soul) and natural right with the Socratic view of philosophy: "Plato eventually defines natural right with direct reference to the fact that the only life which is simply just is the life of the philosopher" (156). Absent from Strauss's account of classical natural right is Aristotle's teleological view of nature or of the "whole" and the moral theory that necessarily goes with it. Strauss views Aristotelian natural right as "vulgar" when compared with the Socratic-Platonic account of natural right.

36. Strauss, *Natural Right and History*, 32; *What Is Political Philosophy?* 38–39; Strauss, "On a New Interpretation of Plato's Political Philosophy," *Social Research* 13, no. 3 (September 1946): 351.

37. Strauss, *Natural Right and History*, 32; *What Is Political Philosophy?* 39.

38. Strauss, *Natural Right and History*, 35.

39. Leo Strauss, "Farabi's *Plato*," in *Louis Ginzberg: Jubilee Volume on the Occasion of His Seventieth Birthday*, ed. Saul Lieberman, Shalom Spiegel, Solomon Zeitlin, and Alexander Marx (New York: American Academy for Jewish Research, 1945), 359 (emphasis added); Strauss, *The Rebirth of Classical Political Rationalism*, 68.

40. Strauss, *Natural Right and History*, 11–12; *Liberalism Ancient and Modern*, 13, 20; *Natural Right and History*, 12.

41. Strauss, *On Tyranny*, 278–79 (emphasis added).

42. Ibid., 197–200, 212; *Natural Right and History*, 122; *On Tyranny*, 212 (emphasis added). See also Strauss's essay "On the *Euthyphron*" in *The Rebirth of Classical Political Rationalism*, 187–206. Strauss often refers to something he calls the "whole." He never defines the term, but it seems clear from the context in which he uses it that it refers to the traditional Platonic realm of Ideas and the Form of the Good.

43. Strauss, *Natural Right and History*, 123.

44. Strauss, *Thoughts on Machiavelli* (Glencoe, IL: The Free Press, 1958), 13; *Natural Right and History*, 123, 124; *The City and Man*, 20.

45. Strauss, *The Rebirth of Classical Political Rationalism*, 169. Stanley Rosen draws somewhat similar conclusions about Strauss's ascent to the "eternal order of the whole" in his *Hermeneutics as Politics* (Oxford: Oxford University Press, 1987), 126–27. For

Rosen's Strauss, "divine madness" is "an act of the will," which he suggestively characterizes a Kantian rather than a Platonic move.

46. Strauss, *Natural Right and History*, 75; *What Is Political Philosophy?* 38–39; *Natural Right and History*, 75.

47. Leo Strauss, "Why We Remain Jews: Can Jewish Faith and History Still Speak to Us?" in *Leo Strauss: Political Philosopher and Jewish Thinker*, ed. Kenneth L. Deutsch and Walter Nicgorski (Lanham, MD: Rowman & Littlefield, 1994), 61 (emphasis added).

48. Strauss, *Natural Right and History*, 12, 130, 12–25 (emphasis added), 5, 128; *On Tyranny*, 279; *Natural Right and History*, 125. For Strauss on divination, see also Leo Strauss, *On Plato's Symposium*, ed. and with a foreword by Seth Benardete (Chicago: University of Chicago Press, 2001), 106–15, 288.

49. Leo Strauss to Alexandre Kojève, April 22, 1957, in *On Tyranny*, 274–76.

50. Strauss, *Xenophon's Socrates* (Ithaca, NY: Cornell University Press, 1972), 124–26. See also Strauss, *The Rebirth of Classical Political Rationalism*, 138.

51. Leo Strauss, *Philosophy and Law: Essays Toward the Understanding of Maimonides and His Predecessors*, trans. Fred Baumann and with a foreword by Ralph Lerner (Berlin: Schocken Verlag, 1935; reprint, Philadelphia: Jewish Publication Society, 1987), 3, 52 (page references are to the reprint edition).

52. Strauss, *Philosophy and Law*, 46–47, 44, 51, 85 (emphasis original). Plato's *Symposium* (and Strauss's interpretation of it) may hold the key to a deeper understanding of Plato-Strauss's view on how the Ideas can be accessed. As Seth Benardete, one of Strauss's best students has written, the Socratic discovery of and education to the Ideas was temporarily halted by Parmenides, who seemed to prove the impossibility of the Ideas. According to Parmenides, the problem with the doctrine of Ideas is not that they don't exist, but rather that they can't be known with certainty. The gap between divine and human knowledge is permanent and too great. In other words, the epistemological problem is *the* problem. In the *Symposium*, Diotima, Socrates's teacher, provides Socrates with the solution to the problem: namely, through "her notion of the in-between or the demonic"—that is, with the *daimonion* and divination. *Plato's Symposium*, trans. by Seth Benardete with commentaries by Allan Bloom and Seth Benardete (Chicago: University of Chicago Press, 2001), 191.

53. See Strauss, *Thoughts on Machiavelli*, 296. See also Tanguay, *Leo Strauss: An Intellectual Biography*, 137.

54. Strauss, *What Is Political Philosophy?* 32. See also Strauss, *The Rebirth of Classical Political Rationalism*, 138, where Strauss likens divination to Socrates's "demonic thing"; *Natural Right and History*, 156.

Chapter 6

1. Leo Strauss, *Persecution and the Art of Writing* (Chicago: University of Chicago Press, 1952), 34; Strauss, *The Rebirth of Classical Political Rationalism: An Introduction to the Thought of Leo Strauss* (Chicago: University of Chicago Press, 1989), 68. A helpful article disentangling Strauss's views and those of his students is Ralph C. Hancock, "What Was Political Philosophy? Or: The Straussian Philosopher and His Other," *Political Science Reviewer* 36 (2007): 13–46.

2. Leo Strauss, *Natural Right and History* (Chicago: University of Chicago Press, 1953), 142.

3. Leo Strauss, *An Introduction to Political Philosophy: Ten Essays by Leo Strauss*, ed. and with an introduction by Hilail Gildin (Detroit: Wayne State University Press, 1989), 85–86.

4. Leo Strauss, *What Is Political Philosophy?* (Chicago: University of Chicago Press, 1959), 12, 15. Classical natural right, as Strauss understands it, is different from natural law and natural rights. Natural law is made up of commandment and punishment. It commands obedience to God's laws and it punishes in the afterlife those who break God's laws. For Strauss, the natural-rights doctrine, by contrast, is synonymous with the subjective freedom to pursue one's values free of any moral constraint except the constraint to not violate the freedom of others to choose whatever values they please.

5. Strauss, *Natural Right and History*, 127.

6. Leo Strauss, "Notes on Carl Schmitt, *The Concept of the Political*," in Heinrich Meier, *Carl Schmitt and Leo Strauss: The Hidden Dialogue, Including Strauss's Notes on Schmitt's Concept of the Political & Three Letters from Strauss to Schmitt*, with a foreword by Joseph Cropsey (Chicago: University of Chicago Press, 1995), 119.

7. Strauss, *Natural Right and History*, 249–50, 251, 42.

8. Strauss, *Liberalism Ancient and Modern* (Chicago: University of Chicago Press, 1968), 21.

9. Strauss, *Natural Right and History*, 186.

10. Ibid., 140–41.

11. Ibid., 140–41, 139.

12. Strauss, *Liberalism Ancient and Modern*, 225.

13. Strauss, *Natural Right and History*, 162, 160–61. It should be clear now that Irving Kristol's notion of a "governing philosophy" is a watered-down version of Strauss's understanding of classical natural right. In the next chapter, we shall demonstrate how this element of classical natural right and prudence blends into Machiavellian prudence.

14. Ibid., 162.

15. Ibid., 129; Leo Strauss to Karl Löwith, August 15, 1946, in "Correspondence Concerning Modernity: Karl Löwith and Leo Strauss," *Independent Journal of Philosophy* 4 (1983): 107; Strauss, *Philosophy and Law: Essays Toward the Understanding of Maimonides and His Predecessors*, trans. Fred Baumann and with a foreword by Ralph Lerner (Berlin: Schocken Verlag, 1935; reprint, Philadelphia: Jewish Publication Society, 1987), 53.

16. See Strauss, *Natural Right and History*, 193; Walter Berns, *Making Patriots* (Chicago: University of Chicago Press, 2001).

17. Strauss, *What Is Political Philosophy?* 40; *The Rebirth of Classical Political Rationalism*, 164; *Natural Right and History*, 160–61.

18. Strauss, *Natural Right and History*, 134.

19. Ibid., 248–49, 251. At the deepest philosophical level, Strauss sees the difference between classical and modern natural right as hinging on the difference between the ancients' reliance on "a teleological view of the universe" and the moderns' denial of teleology and its reliance on a mechanistic view of science. Strauss understands that his attempt to revive classical natural right is rendered problematic in the light of "the victory of modern natural science." (See *Natural Right and History*, 7–8.)

20. Strauss, *Liberalism Ancient and Modern*, x; Leo Strauss to Karl Löwith, *Independent Journal of Philosophy* 4 (1983): 107–08.

21. Strauss, *Natural Right and History*, 130–33.

22. Ibid., 133.

23. Strauss, *The Rebirth of Classical Political Rationalism*, 68–69; Strauss, "Why We Remain Jews," in *Leo Strauss: Political Philosopher and Jewish Thinker*, ed. Kenneth L. Deutsch and Walter Nicgorski (Lanham, MD: Rowman & Littlefield, 1994), 52.

24. See Strauss, *On Tyranny. Including the Strauss-Kojève Correspondence*, ed. Victor Gourevitch and Michael Roth (Chicago: University of Chicago Press, 1991), 205–06.

25. Leo Strauss, *Studies in Platonic Political Philosophy*, with an introduction by Thomas L. Pangle (Chicago: University of Chicago Press, 1983), 139. In chapter 7, we explore in much greater depth the relationship between classical and Machiavellian prudence.

26. Strauss, *What Is Political Philosophy?* 14; *Natural Right and History*, 142; *What Is Political Philosophy?* 28.

27. Strauss, *The Rebirth of Classical Political Rationalism*, 144.

28. Plato, *The Laws of Plato*, trans., notes, and introduction by Thomas L. Pangle (Chicago: University of Chicago Press, 1980), 875c–d. Plato says that the man born with such wisdom is born "with a divine dispensation," 271.

29. See Waller R. Newell, *Ruling Passion: The Erotics of Statecraft in Platonic Political Philosophy* (Lanham, MD: Rowman & Littlefield Publishers, 2000).

30. Strauss, *Liberalism Ancient and Modern*, 24.

31. Strauss, *What Is Political Philosophy?* 28; *On Tyranny*, 200. See also Harry Clor, *On Moderation: Defending an Ancient Virtue in a Modern World* (Baylor, TX: Baylor University Press, 2008). One of Strauss's recent public defenders, the neoconservative Peter Berkowitz, has attempted to infuse the conservative intellectual movement and the Republican Party with Strauss's understanding of moderation and prudence. See Berkowitz, "Moderation is No Vice, and Extremism is No Virtue in Politics," *Weekly Standard*, July 27, 2009.

32. In his essay of tribute to Kurt Riezler, Strauss clearly seems to support Riezler's preference for the nobility of "nationalism" over the techno-hedonism associated with "cosmopolitanism." Strauss was not a "nationalist" in a strict philosophical sense. He was an advocate of the small "polis," but in the context of the modern world he saw the nation as a "half-way house between the polis and the cosmopolis." More to the point, the nation was a halfway house on the road to the polis. Strauss found nationalism to be "theoretically unsatisfactory," but he also thought it might "supply us with the best available framework for understanding the present political situation and for enlightening political action within a world that is dominated for all the foreseeable future by nationalism." At the very least, Strauss saw nationalism as an antidote to the modern ideal, which "does not leave room for reverence, the matrix of human nobility." "Reverence is primarily," Strauss noted, "reverence for one's heritage, for tradition." See Strauss, "Kurt Riezler (1882–1955)," chap. in *What Is Political Philosophy?* 235–41.

33. Strauss, *What Is Political Philosophy?* 222.

34. Strauss, *Liberalism Ancient and Modern*, 100, 85; *Natural Right and History*, 260; *What Is Political Philosophy?* 221–22; *Thoughts on Machiavelli* (Glencoe, IL: The Free Press, 1958), 230–31. Readers of Strauss's discussion on Rousseau in chapter 6 of *Natural Right and History* can't help but be struck by Strauss's seeming sympathy with Rousseau's *First Discourse* and its anti-Enlightenment posture.

35. Strauss, *Liberalism Ancient and Modern*, 206.

36. Strauss, *Persecution and the Art of Writing*, 16–17. For readers unfamiliar with Plato's *Republic*, Thrasymachus is a central interlocutor of Socrates. Thrasymachus is famous in the history of philosophy for defending the position that justice should be defined as the advantage of the stronger. Strauss's Thrasymachus is the representative

of the strictly conventional view of justice—"that justice consists in obeying the law or that the just is identical with the lawful or legal, or with what the customs or laws of the city prescribe." Strauss calls Thrasymachus's view of justice "the most obvious, the most natural, thesis regarding justice." Strauss, *The City and Man* (Chicago: University of Chicago Press, 1964), 74–75.

37. Strauss, *Persecution and the Art of Writing*, 16–17; *The Rebirth of Classical Political Rationalism*, 159.

38. See Strauss, *Thoughts on Machiavelli*, 288–92.

39. Strauss, *Natural Right and History*, 162–63.

40. Strauss, *What Is Political Philosophy?* 90, 80–83 (emphasis added).

41. Readers should compare Strauss's view of statesmanship with those views of his discussed in chapter 9. It is precisely on these grounds that Strauss could appear to support "fascism" in 1933 *and* liberal democracy once he had moved to America.

42. Strauss, *What Is Political Philosophy?* 10; *The City and Man*, 29; *What Is Political Philosophy?* 86, *Natural Right and History*, 321; "What Can We Learn from Political Theory," *The Review of Politics* 69 (2007): 522. See also Strauss, *Liberalism Ancient and Modern*, 205–06. In his introduction to Strauss's *Studies in Platonic Political Philosophy*, Thomas L. Pangle sums up Strauss's central point this way: "The conflicts among the various 'regimes' are the decisive conflicts at the root of all political life; and it is the aim of Platonic political philosophy in the narrow or strict sense to arbitrate these conflicts" (7).

43. Strauss, *Persecution and the Art of Writing*, 16–17.

44. Leo Strauss, "What Can We Learn from Political Theory," 522.

45. Leo Strauss to Karl Löwith, August 15, 1946, *Independent Journal of Philosophy* 4 (1983): 107–08.

Chapter 7

1. Irving Kristol, *Reflections of a Neoconservative: Looking Back, Looking Forward* (New York: Basic Books, 1983), xii.

2. Readers should note, however, that the neocons are disingenuous on this point. They appeal to the past all the time. As we have seen, their deepest philosophic commitments are drawn from a premodern world of ideas.

3. Daniel Bell, *The End of Ideology: On the Exhaustion of Political Ideas in the Fifties* (New York: Free Press, 1965).

4. Kristol, *Reflections of a Neoconservative*, xii.

5. Ibid., xii, 75 (emphasis added).

6. See Irving Kristol, *Neoconservatism: The Autobiography of an Idea* (New York: Free Press, 1995), 158.

7. Leo Strauss, *Persecution and the Art of Writing* (Chicago: University of Chicago Press, 1952), 16. See Strauss's essay on "Niccolo Machiavelli," in *History of Political Philosophy*, 2nd ed., ed. by Leo Strauss and Joseph Cropsey (Chicago: Rand McNally, 1972), 292, where Socrates and Machiavelli merge into one. Further study is warranted on Strauss's understanding of Thrasymachus and his possible relationship to Machiavelli in Strauss's thought.

8. Irving Kristol, review of *Persecution and the Art of Writing*, by Leo Strauss, in *Commentary* (October 1952): 394.

9. See Leo Strauss, *Thoughts on Machiavelli* (Glencoe, IL: The Free Press, 1958), 185, 254, 258, 288–94. We recognize, of course, that Strauss understood there to be serious if not decisive differences between Plato and Machiavelli. Strauss clearly disapproved of the openness with which Machiavelli exposed the unsavory truths of politics and morality. (See Strauss, *Thoughts on Machiavelli,* 10.) Strauss also rejects Machiavelli's denigration of the philosophic way of life as the true and natural end of human life. Does this mean, however, as some claim, that Strauss thought the chasm between Plato and Machiavelli unbridgeable? (See Catherine H. Zuckert and Michael Zuckert, *The Truth about Leo Strauss* [Chicago: University of Chicago Press, 2006], 183.) In our view, Strauss's understanding of philosophy is such that Machiavelli can be subsumed under or reconciled with Plato. It is true that Machiavelli neutered and rejected the traditional view of philosophy, but the more fundamental point is that Plato's philosophy makes room (even if it's the smallest space) for Machiavelli's account of political reality.

10. See Strauss, *Thoughts on Machiavelli,* 43.

11. Ibid., 296.

12. Leo Strauss, "Niccolo Machiavelli," in *History of Political Philosophy,* 2nd ed., ed. Leo Strauss and Joseph Cropsey (Chicago: Rand McNally College, 1972), 291–92.

13. See Strauss, *Thoughts on Machiavelli,* 11; Strauss, *The City and Man* (Chicago: University of Chicago Press, 1964), 5; Strauss, *Natural Right and History* (Chicago: University of Chicago Press, 1953), 106. We do not here claim that Strauss is a "Machiavellian" (at least not in the crude sense of the term), but only that he believed that Machiavelli taught some enduring truths that could and should be used by Straussian-trained philosophic statesmen in the appropriate situations. To the extent that Strauss accepted some of Machiavelli's ideas, it is important to note that he was not advising future rulers to use Machiavellian prudence for the sake of personal advancement or gain. Strauss does seem to lend support to the idea that amoral Machiavellian means can be used in order to promote the common good during extreme circumstances. See Zuckert and Zuckert, *The Truth about Leo Strauss,* 183–84.

14. Leo Strauss to Alexandre Kojève, April 22, 1957, in Strauss, *On Tyranny, Including the Strauss-Kojève Correspondence,* ed. Victor Gourevitch and Michael Roth (Chicago: University of Chicago Press, 1991), 274–76.

15. Kristol's quip is probably the best known and certainly the most frequently quoted description of neoconservatism. The actual origin of the term is less well known. See "Neo-conservative Guru to America's New Order: Q and A: Irving Kristol," *MacLeans,* January 19, 1981, 9.

16. Niccolï Machiavelli, *The Prince,* trans. and with an introduction by Harvey C. Mansfield (Chicago: University of Chicago Press, 1998), 61.

17. Irving Kristol, *Two Cheers for Capitalism* (New York: New American Library, 1978), 222; *Reflections of Neoconservative,* 117, 50–51; David Brooks, "A Partnership of Minds," *New York Times,* July 20, 2007; Brooks, "The Kennedy Mystique," *New York Times,* January 29, 2008, www.nytimes.com/2008/01/29/opinion/29brooks.html. The notion of a "public household" comes from Daniel Bell's *The Cultural Contradictions of Capitalism* (New York: Basic Books, Inc., 1976): 220–82.

18. Daniel Bell and Irving Kristol, "What Is the Public Interest? *Public Interest,* no. 1 (Fall 1965): 1.

19. See Carnes Lord, *The Modern Prince: What Leaders Need to Know Now* (New Haven: Yale University Press, 2003), 42–43.

20. Leo Strauss, *What Is Political Philosophy?* (Chicago: University of Chicago Press, 1959), 235–40, 260.

21. David Brooks, "The McCain Insurrection," *Weekly Standard*, February 14, 2000; Irving Kristol, *Two Cheers for Capitalism*, 221–22; Kristol, *Reflections of a Neoconservative*, 51.

22. Irving Kristol, *Two Cheers for Capitalism*, 253.

23. David Brooks, "The Republican Collapse," *New York Times*, October 5, 2007, www.nytimes.com/2007/10/05/opinion/05brooks.html; "The Social Animal," *New York Times*, September 12, 2008, www.nytimes.com/2008/09/12/opinion/12brooks .html.

24. David Brooks, "Harmony and the Dream," *New York Times*, August 12, 2008.

25. Michael Novak, *The Rise of the Unmeltable Ethnics* (New York: Macmillan, 1972), 235.

26. Irving Kristol, *Reflections of a Neoconservative* (New York: Basic Books, 1983), 51, xiii.

27. Niccolo Machiavelli, *The Prince and the Discourses*, with an introduction by Max Lerner (New York: Modern Library, 1950), 129. This view is endorsed by Carnes Lord in *The Modern Prince*, 19.

28. Michael Ledeen, *Machiavelli on Modern Leadership: Why Machiavelli's Iron Rules Are as Timely and Important Today as Five Centuries Ago* (New York: St. Martin's Press, 1999), 8, 26.

29. Irving Kristol, "Skepticism, Meliorism, and *The Public Interest*," *Public Interest* no. 81 (Fall 1985): 41; Adam Wolfson, "Conservatives and Neoconservatives," chap. in *The Neocon Reader*, ed. and with an introduction by Irwin Stelzer (New York: Grove Press, 2004), 222.

30. Kristol, *Two Cheers for Capitalism*, 22.

31. Machiavelli, *The Prince and the Discourses*, 441; *The Prince*, 99. Machiavelli's point is indicated by one chapter title from the *Discourses on Livy* ("Whoever Desires Constant Success Must Change His Conduct with the Times"), 441–43. See also Lord, *The Modern Prince*, 19.

32. For a succinct presentation of Machiavelli's understanding and use of the concept "fortuna," see Harvey C. Mansfield's introduction to his translation of *The Prince*, vii–xxiv. In the end, Plato's view of the reality of this world is remarkably similar to Machiavelli's view of the world as it is lived day-to-day by ordinary men. See Lord, *The Modern Prince*, 19.

33. Irving Kristol, review of *Persecution and the Art of Writing*, 394.

34. Kristol, *Two Cheers for Capitalism*, 54–55.

35. Irving Kristol, review of *Persecution and the Art of Writing*, 394.

36. David Brooks, "An Economy of Faith and Trust," *New York Times*, January 16, 2009, www.nytimes.com/2009/01/16/opinion/16brooks.html; "The Empathy Issue," *New York Times*, May 29, 2009.

37. See, for instance, Strauss's essay "Progress or Return?" chap. in *The Rebirth of Classical Political Rationalism: An Introduction to the Thought of Leo Strauss*, with an introduction by Thomas L. Pangle (Chicago: University of Chicago Press, 1989), 227–77.

38. David Brooks, "The Empathy Issue." For a devastating critique of Brooks on this point, see Harry Binswanger, "David Brooks—A Modern Day Peter Keating," *Capitalism Magazine*, June 11, 2009.

39. David Frum and Richard Perle, "Beware the Soft-Line Ideologues," *Wall Street Journal*, January 7, 2004, www.opinionjournal.com/editorial/feature.html? id=110004537.

40. Kristol, *Neoconservatism*, 8.

41. Kristol, *Two Cheers for Capitalism*, 129.

42. Neo-Kantianism was a movement in the second half of the nineteenth century and the first quarter of the twentieth century that sought to revive and modify the ideas of the eighteenth-century German philosopher Immanuel Kant. Interestingly, Leo Strauss's earliest and most formative intellectual influences came from neo-Kantianism. He was a graduate student at the University of Marburg, the intellectual center of early-twentieth-century neo-Kantianism. Strauss wrote his dissertation on Hermann Cohen, the philosophic doyen of neo-Kantianism, which he wrote under Ernst Cassirer, a leading neo-Kantian philosopher. Curiously, though, as with Plato's doctrine of Ideas, Strauss wrote virtually nothing on Kant's political philosophy, which surely makes the connection an avenue worth exploring.

43. Walter Berns, *Freedom Virtue & the First Amendment* (Baton Rouge: Louisiana State University Press, 1957), 251.

44. Irving Kristol, *Reflections of a Neoconservative*, 50–51 (emphasis added).

45. A simple but poignant example of how the neocons package and repackage their political philosophy for public consumption can be seen in the different names they have given to their creed. In recent years they have gussied themselves up as "One-Nation Conservatives," "National-Greatness Conservatives," "Big-Government Conservatives," and, most recently, as "Fresh-Start Conservatives."

46. Kristol, *Two Cheers for Capitalism*, 129.

47. Irving Kristol quoted in Ronald Bailey, "Origin of the Specious," *Reason*, July 1997, www.reason.com/news/show/30329.html (emphasis added).

48. Richard Neuhaus, "Encountered by the Truth," *First Things* (October 1998): 82. Presumably this explains, then, why the leading postmodernist philosopher, Michel Foucault, became enraptured at the end of his life with the Iranian Revolution of the Ayattolah Komeini.

49. See Gertrude Himmelfarb, *On Looking Into the Abyss: Untimely Thoughts on Culture and Society* (New York: Vintage, 1995); *The De-moralization Of Society: From Victorian Virtues to Modern Values* (New York: Vintage, 1996); *One Nation, Two Cultures: A Searching Examination of American Society in the Aftermath of Our Cultural Revolution* (New York: Vintage, 2001); *The Moral Imagination: From Edmund Burke to Lionel Trilling* (Chicago: Ivan R. Dee, 2007).

50. David Brooks, "The End of Philosophy," *New York Times*, April 7, 2009, www.nytimes.com/2009/04/07/opinion/07Brooks.html.

51. This point was made clear to me several years ago through personal experience. I once knew a Straussian professor at Ashland University who proclaimed publicly that he had "chosen to live the philosophic way of life." The claim was laughable on its face, but it took on a much more ominous meaning when I witnessed this same man commit a series of profoundly immoral acts. When I demanded that he justify his actions and when I subsequently judged and condemned him morally, he looked at me quizzically and wondered how I could be so naïve as to not see and appreciate that his actions were so obviously, as he said, to acquire "money and power." It was at that precise moment that I began to question and understand the meaning of the Straussian split between theory and practice, between the "realm of theoretical truth" (i.e., the realm inhabited

by philosophers) and the "realm of practical moral guidance" (i.e., the realm inhabited by nonphilosophers). The professor in question saw no contradiction, no problem between his chosen public profession (i.e., "the philosophic way of life") and his private actions.

52. David Brooks, "The End of Philosophy."

53. Leo Strauss, *Thoughts on Machiavelli*, 9. See Irving Kristol's essay, "Machiavelli and the Profanation of Politics," in *Neoconservatism: The Autobiography of an Idea*, 158.

54. Ledeen, *Machiavelli on Modern Leadership*, xvi, 188, xix.

55. Robert D. Kaplan, *Warrior Politics: Why Leadership Demands a Pagan Ethos* (New York: Vintage Books, 2003), 14, 52–64, 69, 77, 82. Kaplan, we should note, is not always identified as a neoconservative. His *Warrior Politics*, however, certainly reads as a standard neocon tract. This is particularly true if one follows his footnotes, which read as a "who's who" of Straussian A-team influences.

56. Lord, *The Modern Prince*, xiv; Irving Kristol, "The End Game of the Welfare State," *Wall Street Journal*, September 11, 1989, and "The Trouble With Republicans," *Wall Street Journal*, April 22, 1988.

57. Strauss, *Natural Right and History*, 130–33; Ledeen, *Machiavelli on Modern Leadership*, 89–90.

58. Irving Kristol, *Reflections of a Neoconservative*, 129.

59. See Kristol, "The End Game of the Welfare State," *Wall Street Journal*, September 11, 1989; and "Machiavelli and the Profanation of Politics," chap. in *Reflections of a Neoconservative*, 128–29, 130, 134 (emphasis added).

60. Strauss, *The City and Man*, 5.

61. Kristol, *Reflections of a Neoconservative*, 76.

62. David Brooks, "The McCain Transition," "The Kennedy Mystique," and "Snapping to Attention," *New York Times*, February 1, 2008, www.nytimes.com/2008/02/01/opinion/01brooks.html; January 29, 2008, www.nytimes.com/2008/01/29/opinion/29brooks.html; and August 3, 2004, www.nytimes.com/2004/08/03/opinion/03broo.html. Brooks's call for a national service program and his glamorization of the Prussian virtues reminds one of Strauss's essay on "German Nihilism" discussed in chapter 9. We shall discuss the neocons' national service programs at greater length in chapter 10.

63. Kristol quoted in Ronald Bailey, "The Voice of Neoconservatism," *Reason Magazine*, October 17, 2001, at www.reason.com/news/show/34900.html; Kristol, *Reflections of a Neoconservative*, 315. Kristol's posture toward religion was, in part, learned from Strauss. Strauss was not embarrassed to give public lectures on subjects such as "Why We Remain Jews: Can Jewish Faith and History Still Speak to Us?" at the same time that his best students knew very well that "No competent student of Leo Strauss was ever in doubt" as to Strauss's atheism. Such lectures were part and parcel of Strauss's political rhetoric to convince the people, and conservatives in particular, that philosophers are not atheists. See Stanley Rosen, *Hermeneutics as Politics* (Oxford: Oxford University Press, 1987), 112.

64. Ledeen, *Machiavelli on Modern Leadership*, 109. See Lord, *The Modern Prince*, 65; Machiavelli, *The Prince*, chapter 18 (emphasis added).

65. See Irving Kristol, "A New Look at Capitalism," *National Review*, April 17, 1981, 414.

66. This position is staked out most clearly in the writings of the Catholic neoconservative Michael Novak. See Novak's *The Universal Hunger for Liberty: Why the Clash*

of Civilizations Is Not Inevitable (New York: Basic Books, 2004), particularly chapter 9. Remarkably, in a post–September 11 world, Novak has called for the brotherhood of Muslims, Christians, and all other peoples of faith to fight humankind's real enemy—secularization. See our chapter 8 on foreign policy for further evidence of the neocons' support for religion.

67. David Brooks, "A Moral Philosophy for Middle-Class America," *New York Times*, October 15, 2006, 12.

68. Kristol, *Reflections of a Neoconservative*, 300 (emphasis added). Kristol's comment bears a striking resemblance to the views of Strauss. Interestingly, Kristol's essay was first published in 1949, which suggests that Kristol may have come into contact with Strauss's thought several years before his review of *Persecution and the Art of Writing*.

69. Ibid., 51.

70. Ibid., 50–51.

71. The pragmatic metaphysics and intellectual technique of John Dewey has more in common with the Platonic-Machiavellian understanding of reality than it does with the Enlightenment view of reality. Strauss shares with Dewey a moral revulsion of classical-liberal principles. Like Dewey, Strauss sought to overturn the Founders' individual-rights republic, but unlike Dewey, Strauss was backward-looking while Dewey was forward-looking.

72. On the Straussian and neoconservative conflation of Aristotelian and Machiavellian prudence, see Lord, *The Modern Prince*, 21–32. As Lord writes: "It would be a mistake ... to draw too sharp a contrast between Aristotle and Machiavelli on these fundamental issues" (32).

73. For an excellent discussion of Machiavelli on prudence, see Harvey C. Mansfield, *Machiavelli's Virtue* (Chicago: University of Chicago Press, 1996), 38–45.

74. Lord, *The Modern Prince*, 67–68, 225–26.

75. Machiavelli, *The Prince*, chapter 18.

76. See Irving Kristol, "Machiavelli and the Profanation of Politics," chap. in *Reflections of a Neoconservative*. Carnes Lord has stated in *The Modern Prince* that it would be a "mistake" to draw "too sharp a contrast between Aristotle and Machiavelli" on the nature of prudence (32). Also see Ledeen, *Machiavelli on Modern Leadership*, 61, 69, 112–41.

77. Ledeen, *Machiavelli on Modern Leadership*, 173–74, 19–20. Ledeen's call for a "strong, resolute, and virtuous leader" reminds one of Heidegger's praise of "resoluteness" in his most important work, *Being and Time*. Strauss attributed Heidegger's fascism to his notion of "resoluteness" (Leo Strauss, "A Giving of Accounts" in *Jewish Philosophy and the Crisis of Modernity*, ed. Kenneth Green [New York: State University of New York Press, 1997], 461.)

78. Kristol, *Two Cheers for Capitalism*, 54–55.

79. Ibid.

80. David Brooks, "The Behavioral Revolution," *New York Times*, October 28, 2008 (emphasis added), www.nytimes.com/2008/10/28/opinion/28iht-edbrooks.1.17312377.html.

81. Ledeen, *Machiavelli on Modern Leadership*, 89–90 (emphasis added). See George F. Will, *Statecraft as Soulcraft: What Government Does* (New York: Simon & Schuster, 1983).

82. Irving Kristol, *Two Cheers for Capitalism*, 54.

83. Ledeen, *Machiavelli on Modern Leadership*, 188.

84. David Brooks, "How to Reinvent the GOP," *New York Times,* August 29, 2004, www.nytimes.com/2004/08/29/magazine/29REPUBLICANS.html? pagewanted=al.
85. Kristol, *Two Cheers for Capitalism,* 4.
86. Alexis de Tocqueville, *Democracy in America,* trans., ed., and with an introduction by Harvey C. Mansfield and Delba Winthrop (Chicago: University of Chicago Press, 2000), 661–65.

Chapter 8

1. George W. Bush, Second Presidential Debate, October 11, 2000, www.debates .org/pages/trans2000b.html.
2. Ibid.
3. It is no wonder that in the 2000 Republican primaries, neoconservatives, for the most part, did not support Bush, but rather the far more interventionist candidate, John McCain.
4. George W. Bush, "Address Before a Joint Session of the Congress on the State of the Union," January 31, 2006, as transcribed in John T. Woolley and Gerhard Peters, *The American Presidency Project,* www.presidency.ucsb.edu/ws/index.php?pid=65090.
5. William Kristol and Robert Kagan, "Toward a Neo-Reaganite Foreign Policy," *Foreign Affairs* 75 (July/August 1996): 20.
6. See, for example, Kristol and Kagan, "Toward a Neo-Reaganite Foreign Policy"; Charles Krauthammer, "The Neoconservative Convergence," *Commentary* 120, no. 1 (July/August 2005); William Kristol and Robert Kagan, eds., *Present Dangers: Crisis and Opportunity in American Foreign Policy* (San Francisco: Encounter Books, 2000); Joshua Muravchik, *Exporting Democracy: Fulfilling America's Destiny* (Washington, DC: AEI Press, 1992); Donald Kagan and Frederick W. Kagan, *While America Sleeps: Self-Delusion, Military Weakness, and the Threat to Peace Today* (New York: St. Martin's Press, 2000).
7. Kristol and Kagan, "Towards a Neo-Reaganite Foreign Policy," 19.
8. Kristol and Kagan, *Present Dangers,* 4.
9. Kristol and Kagan, "Towards a Neo-Reaganite Foreign Policy," 20.
10. Ibid.
11. Ibid., 26–27.
12. Robert Kagan, "Power and Weakness," *Policy Review* no. 113 (June/July 2002): 11.
13. J. Bottum, "A Nation Mobilized," *Weekly Standard,* September 24, 2001, 8.
14. George W. Bush, "Address Before a Joint Session of the Congress on the United States Response to the Terrorist Attacks of September 11," September 20, 2001. As transcribed in Woolley and Peters, *The American Presidency Project,* www.presidency .ucsb.edu/ws/index.php?pid=64731.
15. "How Wide a War?," PBS interview, 9/21/01, www.pbs.org/newshour/bb/ terrorism/july-dec01/wide_war.html.
16. George W. Bush, "Remarks on the 20th Anniversary of the National Endowment for Democracy," November 6, 2003, as transcribed in Woolley and Peters, *The American Presidency Project,* www.presidency.ucsb.edu/ws/index.php?pid=844.
17. Charles Krauthammer, "The Neoconservative Convergence," 26.

18. "Bush calls end to 'major combat,'" CNN.com, May 2, 2003, www.cnn .com/2003/WORLD/meast/05/01/sprj.irq.main.

19. Anonymous, "Parody," *Weekly Standard,* April 21, 2003, 40.

20. Robert Kagan and William Kristol, "The Right War for the Right Reasons," *Weekly Standard,* February 23, 2004, 20.

21. George W. Bush, "Remarks on the 20th Anniversary of the National Endowment for Democracy."

22. Max Boot, *The Savage Wars of Peace,* repr. ed. (New York: Basic Books, 2003), 350.

23. Kristol and Kagan, *Present Dangers,* 16.

24. Max Boot, "The Case for American Empire," *Weekly Standard,* October 15, 2001, 30.

25. Boot, "The Case for American Empire," 27.

26. George W. Bush, "Address Before a Joint Session of the Congress on the State of the Union," February 2, 2005, as transcribed in Woolley and Peters, *The American Presidency Project,* www.presidency.ucsb.edu/ws/index.php?pid=58746.

27. This truth was elaborated by Ayn Rand in her landmark essay, "The Roots of War," reprinted in her anthology *Capitalism: The Unknown Ideal* (New York: Signet, 1967), 35–44.

28. While there is no doubt that a freer world is good for America—more trade with more productive people—the question is, at what cost? And of course this is not the neoconservative argument. Americans, justifiably, will not sacrifice their lives for the sake of more trade, but they will take on real burdens if their very security is at stake.

29. Max Boot, "What the Heck Is a 'Neocon'?" *Wall Street Journal,* December 30, 2002, A12.

30. For an excellent elaboration on this point, see John Lewis, "No Substitute for Victory: The Defeat of Islamic Totalitarianism," *Objective Standard* 1, no. 4 (Winter 2006).

31. Paul Wolfowitz, "Statesmanship in the New Century," in Kagan and Kristol, eds., *Present Dangers,* 321.

32. To read how we think the Islamic Totalitarian threat made evident by the September 11 attacks should have been dealt with, see John David Lewis's forthcoming *Nothing Less than Victory: Decisive Wars and the Lessons of History* (Princeton: Princeton University Press, 2010); and Elan Journo, ed., *Winning the Unwinnable War: America's Self-Crippled Response to Islamic Totalitarianism* (Lanham, MD: Lexington Books, 2009).

33. For an extensive discussion of Strauss's views on the importance of "regime," see chapter 7.

34. For a discussion of this point, see Irving Kristol, "An Autobiographical Memoir," *Neoconservatism: The Autobiography on an Idea* (Chicago: Elephant Paperback, 1999), 8.

35. George W. Bush, "Remarks on the 20th Anniversary of the National Endowment for Democracy."

36. For further discussion of this point, see Yaron Brook and Elan Journo, "The Forward Strategy for Failure," *Objective Standard* 2, no. 1 (Spring 2007). Also see Journo, *Winning the Unwinnable War.*

37. Joshua Muravchik, "Neoconservative Cabal," *Commentary* 116, no. 2 (September 2003): 26–33.

38. Full Text of Iraqi Constitution, courtesy of the Associated Press, October 12, 2005,

www.washingtonpost.com/wp-dyn/content/article/2005/10/12/AR2005101201450.html.

39. Kristol and Kagan, *Present Dangers*, 23.

40. Angelo M. Codevilla, "Some Call it Empire," *Claremont Review of Books* (Fall 2005), www.claremont.org/publications/crb/id.842/article_detail.asp.

41. Boot, "What the Heck Is a 'Neocon'?"

42. Mark Gerson, *The Neoconservative Vision: From the Cold War to the Culture Wars* (Lanham, MD: Madison Books, 1997), 181.

43. Kristol and Kagan, *Present Dangers*, 15.

44. Robert Kagan, "Power and Weakness," *Policy Review* no. 113 (June/July 2002): 3–28.

45. See Peter Schwartz, *The Foreign Policy of Self-Interest: A Moral Ideal for America* (Irvine, CA: Ayn Rand Institute Press, 2004); John David Lewis, *Nothing Less than Victory*); and Journo, *Winning the Unwinnable War*.

46. Joseph Bottum, "A Nation Mobilized," *Weekly Standard*, September 24, 2001, 8.

47. For further elaboration and explanation on this point, see Yaron Brook and Alex Epstein, "'Just War Theory' vs. American Self-Defense," *Objective Standard* 1, no. 1 (Spring 2006): 44. Also see, Journo, *Winning the Unwinnable War*.

48. It must be noted that many neoconservatives do not have any moral problem with the United States fighting a more aggressive war. They do not, however, think they can convince the American people of this course. As Norman Podhoretz wrote in "The War Against World War IV," *Commentary* 119, no. 2 (February 2005): "Of all the attacks on the Bush Doctrine, this set of arguments is the only one that resonates with me, at least on the issue of how to wage war. I have no objection in principle to the ruthlessness the superhawks advocate, and I agree that it would likely be very effective. [The trouble is that] the more closely I look at their position, the more clearly does it emerge as fatally infected by the disease of utopianism—the very disease that usually fills critics of this stripe with revulsion and fear. When these critics prescribe all-out war—total mobilization at home, total ruthlessness on the battlefield—they posit a world that does not exist, at least not in America or in any other democratic country" (30). Ultimately, however, such a course does not serve the neoconservatives' deeper goals. After all, if America were ruthless in its dealing with its enemies, where is the sacrifice? And how would the neoconservatives then define this as a moral war? Their vision of a morally based foreign policy strategy requires American sacrifice. A short, decisive, ruthless war—even if it ends in victory over the enemy—would not advance their foreign policy agenda. They need a long, difficult war of sacrifice.

49. Stephen Hayes, "Beyond Baghdad," *The Weekly Standard*, April 21, 2003, 14.

Chapter 9

1. Strauss's detractors have made all kinds of remarkable claims about this unassuming professor who liked to read old books. Shadia Drury, Strauss's most vociferous public detractor, has been publicly quoted as calling Strauss a "'Jewish Nazi.'" In the Tim Robbins play "Imbedded," actors playing the roles of Paul Wolfowitz and Richard Perle are portrayed shouting "Hail Leo Strauss." Drury was interviewed by and is quoted in Jeet Heer, "The Philosopher," *Boston Globe*, May 11, 2003.

2. For a comprehensive, systematic, and philosophically sophisticated defense of Strauss, see Catherine H. Zuckert and Michael Zuckert, *The Truth about Leo Strauss: Political Philosophy and American Democracy* (Chicago: University of Chicago Press, 2006), 54–57, 199, 261. Another work attempting to prove Strauss's democratic bona fides is Thomas Pangle, *Leo Strauss: An Introduction to His Thought and Intellectual Legacy* (Baltimore: Johns Hopkins University Press, 2006), 7–42, 43–44, 74–86.

3. Steven Smith, *Reading Leo Strauss: Politics, Philosophy, Judaism* (Chicago: University of Chicago Press, 2006), ix.

4. Liberal democracy is a political ideology that promotes democratic processes and permits a wide range of political parties to participate in the electoral process. Liberal democracies may take a variety of political forms, such as republics and constitutional monarchies, as well as presidential and parliamentary forms. Liberal democracy upholds the doctrine of majority rule over that of individual rights. Liberal capitalism, on the other hand, is the political theory of a free society. As a political ideology, it advocates a strictly limited form of government, the purpose of which is to protect individual rights. Politically, it upholds the separation of the State from private, noncoercive actions between individuals, like the separation of economy and State, separation of religion and State, separation of school and State, and separation of culture and State.

5. Since this is a book on neoconservative political thought, the placement of this chapter here should become absolutely clear after readers have read chapter 10 and the conclusion. Had we set out to write a book solely on Leo Strauss's political thought, we surely would have presented the material of this chapter in a different order and manner.

6. Leo Strauss to Karl Löwith, June 23, 1935, in "Correspondence Concerning Modernity: Karl Löwith and Leo Strauss," *Independent Journal of Philosophy* 4 (1983): 183. Strauss wrote very little directly on Nietzsche, but most scholars recognize that his entire corpus is, on one level, an indirect engagement with Nietzsche. See Strauss's "Note on the Plan of Nietzsche's *Beyond Good and Evil*," chap. in *Studies in Platonic Political Philosophy*, with an introduction by Thomas L. Pangle (Chicago: University of Chicago Press, 1983), 174–91. On Strauss's relationship to Nietzsche, see Laurence Lampert, *Leo Strauss and Nietzsche* (Chicago: University of Chicago Press, 1997). Also see Catherine H. Zuckert, *Postmodern Platos: Nietzsche, Heidegger, Gadamer, Strauss, Derrida* (Chicago: University of Chicago Press, 1996).

7. Strauss, *The Rebirth of Classical Political Rationalism: Essays and Lectures by Leo Strauss*, with an introduction by Thomas L. Pangle (Chicago: University of Chicago Press, 1989), 27–28, 31, 30. In his essay on Kurt Riezler, Strauss had this to say about Heidegger: "One has to go back to Hegel until one finds another professor of philosophy who affected in a comparable manner the thought of Germany, nay, of Europe. But Hegel had some contemporaries whose power equaled his or at any rate whom one could compare to him without being manifestly foolish. Heidegger surpasses all his contemporaries by far. This could be seen long before he became known to the general public. As soon as he appeared on the scene, he stood in its center and he began to dominate it. His domination grew almost continuously in extant and in intensity. He gave adequate expression to the prevailing unrest and dissatisfaction because he had clarity and certainty, if not about the whole way, at least about the first decisive steps. The fermentation or the tempest gradually ceased. Eventually a state has been reached which the outsider is inclined to describe as paralysis of the critical faculties; philosophizing seems to have been transformed into listening with reverence to the incipient *mythoi* of Heidegger."

See Strauss, *What Is Political Philosophy?* (Chicago: University of Chicago Press, 1988), 246.

8. Strauss's connection to Nietzsche is examined in Lawrence Lampert, *Leo Strauss and Nietzsche* (Chicago: University of Chicago Press, 1997). Strauss's philosophic debt to and differences from Heidegger are ably discussed in Gregory Bruce Smith, *Martin Heidegger: Paths Taken, Paths Opened* (Lanham, MD: Rowman & Littlefield, 2007), 239–46.

9. In order to know the intellectual context in which Strauss's thought developed, see Richard Wolin, *Heidegger's Children: Hannah Arendt, Karl Löwith, Hans Jonas, and Herbert Marcuse* (Princeton: Princeton University Press, 2001); Richard Wolin, ed., *The Heidegger Controversy: A Critical Reader* (New York: Columbia University Press, 1991); Karl Löwith, *My Life in Germany Before and After 1933* (Urbana: University of Illinois Press, 1986); Victor Farías, *Heidegger and Nazism* (Philadelphia: Temple University Press, 1987); Mark Lilla, *The Reckless Mind: Intellectuals in Politics* (New York: New York Review of Books, 2001); Luc Ferry and Alain Renaut, *Heidegger and Modernity*, trans. Franklin Philip (Chicago: University of Chicago Press, 1990); Gregory Smith, *Martin Heidegger*.

10. For a strained but thoughtful analysis of Strauss's lecture, see Susan Shell, "'To Spare the Vanquished and Crush the Arrogant': Leo Strauss's Lecture on 'German Nihilism,'" in *The Cambridge Companion to Leo Strauss*, ed. Steven B. Smith (Cambridge, UK: Cambridge University Press, 2009), 171–92.

11. See George L. Mosse, *The Crisis of German Ideology: The Intellectual Origins of the Third Reich* (New York: Schocken Books, 1964); Fritz K. Ringer, *The Decline of the German Mandarins: The German Academic Community, 1890–1933* (Hanover, CT: Wesleyan University Press, 1969); Roger Woods, *The Conservative Revolution in the Weimar Republic* (New York: St Martin's Press, Inc., 1996); Jeffrey Herf, *Reactionary Modernism: Technology, Culture, and Politics in Weimar and the Third Reich* (New York: Cambridge University Press, 1984); Martin Travers, *Critics of Modernity: The Literature of the Conservative Revolution in Germany, 1890–1933* (New York: Peter Lang, 2001); Fritz Stern, *The Politics of Cultural Despair* (New York: Anchor, 1965); and Kurt Sontheimer, "Anti-Democratic Thought in the Weimar Republic," in *The Road to Dictatorship: Germany 1918–1933*, trans. Lawrence Wilson (London: Oswald Wolff, 1964), 41–56.

12. Leo Strauss, "German Nihilism," *Interpretation* 26 (Spring 1999): 363, 359.

13. Strauss, "German Nihilism," 362. Also see Strauss's essay titled "Living Issues of German Postwar Philosophy," in Heinrich Meier, *Leo Strauss and the Theologico-Political Problem*, trans. Marcus Brainard (Cambridge, UK: Cambridge University Press, 2006), 115–39. The autobiographical nature of Strauss's essay on German nihilism is supported by his later claim that "Nothing so affected our minds as profoundly in the years in which they took their lasting directions as the thought of Heidegger.... Heidegger who surpasses in speculative intelligence all his contemporaries ... attempts to go a way not yet trodden by anyone or rather to think in a way in which philosophers at any rate have never thought before." Jacob Klein and Leo Strauss, "A Giving of Accounts," *The College* 22, no.1 (1970): 1–5.

14. Strauss, "German Nihilism," 358, 370–71.

15. Strauss, "German Nihilism," 358, 370, 371, 358, 371 (emphasis original). See Strauss's essay "Note on the Plan of Nietzsche's *Beyond Good and Evil*," chap. in *Studies in Platonic Political Philosophy* (Chicago: University of Chicago Press, 1983), 188. Readers should know that the "egoism" defended by the nineteenth-century English

Utilitarians is very different from the philosophy of rational egoism advocated by Ayn Rand. See Ayn Rand, "The Objectivist Ethics," chap. in *The Virtue of Selfishness: A New Concept of Egoism* (New York: New American Library, 1964), 13–35.

16. Strauss, "German Nihilism," 358, 370 (emphasis original). Strauss's attachment to the closed society was explored more fully in chapter 6.

17. Strauss, "German Nihilism," 358, 368, 371, 358. "M-Day" refers to mobilization day. Near the end of his life, Strauss picked up the theme of virtue, sacrifice, and death, but he draped it in a discussion of *eros* in Plato's *Symposium*. There Strauss wrote that "Everything ennobling is connected with one's transcending one's poor self. The most visible and the most impressive form of self-sacrifice is accepting death, willingness to die." Leo Strauss, *On Plato's Symposium*, ed. and with a foreword by Seth Benardete (Chicago: University of Chicago Press, 2001), 208.

18. Strauss, "German Nihilism," 371 (emphasis original). In a review of John Dewey's book *German Philosophy and Politics*, Strauss revisits some of the themes first advanced in his talk on "German Nihilism." There Strauss focuses on how German philosophers and intellectuals in the period during and immediately after World War I attempted to denigrate the moral philosophy of self-interest and to replace it with a duty-based ethics. The whole tone and substance of the review is similar to the "German Nihilism" lecture, in that Strauss clearly sympathizes with the German defenders of duty and self-sacrifice. The seeming "danger" of the German approach, despite its inherent attractiveness, according to Strauss, is that it goes too far: Its "moralism is unmitigated by sense of humor or sense of proportion." Still, Strauss makes it clear that he sides with a moral philosophy of "duty" over "self-interest" when he writes of the "important truth that self-denial is as a rule a safer guide to decency than is 'self-realization.'" See Leo Strauss, review of *German Philosophy and Politics*, by John Dewey, in Strauss, *What Is Political Philosophy?* (Chicago: University of Chicago Press, 1988), 279–81.

19. For an excellent account of the development of Moeller van den Bruck's political philosophy, see Stern, *The Politics of Cultural Despair*, 231–325.

20. Werner Sombart, *Händler und Helden: Patriotische Besinnungen* [*Merchants and Heroes*] (Munich: 1915). See Ringer, *The Decline of the German Mandarins*, 183–84; Jerry Z. Muller, *The Mind and the Market: Capitalism in Modern European Thought* (New York: Alfred A. Knopf, 2002), 256–57; Richard M. Ebeling, "Free Markets, the Rule of Law, and Classical Liberalism, *The Freeman: Ideas on Liberty* (May 2004): 10; F. Y. Edgeworth, "Economists on War," *Economic Journal* (December 1915): 604. Likewise, Ernst Jünger, whom Strauss mentions as one of the leading influences on his generation of "young nihilists," published in 1920 an account of World War I that strikes the same themes as Sombart's *Merchants and Heroes*. See Jünger's *In Stahlgewittern* [*Storm of Steel*] (Hanover: published privately, 1920; reprint, New York: Penguin Classics, 2004).

21. On the development of Schmitt's political thought, see John P. McCormick, *Carl Schmitt's Critique of Liberalism* (Cambridge, UK: Cambridge University Press, 1997); and Joseph W. Bendersky, *Carl Schmitt: Theorist for the Reich* (Princeton: Princeton University Press, 1983).

22. McCormick, *Carl Schmitt's Critique of Liberalism*.

23. Carl Schmitt, *The Concept of the Political*, trans. and with an introduction by George Schwab, and with a foreword by Tracy Strong (Chicago: University of Chicago Press, 1996), 26, 29.

24. Smith, *Reading Leo Strauss*, ix.

25. At Strauss's request, Schmitt wrote a letter of recommendation for his young admirer, which helped Strauss to secure a grant from the Rockefeller Foundation to go to Paris and then to England. Strauss used these years in France and England to search philosophically for that horizon beyond liberalism. He found it in the thought of the medieval Jewish philosopher Moses Maimonides and published his results in *Philosophy and Law* (1935).

26. Strauss, *Natural Right and History* (Chicago: University of Chicago Press, 1953), 318.

27. Leo Strauss, "Notes on Carl Schmitt, The Concept of the Political," in *Carl Schmitt and Leo Strauss: The Hidden Dialogue*, ed. Heinrich Meier, trans. J. Harvey Lomax (Chicago: University of Chicago Press, 1995), 119, 110.

28. Ibid., 111. Strauss put extra emphasis on the word "entertainment."

29. Ibid., 96–97.

30. Ibid., 114–15.

31. Ibid., 112–13.

32. Ibid., 119.

33. Ibid., 119.

34. Leo Strauss to Carl Schmitt, September 4, 1932, in Heinrich Meier, *Carl Schmitt and Leo Strauss: The Hidden Dialogue*, including "Leo Strauss: Notes on Carl Schmitt, Concept of the Political,* and "Leo Strauss: Three Letters to Carl Schmitt," trans. by J. Harvey Lomax, foreword by Joseph Cropsey (Chicago: University of Chicago Press, 1995), 124–26. I should like to thank Professor John McCormick of the University of Chicago for reminding me of the importance of Strauss's "Schmitt" letter.

35. It should also be noted that Strauss, while in Paris, wrote to Schmitt less than two months after sending the Löwith letter in order to ask Schmitt for an introduction to the French nationalist and monarchist Charles Maurras, who was the principal thinker behind the *Action Française*, France's leading right-wing movement and periodical during the years leading up to the Second World War. Maurras was also a supporter of Mussolini's fascist regime. See Leo Strauss to Carl Schmitt, July 10, 1933, in Meier, *Carl Schmitt and Leo Strauss: The Hidden Dialogue*, 127–28.

36. Leo Strauss to Karl Löwith, May 19, 1933, in *Gesammelte Politsche Schrifte*, ed. Heinrich Maier, vol. 3: 624–26. I have used the translation provided by Scott Horton appearing on the Balkinization website, http://Balkin.blogspot.com/2006/07/letter_16 .html, in July 2006.

37. Strauss's remarkable 1933 letter has only just recently become the subject of scholarly discussion. See, for instance, Eugene R. Sheppard, *Leo Strauss and the Politics of Exile: The Making of a Political Philosopher* (Waltham, MA: Brandeis University Press, 2007), 60–67; Harvey C. Mansfield, "Timeless Mind," review of *Leo Strauss and the Politics of Exile: The Making of a Political Philosopher*, by Eugene R. Sheppard; and Mansfield, *Leo Strauss: An Intellectual Biography*, by Daniel Tanguay, in *Claremont Review of Books* 8 (Winter 2007/08): 23–36; Richard Wolin, "Leo Strauss, Judaism, and Liberalism," in *Chronicle of Higher Education*, April 14, 2006; Nicholas Xenos, *Cloaked in Virtue: Unveiling Leo Strauss and the Rhetoric of American Foreign Policy* (New York: Routledge, 2008); Alan Gilbert, "Leo Strauss and the Principles of the Right: An Introduction to Strauss's Letter," *Constellations* 16 (2009): 78–81; and James Costopoulos, "What Is a Fascist? Goldberg and Xenos on Fascism and Leo Strauss," *Interpretation* 36 (2009): 253–72. The most thoughtful defense of Strauss and his letter to Löwith is Catherine H. Zuckert, "Leo Strauss: Fascist, Authoritarian, Imperialist?" paper presented at the

annual meeting of the American Political Science Association, Chicago, IL, August 30–September 2, 2007.

38. Strauss's defenders typically respond to the Löwith letter in one of seven ways. Some want to pretend that Strauss did not write the letter and therefore refuse to talk about it. Others evade the principal question as to whether Strauss was attracted to fascism in the early 1930s and quickly change the terms of debate so that Nazism is used interchangeably with fascism, and since Strauss was known to be anti-Nazi, then the letter can have no meaning. Some argue that Strauss may have been attracted to fascism in the early 1930s, but "so what," they say, "so were a lot of people." Others argue that Strauss is really only saying that Germany should follow the respectable model of ancient imperial Rome. Some argue that Strauss was really only kidding so as to provoke his friend Löwith into taking a stronger stand against the Nazis. Others argue that Strauss's call for fascism was a prudential and tactical move in order to provide a benign alternative to the Nazis. And finally, some argue that Strauss may have been attracted temporarily to fascism as the only meaningful alternative to Nazism in the early 1930s, but that he later rejected those principles once he came to England and then to America.

39. Catherine Zuckert, one of Strauss's best students and defenders, has attempted to explain away the import of Strauss's support for fascism in the Löwith letter by suggesting that this was an example of Strauss's prudence. According to Zuckert, Strauss's letter "concerns a question of political practice, i.e., what should be done by certain individuals or kinds of human beings in a specific set of circumstances." She continues: "It is not a statement, much less an explanation of his political principles." (See Zuckert, "Leo Strauss: Fascist, Authoritarian, Imperialist?") In other words, we can feel better knowing that Strauss could be a fascist in practice but not one in theory. Presumably, then, we should also assume that Strauss's defense of liberal democracy in later years was a prudent accommodation to the fact that he was living in the United States and should not be taken as a sign of his theoretical commitment to the philosophy of liberal democracy. We believe that Zuckert has properly identified and understood Strauss's larger project. We disagree, however, with her judgment that it was somehow understandable or acceptable for Strauss to be opposed to fascism in theory but not in practice. We also believe that Strauss was much more sympathetic to fascist principles and the fascist critique of classical liberalism than he was to the principles and practice of classical liberalism.

40. One student of Strauss's who recognizes the importance of the 1933 letter to Löwith and whose interpretation of the letter takes seriously Strauss's attraction to fascism is Werner Dannhauser. "The reading of such a passage causes pain," writes Dannhauser. He continues: "It is true that the fascism to which Strauss alludes is that of Mussolini and not of Hitler." Dannhauser, "Leo Strauss in His Letters," in *Enlightening Revolutions: Essays in Honor of Ralph Lerner*, ed. Svetozar Minkov (Lanham, MD: Lexington Books, 2007), 359. Even Steven B. Smith, the man who wrote that Leo Strauss was a great friend to liberal democracy, "one of the best friends liberal democracy ever had," has written more recently that it "is entirely conceivable that the young Strauss was a conservative authoritarian who saw the renewal of imperial rule where 'the subjected are spared and the proud are subdued' as the only practical antidote to Hitler's national socialism" ("A Skeptical Friend of Democracy," *New York Sun*, March 14, 2007, www.nysun.com/arts/skeptical-friend-of-democracy/50399/). More recently, another Strauss defender, James Costopoulos, has conceded that Strauss may have "sympathized with Italian Fascism" ("What Is a Fascist? Goldberg and Xenos on Fascism and Leo Strauss," *Interpretation* 36 (2009): 271). Peter Minowitz has also written that Strauss "conveys unmistakable

sympathy" for the principles of fascism (Minowitz, *Straussophobia: Defending Leo Strauss and Straussians against Shadia Drury and Other Accusers* [Lanham, MD: Lexington Books, 2009], 156).

41. Giovanni Gentile, *Origins and Doctrine of Fascism, With Selections from Other Works*, trans., ed., and annotated by A. James Gregor (New Brunswick, NJ: Transaction Publishers, 2002). The full text of this document is available at www.worldfuturefund .org/wffmaster/Reading/Germany/mussolini.htm, which has been used for purposes of quotation in this text. On Giovanni Gentile, the intellectual godfather of fascism, see A. James Gregor, *Giovanni Gentile: Philosopher of Fascism* (New Brunswick, NJ: Transaction Publishers, 2001).

42. In the paragraph that follows and in the accompanying footnotes, we shall compare and contrast Strauss's basic philosophic principles with those of Mussolini's "The Doctrine of Fascism."

43. Benito Mussolini, *The Doctrine of Fascism*: Fascism is "a spiritual" movement, "arising from the general reaction of the century against the materialistic positivism of the XIXth century.... Fascism is therefore opposed to all individualistic abstractions based on eighteenth century materialism." Fascism "is opposed to classical liberalism." Fascism "is definitely and absolutely opposed to the doctrines of liberalism, both in the political and the economic sphere."

44. Mussolini, *The Doctrine of Fascism*: Fascism "denies the materialistic conception of happiness as a possibility, and abandons it to the economists of the mid-eighteenth century. This means that Fascism denies the equation: well-being = happiness, which sees in men mere animals, content when they can feed and fatten, thus reducing them to a vegetative existence pure and simple."

45. Mussolini, *The Doctrine of Fascism*: Fascism, according to Mussolini, begins with "an organic conception of the world," and it rejects the idea that government's functions can "be limited to those of enforcing order and keeping the peace, as the liberal doctrine had it." The fascist state "is no mere mechanical device for defining the sphere within which the individual may duly exercise his supposed rights."

46. Mussolini, *The Doctrine of Fascism*: "If the XIXth century was the century of the individual (liberalism implies individualism) we are free to believe that this is the 'collective' century, and therefore the century of the State." And, "Anti-individualistic, the Fascist conception of life stresses the importance of the State and accepts the individual only in so far as his interests coincide with those of the State, which stands for the conscience and the universal, will of man as a historic entity.... Liberalism denied the State in the name of the individual; Fascism reasserts the rights of the State as expressing the real essence of the individual."

47. Mussolini, *The Doctrine of Fascism*: "Fascism ... sees not only the individual but the nation and the country; individuals and generations bound together by a moral law, with common traditions and a mission which suppressing the instinct for life closed in a brief circle of pleasure, builds up a higher life, founded on duty ... in which the individual, by self-sacrifice, the renunciation of self-interest, by death itself, can achieve that purely spiritual existence in which his value as a man consists."

48. Mussolini, *The Doctrine of Fascism*: "Fascism does not, generally speaking, believe in the possibility or utility of perpetual peace.... War alone keys up all human energies to their maximum tension and sets the seal of nobility on those peoples who have the courage to face it.... The Fascist accepts and loves life; he rejects and despises suicide as cowardly. Life as he understands it means duty, elevation, conquest; life must be lofty

and full, it must be lived for oneself but above all for others, both near bye and far off, present and future. Fascism believes now and always in sanctity and heroism, that is to say in acts in which no economic motive—remote or immediate—is at work."

49. Mussolini, *The Doctrine of Fascism*: "The Fascist conception of the State is all embracing; outside of it no human or spiritual values can exist, much less have value. Thus understood, Fascism, is totalitarian, and the Fascist State—a synthesis and a unit inclusive of all values—interprets, develops, and potentates the whole life of a people.... The Fascist State is not a night watchman, solicitous only of the personal safety of the citizens.... The State, as conceived and realized by Fascism, is a spiritual and ethical entity for securing the political, juridical, and economic organization of the nation, an organization which in its origin and growth is a manifestation of the spirit.... If liberalism spells individualism, Fascism spells government."

50. Mussolini, *The Doctrine of Fascism*: "We are, in other words, a state which controls all forces acting in nature. We control political forces, we control moral forces we control economic forces, therefore we are a full-blown Corporative state."

51. Mussolini, *The Doctrine of Fascism*: "The Fascist State, as a higher and more powerful expression of personality, is a force, but a spiritual one. It sums up all the manifestations of the moral and intellectual life of man.... The Fascist State is an inwardly accepted standard and rule of conduct, a discipline of the whole person; it permeates the will no less than the intellect. It stands for a principle which becomes the central motive of man as a member of civilized society, sinking deep down into his personality; it dwells in the heart of the man of action and of the thinker, of the artist and of the man of science: soul of the soul."

52. Mussolini, *The Doctrine of Fascism*: "The State educates the citizens to civism, makes them aware of their mission, urges them to unity; its justice harmonizes their divergent interests; it transmits to future generations the conquests of the mind in the fields of science, art, law, human solidarity; it leads men up from primitive tribal life to that highest manifestation of human power, imperial rule. The State hands down to future generations the memory of those who laid down their lives to ensure its safety or to obey its laws; it sets up as examples and records for future ages the names of the captains who enlarged its territory and of the men of genius who have made it famous."

53. Mussolini, *The Doctrine of Fascism*: "This positive conception of life is obviously an ethical one.... Therefore life, as conceived of by the Fascist, is serious, austere, and religious.... The Fascist disdains an 'easy' life. The Fascist conception of life is a religious one, in which man is viewed in his immanent relation to a higher law, endowed with an objective will transcending the individual and raising him to conscious membership of a spiritual society."

54. Jonah's Goldberg's *Liberal Fascism: The Secret History of the American Left from Mussolini to the Politics of Means* (New York: Doubleday, 2007) is quite helpful in explaining just how widespread fascist ideas were in respectable intellectual circles prior to the rise of Hitler and the Nazis. Also see John P. Diggins, *Mussolini and Fascism; The View from America* (Princeton: Princeton University Press, 1972); Leonard Peikoff, *The Ominous Parallels* (New York: Mentor, 1982).

55. Hans Jonas, *Memoirs*, trans. Krishna Winston and ed. by Christian Wiese (Waltham, MA: Brandeis University Press, 2008), 48, 161. The Jonas reference was first brought to my attention in Nicholas Zenos's *Cloaked in Virtue: Unveiling Leo Strauss and the Rhetoric of American Foreign Policy* (New York: Routledge, 2008), 149, n55.

56. Leo Strauss to Gerhard Krüger, July 23, 1933, in *Gesammelte Politsche Schrifte*, ed.

Heinrich Maier, vol. 3: 432–33. I would like to thank Professor Jeff Love of Clemson University for his felicitous translation of the Krüger letter.

57. Leo Strauss, "The Re-education of Axis Countries Concerning the Jews," *The Review of Politics* 69 (2007): 531, 536, 532.

58. Strauss, "The Re-education of Axis Countries Concerning the Jews," 532–33.

59. Catherine H. Zuckert and Michael Zuckert (two scholars for whom I have enormous respect and from whom I have learned much) have drawn a line in the sand on this issue. In *The Truth About Leo Strauss*, they wrote: "Those who claim that Strauss sympathizes with fascism commit the very elementary but, we believe, irresponsible error of concluding that because Strauss is critical of some of the theoretical premises of liberal democracy, he is a critic of liberal democracy tout court, and that therefore he (being a conservative and not a leftist critic) must be sympathetic to fascism. None of this chain of reasoning is grounded in what Strauss actually said or thought" (185–86). When the Zuckerts published this in 2006, it was reasonable to insist that the burden of proof rested with those who claimed that Strauss was a Nazi sympathizer or a fascist. With the publication of Strauss's letters from the 1930s and other available evidence from the period and by pursuing new lines of philosophic investigation, that burden of proof is inching closer to having been met.

Chapter 10

1. Irving Kristol, *Two Cheers for Capitalism* (New York: New American Library, 1978), 235.

2. Adam Myerson, "Conservatives and Neoconservatives," *Public Interest* no. 154 (Winter 2004): 41; Kristol, *Two Cheers for Capitalism*, 237.

3. Kristol, *Two Cheers for Capitalism*, 65.

4. Kristol, *Two Cheers for Capitalism*, 239–53.

5. Irving Kristol, *Neoconservatism: The Autobiography of an Idea* (New York: Basic Books, 1995), 99–100, 124, 100.

6. Irving Kristol, *Reflections of a Neoconservative: Looking Back, Looking Ahead* (New York: Basic Books, 1983), xiii; *Neoconservatism*, 365. Kristol almost certainly came to see nationalism as the anodyne to liberalism via Strauss, who very subtly advocated nationalism in many of his writings. We shall recall from chapter 7 that Strauss believed in nationalism as an antidote to modern liberal capitalism and as a means of providing a temporary shelter on the road back to the ancient polis. Readers should also consider Strauss's remarkably sympathetic reading of Rousseau's *First Discourse* in *Natural Right and History* (Chicago: University of Chicago Press, 1953), 255–59, which should be read along with his discussion of classic natural right in the same work.

7. See David Brooks, "One Nation Conservatism," *Weekly Standard*, September 13, 1999, www.jewishworldreview.com/weekly/standard091099.asp.; "A Return to National Greatness," March 3, 1997; "Bush's Patriotic Challenge: From Compassionate Conservatism to Courageous Conservatism," *Weekly Standard*, October 8, 2001.

8. Brooks, "One Nation Conservatism"; "Bully for America," *Weekly Standard*, June 23, 1997.

9. Carnes Lord, *The Modern Prince* (New Haven: Yale University Press, 2003), 140; Walter Berns, *Freedom, Virtue & The First Amendment* (Baton Rouge: Louisiana State University Press, 1957), 252–53. See also Harry M. Clor, *Obscenity and Public Morality*

(Chicago: University of Chicago Press, 1975), and *Public Morality and Liberal Society: Essays on Decency, Law, and Pornography* (South Bend, IN: University of Notre Dame Press, 1996); and David Lowenthal, *No Liberty for License: The Forgotten Logic of the First Amendment* (Dallas, TX: Spence Publishing Company, 1997).

10. David Brooks, "Politics and Patriotism: From Teddy Roosevelt to John McCain," *Weekly Standard,* April 26, 1999, 16f. The connection here between Strauss's 1941 lecture titled "German Nihilism" and Brooks's call for a "National Greatness" conservatism is too obvious to go unnoticed.

11. Brooks, "National Greatness: Teddy Roosevelt's Vision for the Twenty-First Century," *American Quarterly Experiment* (Winter 1998–99): 19–28; "Bully for America"; "Politics and Patriotism," 16f.

12. David Brooks, "Politics and Patriotism."

13. Brooks, "A Return to National Greatness; A Manifesto for a Lost Creed," *Weekly Standard,* March 3, 1997; "National Greatness: Teddy Roosevelt's Vision for the Twenty-First Century," 19–28; "Bully for America"; "A Return to National Greatness."

14. Brooks, "Pabulum with a Purpose," *Weekly Standard,* August 14, 2000; "A Return to National Greatness; A Manifesto for a Lost Creed"; "The Coming Activist Age," *New York Times,* July 18, 2008, www.nytimes.com/2008/07/18/opinion/18brooks.html.

15. Brooks, "A Return to National Greatness; A Manifesto for a Lost Creed; "Bully for America."

16. See Stewart H. Holbrook, *The Story of American Railroads* (New York: Crown Publishers, 1947), 8–9.

17. David Brooks, "Politics and Patriotism"; Michael Ledeen, *Machiavelli on Modern Leadership: Why Machiavelli's Iron Rules Are As Timely and Important Today As Five Centuries Ago* (New York: St. Martin's Press, 1999), 115.

18. William James, "The Moral Equivalent of War," a speech delivered at Stanford University, 1906. An online version is available at www.constitution.org/wj/meow.htm.

19. Brooks, "A Return to National Greatness; A Manifesto for a Lost Creed"; "Politics and Patriotism"; "One Nation Conservatism"; "The McCain Insurrection," *Weekly Standard,* February 14, 2000.

20. Brooks, "National Greatness: Teddy Roosevelt's Vision for the Twenty-First Century"; "The McCain Insurrection."

21. Brooks, "The Politics of Creative Destruction," March 13, 2000; "The McCain Insurrection," February 14, 2000.

22. Brooks, "The Politics of Creative Destruction"; "The McCain Insurrection."

23. Senator John McCain, "Putting the 'National' in National Service," *Washington Monthly* (October 2001) at www.washingtonmonthly.com/features/2001/0110.mccain.html.

24. Berns, *Freedom, Virtue and the First Amendment* (Chicago: Regnery, 1965), 253.

25. David Brooks, "Politics and Patriotism."

26. Ibid.

27. David Brooks, "A Return to National Greatness: A Manifesto for a Lost Creed."

28. William Kristol and Robert Kagan, "Toward a Neo-Reaganite Foreign Policy," *Foreign Affairs* 75, no. 4 (July/August 1996; emphasis added), www.foreignaffairs.com/articles/52239/william-kristol-and-robert-kagan/toward-a-neo-reaganite-foreign-policy.

29. Ibid.
30. Ibid.
31. Ibid.
32. Brooks, "Bully for America."
33. Brooks, "Politics and Patriotism."
34. Ibid.
35. Max Boot, "True Believer: TR, McCain, and Conservatism," *World Affairs* 171, no. 2 (Fall 2008), www.worldaffairsjournal.org/2008%20-%20Fall/full-Boot.html.
36. Ibid.
37. Brooks, "Bully for America."
38. William Kristol and Robert Kagan, *Present Dangers: Crisis and Opportunity in American Foreign Policy* (San Francisco: Encounter Books, 2000), 83.
39. Max Boot, "The Case for American Empire," *Weekly Standard* 7, no. 5 (October 15, 2001), www.weeklystandard.com/Content/Public/Articles/000%5C000%5C000%5C318qpvmc.asp.
40. Carnes Lord, *The Modern Prince*, 24.
41. Michael Ledeen, *Machiavelli on Modern Leadership* (New York: St. Martin's Press, 1999), 71, 70.
42. See speech delivered by President Bush at the National Endowment for Democracy, November 6, 2003, www.whitehouse.gov/news/releases/2003/11/20031106-2.html.
43. For a powerful antidote to the neoconservative's view of foreign policy, see Elan Journo, ed., *Winning the Unwinnable War: America's Self-Crippled Response to Islamic Totalitarianism* (Lanham, MD: Lexington Books, 2009).
44. Irving Kristol, *Reflections of a Neoconservative* (New York: Basic Books, 1983), xiii; Kristol and Kagan, "Toward a Neo-Reaganite Foreign Policy," *Foreign Affairs*, www.foreignaffairs.com/articles/52239/william-kristol-and-robert-kagan/toward-a-neo-reaganite-foreign-policy.
45. Strauss, "German Nihilism," *Interpretation* 26 (Spring 1999): 358.
46. Joseph Bottum, "A Nation Mobilized," *Weekly Standard* 7, no. 2 (September 24, 2001): 8.
47. Brooks, "Bush's Patriotic Challenge"; Croly quoted in Arthur A. Ekirch, Jr., *The Decline of American Liberalism* (New York: Longmans, Green and Company, 1955), 202.
48. Michael Ledeen, *Machiavelli on Modern Leadership*, 159–60, 69–70.

Conclusion

1. Alexander Hamilton, "Federalist No. 1," *The Federalist*, ed. and with introduction and notes by Jacob E. Cooke (Hanover, NH: University Press of New England, 1961), 3.
2. Thomas Jefferson, *Notes on the State of Virginia*, in *The Portable Thomas Jefferson*, ed. Merrill D. Peterson (New York: Penguin Books, 1975), 211; Thomas Jefferson to Peter Carr, August 10, 1787, in *The Portable Jefferson*, 425.
3. James Madison, "Federalist No. 14," *The Federalist*, 89.
4. Robert Green McCloskey, ed., *The Works of James Wilson*, vol. 2 (Cambridge: Harvard University Press, 1967), 585.

5. James Madison, "Speech in the House of Representatives, June 8, 1789," in M. Meyers, ed., *The Mind of the Founder: Sources of the Political Thought of James Madison* (Hanover, NH: University Press of New England, 1981), 164.

6. Irving Kristol, "The Capitalist Future," 1991 Francis Boyer Lecture delivered at the American Enterprise Institute (December 1991) (emphasis added).

7. We believe that it is both necessary and possible to establish an *absolute, permanent, certain,* and *secular* moral code that grounds individualism and economic laissez-faire and that is derived from and is consonant with man's nature as a rational and volitional being. Interested readers will find this demonstrative science of ethics presented in the novels and nonfiction writings of Ayn Rand. See Ayn Rand, *Atlas Shrugged* (New York: Random House, 1957); *The Virtue of Selfishness: A New Concept of Egoism* (New York: New American Library, 1964); *Capitalism: The Unknown Ideal* (New York: Signet, 1986); *Philosophy Who Needs It?* (New York: Signet, 1984). The first and only systematic presentation of Ayn Rand's philosophy is contained in Leonard Peikoff's *Objectivism: The Philosophy of Ayn Rand* (New York: Dutton Books, 1991). The fullest discussion of Ayn Rand's moral philosophy will be found in Tara Smith's *Ayn Rand's Normative Ethics: The Virtuous Egoist* (Cambridge, UK: Cambridge University Press, 2006). For two excellent presentations of Rand's philosophic system written for a popular audience, see Craig Biddle, *Loving Life: The Morality of Self-Interest and the Facts that Support It* (Richmond, VA: Glen Allen Press, 2002); and Andrew Bernstein, *Objectivism in One Lesson: An Introduction to the Philosophy of Ayn Rand* (Lanham, MD: Hamilton Books, 2008).

8. William Kristol, "On the Future of Conservatism: A Symposium," *Commentary* 83, no. 2 (February 1997): 32–33; David Brooks, "Harmony and the Dream," *New York Times,* August 12, 2008, www.nytimes.com/2008/08/12/opinion/12iht-edbrooks.1.15207937.html.

9. Michael Ledeen, *Machiavelli on Modern Leadership: Why Machiavelli's Iron Rules Are as Timely and Important Today as Five Centuries Ago* (New York: St. Martin's Press, 1999), 112–13.

10. The idea of "soft despotism" comes from Alexis de Tocqueville's *Democracy in America,* trans., ed., and with an introduction by Harvey C. Mansfield and Delba Winthrop (Chicago: University of Chicago Press, 2000), 661–65. See Paul A. Rahe, *Soft Despotism, Democracy's Drift: Montesquieu, Rousseau, Tocqueville, and the Modern Prospect* (New Haven: Yale University Press, 2009).

11. It should be made clear here that we do not regard freedom as a primary nor as a starting point, nor do we think that freedom is compatible with just any moral philosophy. Freedom in a free society does not mean the freedom to do whatever one wants. We reject the idea that *any* use a man makes of his freedom is necessarily a moral use. Freedom is a conclusion, not a starting premise. It must rest on a logically ordered structure of ideas. In a sentence, a proper definition and defense of freedom must be grounded hierarchically on a code of rights, which in turn must rest on a proper code of ethics. In other words, freedom or the free society can be validated philosophically only if it is grounded objectively on the nature and the requirements of human survival and flourishing. A properly free society cannot be an amoral society as advocated by some libertarians.

12. In 2005 the neoconservative David Gelernter wrote a rather clever essay for *Commentary* magazine in which he attempted to define the nature and meaning of "Americanism." According to Gelernter, the "idea of a 'secular' Americanism based on

the Declaration of Independence is an optical illusion." Instead, he argues, the "American creed" is synonymous with a "certain approach to Protestantism." Gelernter goes on to describe what he thinks is unique about Americans and the essence of their nation: "The fundamental fact: the Bible is God's word. Two premises: first, every member of the American community has his own individual dignity, insofar as he deals individually with God; second, the community has a divine mission to all mankind. Three conclusions: every human being everywhere is entitled to freedom, equality, and democracy." (David Gelernter, "Americanism—and Its Enemies," *Commentary* 120, no. 5 [December 2005]: 41, 43.) The unstated logical conclusion of Gelernter's essay is that Americans have a moral duty to sacrifice their freedom in order to carry out their divine mission to deliver freedom, equality, and democracy to those people around the world who don't have it. At the center of Gelernter's "Americanism" stands Woodrow Wilson, a man who did as much as anyone to explicitly reject the principles of the Declaration of Independence and the Constitution. Gelernter's "Americanism" is, in other words, put in the service of neoconservative foreign policy and the Bush administration's policy in Iraq. Let us quickly address here what is often but mistakenly thought to be at the heart of or synonymous with Americanism: Christianity. It is obviously true that there are and always have been a good many Christians in America, but the United States of America is not nor has it ever been a "Christian nation." (By way of analogy, we might say that Iran is an Islamic nation but Turkey is not, despite the fact that most Turks are Muslim.) Christianity is not nor has it ever been what makes America unique in comparison to, say, the Christian nations of Europe. What makes America historically unique is not the Salem witch trials, the Christian defense of slavery, or the Scopes trial. These kinds of events are all remnants of the Old World. The Declaration of Independence could not and would not have been written by the Puritans, who did not understand and certainly would never have tolerated the radical individualism, the economic freedom, and the limited government promoted by the Revolution.

13. Given the very public criticisms of their foreign policy since the beginning of the Iraq War, the neoconservatives have recently launched a PR campaign to justify and rehabilitate their ideas and policies. Their strategy works something like this: Phase one, define neoconservatism as being "in" the "American grain" (see Irving Kristol, "The Neoconservative Persuasion," *Weekly Standard,* August 25, 2003); phase two, define the "American grain" or Americanism as the "divine mission" of Americans to spread democracy around the world (see David Gelernter, "Americanism—and Its Enemies, 41–48); phase three, equate America's divine mission and its greatness with the neoconservative policy of using force against other nations around the world that are not democratic (see Robert Kagan, "Neocon Nation: Neoconservatism, c. 1776," *World Affairs* [Spring 2008]: www.worldaffairsjournal.org/Spring-2008/full-neocon.html).

14. David Brooks, "The Social Animal," *New York Times,* September 12, 2008, www.nytimes.com/2008/09/12/opinion/12brooks.html.

15. See, for instance, Peter Berkowitz, "Moderation is No Vice, and Extremism is No Virtue in Politics," *Weekly Standard,* July 27, 2009.

16. Jonah Goldberg, *Liberal Fascism: The Secret History of the American Left from Mussolini to the Politics of Meaning* (New York: Doubleday, 2007), 23.

17. Leo Strauss, *An Introduction to Political Philosophy: Ten Essays by Leo Strauss,* ed. and with an introduction by Hilail Gildin (Detroit: Wayne State University Press, 1989), 98.

INDEX

195; death of, 73; demands of, 129; of duty, 85; GOP, 24; government sponsored, 245; kingly, 93; of Kristol, I., 103; Machiavelli hiding, 64–65; Occidental, 71; of Plato, 28; politics cut from, 113; pragmatist, 224; purpose of, 97; of Strauss, 98; Strauss defining, 106; working man's, 126

Plato: allegory of, 65; dichotomy of, 157; epistemology of, 13; fascism inspired by, 251; getting back to, 220; on ignorance, 85; interpretation of, 8; Kristol, I., on, 60; law conceived by, 118; learning from Socrates, 67; Locke vs., 168; on loyalty, 56; Machiavelli reconciled with, 128; metaphysics of, 92, 97; neoconservatives learning from, 164; philosophy of, 28; Strauss on, 60, 96, 104

the Pledge of Allegiance, 250
Podhoretz, John, 173
Podheretz, Norman, 3, 9, 10, 15, 39, 44
polemic, 59, 211
policy: Iraqi, 228; prescriptions, 5; wonks, 3. *See also* domestic policy; foreign policy
polis, 114, 122
politics, 139; advantage in, 37; art of, 32; competing, 39; contemporary, 35; day-to-day, 138; economics under, 143; Kristol, I., on, 34; moderate, 246; neoconservative, 162–169; nostalgia, 28; organization of, 100; philosophy cut from, 113; principle trumped by, 34; students of, 58; subterfuge of, 251
polity, 130
power: entrenched, 30; liberty vs., 43; perception's, 121; police, 162, 250; prerogative, 168
practice: theory distinct from, 101; theory's tension with, 95
pragmatism, 35; cloaked, 37; social version of, 160
Pragmatism Obama Style (Berkowitz), 36
prayer, 131
principle, 5; compromising, 52; disposition replacing, 25; The Enlightenment's, 77; fixed, 32; of Marxism, 48; nineteenth-century, 135; old-fashioned, 35; ontological, 100; rhetorically used, 37; value-laden, 243
profit motive, 83

proletariat, 181
Protestant, 84
prudence: Aristotelian, 38; guiding, 125
public: ethos, 143; knowledge, 7; religion supported by, 41; unwary, 36

al Qaeda, 78, 179, 193–194

rationalism: ancient, 67; communism extended from, 76
Reagan, Ronald, 4, 17, 31, 442, 43, 56
reason: Brooks discouraging, 49–50; Enlightenment and, 66–67, 74, 78, 86, 152, 239–241; faith in, 72; liberty related to, 237–238; limiting, 87, 110; neoconservatives and, 23, 25, 68, 73, 79, 85, 146; transcending, 147; unassisted, 107; validity, 110
regime: analysis, 186; collectivism, 93; components of, 216; entitlement, 49; improving, 117; Middle East changing, 141; mixed, 95; totalitarian, 67
regulation, 39; choice, 167; government, 168; material, 242; state of, 166; uniformity through, 248; wisdom hampered by, 116
relativism, 73, 152
religion, 4, 141, 207, 220, 240, 248; capitalism based on, 161; civic, 85–87, 94, 124, 126–127, 160; civil, 37, 214, 224–225, 250; imposed, 127; Kristol, I., on, 162; Lord on, 161; Marx on, 161–162; neoconservatives and, 18–19, 35, 38, 68–69, 79, 150, 155, 186; public supported, 41
Republic (Plato), 93
Republican Party, 35; conversion of, 23; Democratic Party absorbed by, 42; Kristol, I., call to, 156; Machiavelli heeded by, 33; neoconservative advice to, 52; outdated, 28
responsibility, 49, 128
rhetoric: of Berkowitz, 139–140; contrarian, 33; exotic, 243; neoconservative, 31; noble, 110; principle of, 37; tropes of, 250
the Right, 10; elements of, 227; old, 13
righteousness, 28
rights: concept of, 49; duty emphasized over, 240; individual, 29; needs synonymous with, 48
role: government's, 87; subservient, 144

ABOUT THE AUTHORS

C. Bradley Thompson is the BB&T Research Professor in the Department of Political Science at Clemson University and the Executive Director of the Clemson Institute for the Study Capitalism. He is the author of the award-winning book *John Adams and the Spirit of Liberty*. He also edited *The Revolutionary Writings of John Adams* and *Antislavery Political Writings, 1833-1860: A Reader*.

Yaron Brook is executive director of the Ayn Rand Institute. He appears regularly on national TV and radio to discuss business, economic, and foreign policy issues. He has written and spoken extensively on U.S. foreign policy in the Middle East and on the role of neoconservatives in formulating that policy.